Vice and the Victorians

Vice and the Victorians

MIKE HUGGINS

Bloomsbury Academic
An imprint of Bloomsbury Publishing Plc

B L O O M S B U R Y
LONDON · OXFORD · NEW YORK · NEW DELHI · SYDNEY

Bloomsbury Academic
An imprint of Bloomsbury Publishing Plc

50 Bedford Square	1385 Broadway
London	New York
WC1B 3DP	NY 10018
UK	USA

www.bloomsbury.com

BLOOMSBURY and the Diana logo are trademarks of Bloomsbury Publishing Plc

First published 2016

© Mike Huggins, 2016

Mike Huggins has asserted his right under the Copyright, Designs and Patents Act, 1988, to be identified as Author of this work.

All rights reserved. No part of this publication may be reproduced or transmitted in any form or by any means, electronic or mechanical, including photocopying, recording, or any information storage or retrieval system, without prior permission in writing from the publishers.

No responsibility for loss caused to any individual or organization acting on or refraining from action as a result of the material in this publication can be accepted by Bloomsbury or the author.

British Library Cataloguing-in-Publication Data
A catalogue record for this book is available from the British Library.

ISBN: HB: 978-1-4725-3042-4
       PB: 978-1-4725-2973-2
       ePDF: 978-1-4725-2522-2
       ePub: 978-1-4725-2556-7

Library of Congress Cataloging-in-Publication Data
Huggins, Mike.
Vice and the Victorians / Mike Huggins.
 pages cm
Includes bibliographical references and index.
1. Vice control–Great Britain–History–19th century. 2. Great Britain–Social life and customs–19th century. 3. Alcoholism–Great Britain–History.
 4. Great Britain–History–Victoria, 1837-1901. I. Title.
 HV8067.H84 2015
 364.1'7094109034–dc23
 2015010998.

Typeset by RefineCatch Limited, Bungay, Suffolk

CONTENTS

Acknowledgements vi
Introduction vii

1 The Language of Vice 1

2 The Spatial Dimension of Vice 31

3 The Vice of Drunkenness 59

4 Vice and Profligacy: Betting and Gaming 87

5 Sexuality, Pornography and Prostitution 117

6 From Vice to Virtue 147

7 Vice and Respectability 173

Epilogue 197

Notes 203
Suggestions for Further Reading 231
Index 235

ACKNOWLEDGEMENTS

I would first like to thank John Walton who first gave me the idea for this book many years ago, over discussions in a bar, a context highly appropriate for this topic. The enthusiasm, dedication and professionalism of the History staff at St Martin's College and the University of Cumbria gave me the impetus to keep going on the topic – they took the project seriously when some other academics saw study of such an unrespectable topic as being rather inappropriate. Pamela Robson, Erica Munkwitz, Tony Mangan, Lesley Hall, Craig Stafford, Keith Gregson and Michael Brown, together with Frances Arnold and Emma Goode at Bloomsbury and the publisher's anonymous readers all offered helpful insights and suggestions during the writing of the book.

INTRODUCTION

This book is about vice, a word we all know, saturated with powerful meanings, though these are often debated. The complex and fluid relationships between vice, virtue and respectability were very significant features of the Victorian period. So there have been many studies of aspects of particular leisure activities then seen as vices, especially in relation to topics such as sex, drink, gambling or the temperance movement. There is, however, no one book which addresses this theme. Much of the recent scholarship in this area is fairly dense and specialized and often heavily theory-laden. Therefore this book has the modest aim of bringing together some of the evidence and insights from this research in a readable and accessible synthesis and it should appeal both to undergraduates taking courses in Victorian history or literature, and to a broader educated audience outside higher education.

In places too, it takes a cultural approach, exploring themes of vice's contested representations and meanings, the expressive language in which vices were described, and the assumptions and judgements about vice which shaped people's lives. It looks at vice in the context of everyday Victorian life and experience, across the classes and for both men and women. As well as contributing to our understanding of the struggles over vice's cultural meanings and significance, the book has much to say about other Victorian themes such as leisure, class, gender, sexuality, crime, print culture, policing, urban history, religion and consumption. Though this is not an economic study, Victorian vice had economic features: significant commercialization, forces of demand and supply, markets, consumers, investment, and technologies, and these are touched upon in passing. It created very significant employment within Victorian society: prostitutes, publicans, tipsters, barmaids, bookmakers and the like. Though heavily reliant on existing secondary studies, its illustrative examples draw on a wide variety of sources: newspapers, magazines, art, literature, sermons, memoirs, court reports, banners and pledges, to mention but a few.

Vice's meanings are not fixed. They regularly changed over time and across place. During the medieval period, Christians attacked certain 'capital vices', or 'cardinal sins', such as wrath, greed, sloth, pride, lust, envy, and gluttony. These powerful vices in turn created further sins. Vice shifted meaning as Britain became more secular. By the Victorian period, vice formed a key part of the imagination, common and widespread across its archival remains, something regularly thought about and discussed verbally and in print, and under constant surveillance. Generally the term applied to those behaviours, actions and habits that by general consensus amongst the respectable were considered immoral, degrading or depraved. Others saw vices as merely something regarded as a fault, a negative character trait or unhealthy habit. For yet others, however, so-called vices were merely pleasurable leisure activities.

More recently, in twentieth-century British law enforcement, vice crimes have tended to refer specifically to prostitution and pornography, as in the case of London's famous Metropolitan Vice Squad, the Clubs and Vice Unit first formed in 1932. In America, usage has often referred more to gambling and alcohol, though the Los Angeles Police Department's Vice Division focused on gaming, bookmaking, pornography and prostitution. Vice crimes were specifically identified as part of the penal code in some countries.

We all disapprove of the public vices of others, but sometimes quite enjoy our own private ones, even if with at least a frisson of guilt. We also 'know' about the Victorians, though the Victorians are seen as either similar or different or both depending on the various lens through which they have been viewed, be that nostalgia, affinity, admiration or condescension. Historians have debated how far a dark and decadent Victorian life existed behind a supposed façade of respectability, and indeed if respectability was less powerful than supposed, or even merely a myth.

Certainly the Victorians, like modern society, were divided both about what vice was, and what should be done about it. People had to locate their behaviour, attitudes and language, and that of others, somewhere on a linguistic continuum: vice or virtue; villain or victim; impure or pure; dirty or clean; sin or salvation; the 'demon drink' or total temperance; sexual dalliance or continence; over-indulgence or abstinence; corruption or purity; disreputability or solid reputation; un-respectability or respectability. Those who virtuously campaigned against vice tried to categorize its repugnant behaviours, and those individuals and groups in Victorian society attracted to them, using such language. By so doing, they felt it would assist and enforce changes in attitudes and behaviour. Yet at the local level such definitions were debated, and laws variously enforced or actions tolerated by police and magistrates.

So this book sets out to examine, deconstruct and reconstitute some of the complexity of Victorian perceptions and representations of vice and explore the cultural contexts of vice-related activity; to look at the many ways the 'war' against vice was waged and evaluate the extent of their success; and to come to tentative conclusions about the relationship between respectability and vices in Victorian life.

The book's structure

Chapter 1 introduces the topic in more detail and provides a context for later chapters. Its main emphasis is on unpacking the various meanings of vice. It shows that debates over vice already stretched deep into the past. It looks at the inter-relationships of vice and virtue, and those relating to vice, social class and gender. It also provides a brief summary of the more significant fluctuations in British attitudes to vice over the nineteenth century.

Vice had a spatial dimension, a social and moral geography, dealt with in Chapter 2. People had to seek out its public manifestations, to enjoy it or to attempt to regulate it. Cruelty to animals, for example, was really only regulated in areas where public controls could be applied. Fox-hunting, hare-coursing or shooting of game birds on landowners' own property were ignored. Vice was mentally mapped by everyone from social *flaneurs* to social reformers. It was seen as particularly concentrated spatially in distinctive areas, 'immoral landscapes' where it was less easily mastered and controlled.[1] City streets, public houses, brothels, clubs, music halls, fairs and race meetings all came under attack from moral, religious and political groups which saw popular leisure as idleness, to be discouraged and censured especially if associated with vice.

The Victorians, like modern parents, saw opportunities for vice as more common at night. As night fell, lamplighters lit up the main streets and those who had finished work started making their way through the town. Street girls, hiding in the shadows, looked more attractive in the flickering and tremulous gaslight. As evening drew on they became more importunate. Shop girls out on the spree became more light-hearted and sought companionship. Young men roamed the urban streets looking for adventure.

Gambling clubs, public houses, theatres and music halls began to fill up for the evening, and there were more temptations to vice in places like the pleasure gardens. Young men and girls could find themselves caught up in these urban excitements, and their desire could grow as alcohol took more effect. Back streets and slums remained unlit, and there darkness concealed movement and could conceal crime. In London's parks, so-called 'park women' wandered along those paths most frequented after nightfall, consenting to any species of humiliation for the sake of acquiring a little money.

Vices could be of many sorts, yet in its cultural discourses, and the ideas, beliefs and meanings applied to it, clear clustering was discernable in the ways it was presented and interpreted in the media, Parliament, government commissions and elsewhere. Three central vices dominated discourse: the unholy trinity of drink, gambling and sex.

Chapter 3 explores the drinking of alcohol, its contexts and the issues arising from it. These were continual concerns across the Victorian age. Phrases associating drink and vice were extremely frequent, revealing the assumptions about alcohol's effects that many moral reformers shared. Variously described, it was most often the 'vice of drunkenness', or even worse 'the vice of habitual drunkenness', of 'intemperance', 'dissipation', and 'intoxication'. It was almost always applied to alcohol, and the 'vice of opium smoking' or tobacco smoking was rarely attacked before the

1890s. Drunkenness had clear consequences. The report of the Commission on the Sanitary Condition of the Labouring Poor in 1840 saw the 'vice of intoxication' as a 'fearful vice' leading inexorably to pauperism and crime.[2] The latter was a further dominant theme, and chaplains of prisons, city magistrates and chiefs of police all regularly made explicit connections between the two. Drink was also linked to health, to alcoholism, brain and liver damage. There was even, thought the General Board of Health in 1850, an increased chance of falling victim to cholera, if one drank and had dissipated and intemperate habits.[3]

Yet at the same time, alcoholic drink was all-pervasive, associated with a wide variety of activities in public houses and beer shops, clubs and private houses, and linked closely to some forms of work as well as leisure. Brewers and publicans were powerful interest groups, prominent on local authorities, and able to exert strong parliamentary pressure.

Chapter 4 examines the complex and changing nature of betting and gaming in Victorian Britain. Both were associated with vice and profligacy, most especially when individuals' attachment became obsessive and addictive. Its consequences for families and for tempting theft from businesses were regularly emphasized. Gambling to some was exciting and thrilling, yet, because of its sinful associations, often also shameful. Like the drinking of alcohol, betting could be seen as a popular cultural phenomenon, certainly cross-class and sometimes attractive to both sexes. It was associated with a wide variety of sports, from horse- and dog-racing to football, cricket and rowing, as well as with other gaming activities such as card playing or coin tossing. Attitudes to it were shaped once again by class and gender as much as by the specific nature and extent of the gambling, and whether it was cash or credit. By the 1890s, as interest and support fell away from the temperance movement, moral reformers increased their active opposition to betting, which was portrayed as the 'last and greatest of social evils'.

The theme of Chapter 5 is the sets of discourses and behaviours collected around sexuality and vice. This was an area where the arguments of Victorian moralists were particularly characterized by power relationships, paradoxes, contradictions and inconsistencies. Sex was a topic regularly discussed by the medical profession, portrayed in art and sculpture, and covered in the columns of newspapers, but the thrust of much coverage was on prostitution, its defiling of moral purity and the consequent need to regulate (though not completely suppress) women's sexual experience outside marriage. The term vice was also applied to such topics as premarital sex, same-sex relationships, 'free love', women's sexuality, masturbation, pornography and prostitution. There were associated debates related to the changing basis of knowledge about sex, sexually transmitted diseases, birth control, legislation and censorship, sex education, the separation of pleasure from procreation, and the extent to which abstinence should be or was promoted by women and men.

Chapter 6 focuses on the formal, organized fight against vice. Vice had its corollary in the world of virtue and there were key contexts where virtue was lent the strongest of support, and moral reformers waged war upon vice. Parents, employers and the community, societies and organizations, chapels, churches and the mechanics' institutes formed part of this world. Preachers, municipal leaders, industrialists and other well-connected guardians of urban respectability all attacked vice. Evangelical groups played a key role. Their faith in God offered a moral absolute and in attacks on vice, discipline, morality and spirituality overlapped. Their world was devoted to saving those who had sinned, and calling them to repentance and redemption. They sought to do this in ways that included argument, education, preaching, lobbying and the formation of a huge variety of organizations and groups.

Chapter 7 brings together notions of vice and respectability, attempting a reassessment of their relationship and the place of vice in Victorian life. For many historians, the ideological power of respectability, despite its complexities and nuances of interpretation, has been a key feature of the Victorian age. Indeed, in 1988 the historian F.M.L. Thompson summarized the period as 'the rise of respectable society'.[4] Yet the extent to which the same homilies against vice were repeated suggests that in the contest between what we can call 'disreputable' and respectable leisure the anti-vice attacks sometimes fell on stony ground. This chapter also explores the limitations of respectability's power. Certainly a counter-discourse supporting more traditional notions of pleasure and hedonism retained its appeal in particular cultural contexts. The social and moral signifiers of vice proved highly complex, while virtue and respectability were rarely identities to be totally assumed. For the middle classes, as for the working classes too, respectability often became a role to be practised and played, although sometimes in a more limited and situational sense, increasingly so in the later nineteenth century. It was context that determined behaviour, and decided whether particular actions were vices or pleasures.

The book ends with a short epilogue, exploring some of the reasons why the Victorian campaigns against vice were only partially successful, and the extent to which these campaigns were different from those in other recent periods of history and successfully carried into and across the twentieth century.

Many of the chapters begin with a short illustrative case study. These case studies provide a useful starting point for discussion and reflection for groups and individuals before reading further. A guide for further reading is also provided at the end of the book.

Historiography

Vice has had multiple manifestations across the Victorian world. Rather surprisingly, its various dimensions, regulatory responses, popularity, social roles and cultural significance have never been the subject of detailed study. No monograph has brought its examples together to study its meanings, locations, what exactly it incorporated and its relationship to respectable culture. British academic research has paid much more attention to social and moral reform, to Victorian attempts to curtail vice's evils and to 'respectability'.[5] So the specific historiography of vice is, at present, fairly limited, though so much secondary material touches on it in part that only a few key works can be mentioned here.

In recent years, what might be termed the 'low life' of Victorian Britain has attracted some attention, and two studies of vice in London have addressed the Victorian period as part of a longer study.[6] Indeed, London, especially in terms of themes like slumming, crime or sexual activity, has dominated the bulk of scholarly work.[7] Policing of street behaviour has also been of interest.[8] By contrast, focused studies of urban areas outside the capital are few, though there have been useful studies of Liverpool and Merthyr.[9] Locations associated with vice such as music halls, race-courses or fairs all have their own specialist literature, which for reasons of space cannot be mentioned here.

Studies of alcohol, temperance and its reform movements are dominated by Harrison's *Drink and the Victorians: The Temperance Question in England, 1815–72* (1971). Indeed, its definitive scope, based on detailed analysis of archival sources and focus on organizational histories, leading individuals, pressure-group politics and legislation discouraged substantial further work. The bulk of work has been on the specific relationship between drink, addiction and social policy,[10] and the various Victorian campaigns against drink.[11] There have been several longitudinal studies of attitudes towards the drinking of alcohol or liquid refreshment more generally which include the period[12] and the Victorian public house has also attracted attention.[13] There are also some useful regional and local studies.[14]

Studies of gambling are fairly limited and are focused on working-class gambling, though its regulation has also been of sustained interest.[15] Social and economic monograph-length studies of its role are few.[16] Scholarship on horse-racing has included its role in sustaining betting, and there have also been some studies of bookmakers and tipsters.[17]

By contrast, a very substantial body of scholarship, from a wide variety of disciplines, has covered sexual vices. The world of Victorian sexual behaviour has been increasingly explored by feminist historians,[18] and there have been a significant number of works on aspects of prostitution, for example, covering urban areas across Britain.[19] Literary critics, sociologists, medical experts, psychologists and specialists in cultural studies have all contributed to the field.[20] There are also emerging interdisciplinary academic fields such as 'queer studies', which explores issues relating to sexual orientation and gender identity.[21] Earlier views that the Victorians were prevailingly ignorant, inhibited, prudish and hypocritical about sex have been increasingly challenged.[22] Most recent work implies a complex picture, while emphasizing that prudery's values always commanded wide assent especially amongst the respectable middle and working classes.[23]

Studies of drink, gambling and sexual vices often include much on social reformers and their strategies and tactics. For temperance, for example, books by A.E. Dingle, Brian Harrison and Lilian Shiman have much on the campaigns, as does Allan Harty's local study of Sunderland.[24] Respectability has been a theme running through many broader studies of the period, ever since the work of Geoffrey Best in the 1970s and F.M.L. Thompson in the 1980s.[25] A number of monographs have also used it as a major focus.[26]

Finally

Writing this book has had many challenges. Spending five days reading Victorian pornography in the British Library can turn you off, not turn you on. And you have to sit in a special area to access these 'special books' so you are singled out! The voluminous temperance literature, though fascinating, was also serious, earnest and heavy going, usually lacking any humour to lighten it. Reading about vice, and all the Victorian societies dedicated to eradicating it, soon revealed that the word vice constantly changed its tone, its meanings, its audience and its focus, as it was manipulated in its various media-framed discourses. Such complexity will need in the future a more sophisticated, nuanced and in-depth study to do it justice, and avoid the dangers of over-simplification and over-generalization inevitable in an introductory work. The same effort needs to be devoted to unpacking the materials and articles devoted to vice, as has been spent on the Victorian reform movements, politics and religion. Nevertheless, this study provides a first foray into a fascinating area, one that has been really enjoyable to explore.

CHAPTER ONE

The Language of Vice

Introduction

The darker side of Victorian society shocked and provoked people then as it does to this day. For the Victorians, vice was a major obsession, a key point of tension and an important cultural continuity. Vices were less legitimated social practices. Some enjoyed their excitements and pleasures but others felt repulsion and horror at the moral, social, financial and physical impact of vice, and its possibly addictive consequences. The various Victorian anti-vice movements were a highly significant feature of the period. They directly affected the lives of millions. They contributed significantly to the wider cultural landscape.

At the same time vice was, to use a medical term, endemic in British society. It had what historians call a *longue durée*. Its habits of behaviour, attitude and thought were deep-rooted. They were resistant to change. Drink, sexual misbehaviour and gambling were always targets, but every now and then their specific manifestations would be publicized by campaigning groups and the press, and there would be a reaction from police and Parliament, only for public interest to then slowly dissipate. The activities would then tacitly continue once more.

This makes the study of vice a key element of any understanding of Victorian society. Vice was surrounded by vociferous discourses, all demanding attention. It had multiple meanings, ambivalences and contradictions. It was mediated through variables such as social class, gender, age, town and country or specific pastimes. For the historian, the sources available, links with Victorian themes such as purity and respectability, and its difficult chronology all make vice well worth exploring, despite the perils of generalization.

The term 'Victorian' itself, still actively found in popular use, is similarly nuanced. It covers a long and changing transitional industrial, economic, socially and politically important period, whose cultures were dauntingly complex. It was an age of contradictions, variously dominated by Evangelical, utilitarian and imperialist trends. It has been represented in different ways ever since 1901. It has come to refer to a specific set of attitudes whose influence has extended geographically well beyond the shores of Britain and its empire, and chronologically further by far than the nineteenth century. Sometimes it has been applied to specific 'respectable' characteristics, such as moral rectitude or to so-called Victorian values, but at others to prudishness and hypocrisy. The term 'Victorian' has also been applied, in terms of style, to novels, architecture, art and furniture.

Attitudes to vice varied culturally across Victorian Britain, with strongly Calvinist or Free Church-dominated areas most strong in their opposition. As foreign visitors noted, the British attitudes to vice contrasted with those found in Paris, Vienna or Rome, where modernity took different forms.[1] So an exploration of the Victorian ideas about vice can offer insights into the way issues such as pleasure and its consequences, reason and respectability or freedom and liberty were viewed across the United Kingdom. This was particularly significant in relation to topics such as strong drink, gambling and sex.

Chapter outline

This chapter provides a context for later chapters. It begins by showing how debates over vice already stretched deep into the past by 1837. During the Victorian period, the word 'vice' was exploited in many different topics and debates. It was found in different contexts, in speech and in various print media, but most commonly it was used by moral and social reformers to attack socially-disapproved-of leisure activities, especially those of the poor. The material such reformers produced has been heavily exploited by historians. Consequently, we know more about the reform movements than about those who took part in vice-related activity. The biases of such material distort attempts at analysis.

What Victorians defined as vice was related to the ways in which they defined virtue so these inter-relationships are next explored, before the chapter introduces the complex relationships between vice, social class and gender. These are themes that reoccur throughout the book. Finally, a succinct summary of the more significant fluctuations over the nineteenth century is attempted, in the context of changing practices, ideas and global influences.

Vice debates had a long history

To understand where debates about vice fitted into the Victorian world perhaps we should begin in June 1837. The young queen, Victoria, quickly issued a Proclamation against Vice for the 'encouragement of piety and virtue' and the discouragement, suppression and punishing of 'vice, profaneness, debauchery and immorality'. These, said her Proclamation, were 'highly displeasing to God' and 'a reproach' to religion and government. All 'persons of honour or in place of authority' were to provide good example by their own virtue and piety. This Proclamation became a fixture, regularly read out during her reign in churches, council chambers, courts and other national institutions.[2] Readings were highly solemn, ritualistic and symbolic acts.

To some, it reflected a judgement about earlier Georgian immorality, aristocratic debauchery, excess and dissolute behaviour. It appeared to embody a new morality, a deliberate attempt by the Queen, the head of the Church of England, to call people back to a life of piety and virtue. Others saw it as a response to concerns over Chartism, male suffrage demands, or fears of moral decay associated with urbanization and industrialization.

In reality, the roots of her Proclamation went deep into the past. Victoria followed a tradition long heavy with symbolic meaning and impact. It told the British that moral concerns were being addressed. Polite language had shifted away from earlier Puritan and biblical images of 'odious and loathsome sinnes' and 'temptations'. The focus had become more secular, using vices and evils to symbolize immoral behaviour. In 1660, King Charles II, privately a lover of more sinful pleasures, had issued a solemn public Proclamation against drinking, swearing and debauchery, perhaps to gain support from subjects with strong Puritan sympathies. One of the first Acts of Queen Anne's reign was a Proclamation against Vice and Debauchery, to suppress 'profaneness' and 'immoralities'. She imposed a strict court morality.

By the 1780s, reform of manners movements had begun to attack the perceived immorality of the upper and lower classes, and the more boisterous, bawdy, convivial and pleasure-seeking aspects of Georgian life. In 1787, George III issued another Proclamation Against Vice, and 'the Encouragement of Piety and Virtue', urging his subjects to suppress 'excessive drinking, blasphemy, profanation of the Lord's day, and other dissolute, immoral or disorderly practices' such as 'all public gaming houses'.

The founding of the Proclamation Society, dominated by fervently religious Evangelical groups, quickly followed. Its purpose was to 'enforce a stricter execution of the laws against vice and immorality' and 'to afford the Magistracy such assistance in the discharge of their duty as the nature of the case may require'. The Society issued legal proceedings against blasphemous and indecent publications, and aimed to suppress prostitution, swearing and abuse of the Sabbath. Its successor, the Society for the Suppression of Vice and the Encouragement of Religion, was founded in 1802. It wanted the complete suppression of Sabbath breaking, blasphemous and licentious publications and private theatricals, fairs, brothels, dram-shops, gaming houses and fortune-tellers. In its first two years, 623 of its 678 prosecutions were for Sabbath breaking. It paid little attention to the sex industry. The issue was perhaps too close to home for some of its upper-class financial supporters, and such vices were important to London's economy and to its businessmen.

There was also a moral reaction against the scandals associated with the Prince of Wales, his mistresses and illegitimate offspring, and upper-class libertines, excessive drinkers and gamblers. Consumer demand for vice, however, was simultaneously fostered by the socially aspirant middling sort of people – manufacturers, merchants, wealthier tradesmen, lawyers, doctors, teachers and other professional men. They had surplus wealth to spend and free time to enjoy it, a demand driven most of all by the capital city, London, a popular venue for many forms of commercial leisure. It had sufficient forms of vice to satisfy everyone. London was a centre for prostitution, turning over perhaps about £20 million a year (about £1.5 billion today), from girls offering a 'three-penny upright' to high-class courtesans retained by rich aristocrats.[3]

Many people were strongly opposed to such behaviour, on the grounds of religion, morality or social conscience. During the Evangelical revival, flourishing from the 1790s to the 1840s, sin became particularly identified with specific activities like excessive drinking or fornication. The reformist High Church Oxford Movement, with its strong views on sin, had a similar major impact within Anglicanism in England in the 1830s.

The Evangelical revival was a complex phenomenon, taking different forms in England, Scotland, Ireland and Wales. It provided an anti-vice vocabulary, philosophy and moral force. Its power was limited, thanks to doctrinal and social class differences, but there was substantial co-operation amongst groups aiming at moral change and religious conversion. Social and political pressures brought such concerns to a peak. Strong objections to vices and related social abuses came from within the growing numbers of the middle classes, a small minority but growing in numbers. Even here, *active* middle-class reformers were always a small, highly vociferous, minority. Some aspired to ape upper-class life and mingle with them socially; others were keen to distance themselves from the *working* classes but they also wanted to demonstrate that they were socially and morally superior to the *upper* classes, their supposed wasteful luxury, endemic bribery and corruption, and the way government sinecures could be given to cronies and hangers on.

At a time when industrialization and urbanization were placing traditional certainties under threat, there was a whole litany of further beliefs about a decline in British behaviour and values. Society needed to govern its impulsive behaviour. People needed to exercise more self-control and restraint. Concerns often mirrored those reflected in the tabloid press in the twenty-first century. The expanding industrial towns were filled with the poor and vicious, threatening a breakdown of law and order and the social fabric. Some were viewed as the 'idle' poor, failing to find work, or doing nothing constructive with their free time. Others were 'wasting' what little wages they had on folly, extravagance, pleasure, intemperance and distraction, or on dress and clothing. They demonstrated their irresponsibility in the streets rather than working hard to improve their poverty-stricken lives and taking care of their homes and families. Unitarians, for example, believed drink, moral destitution and parental neglect largely caused poverty, not economic or political structures.

The battle against vice was a battle to raise standards, to move towards a more civilized, orderly and polite society. Vice threatened social order, good government and respectable life. For reformers, society needed a stronger and healthier work ethic. Vice was often associated with commercial forms of leisure, such as public houses and brothels. Such enjoyments were viewed as an unacceptable use of the time of the Victorian workforce.

So when Victoria became queen in 1837, parts of British society welcomed her Proclamation. The word 'vice' provided a culturally-significant target to overthrow. Evangelical and Enlightenment thinking encouraged increasingly genteel behaviour, and moral and sexual earnestness amongst more respectable and responsible sections of the middle classes, artisans and working-class radicals. New sets of manners and codes surrounded personal behaviour. Social distancing and anti-vice persecutions had increased. Many Britons were becoming more respectable, sober, orderly and restrained, more censorious or hypocritical.[4] As Lord Melbourne, Victoria's first prime minister, gloomily observed to the young queen: 'Nobody is gay now; they are so religious.'

Yet in the very month in which Victoria's Proclamation was issued a new London periodical was produced. This was *The Town*, described by editor Renton Nicholson in its preface as 'one of the most racy, spicy and figging productions of literature ever produced'. 'Figging' was a word bearing a variety of usually vulgar meanings, from the insertion of a prepared piece of peeled ginger root into the anus to increase sexual or sadomasochistic pleasure (a possible meaning here), to thieves' slang for pocket picking. *The Town* was prurient and pornographic, indecorous and indecent. Its gossip, titillation and *double entendres* covered a bawdy London world of nocturnal pleasures featuring peers and policemen, prostitutes and pickpockets and the sporting 'Fancy'. Sold at two-pence an issue, and aimed at the urban artisan market at a time of considerable social fluidity, *The Town* found sufficient metropolitan readership for commercial success, despite the Proclamation against Vice.[5]

The language of vice

So what did this word 'vice' in Victoria's Proclamation mean? It was a well-recognized theme, yet its definition was problematic. The Victorian middle classes spent much time in attempting to map, categorize and classify unacceptable 'vicious' behaviour and what was respectable and proper, especially in relation to what they saw as a declining aristocracy and sometimes degenerate working class. So vice discourses exerted a powerful influence on Victorian culture. Yet the word 'vice' was elusive, difficult to pin down and subject to huge variation in its social categories, purposes, metaphors and meanings in different cultural contexts. Vice was like quicksilver. It constantly changed its nuances, its audience and its focus as it was manipulated. Vice was opaque, not transparent, with diverse readings, meanings and interpretations. We cannot access what people felt directly, but we *can* explore the meanings and issues most broadly and prominently circulated, and the ways they were framed. Vice elicited strong feelings, powerful emotions and extreme reactions.

Queen Victoria's Proclamation's specific examples of vice were largely linked to three dominant themes: sexual immorality, gambling and the drinking of alcohol. It contrasted vice with 'proper' Sunday behaviour and thus provided support for the Sunday Observance movement. 'Playing on the Lord's day at dice, cards or any game whatever, either in public or private houses' was blasphemous and to be discouraged. 'All public gaming houses and places, and lewd and other disorderly houses' were to be suppressed. The selling of 'wine, beer or other liquors or receiving or permitting guests' at taverns or other public houses during 'the time of divine service' was also mentioned. The Proclamation also linked vice explicitly with 'dissolute, immoral and disorderly conduct'. Such activities were clearly offences against good order and Christianity, hinting vaguely at sexual misbehaviour.

The deceptively simple questions about vice, its definition and its Victorian meanings are not easy to answer. One man's abhorrent licentious 'vices' could be another man's simple habitual 'pleasures'. Perception was all. What is very clear, immediately, is the sheer number and variety of voices and perspectives on vice throughout the Victorian age. There was *no* consensus. Texts addressing vice were written with different intentions, for different audiences and from almost unique perspectives. They were read and used differently, and with different meanings, according to context.[6] Equally, individuals adopted very different projects of moral regulation.

The term was regularly appropriated by moral and social reformers with an absolute confidence in moral absolutes, their own moral superiority and the immorality of those needing moral improvement. They believed that virtue and vice were knowable, instantly recognizable and universal. Certain actions were, by their very nature, totally abhorrent symbols of immorality, evil and degeneracy. Though drinking, 'fornication' outside marriage or gambling were dominant themes, constantly under attack, they stood alongside debatable 'minor vices' such as smoking tobacco or opium taking. Young girls were 'rescued from vice', but so were the pupils of Ragged Schools, those charity organizations which sought to provide free education to destitute, vagrant and very poor children. The major 'sins' like drinking, almost automatically linked people to further vices, beginning with the 'vice of improvidence', a word applied to those 'wasting' their money in non-rational forms of recreational pleasure. They could then be 'tainted with the vice of pauperism', which an assistant Poor Law Commissioner discerned in 1841.[7] This in turn created another vice, appalling to the better-off: the vice of 'dependence on the rates'. So there were many forms of 'temptations to vice'. Governors of prisons and reformatory schools claimed crime and vice were closely associated. Young criminals were 'schooled in vice' before embarking on 'careers of vice'. The slums were full of 'dens of vice and infamy', as were drinking houses. A whole range of activities offered 'encouragement to vice'.

The world of vice spread its tentacles widely. The Victorians were 'tempted' by vice. They 'fell into' it. They acquired 'vicious' habits. At the annual general meeting of the National Temperance League in 1865 public houses were denounced as places where 'every sort of viciousness was engendered'. At a weekly gospel temperance meeting in Central Hall, Newcastle, in November 1891, a 'vicious exhibition' was described by Colonel W.L.B. Coulson. He had seen miners with their whippets held on leashes, carrying rabbits in a sack, which were then given twenty-five yards start before being chased by the dogs.[8] The event linked to the further vice of betting.

By the 1840s tobacco was being attacked as a wasteful and stupefying vice, a 'tobacco mania'. Thomas Cook, the entrepreneurial travel agent, tried to start an anti-smoking movement in the 1840s, and Thomas Reynolds founded the British Anti-Tobacco Society in 1853. Its *Anti-Tobacco Journal* remained strong from 1850 to 1870. Amongst doctors a 'Great tobacco controversy' raged in *The Lancet* in 1853, and there was continued opposition to smoking as 'the source of unnumbered evils' through the century.[9]

In the 1860s, slumming journalists published the first sensationalist and mythologized accounts of supposedly mysterious and evil opium dens in London's East End, especially in Shadwell, titillating and creating anxiety in equal measure about the 'vice of opium smoking'. They painted a picture of such dens as commercial organizations in which depraved people gathered together to enjoy opium communally. There were claims that 'distinguished members of the nobility and aristocracy of Great Britain, and, it is rumoured even that royalty has condescended to visit'.[10] In reality, they catered almost entirely for the small Chinese community but the stories journalists spawned, and their use by Englishmen seeking new experiences, were soon being picked up in popular fiction, such as Dickens's *The Mystery of Edwin Drood* (1870). Increasingly, such fiction drew on racist sentiments and the broader late-Victorian sensationalization of the Orient, suggesting that the small Chinese community in the East End and their supposed addictions and dependency on opium were a social evil, a bad influence. Novelists exploited images of addiction and drug dependency, fear and desire, decadence and immorality, excessive inhuman pleasures and even a sinister Oriental underground.

There were many other potential vices. Preachers often targeted the 'inordinate vice of ambition'. According to the *Daily News* of 3 September

1851 the 'vice' of the yachting system was carrying too much canvas. To the *Plymouth and Cornish Advertiser* of 3 December 1857, the chief cause of the Indian Mutiny was the 'vice and cruelty of heathenism'. Even young children could fall into vice. Long after the late century education acts, in some areas of London, such as Tower Hamlets, the 'vice of truancy' was apparently ingrained.[11]

Churches and churchmen sometimes became the target of accusations couched in terms of vice. One witness to the Select Committee on the Sale of Liquors on Sunday in 1867–8, for example, attacked the churches for displaying their 'vice of hypocrisy'. At a select committee of the House of Lords in 1874 the Earl of Harrowby attacked the 'vice of simony in church'.[12] The involvement of churches in educational provision led to 'the vice of denominationalism' according to the Royal Commission enquiring into the working of the Elementary Education Acts in 1886. Even eating could not escape censure. Augustus John Harvey's pamphlet on *Intemperance in Food: A National Vice* (1876) prefigured more recent debates about obesity in attacking Britain's excessive appetites for food. To engineer and social commentator Thomas Wright (1839–1909), selfishness and love of money were vices.[13]

Despite the ubiquity of the word, the language of vice was a powerful leitmotif. It allowed reformers to create self-serving binary identities – 'refined' and 'rough' – within a polarized world of absolutes: virtue and vice, morality and immorality, good and evil, sanctity and sin, purity and impurity, Puritanism and pleasure, even while disputing the relative evil of particular vices.

For the Victorians, views, visions and representations of vice, sometimes luridly hysterical and sensationalist and embodying fears of moral panic, helped define social life. They illuminated Victorian society. They shed interpretative light on gender, class and identity. In the world of vice, social and moral categories overlapped. Their polarized moral struggles were represented in Victorian paintings and posters, literature and theatrical melodrama, sermons, pamphlets, tracts and investigations, newspaper court reports, Gothic romances, or magazines and periodicals. Vice was discussed in Parliament, reported on by Select Committees, or addressed in legislation. These generated and circulated particular notions of vice, often locating them as on the borders of social imagination to point up the 'true path' of virtue, morality and goodness. The respectable middle classes emphasized the character-building attitudes described by Samuel Smiles in his 1859 *Self-Help* book: the Protestant work ethic, thrifty saving, self-discipline and self-denial. They sought to transfer these to the new and expanding leisure market, and encourage the working classes to embark on moral and social improvement and more 'rational' recreations.

Notions of 'dangerous vice' were also linked to specific fears of an uneducated, vice-ridden and improvident proletariat. Campaigners were concerned about the potential costs to ratepayers, potential violence and political instability, and by fears of degeneration. Earnest, pious churchmen, driven by their sense of sin and guilt, were afraid for the immortal souls of their charges. Industrialists stressed the impact of drink or gambling on production and profit. Such themes gripped Victorian social scientists such as Weber and Freud, and challenged and threatened society. The reformers stressed their moral mission and civic duty to address vicious behaviour, not the economic and structural forces that made it difficult for the poor to cope. Newspapers generally gave prominence to the vices of individuals, not the structural and systemic circumstances that sometimes forced them into vice.

For reformers, the battle against vice lent meaning and gave order to their daily lives. We can see how the dominant themes of vice were actually employed by looking at one reformer's life in more detail. Francis Close (1797–1882) was the son of a vicar, a former student at St John's College, Cambridge, a man who spent his life concerned about and fighting against 'the follies and vices of society'.[14] In his early youth he had experienced an evangelical conversion and soon became a leading radical, strongly opposed to National Society education, ritualism in the Church of England, Romanism and Popery, and a thorn in the side of race meetings, theatres and other places of 'idle play'. He believed firmly in total abstinence from drink. He was strong on Sabbath observance as a day of rest. Any breach was a 'national evil'. Sunday papers were 'for the most part of an evil, polluting, ungodly and licentious character', a 'pernicious literature'.[15] Ungodliness was the ultimate vice, and in 1842 he had Manchester atheist G.J. Holyoake imprisoned for libelling Christianity.

Close became perpetual curate of Cheltenham in 1826, and his popularity grew rapidly. He was a big man, with a commanding voice, and a forceful and effective preacher without notes. Opponents saw him as a bigot, but his strong views and forceful personality, general geniality and humour attracted large congregations and the support of leading local figures. He was adept at raising money and managing publicity, and was the prime mover behind the formation of the *Cheltenham Chronicle*. It publicized his views and attacked his enemies.

The local races provided an early target. According to Close, they were filled with licentiousness, prostitution and drunkenness, a 'torrent of vice'. Their consequences were 'deadly', evil and ruinous, and they were supported by the leading local aristocratic family, the Berkeleys, whom he condemned for their wild orgies and escapades.[16] Profligacy and pleasure were sinful. His sermons, tracts and lectures against Sabbath-breaking, theatres, drink and smoking were regularly printed. Cheltenham gained a reputation as one of the most sober and religious towns in Britain.

He became Dean of Carlisle in 1856. Arriving in Cumberland, he perceived Carlisle as a wicked city, full of temptation and a morally blind population. Working with his bishops he made the area more protestant and Low Church, and introduced Bible classes and adult night schools. Close was a committed teetotaller, a leading figure in the British and Foreign Bible Society and the Church of England Temperance Society. He linked himself with the United Kingdom Alliance, which in the 1860s helped circulate his long sermons such as 'Teetotalism: A Christian's Duty or Why I Have Taken the Pledge'. Temperance became his major crusade. He travelled the country in support of the cause, telling Glasgow abstainers in 1861 that alcohol was 'mischievous, deleterious, injurious to your constitution, to your health, to your mental powers and your moral character'.[17] He wrote papers for the International Temperance and Prohibition Convention.

Close's antagonism to vices extended even to tobacco smoking, which he saw as far more than an impure habit. Excessive youthful smoking was a 'great national evil', with 'the most serious and distressing consequences'.[18] To combat the 'moral evils' of smoking he became President of the Anti-Tobacco Society in the 1850s.

Despite or because of his popularity with female members of his congregation, he was reluctant to discuss sexual sin. He was happily married, had a large family and, unusually for the time, was opposed to double standards. No breath of scandal ever touched him, even if his strong opinions made him enemies, sometimes from within the clergy. Even so, Close saw society as divided into the 'virtuous classes' and the 'dangerous classes', predominantly working-class, with many illegitimate children. Sin and crime were almost universal amongst them, and children were 'trained in vice' by their parents.

Although drink and gambling were seen as vices by reformers like Close, there was little evidence that their views were those of a majority, even when, as in the case of ready-money gambling, this was against the law. Reformers' views did not always go unchallenged. For example, on 4 August 1866 a letter to *The Wrexham Advertiser* wrote:

> Sir,
>   Allow me . . . to call the attention of the authorities to the demoralising practices indulged in on the outskirts of this town on Sunday afternoons, by persons whose delight (apparently) is the desecration of the Sabbath. On Sunday last . . . we found the thoroughfare nearly blocked by a number of young men busily engaged in the unlawful game of *pitch and toss*. This is by no means the only instance that these degrading practices have been witnessed by us. Being under the impression that the police authorities are not aware of this fact I have taken the liberty of trespassing on your valuable space.

The complaint, from the anonymous 'B', could have been made directly to the police but, in general, pitch and toss, a game involving the toss of coins, was rarely prosecuted and the writer presumably hoped to get more action by giving it publicity. And clearly the offence, however 'demoralising' and 'degrading', was made greater by being on a Sunday even if it was in the afternoon after divine service. It was 'young men' who blocked the writer's route instead of courteously letting him through, and there was often a generational aspect to reformers' complaints.

However, the writer's views met with resistance. The very next week a letter from 'XYZ' argued strongly against 'B's view, claiming that 'on the whole it is a very innocent amusement' and that 'XYZ' 'could not help regretting that [his] indignation is not vented on something more serious'.

The media

Such vice discussions and exchanges caused debate, distress and strong feeling. This forced the Victorian media into difficult positions. Victorian newspapers generated substantial coverage of vice, because they catered for readership demands, but were very careful in their presentation. They tried to sound disapproving even when editors' personal lives were disreputable. Many editorials were written in a manner that conveyed the assumption that all a paper's readers were reticent, reserved and restrained. They avoided being explicit. Wherever their main readership was perceived as the more literate, better-educated and respectable, the voices of articulate moral reformers dominated their columns, raising their voices in opposition to vice and demanding action. For editors, a mixture of delicacy, squeamishness, modesty, dignity, concerns about possible offence to listeners or readers, or of putting ideas into people's heads, and a consciousness of possible complaints if they went into too much detail all meant that some vices were *not* described. Indeed, they might not even be named. Instead, words such as 'unspeakable' or 'unnameable' mixed hints of horror, shame and disgust.

Reticence accompanied tacit understandings of what could or could not be voiced. Much comment was carefully coded, brief and guarded. The knowing reader would comprehend exactly what was being discussed by reading between or beyond the lines. The unknowing, naïve or 'too delicate' would be sheltered from unseemly contamination.

As the crusading editor of the *Liverpool Mercury* recognized in 1856, informing readers about the moral evils that reigned unchecked in their streets was an 'arduous and repulsive task'. Reporting gave publicity to 'much we would gladly have withheld from the eyes of our readers'. But he felt that such 'morally repulsive facts' helped put 'imperilled innocence on its guard'. They deterred offenders and encouraged better administration of justice. In short, 'informed and awakened opinion' would 'purify and regenerate Liverpool life'.[19] The dilemma for 'decent' reformers was that publicizing vice might imply that it was appealing and raise awareness of how to purchase vicious pleasures.

Like vice, the related term 'impurity' covered a range of actions, always sinful yet often tempting. So impurity too was rarely defined in any detail. *Tempted London*'s 1882 warning to young men about impurity, seen as doing 'more than any other sin to injure and destroy them', indicated the difficulty reformers faced. It left much 'under the seal of silence', and accepted the need to be guarded and reserved. The book's examples of impurity included 'obscene conversation', 'loose reading', 'the influence of theatres, music halls, etc.', and 'drink'. Two further topics, masturbation and sex with young women, were described in very brief and guarded terms, since, the writer believed (or hoped) that 'the interpretation will not be found difficult by those it is meant to reach'. Masturbation was the 'secret vice', a 'ruinous practice', with apparently awful results. Pre-marital sex was 'the social evil', even more vaguely addressed, taking almost two pages to warn of 'glib male friends' before women were actually mentioned, followed by a page showing how young women might 'pick up' foolish youths, and then a short paragraph discussing women 'plying a hideous trade'. Its advice to young men was to 'never . . . enter a doubtful house', 'leave drink alone', 'cultivate good company' and learn 'the awful results of immorality', such as disease, ill health and accelerated death.[20]

Likewise, when a staunch supporter of the Social Purity Alliance, Rev. E. Lyttelton, headmaster first of Haileybury and later of Eton, wrote his *Causes and Prevention of Immorality in Schools* in 1887, it was a very carefully guarded and phrased attempt to provide advice to young boys. 'Of all the sins to which a boy is tempted at school', he announced, 'the most prevalent, the most alluring and the most enduring and deadly . . . is impurity', caused by 'dirty talk' and 'curiosity'. His lack of clarity about what exactly 'impurity' entailed probably stimulated curiosity rather than curtailed it.

Advice to women was even more guarded, since male double standards suggested it was a measure of a woman's personal virtue to lack knowledge (or pretend ignorance) of the wider world. Many men expected their wives and daughters to know nothing of vices such as prostitution, and by no means to get involved in helping to remedy them. But some female social reformers attempted this, a point made forcibly in one letter, apparently from a woman, to *The Times* in 1857:

> We have been told that, in virtuous women, it is a breach of feminine delicacy even to suppose the existence of certain outcasts of our own sex, or of certain exemptions in regard to vicious indulgence assumed by yours; in short, that, as women of virtue, we have nothing to do with such questions, though we know, too well, how deeply they affect us, how terribly near they approach us personally, how the far-reaching contagion of such covert vice involves in some form or other the peace of our 'virtuous' homes, the fidelity of our husbands, the health and morality of our sons, the innocence of our daughters. We have been allowed, indeed, to patronize penitentiaries, to read chapters of the Bible, and distribute lugubrious tracts to wretched, sullen, disordered victims; but, meantime, we are told – I have myself been told, half pityingly, half sneeringly – that for every one unhappy creature we rescue out of the streets two will be at

once supplied to fill up the vacancy; that this 'state of things' is a necessary social evil; and that we virtuous women had better not meddle with it, lest worse befall us.[21]

In newspaper reportage, the presence of prostitutes at events that middle-class husbands might attend was usually passed over in silence to avoid any potential domestic disharmony, or tactfully hinted at for those who could interpret the allusion. A reporter at one Manchester race meeting in 1867, describing the scene to his readers, simply asked rhetorically: 'Shall we describe to you the numerous ladies in numerous barouches? ... They do not belong to the most respectable families in Manchester'.[22] The following year *The Star* equally carefully described prostitutes as 'that unhappy class for which we have no name one does not shrink from writing'.[23]

But if some newspaper editors were careful not to offend their respectable readers, there were also popular papers whose editors were well aware that providing their readers with a diet of material related to vice would encourage sales. As the reading public expanded, the popular Sunday press, such as *Reynolds's News* or *Lloyd's Weekly Newspaper*, increasingly filled their columns with sensationalist 'human interest' stories, personalizing good and evil, vice and virtue. They drew heavily on police court reports, using criminality, and themes such as sex and drunkenness. This displayed for the moral instruction, delectation and imaginary worlds of readers the comfortably-distant immorality and evil of others. The popularity of the penny weekly, *Illustrated Police News*, founded in 1864, hypocritical and sensationalist, full of descriptions of the sexual misconduct, criminality and vice it campaigned against, likewise demonstrated public appetite for its material.

By the 1880s, newspapers had realized that signalling such reports with a caveat against reading them would actually simply draw more readers in. The *Pall Mall Gazette* of 4 July 1885, for example, began its sensational report with 'A frank warning'.

> We have no desire to inflict upon unwilling eyes the ghastly story of the criminal developments of modern vice. Therefore we say quite frankly to-day that all those who are squeamish, and all those who are prudish, and all those who prefer to live in a fool's paradise of imaginary innocence and purity, selfishly oblivious to the horrible realities which torment those whose lives are passed in the London Inferno, will do well not to read the Pall Mall Gazette of Monday and the three following days. The story of an actual pilgrimage into a real hell is not pleasant reading, and is not meant to be. It is, however, an authentic record of unimpeachable facts.

There were even more unrespectable newspapers throughout the Victorian age that used delicacy as an ironic critique of respectability. *Town Talk*, which gained a readership despite or because of being seen as a work of 'vicious literature' by the more respectable, regularly pretended to be attacking vice. On 7 June 1879 its editor mischievously assured readers that its lines were:

> ... intended only to place fathers of families in their guard and not to gratify an idle curiosity. Rival journalists ... may write as many leaders as they like on what they are pleased to call 'garbage journals', but they will not prevent me and my colleagues doing our duty to society ... we are in receipt of numerous letters from clergymen and educationalists from all parts of the country, congratulating us on our honesty and outspokenness and our many endeavours to uproot vice.

Town Talk was attacked by more respectable newspapers on the grounds of being 'indecent'. Attempts were made to damage its circulation, with rumours that vendors would be prosecuted. *Town Talk*, in response, virtuously claimed in its innocent, heavily tongue-in-cheek leader:

> As the intentions of *Town Talk* have been misunderstood, or misconstrued, in certain quarters, we beg to state that it is the policy and object of this journal to expose vice, fraud and filth of every sort, undeterred by any fear. We wish to drive immorality from our streets, and wherever temptation for the young may exist, we have resolved to expose it ... It has been suggested by some of our enemies – and success always commands enemies ... that we are really advertising the horrible places and practices we describe. If the publicity we afford to the vile dens we have written of is likely to do them any good, all we can say is that we are very much surprised.[24]

The meanings of vice were constructed by individuals within a wide range of identities such as class, gender and generation, or religious, economic, military and political structures. This undermines over-simplistic attempts to locate vice in Victorian culture. The frequency of the word's appearance in Victorian sources suggests that attacks on vice represented a dominant discourse. In part, it was used as a term of abuse, reflecting the changing preoccupations and compulsions of the powerful. It had a constellation of overlapping and occasionally contending meanings and associations levelled at those whose behaviour challenged context-specific notions of respectability, or threatened to dislocate and destroy society.

It played an important symbolic function in Victorian society. It helped to define what the more respectable saw as its moral centre. Definitions were often presented as binary ones, contrasting vice with virtue, and goodness with evil. Such divisions were a focus of intense debate, with little consensus. Some approved of that which others disapproved of. The more reflective or self-critical suffered and agonized over the moral dilemmas of the age.

Problems of data

Modern understanding of the world of Victorian vice and virtue is driven and limited by record availability. Respectable churches, chapels, cooperative societies, friendly societies and temperance societies used print to support their lobbying efforts against vice. Their records often survive. The drive to moral reform, respectability and self-improvement was linked to education and literacy. Such written sources have attracted the bulk of academic historical attention. So, for example, as a recent study of sport and alcohol admitted, 'the social and cultural role played by alcohol is still underdeveloped', while 'the temperance movement and attempts to restrict the consumption of alcohol . . . have attracted the attention of scholars'.[25] How *deeply* 'respectable' moral attitudes penetrated, encapsulated and transmitted the assumptions of Victorian middle-class society, however, is extremely difficult to quantify. Information on actual experience has to be inferred from sources such as police files and divorce court records. Some vices operated at the margins of Victorian culture, serving merely to define the shape of 'normal' activity as it moved and shifted over time in various places across Britain: the preserve of the few, not the majority. Yet at times it was the reformers who were more towards the margins, and the behaviours they attacked, like alcohol drinking, were those of the many.

If definitions of what constituted vice are problematical, then finding hard data on vice proves even more difficult. The common currency was assertion rather than reasoned argument. So whilst to J.C. Fowler, a lawyer and magistrate giving evidence to the Select Committee on the Regulation of Public Houses in 1852, 'the vice of drunkenness' had reached the dimensions of 'a national calamity', his contemporary the Rev. John Clay believed that 'drunkenness as a vice has diminished', and that 'the more intelligent classes resort less to drink than they formerly did [while] the better classes never indulge themselves so far as to make themselves amenable to the law'.[26]

Another major problem for studying vice is the overlap between vice in general and those vices actually criminalized at different stages through the century, many of which, such as those relating to drunkenness or gambling, were widespread across society, and sometimes tacitly accepted. This created serious problems with official crime statistics relating to prosecutable vices. The new police forces in Glasgow (established 1800), London (1829), the new borough councils (from 1835) and the rural constabularies (from 1849) were enlisted in support of attempts to impose order and tame some of the excesses of commercial leisure, and to crack down on the vicious and immoral entertainments, pastimes and activities of the lower classes. Quite often, the new police were, if anything, more concerned with propriety than property. In the small country town of Horncastle, for example, its tiny early-Victorian police force spent much of its time ensuring its respectable citizens were not bothered by the drunken brawls, riotous behaviour, begging and prostitution created by its disorderly pubs and beer houses and circa twenty brothels. They tried, rather, to keep working people's immoral excesses away from public view and prominent concern.[27]

The police may have had some success in suppressing vice-related behaviour. But as research on policing has showed, this is open to debate, and crime statistics are variable, distorted by changes in legislation, different patterns of policing in different localities and the attitudes of particular chief constables, sergeants and constables, and those sitting on the magistrate's bench at any one time towards specific behaviours. Prosecutions rose when officials were zealous. They dropped with a change of personnel. Brief moral panics would flare up after letters of complaint were published or a newspaper had some anti-vice campaign. The police response soon lessened once public interest tailed off, with little change resulting. Ordinary constables were subject to temptation, with substantial numbers regularly having to be dismissed for drunkenness on duty, and others for various forms of sexual impropriety, while their low wages led some to be vulnerable to inducements to look the other way.

Reformers reacted by adopting different arguments depending on the figures produced. So, for example, when defenders of fairs or horse-racing pointed out that police prosecutions were usually quite low, given the size of crowds which could range from a few thousand at small events to an estimated hundred thousand or more at the larger ones, reformers would accuse police of adopting soft policing tactics, only taking notice of the very riotous cases and not enforcing the law to the maximum extent. When figures were high this 'proved' the real extent of the problem.

Even more crucially, there were multiple perceptions of the same behaviour, which could be interpreted differently by different people and in different contexts. Within different religious groups the extent to which specific behaviours were seen as vice varied. Catholic Ireland had far lower drink-related prosecutions than Protestant Scotland or north Wales. Evangelicals were generally the most opposed to drink. By contrast, amongst Catholics support for full temperance was weak, though there was some support for abstention on Saturday nights and Sundays. But even so, the 'failings and vices of the present day', according to the Catholic confraternity of St Joseph in 1873, included 'frequenting public houses and improper places of amusement'.[28]

Neither reformers' complaints nor police reactions can be taken at face value, not least since practical policing forced a compromise between middle-class concerns and the problematic realities of policing and the enforcement of legislation relating to issues such as street bookmaking or pub opening hours. Very differing perceptions and cultural expectations can be clearly seen when comparing reformers' complaints with written police responses. In 1858, for example, there were a series of complaints to the Home Office about London prostitution, brothels and 'night houses' (late night places of entertainment, such as supper rooms, most busy from 11 p.m. to 5 a.m.) from metropolitan vestries and the Society for the

Suppression of Vice. These included a letter from Henry Rowley, of Well Close Square in London, attacking these 'night houses'.

The two divisional police responses to his letter survive. Rowley alleged that there were 'upwards of 50 licensed public houses' having music licences in the East End dock areas. The police said that there were only twenty-four. Rowley described the women as variously 'fallen women' in a state of dress that would 'not be tolerated ', 'abandoned women encouraged to assemble and act as decoys' and 'indecently clad'. K-Division admitted some were prostitutes but they were not decoys. Many others were 'sailors' wives' or girlfriends. Both divisions said women's clothing was 'respectable, dressed same as elsewhere', 'well dressed', admittedly 'with no bonnets, but imitate style of dress of ladies at evening parties and theatres'. Rowley claimed 'shameless scenes' were often exacted. K-Division said the assertions were untrue, Whitechapel Division said that they were 'rare', with no arrests in the past five years. Rowley said the streets were 'polluted by the foulest of words and deeds', and at night there were 'scenes past description'. This was seen as 'untrue'. To Rowley, the women's language and manners were 'revolting', and some 'excited by drink, give expression to their lust in words odious as hell itself'. The police argued that Rowley was an outsider, with no cultural understanding, and felt that while offended women were likely to retaliate with offensive language, it was not as bad 'as strangers believe it to be'. Rowley thought that a majority of the prostitutes were local girls, and under eighteen. The police said prostitutes were 'generally much older', some 'from port towns elsewhere', and variously English, Irish, Dutch and German. In sum, the police said behaviour was 'normal' for dock areas. There was however some agreement. Rowley had alleged that in some streets 'every house is a brothel'. K-Division said this was untrue, but at Whitechapel they said 'there are streets in the division where every house is a brothel'.[29]

Likewise, in 1886 there were local Vigilance Association complaints of large numbers of prostitutes on Clapham Common, leading to nightly 'disgusting exhibitions of vice' but the police response suggested that numbers were very much exaggerated and the Common was mainly full of respectable women and courting couples. They took the view that the few prostitutes were quite discreet, only soliciting men who approached them.[30]

Vice and virtue

Behaviours such as hard work, perseverance, honesty, thrift, prudence and self-reliance were presented as virtues, maxims to be displayed on the town hall walls, on samplers and in children's books. They were ascribed to individuals, though the middle classes were portrayed as more virtuous than other classes. The coupling of Victorian vice with notions of virtue paradoxically linked both to potential personal pleasure, although any supposedly immoral pleasures were often described using the less neutral term 'lasciviousness'. Indeed, the Rev. Sydney Smith (1771–1845), preacher, journalist and wit, once reportedly sadly remarked that 'we have no amusements in England but vice and religion'. Some were attracted to one, some the other, some to both, depending on age, temperament and circumstance.

Virtue's key role was to resist vice. As Anne Brontë reminded readers of *The Tenant of Wildfell Hall* in 1848, virtue lay more in 'the circumstance of being able and willing to resist temptation', than in 'having no temptation to resist'. Yet vice was attractive. The poet Algernon Charles Swinburne famously preferred in 1866 to alliteratively swap 'the lilies and languor of virtue', with its funereal inertia and passive idleness, for the more exciting 'raptures and roses of vice'.[31] A good example of the inner tensions and ambivalence generated by the attractions of vice can be found in Robert Louis Stevenson's 1886 novella, *The Strange Case of Dr Jekyll and Mr Hyde*. It illustrates well how such fiction provided the Victorians with a fantasy outlet, an alternative world where vice had a clear place.

The novella was set in the festering and foetid air and swirling fog of London, a stereotypical vice image. It brought out co-existing aspects to Stevenson's character, the respectable and the unrespectable, and the virtuous and the vicious. In the book, Dr Jekyll had been conducting experiments to explore his identity, and developed a cocktail of drugs that separated these two sides of his nature. So despite his surface respectability as a medical man, taking the drug allowed him occasionally to change his nature. He became the evil Mr Hyde, and turned to the most secret, corrupt and monstrous of his inner inclinations. Hyde gained pleasure and satisfaction out of senseless cruelty and violence, attacking the innocent without provocation, and was portrayed as depraved and evil. Hyde also enjoyed the pleasures of immoderate alcohol. Stevenson's book was full of metaphors and images associated with drugs and drink yet combined them with imagery associated with the temperance movement.[32] The book hinted strongly at sexual encounters and transgressions too. It captured Stevenson's occasional bouts of shame and self-loathing, and wish for a more balanced approach to life. The more respectable could read it as a moral tale, an allegory about drink's dangers. To sober reformers the book demonstrated the fate of those who tried to abandon the standards of respectability and escape into addiction, excess and social self-abandonment. Yet others, appearing equally respectable, could have bought the book because they were ambiguous about vice, and the book offered a way of vicariously fulfilling their own fantasies.

The baseness of vice and the beauty of virtue were two sides of the same coin. They interacted, were interdependent and gave energy to each other's definition. For someone to claim moral strength and virtue there had to be moral dangers to resist.

The problem for those preaching the primrose path of virtue was that temptations to vice and profligacy were widespread and scattered. It was difficult to avoid them, and equally difficult to resist their allure. Whilst attractive to all age groups, vice was especially problematic when it seduced the young and gullible middle classes, not just the poor and uneducated. Such moral corruption threatened social position and offered the prospect of unacceptable future generations. Concerns about the availability of strong drink to medical students forced respectable governors of London hospitals in the 1840s to buy surrounding land to remove 'any temptation to vice in consequence of the contiguity of public and other houses'.[33]

The definitions and uses of vice were shaped by power relationships, and the struggles, negotiation and accommodation between members of groups asserting their own chosen forms of moral order, as did, for example, one letter to *The Times* in 1847:

> Sir, – Allow me to call your attention as well as that of your readers, to a very serious nuisance which exists of an evening in the neighbourhood of the Regent's-park – viz., in Albany-street, Norton-street, &c. At the corners of these streets are congregated of a night parties of six or seven of the very lowest class of prostitutes, who make it their business to insult every passer-by, whether lady or gentleman, with the vilest and most obscene language, and often committing acts of the greatest indecency, thereby making these streets quite impassable for ladies after 10 o'clock at night. Surely the police have power to interfere in these matters! We pay for having the streets kept in order, and for their lighting; and surely we ought to have them clear of such very disgusting and revolting nuisances.[34]

Such complaints had some impact on legislation. It was much easier, in an avowedly Christian country, to defend virtue and attack vice, especially if you were middle class. In much of the rhetoric, vice was projected as something found only amongst the lower working class and the upper class, and not amongst the supposedly respectable middle classes, with their emerging political, social and economic power.

Vice, gender and class

Vice was a highly gendered topic, and here too power was the key, and gender differences in approach were linked to class divides. Articulate women moral reformers from the middle classes often played roles in anti-vice organizations as speakers and organizers. Women were more overtly religious, going to church more than men. Almost two-thirds of most congregations were female, but males dominated much reform society membership, and often targeted working-class female behaviour in their discourses on drink, sexual behaviour and gambling, despite the complex multiplicity of women's gender identity in such situations. Women encountered drink, for example, in a range of contexts, as heavy or moderate drinkers themselves, as possible victims or causes of excessive drinking by men, as temperance reformers or in reading about it. Women novelists as diverse as Elizabeth Gaskell, Anne Brontë and George Eliot explored the 'drink question' regularly. More generally, changes in women's role in British urban society, which offended male notions of superiority or traditional expectations, were often addressed in the language of vice. Men's similar behaviour was more likely to be ignored or played down, thanks to a strong double standard of acceptable behaviour.

Working-class women's roles as drunkards or prostitutes were publicized, suggesting they were weaker or more open to temptation. By contrast, upper-class codes demanded that its members should not enquire too closely into people's private lives, so vices were often hidden. Elite female misbehaviour was rarely publicized. They were supposedly pure. It was usually only upper-class divorce cases that allowed the press to report on dissolution and excess. The story of the marriage breakdown of Lady Jessica Sykes, who had been married at eighteen to the forty-eight-year-old Sir Tatton Sykes, of Sledmere in Yorkshire, was given sensational press reportage. The two had little in common. He was religious, sickly and not a great conversationalist. She was sociable and lively. By the late 1880s she was living in London, he in Yorkshire. From then on she gained an increasing reputation in high society for sexual promiscuity, heavy drinking and excessive spending. The marriage problems became more widely public after Sir Tatton put an advertisement in *The Times* in December 1896 announcing that he would no longer be responsible for her debts. Court cases in 1897 further fuelled the flames of publicity and Jessica's final fall from grace. Jessica's own feelings about the double standard are best summed up in one of her favourite sayings: 'after all I have only a man's vices'.[35]

In civilized Victorian society young girls and respectable middle-class married women were heavily idealized and meant to be sheltered from vicious experiences. In a context of far more male power than today, they were placed metaphorically on pedestals. They were portrayed as innocent, naïve, inexperienced creatures who needed male protection to shelter them from the awful realities of Victorian male life. Only men were supposedly attracted to vice, but paradoxically women were weak creatures and so easily led into temptation. The best way to keep them safe was through marriage to a solid middle-class man who would provide them with a home and family. He would go to work, while she would be confined to a domestic role, to become what an 1854 poem by Coventry Patmore (1823–96) called the 'angel in the house'. Most men and some women represented women as 'natural' home-makers, even though many still worked.

And if a woman thought this unfair, there were the awful warnings of what could happen if she fell into vice, had an affair or became an alcoholic. She could be banished from her home and lose her children, or wander the streets and end up in prostitution, a stock moral tale in reformist literature and art. Men and women were ideally supposed to occupy separate spheres: the 'little woman' as the respectable domestic care-giver and 'ministering angel', taking charge of domestic affairs and providing the children in their turn with a moral code, while the man dealt with a different material morality, that of business, sociability and public pleasures. For the more pious, home and family had privacy, security and devoted sanctity, sometimes reinforced by daily prayers. It was respectable social space. There were austere, stern and puritanical middle-class homes, especially early in Victoria's reign, though middle-class families in general were becoming worldlier through the century.

Even so, there was a clear differentiation between public and private life, especially for men. Men knew that they were meant to display domestic virtue and behaviour at home but there was far less pressure for them to display such behaviour outside. The 'double standard' and sharp separation between the public and domestic contexts allowed some to be seduced by the deviant temptations of vice.

Here again these were stereotypes. In many areas of Britain, and especially when men's wages were low, women had always had little choice but to work to supplement family income. In agriculture, both women and men worked at times such as harvest or potato picking. Some industries relied on female labour: the cotton industry, for example, employed large numbers of women, while many young girls and unmarried women ended up in domestic service, where they were regularly exploited and sometimes sexually abused by their employers. We need to remember, too, that many women were involved in unrespectable occupations, as prostitutes, as entertainers or as barmaids. For the female poor, the provision of respectable standards of material maternal care – being able to provide clothing, shoes, soap and water, haircuts so that people saw them as 'good, respectable' parents – was financially impossible, yet they were unrealistically pilloried as ignorant and degenerate.

So women with disreputable lives were targeted by anti-vice protesters, whilst respectable women were presented as the reason for anti-vice campaigns. Women needed to be sheltered from vice by men's actions. Such views rested on particular views of women, which many but not all men held. During the Victorian period, women were regularly treated very much as second-class citizens. They did not have the vote. On marriage their property belonged to their husband. It was hugely difficult to get a divorce, even if they were physically or sexually abused. Women who became ensnared by vice were represented as far worse than men, seen clearly in the way Victorians defined the 'fallen woman'.

Such double standards were indicated clearly in governmental reactions to the growing recognition in the mid-nineteenth century that venereal disease and drunkenness were causing substantial damage to British levels of military effectiveness. Navy and army doctors did not blame their patients, Britain's valiant soldiers and sailors. After all, men were men, and these were fighting men who could die in the service of their country. Blame was shifted onto the pimps and prostitutes, the publicans and barmaids who supposedly created and furnished the demand for 'vice', and the Contagious Diseases Acts of the 1860s allowed police to arrest suspected prostitutes in certain army towns and naval ports and have them compulsorily checked for venereal diseases. The Act generated opposition, especially as it allowed police to stop any woman, no matter how 'respectable'. Dean Close's pamphlet, *Recent Legislation on Contagious Diseases* (1870), for example, attacked the Contagious Diseases Act as 'infamous', 'bad for women', and 'hypocritical'.

Vice debates were tied to gender, and also to social class, in its more admittedly loose sense of social strata, and with the recognition that class identities were often fluid, uncertain and contested. The Victorian period was a time during which the raw numbers and the overall national proportion of the professional and commercial middle classes rose rapidly. They benefited from increased free time and income. Potent minorities within this group, especially members of church, chapel and later the Liberal Party, were concerned with the corrupting effect of leisure in civic society, but were particularly apprehensive about its effects on the lower orders. They emphasized thrift, responsibility, self-reliance and individual hard work. Better example was needed, a play discipline to complement work discipline.

One result of the way such groups focused on working-class vices has meant that historians have sometimes been deceived into seeing vice as simply reflecting class divisions, leading Niall Ferguson, for example, to represent the proletariat as divided into a labour aristocracy with skills who secured higher wages and a 'lumpenproletariat' with vices who favoured gin.[36] However, attitudes to vice reflected not merely class but another form of social division. Skilled workers drank and bet too. Being a drinker rather than a temperance reformer or a gambler rather than a follower of rational recreations marked a different form of personal identity to that of class. Leisure cultures were not the same as classes, and often merged other identities with those of class. Members of the middle classes often enjoyed their vices, if more often in moderation. At certain times, in certain locations and contexts, the middle classes could be hedonistic too, especially those men less tied to home and work.

It was those middle-class groups who espoused a more reformist leisure culture that most attempted to privilege and legitimate certain forms of behaviour and recreational activity by articulating them as normal, correct, natural and unproblematic, or as duties and responsibilities. Behaviours related to what they perceived as vices were defined negatively, as dangerous, threatening, impure, destabilizing and repulsive 'vices' or 'immoral' acts. They were portrayed as selfish and sinful, carried out for personal gratification by other classes in society, and needing to be regulated.

The most respectable were particularly keen to distinguish themselves from the 'rough' working classes, and the supposedly idle and dissolute landed upper classes, and this latter group became increasingly defensive as a result, with even the 'fast set' enjoying a less publicized and privatized but often hedonistic country house life. Attacks on the vices of the working and upper classes enabled some sections of the middle classes to assert superiority. This was another reason for the foregrounding of 'vice' in Victorian discourse.

In a society where people talked in terms of simple divisions, such as the 'deserving' and 'undeserving' poor, or the 'rough' and the 'respectable', campaigns against vices became part of a broader attempt to 'civilize' Britain's towns, taming and regulating manners and behaviour, and imposing specific forms of middle-class consciousness, values and morality. Reformers believed the poor were often idle, wasteful and improvident, frittering away their already scarce resources and refusing to help themselves despite the efforts of charitable reformers; the vices of the poor were also dangerous, threatening ordered and civilized life.

However, the anti-vice campaigns were directed not just against the working classes but *all* classes who espoused different understandings of what constituted appropriate behaviour. The Nonconformist tradition helped develop the 'Nonconformist conscience', checking corruption in public life. The poor could not be expected to behave better if the wealthy misbehaved. The Rev. Charles Girdlestone, in his essay on 'Rich and Poor' in 1852, was one of many who argued that vice was exacerbated by the example provided by the 'wasteful, selfish and luxurious living, on the part of the higher classes', by the 'dissipation of time, health, means and morals, which is enacted on a more brilliant scale in operas and club-houses, in saloons and drawing rooms, at routs and balls and banquetings'.[37]

Anti-vice reformers mocked the 'dissipated' upper classes, and attacked their conspicuous consumption and free time, their love of blood sports and their moral degeneracy compared to the supposedly hardworking, respectable merchant and professional classes, the more so because the upper classes still attracted traditional deference, becoming potential models for emulation, not censure. In novels, aristocractic characters like Lord Mowbray in Disraeli's *Sybil* were increasingly symbols of corruption and vice.

In 1885, the Nonconformist editor of the *Pall Mall Gazette*, W.T. Stead, began a highly compromised campaign against child prostitution. His supporters in the Liberal press portrayed the apparent seducers of such children as debauched and depraved aristocrats, rather than middle-class businessmen. The *Northern Echo*, for example, pointed the finger at men with 'the proudest names', the 'highest stations', the 'rich' and the powerful.[38] The 'decadent' upper classes were scapegoated, too, for the Jack the Ripper prostitute murders and moral panics in the summer of 1888.

Where the middle classes were strongest in numbers, especially in London, the heart of commerce, banking and trade, attacks on vice were at their strongest, even though some of the middle classes were actively involved as customers or as purveyors of facilities. In the industrial towns, where middle-class numbers were few, attacks were weaker. Even so, attacking vice could be dangerous. For example, when preachers tried to distribute tracts and berate those going to race meetings they could be abused or have clods of earth thrown at them. Attacks on vice were particularly vociferous in those towns where religion allied with middle-class reform power: York, where there was a strong Quaker presence, for example, was a centre for the anti-gambling movement. There was safety in numbers.

The middle classes aspired to suburban villas to get away from the 'wrong' sorts of streets, and kept wives at home rather than at work. They claimed to be more severe in their professional and commercial public morality. To get on in their world they had to maintain at least the appearances of being moral. They went regularly to church or chapel, some because of a strong faith, but others only for appearance's sake. Church attendance distinguished them from those unrespectable workers who, having worked long hard hours over a six-day week, spent their Saturday evenings in pleasure and slept in on the Sunday, and turned to activities like pitch and toss in the afternoons.

Reformers tried not to acknowledge publicly that middle-class culture was not universally disapproving of the vices of the age, or that political, social and sectarian conflict had an impact. Though they often tacitly accepted that the middle classes could also be attracted to vice, and that the domestic hearth, the church or business were not the only contexts of social action and behaviour, this side of Victorian middle-class life remained largely tacit. That avoided alienating financial and cultural support. The Rev. W. Reid was one of the few temperance reformers to admit that 'did ministers and medical men publish to the world the knowledge they have acquired of drink's doings in the homes of the respectable and professedly religious, a revelation would be made'.[39]

Within the middle classes could be found supporters *and* opponents of drink and betting. The leading brewers, like Bass and Worthington, who sold the ale and beer that caused drunkenness, and whose tied-house pubs and beer houses were a feature of later Victorian Britain, were wealthy and politically powerful enough to be known as the 'Beerage'. Yet amongst the brewing trade there were a number of leading Quaker dynasties, such as the Guinness, Hanbury and Buxton families. Frederick Charrington, heir to another brewing dynasty, was not only active in the temperance movement, but also in campaigning against drunken policemen and in closing brothels in the 1880s.[40]

Horse-racing had betting at its heart, but its administrative organizations, race-courses, betting rooms and thoroughbred auction houses were all run by middle-class family dynasties such as the Weatherbys and the Tattersalls. Trainers, stud farm owners and leading bookmakers were also middle class. In racing towns such as Newmarket or Middleham, a majority of trainers bet but also attended Church of England services. Middle-class betting on credit was legal, so did not appear in police statistics. Betting debts were debts only of honour, not legally enforceable, though the private unspecified debt-related prosecutions involving bookmakers probably concealed gambling debts. Middle-class men's gambling surfaced in the sources rarely, as when the 'gentleman' C.H. Parrington in Yarm, North Riding, was assaulted by a 'sporting commission agent' (a synonym for a bookmaker) over a gambling debt of £30.[41]

The reformers could point out that fewer middle-class men appeared in drunkenness statistics than for assault, but the police often treated drunken middle-class men more respectfully, unless they were violent. They often merely found a cab and sent them home, not least since such help often resulted in financial reward.

Even when charged with a vice-related offence, the middle classes could more easily find legal representation, respectable friends to give them a character reference and a sympathetic bench to provide a sympathetic ruling. In 1872, for example, James Richards and the Rev. William Dawson of St John's, Clerkenwell, were jointly charged with visiting five urinals for an unlawful purpose in the early hours. Two constables swore that they had seen them in company over that period and had finally arrested them after the fifth visit. Questioned by the defence lawyer, the constables were certain the two had been together. The vicar claimed that he was regularly in the habit of walking at night, and strongly denied that he knew Richards. He brought testimonials from Lord Hatherley, two well-known clergymen and the Bishop of Carlisle, who said Dawson's life had been one of 'saintly purity'. The police were mistaken. The magistrates dismissed the case because of his 'high character'.[42] Dawson's respectability saved his career, another reminder that respectability sometimes had real currency.

The problematics of chronology

If we survey vice over the whole of Victoria's reign, the anti-vice campaigners regularly appeared to have widespread popular support, judged by positive media coverage. They claimed to dominate discourse and public morality, but their battle was never finally won. The actual effectiveness of any legislation was relatively limited, constantly under challenge from private practices that were usually ignored, and tacitly accepted. And as historians have recognized, changes in education, employment, politics, medicine and the law also acted upon and reflected attitudes.

There were more significant fluctuations over the century, however, albeit difficult to summarize succinctly, and vice debates forced Victorians to grapple with complex, rapidly-changing practices, ideas and global influences. Around 1820, social and political pressures, typified by the infamous Peterloo Massacre in Manchester, created a peak of concern about societal order amongst the elite. During the 1820s and 1830s moral reform voluntary societies such as the British and Foreign Temperance Society and the Lord's Day Observance Society flourished, and church and chapel groups cooperated to challenge religious apathy, and try to legally suppress some perceived problematical customary recreation.

Fears of moral decay were made greater when slight rises in real incomes encouraged the growing commercialization of leisure, although the period was largely one of urban working-class deprivation. Activities such as heavy drinking, infidelity, sexual misbehaviour or gambling were reconstructed as pathological. The political and legislative responses to each of these are given more detailed coverage in later chapters, since possessing sufficient cultural power to construct pleasures as vicious or virtuous was crucial in helping to shape vice and its meanings. The temperance movement and the prevention of prostitution were both major issues between 1837 and the late 1850s.[43]

Vice became a dominant theme in much Victorian discourse, though specific concerns ebbed and flowed. Opinions shifted and waves of moral panic swept over Britain, just as in recent decades. And it was never a single cultural norm. It had multiple manifestations. Moreover, a variety of attitudes always existed even though the sustained campaigns against alcohol and prostitution had some success up to mid-century, so that some middle-class English at least were more inhibited in their behaviour, more polite, more orderly and more tender-minded. They practised sexual restraint, but probably more to limit family size than for any moral reason. They worked hard, had a sense of duty, gave to 'good' causes, and took care of their money rather than spent it extravagantly. Charles Dickens, working with the rich philanthropist Angela Burdett-Coutts, managed Urania Cottage in the 1840s and 1850s. This was a refuge for women who had lapsed sexually or become prostitutes, or even some just considered to be at risk. However, he only accepted those who agreed to emigrate to Australia after their 'reformation', an indication that their contagion and removal from respectable society was often seen as important by reformers.

But even while reformers pressured Parliament to curb individual liberty and choice of leisure in the cause of a greater good, reformist movements began to fracture as denominational divisions became stronger, and campaigns and petitions against vice became more politicized. Standards of living were rising, but only slowly. The average Briton was already about 13 per cent better off in 1851 than he was in 1801, and powerful secular and commercial interests were able to challenge the reformers' right to insist on legislation rather than leave such issues to personal choice.

During Victoria's reign, a further major wave of revivalism swept Great Britain and Ireland between 1857 and 1860. The increased availability of commercial leisure forms, the expansion of the suburbs, and the growth of railways all had an impact, even if the constraints of respectability placed limits on middle-class public behaviour.

In 1867, a broader franchise was introduced, and in general the 1860s briefly appeared to be slightly more 'permissive', as was the same decade in the twentieth century. Britain had become the leading economic and military power with an ever-expanding empire. Its expansion saw the discovery of new forms of alcohol, new forms of sexual expression, and a larger army and navy that had to respond to problems of sexual disease.

The economy continued to boom through the decade and on into the early 1870s, and employment was high. The industrial might of the north and Midlands had made Manchester, Birmingham and Leeds prideful, powerful, and potentially pleasure-filled places. The earlier difficulties created by industrialization and urbanization appeared to be lessening. From the 1870s onwards, middle-class numbers increased and their incomes rose. Many became more prone to enjoyment, spending money on commercial entertainments, perhaps widely relished, like gambling, that others attacked as vices. Some of the middle classes participated in recreations that excluded the working classes, but in general they were perhaps less smug, less complacent and sometimes savoured the new celebrity culture that was permeating society.

Society appeared to be settling down. Many believed that the more skilled and hard-working amongst the lower classes had become less militant and more respectable. But this led to more concern about the residuum, what are today sometimes described as the 'undeserving' poor, seen as 'dangerous' and difficult to reform, who were increasingly organizing leisure in terms of their own aspirations.

Some moral reformers shifted ground to stress the importance of moral choices and individual moral responsibility within what was now more clearly a capitalist but democratic market economy. As reformers became rather more politically marginalized from the mainstream, there was more commitment to individual and family reclamation at the local level. The efforts of William Gladstone and his wife to rescue 'fallen women', or the activities of many temperance reformers, now fell into this category.

Vice was always highly politicized. In general, Tories were more supportive of vice-related industries such as brewing and gambling. Lancashire Tory mill-owners who were Anglican were likely to bring paternalistic, cock-fighting, beer drinking attitudes into their management while Liberal, chapel-going owners were likely to enforce temperance and education upon their workforce.[44] When temperance reformers allied with the Liberals, and gained support for anti-drink legislation, this created the potential for an electoral backlash, threatening the Liberals' hold on power, amidst concerns about how legislation undermined individual responsibility.

Moral campaigns made a comeback in the 1880s, partly created by the 'new journalism' which profited from moral crusading, while filling its pages with prurient details for the delectation of the unrespectable as much as the moral crusader. The tensions created by cycles of economic depression after 1872 and the political upheaval and social reorganizations of the period forced a societal reaction. This found a voice in the debates over morality in the 1880s. The late Victorian press sometimes characterized the next decade as the 'Naughty Nineties', an era of decadence when radical new ways of thinking were emerging. There was an explosion of differing and conflicting positions, illustrating the ambiguous nature of Victorian attitudes to vice, as the forces of modernity impacted on society: cultural, political and technological change, growing urbanization, an increasingly politically powerful working class and lingering nostalgia. Rising real wages and increases in leisure time and the standard of living for a majority attracted more spending on the dubious temptations of vice. In the last decade of Victoria's reign, society faced further social, sexual and spatial changes. The late Victorian 'purity' movements clashed with yet also co-existed with vice's more hedonistic supporters. In London, for example, the Metropolitan Police was faced from the 1870s onwards by organized pressure groups variously arguing that criminality, prostitution, drunkenness and betting were all serious threats to public order. Policing was forced to respond, as was the Home Office.[45] Neither side could achieve any significant victory, but most accepted that the overt public face of vice was to be condemned; being caught out in public contexts could be socially disastrous for individuals or families.

After Oscar Wilde's two-year imprisonment for gross indecency following his sensationally-covered arrest and trial he chose to leave England and live in Paris. This raises an important point in relation to discussion of Victorian vice. There was something quite distinctive in relation to the way the Protestant British thought about vice in comparison to people in countries such as France, parts of the Austro-German Empire or Italy. This applied particularly to the way sexual behaviour such as male homosexuality, prostitution or pornography was treated, but also in attitudes to alcohol. France had decriminalized homosexual acts between consenting adults as early as 1791, and it was legalized by the Italians by 1890. The French had state-controlled legal brothels from the Napoleonic period onwards, with a morals brigade which ensured prostitutes were registered, and an attitude of rather more sexual freedom. In many regions of Germany, prostitutes likewise had to register with police or local health authorities. In Italy, there were also state brothels, and by 1891 prostitution was legal in private houses and there were hospitals for sex workers. Similarly, to the French to arise drunk from the table was a reproach, and in Spain or Italy a disgrace. British behaviour, especially when drunk, was noted negatively by many foreign visitors.

Conclusion

This chapter has shown how far vice was a ubiquitous feature of life during the Victorian age. Discourses surrounding vice were a feature of British life of the puritan age of the early seventeenth century, but they grew in importance in the nineteenth century, especially amongst the more respectable. The language of vice was inescapable: a feature of discussion amongst neighbours, read about in the newspapers and attacked in sermons, in print and in Parliament by social reformers and Evangelical preachers. But its definitions and meanings were debateable, and it was the vices of the poor that were most often criticized and emphasized, both then, and sometimes by modern social historians. This chapter has placed stress on the complex interrelationships of vice, virtue, gender and social class, and such themes reoccur in later chapters, often highlighted through the lens of their various narratives, the stories which the Victorians told themselves about vice's manifestations. These offer important clues about vice's contemporary nature, meanings and significance. Their sheer volume and constant repetition helped to shape the perceptions of those reading or hearing them. So in the next chapter we turn to examine Victorian narratives and beliefs about the spatial locations of vice. Examination of the social and cultural geography of vice offers a highly useful insight into its construction in Victorian thought.

CHAPTER TWO

The Spatial Dimension of Vice

Introduction

Cultural notions of physical space and place were important in constructing and defining vice, its multi-sensory intensity and people's associated emotional responses to it. What particularly appalled some Victorians was that vice was so public and so easy to see in their cities and streets. General and specific descriptions of the affront to respectable senses and imagination of such supposedly vicious places provided particular ways of seeing and interpreting the forms of vice. People created mental maps of meaning about the world in which they lived. Print descriptions and gossip together helped people to understand and use this spatial knowledge.

During the Victorian age, descriptions of the extent of vice commonly gave it physical form: almost liquid as in a 'torrent', 'swelling tide' or 'flood of vice'; large in volume, 'huge', 'vast' or of 'considerable amount'; and with sufficient depth that an individual might 'plunge' or 'fall' into its 'lowest' or 'deepest' zones. Sometimes it was spoken of like a disease, offering dangerous possibilities of contamination.

So people tried to define its specific locations where were found its 'lowest haunts', 'objectionable premises', its 'temptations' or 'shames'. 'Haunts' suggested places habitually frequented by those who were 'other', ghost-like, lacking clear definition, beyond respectable understanding – if not supernatural, perhaps sub-human. Another commonly used descriptor, 'dens of vice and iniquity', implied locations which were 'abominable', 'dangerous' and 'filthy', while 'dens' were biblically associated with dangerous wild beasts, such as lions. Human 'dens' were uncivilized, with wilder, excessive, more animal-like behaviour, secret places, where 'normal' rules were suspended and were concealed from the view of the general human population, who rarely visited.

So more respectable Victorians and social reformers mapped and classified vice into a series of immoral and dangerous landscapes, beyond the bounds of respectable society. These subjective mental maps, with their metaphors, images and languages, reveal how certain places at certain times reflected Victorian debates over morality, cultural values and legitimacy. They demonstrated people's apparent need to regulate, control and discipline particular areas of more sensual gratification and movement, as for example, in dealing with prostitution.[1] They became part of middle-class attempts to make sense of and classify criminality. The evangelically-motivated Victorian sociologist Henry Mayhew's mid-century study of London labour and poor even provided maps detailing Metropolitan Police statistics for offenses such as 'persons committed for carnally abusing girls', 'bigamy', or 'keeping disorderly houses'.

Powerfully-written accounts of these spaces which reformers believed vice to occupy aimed at their reform. In Liverpool, in the later 1850s, its Society for the Suppression of Vicious Resorts pursued what it called an 'open crusade against vice' and 'social evil' by amassing evidence and encouraging the police to prosecute the keepers of 'infamous places of public resort': brothels, dancing saloons and other 'dens of iniquity'. This moulding of Victorian social space allowed specific locations to be represented and narrated by reformers in terms of apparently 'objective' truths about immoral behaviour.

Chapter outline

This chapter covers key sites of vice, beginning with Victorian images of vice in the slums and the urge to slum visits and slum clearance, before moving to explore the general urban leisure landscape, and examples of specific locations such as music halls and variety theatres, pleasure grounds and race-meetings. If towns were always problematic, so too could be the countryside, while the anonymity provided by travel away from home to British resorts or abroad provides a further case study.

Vice in the slums

Vice was rarely to be found in those streets and neighbourhoods where anti-vice campaigners themselves lived or which they frequented. Public streets were sites of surveillance and regulation by the police, but all public spaces and thoroughfares of towns were occasionally vulnerable to drunks, prostitutes and other rowdies. Many street-prostitutes solicited openly, negotiating for custom, even in business areas, normalizing their appearance in the urban cultural landscape, even if the respectable pretended not to see them.

The middle classes feared the slums, 'low' neighbourhoods where vice was supposedly more commonly found, places rarely visited, observed or seen at a distance. Most knew the streets which marked the borders of respectability. When they visited such places they were outsiders, prowling prudes often lacking understanding of the 'alien' cultures they described, places where language, behaviour, attitudes, class and incomes were so very negatively different, challenging the expectations and norms of respectable ratepayers.

To the latter, the *ideal* street in Victorian Britain was one which allowed continuous movement, but was neat, clean and tidy, fairly silent and most importantly respectful and safe.[2] The slums possessed none of those attributes. Slum streets were full of the poor, for whom almost all leisure had to be taken outside the home. Unsurprisingly, environmental, moral and criminal determinism meant that the slums, with their want, disease, ignorance, idleness and squalor, were a particular target of reformers attempting to engage with the problems of vice.

The unhealthy 'dirt', 'filth', 'impurity' and insanitary pollution of the slums provided powerful images, which symbolically defined Victorian social and moral boundaries. Such terms could easily be applied to vice and to the morals of inhabitants, especially given the hyperbole and sensationalism employed by many investigators and writers. In 1863, for example, Friar's Mount in London's Bethnal Green was full of 'vice and debauchery', people living through 'a painful and monotonous round of vice, filth and poverty' in ruinous tenements. Their existence was 'half lived by vice'. They were half-starved and working in poor trades.[3]

By mid-century, a majority of the British population were urban dwellers. Britain had become an industrial nation. London had the highest population of any European city, and towns such as Liverpool, Birmingham and Manchester (the 'shock city' of the 1840s), were far larger than their pre-industrial counterparts. They were magnets for rural migrants but through their very size and socio-cultural diversity potentially more lonely, anonymous and lacking in community. Attitudes to these great Victorian cities were ambivalent. They were huge, dark and powerful, attracting superlatives from some for their economic successes and the magnificence of their public buildings. Their main streets showcased splendour and extravagance. Others viewed them as dangerous, alienating and brutal cesspools of vice. Pride in their progress was coupled with an awareness of the drawbacks of urban life, its disease, immorality and overcrowding, though some had an optimistic belief in the urban planning and municipal government of these multi-faceted environments.[4]

Experiences of this new urban life often shaped approaches. The city, with its crowds, spectacle, lights and anonymity, had marginal zones. These morally affronted notions of normality, especially as cities became more socially and functionally separated internally. London's West End was ordered and respectable. Wealthier and more respectable citizens ignored, pretended to ignore and very occasionally discovered, socially peripheral, overcrowded, poverty-stricken urban areas and streets not far from their places of work or neat homes. These were highly challenging places, dark, horrible and painful to look upon. They threatened the certainties of the middle-class world-view, morality and beliefs, and created anxiety and apprehension.

Campaigners applied rhetorical terms of 'immorality', 'indiscipline', 'corruption', 'disreputability', 'laziness' and 'sinfulness' to those living in these 'naturally' unhealthy, poor environments. It was supposedly slum-dwellers themselves who created the conditions and criminality, rather than poverty creating crime. The sheer enormity of the problems and the vital need for sanitation, rebuilding, social reform and education, was not initially widely understood. Ideas of social justice only slowly emerged.

For much of the nineteenth century, reformers only needed to walk a few yards from more fashionable thoroughfares to reach more dangerous slum neighbourhoods such as the stone tenements of Glasgow, the 'old town' of Manchester, the back-to-back houses of Leeds or West Yorkshire and London rookeries. These housed a supposedly criminal underworld, 'the dangerous classes', people who potentially seemed to threaten robbery, attack or mere importunity. Their lives shocked onlookers' sensibilities.[5]

Such overcrowded slums created concern. Outside the constraining pressures created by family and kin, known neighbours or chapel and church congregations, for some, especially amongst the young and single, or the older and unmarried, the temptations of vice proved far less easy to resist than in earlier pre-industrial times. Respectable areas sometimes had red-light districts conveniently close by. Behind London's Westminster Abbey, for example, were Pye Street and Duck Lane, an 'unsightly hell' filled with 'vice the most terrible', with 'women of pleasure', often young girls, 'driven to vice' by the fear of starvation.[6] Slums were 'citadels of vice and crime', housing prostitutes and thieves, the disgusting and the degenerate. They inhabited squalid, broken-down buildings lining the grotesque labyrinthine twists and turns of the city's dark and dirty alleys, damp cellar dwellings, draughty garrets, putrid lanes and festering courts. It was easy to become totally lost and disoriented.

London always figured large in the narratives of vice, as it has also in historians' narratives and representations. Its slow and uncertain piecemeal improvement and the narrow, winding alleys that were slow to be cleared, allowed it to be portrayed as potentially suffering the same fate as Ancient Babylon. 'Narratives of sexual danger' surrounded the 'dark, powerful and seductive labyrinth' of slum streets.[7] Many Victorian novelists exploited London's powerfully symbolic settings, sometimes romanticizing the slums, but others emphasizing a poverty-stricken and often criminal underclass. Dickens's *Oliver Twist* (1837) was located in 'darkest London': a place of lurid fascination, peopled by desperate thieves like Fagin and Bill Sikes. Dickens's preface deliberately challenged the possibility of romanticizing such places, asking:

> The cold, wet, shelter-less midnight streets of London; the foul and frowsy dens, where vice is closely packed and lacks the room to turn; the haunts of hunger and disease; the shabby rags that scarcely hold together: where are the attractions of these things?

William Harrison Ainsworth's novel, *Revelations of London*, published in 1844, portrayed the 'rookery' of St Giles, with its 'squalid inhabitants and wretched and ruffianly occupants', and was 'struck with amazement that such a huge receptacle of vice and crime should be allowed to exist'.[8] There were provincial equivalents. Manchester, Glasgow, Liverpool and Birmingham were all simultaneously inspiring but frightful in the scale of their overcrowding. Mrs Gaskell's *Mary Barton* (1848) evoked powerful pictures of dirty, insanitary northern English slums, linked to prostitution, drug addiction and murder. Manchester's 'old town', sometimes known as Angel Meadow, heavily polluted, with appallingly deteriorated, unventilated, unhealthy, overcrowded housing in an area containing over 20,000 inhabitants, was infamous. Young Friedrich Engels said that he could not paint it 'black enough' to create a true impression. In *The Condition of the Working Class in England* (1845) he portrayed residents there as brutalized by their conditions, their 'labours and hardships', which forced them to 'unbridled' excess and 'a want of providence' in their pleasures. As late as 1896 a survey noted that certain areas still attracted the vicious, wretched and helpless. Liverpool's Chief Constable thought its slums were criminal and demoralized. On Tyneside, in 1855, the *Shields Daily News* described local slum dwellings as the 'refuge of the lowest dregs of society', and asked:

> Who can estimate the amount of immoral conversation that passes, the unlawful schemes plotted, or the low, filthy literature read in common lodging houses and the intemperance that prevails in these nests of vice?[9]

Such 'common' or 'low' lodging houses, hovels which provided literally dirt cheap accommodation for tramping artisans and the indigent poor, were seen as a major location of physical and moral evil, where men, women and children might huddle in a single bed. Social investigator Henry Mayhew described them in a *Morning Chronicle* article of 1850 as 'wretched dens of infamy, brutality, and vice'.[10] The 1854 *Pictorial Handbook of London* labelled them as 'very hotbeds of vice and crime, a disgrace to humanity, a reproach to the Christianity of England ... sinks of iniquity and contamination'. In 1885, Henry Vigar Harris saw the lodging-house dormitories of Commercial Street, Islington, as full of the 'vilest of humanity', 'the apex of low life, boasting vice and debauchery'.[11] To the young Liberal journalist, Howard J. Goldsmid, who made an exploration of the 'inner life' of 'low' lodging houses disguised as a tramp in 1886, the Whitechapel houses were 'dens of misery unutterable and of vice indescribable', full of women who appeared 'prematurely old, gin-sodden and steeped in vice'.[12]

Urban port areas such as London's Limehouse and Rotherhithe, or Cardiff's Tiger Bay area, also perceived as vice-filled, were notoriously difficult to police. Ratcliffe Highway was infamous, a Thames dockland area where Americans, Chinese, Greeks, Italians, Lascars, Malays and other ethnic minorities could be found. Its beer houses and lodging houses, gin palaces and dancing saloons, brothels and opium dens attracted regular unavailing letters of complaint to the *East London Chronicle* from respectable ratepayers urging measures to suppress the 'frightful scenes of debauchery and vice' that continually disgraced the neighbourhood.[13] In Portsmouth, a navy port and garrison town, where service policy discouraged men from marrying, beer houses were notorious for prostitution, with an unenviable reputation.

Foreign visitors to Britain, seeing its city life, also employed the language of vice. When American Henry Coleman visited Manchester in the 1840s, for example, he saw 'utter vice and profligacy', and told a friend he could not describe the events in detail for it would be absolutely offensive.[14] Frenchman Hippolyte Taine concluded that both good and evil were greater than in France and that the spectacle of debauchery left him with an impression of nothing but degradation and misery. For Daniel Kirwan, correspondent of the *New York World*, London's slums in 1870 were 'haunts of vice, misery and crime', where even children of tender age had 'vice in every glance of their eyes' while the costermongers' code of morals 'was beneath mention'.[15]

The views of foreigners, outsiders, might be dismissed, but many respectable British men and matrons were equally shocked, offended and complaining. They were surrounded by urban evils, temptations to vice, depravity and immorality in a wide variety of contexts. At times, 'vicious' (i.e. full of vice) behaviours were excessive, quite intolerable. The annual report of Liverpool's Society for the Suppression of Vicious Practices noted in 1858 that at the Domville Dance Hall in Lime Street, 'vice ran riot'.[16] In Hull, in 1870, the magistrates received what the local paper carefully assessed as 'most reasonable' complaints about the area around Cooks' Buildings in Lowgate. Their shocking moral condition, profanity and depravity, and loathsome and disgusting nuisance meant that no respectable person could pass along the street without being 'polluted by the most horrible and abominable blasphemies'. Though the area was known for prostitution, one magistrate at least was more offended because 'the language employed there was both shameful and disgusting' (an indication here as elsewhere of the importance of discourse in the construction of cultural meaning). Yet here as elsewhere, such attacks were resisted, with a local silversmith arguing that the neighbourhood was not as bad as represented.[17]

New industrial towns like Merthyr or Middlesbrough, with few middle-class residents, were quite often portrayed as uncivilized 'frontier' areas. Overcrowding was regularly put forward as leading to incest, prostitution and generalized indecency. Merthyr was famous for grim conditions and gained a reputation for drink, prostitution and crime, whilst its press debated the behaviour, public drunkenness and relative respectability of different parts of the town.[18] At Middlesbrough, social reformers argued that the hostile iron-working environment had a bleakly disintegrating effect on community life, breeding intemperance and immorality.[19]

As late as 1890, London slums were still seen as vice-ridden. William Booth's *In Darkest England and The Way Out* used the language of vice to describe London's East End slums, colonies of 'heathen and savages', a 'submerged tenth' of the population, some living by crime and yet more by vice, and all sodden with drink. Such areas were 'a jungle of pauperism, vice and despair', containing 'multitudes of slaves of vice'.[20] Arthur Morrison's *A Child of the Jago* (1896) thrilled and appalled readers in Britain and America with graphic and lurid descriptions of the drunkenness, deviancy, degeneration and filth of a small area just beyond London's West End. Contemporary discourses and narratives from the exposure of child prostitution to Jack the Ripper's murders of prostitutes likewise created strongly negative images. Overcrowding was always believed to lead to sexual promiscuity, even if actual statistics failed to reveal a link between illegitimacy and housing density. Beatrice Webb accepted even at the century's end that in the worst of the overcrowded, fetid slums, sexual promiscuity and even sexual perversion – the violation of little children – were almost unavoidable among men and women of average character and intelligence, crowded into the one-room tenements.[21] The worst forms of pollution, such as the large gas manufactories, were generally situated in and blighted the poorest, working-class slums, yet people flocked to them from all over Britain, Europe and the Empire. By 1900, London's sooty, polluted streets held over six million inhabitants.[22]

Such descriptions revealed more about the prejudices of some of the middle classes than they did of the poor. The poor experienced short life expectancy, regular unemployment, social exclusion, poor nutrition, often engaged in heavy labour for long hours and poor pay, lived in poverty and were highly nomadic, moving to avoid debt collectors or to find fresh work. Slum dwellers were forced into externally-imposed categories. They were an almost alien people: 'city savages', the desperate and the daring, idle, drunken and rootless, moving from one rented accommodation to another. Investigators such as Henry Mayhew viewed them as a 'wandering tribe', deviant and potentially criminal, with high cheekbones and protruding jaws, almost 'animal-like' in appearance. Some Victorians drew on the pseudo-sciences of physiognomy and phrenology. These claimed to identify character and criminality through appearance, moralizing physical attributes and linking them to virtue and vice.

Mayhew spent time and effort categorizing the social geography and criminality of London's 'dangerous classes', and later in the century investigative reporters and early sociologists contributed to the mapping task in more detail, revealing the mysteries of 'darkest London' and specifying which quarters should be avoided by decent people. Such reports noted correctly that the very poor were often physiologically different, but failed to acknowledge the effects of nurture and environment. One, two or even three families might live in a single damp, ill-ventilated room. Rents might be demanded by the day because families were not always able to pay by the week or month. The terrible social effects of too-rapid urban expansion with its abject poverty, sexual exploitation, child labour, dirt and drunkenness were shockingly evident.

Moral corruption was sometimes explicitly linked with particular groups of immigrants, as a way of meeting the social threat they posed. Irish fleeing the famine were promptly categorized and diagnosed as the sub-human Catholic 'felon class of Irish cockneys' or the 'low Irish'. St Giles, for example, became identified as a prominent quarter, crowded 'by a half-Irish population, of all occupations, and no occupations, guilty of all manner of vices'.[23] Later, poverty-stricken, uneducated Jews fleeing persecution in Central and Eastern Europe who crammed into London's East End from the 1880s, and living in already appallingly overcrowded slums were portrayed in similar ways.[24]

For many writers, vice was associated with the way human bodies were represented. Beauty was associated with virtue, ugliness with vice. Vice supposedly disfigured, so unattractive physical features were linked to unattractive character. Slum dwellers as an alien, vice-ridden group became a stock theme of the sensational and over-melodramatic penny-dreadful serial novels and magazines widely read by Victorian teenagers. *Shadows of Slum Life*, for example, published in 1889 in Manchester, as part of the Excelsior Library series, used the slums as a fictional setting for an older doctor's slum explorations, his 'rescue' of and later marriage to a young girl. Told in the first person, the story portrayed slum dwellers as separate tribes who defied modern society and its sanitary and social laws, and constantly preyed upon and become a danger to all whose misfortune it was to live nearby.

Slum visits and slum clearance

Socially-conscious novelists, journalists, social investigators and reformers who ventured into slum areas regularly turned to the vocabulary of vice to help explain their experiences to the wider reading public. From their beginnings, middle-class slum visits had complex and contradictory motives, approaches and impulses: genuine Christian sympathy with the poor, philanthropic acts of charity, fear, love, or a wish to dominate and control. Some guiltily mixed their undoubted mission of service, sympathy and action with feelings and anxiety about sexuality and gender, eroticizing poverty while satisfying their morbid and purient curiosity. Some visits were laudibly sympathetic and altruistic, some more a means of working out reformers' own spiritual salvation, yet others perhaps a pleasurable means of egoistic self-gratification and the meeting of forbidden desires, a form of philanthropic hedonism, or experimentation with sexual, class and gender identities. Around mid-century, women were playing an increased role, though their activity concealed a very limited impact in terms of social discipline.[25]

Slum denizens were supposedly helpless to help themselves, 'outcasts' whose cries were ignored by the more powerful. There was only slow but growing recognition that slum conditions were a consequence of economic, social and cultural factors, not caused by deviant subgroups in society. They shamed society and could be improved. After mid-century, it became increasingly 'fashionable' amongst some middle-class respectable philanthropists of both sexes to go 'slumming', venturing gingerly into dangerous streets feeling heroic. Some adopted disguises. Quite often their reports were shaped and filtered by the policemen who were regularly employed to take visitors around the area, protecting them from harm and 'reading' and interpreting the visual spectacle. Policemen's lives and careers were shaped by their dealings with criminals, and they had a vested interest in talking up the difficulties of specific neighbourhoods. The police presence symbolized external regulation and control. They were resented by many slum-dwellers, who made clear that they found visits, even from the well-intentioned, unwelcome interventions into their culture.[26]

Some impersonated the poor to help expose poverty. James Greenwood, working for the *Pall Mall Gazette* in 1866, for example, disguised himself to spend a night in a Lambeth workhouse dormitory. His report mixed shock and evident pleasure, hinting at homoerotic impulses and hearing of 'most infamous' but indescribable 'horrors'. In some towns, temperance societies sponsored outdoor meetings and cottage visitations.

Visits were sometimes described metaphorically as a 'descent' into the 'darkest' areas of a city, an 'abyss', a dangerous and forbidden world.[27] A sermon preached by the Rev. Prebendary W. Rogers in Balliol College Chapel on Sunday 4 February 1883, captured clearly the linkages between descent, vice and slum-dwellers. The congregation were asked to 'descend with him' into East London, where they would experience 'coarseness and vulgarity', 'poverty and meanness written on the countenances of the wayfarers ... vice flaunting itself in gaudy apparel'. If they were to go inside the 'wretched' houses, they would see people 'huddled together like the beasts that perish ... grossly ignorant, semi-paupers'. During the same decade, Oxford-educated journalist Henry Woodd Nevison astutely recognized that his slumming generated a shared sympathy with the poor, but also created an irresistable attraction of repulsion.

But for many, their acts of charity became, in the words of expatriate American novelist, Henry James, a 'passion'. The slums became sites of personal liberation and self-realization for several generations of middle- and upper-class, often well-educated, men and women, some carrying out investigations and studies, some doing forms of religious and charity work, or working as teachers or nurses.[28]

In August 1893, the middle-brow *English Illustrated Magazine* even claimed that some rich philanthropists arrived in the East End so filled with literary preconceptions that actual slums were insufficiently 'slummy'. By the 1890s, slum visits were also attracting more working and lower middle-class female reformers, including the Ranyard Bible nurses and the Salvation Army 'slum lasses'.

Civic fathers wanting a better-ordered city targeted the slums too. From the Parliamentary Select Committee of the House of Commons Report on Metropolitan Improvements of 1837–8 to the Royal Commission on the Houses of the Working Class in 1885 and beyond, defining them in terms of their vice provided an ideological legitimization. The 'cultural cleansing' of such supposedly vice-ridden areas and their morally-challenged inhabitants accompanied their physical demolition and reconstruction. This helped civic leaders to embellish and boost their towns, and promote urban images attracting a respectable reputation, and more industry and commercial development.

From as early as the 1840s and 1850s, the local and national press had increasingly demanded that vestries, Boards of Health and corporations should do more. London got most attention. It was Britain's capital city, the financial and administrative centre of a huge Imperial enterprise, cosmopolitan and prosperous. It became the focus of much journalistic, survey and fictional material concentrating on its poverty, slums and destitution, fears of social unrest or sexual and alcoholic dissipation, and a sense of outraged injustice. Other towns also featured. The 1842 House of Commons Commission on the Sanitary Condition of the Labouring Population of Great Britain noted Brighton slum dwellers as 'perpetrators of vice and crime', and Birmingham lodging houses as the resorts of abandoned characters who were 'sources of extreme misery and vice'. Poor housing and overcrowding were major factors in creating ruined lives. One witness described how a young girl could only find a bed by sleeping with her sister and husband. 'Improper intercourse' had taken place, and thereafter she had become 'more depraved'.[29]

By the 1860s even magazines like *The Builder* were exposing housing conditions, albeit employing the language of vice to help make their point. Schemes of civic 'improvement' began in the major cities. In London, for example, the worst areas of the West End, where the homes of the wealthy and middle classes were predominantly located, were being cleared by the 1860s and 1870s and replaced by better low-cost housing. The 'pestilent slums of Glasgow', which were swept away in the 1860s, were 'plague spots, some of the dens of vice and crime and wickedness'. Their clearance led to 'beneficent' change and 'sanitary and moral good', though there were reportedly still 200 brothels and 150 illicit unlicensed 'shebeens' (drinking houses) in the old city centre in the early 1870s.[30] Local authorities everywhere created 'breathing room' by improving slum areas.

The urban leisure landscape

Common perceptions of the anonymous, confusing and often unfamiliar vice-ridden industrial city contained ambiguity. Cities were places where models of propriety and respectability sometimes appeared less entrenched. They were recognized as places of moral danger, especially to the young. They could be represented as hedonistic and privatized areas of vice, adventure and pleasure, far from the prying eyes of staid church congregations and stern employers or the moral constraints of parents, relations and neighbours. So newspaper explorations of 'the dark side of Glasgow', or 'fast young Birmingham' also publicized their availability.[31] Theatre and music hall areas, or the raffish bohemianism of places like Soho, became the anticipatory focus of urban myth, tall tales and future excitements.

There was also a temporal dimension to urban vice. Streets, public houses or music halls all became more highly-charged places of potential vice as night fell. Lights were lit in the main streets but not the slums. Darkness and shadow cloaked movement. Young people were especially vulnerable then. Vice could become additive. As one anonymous writer complained in 1888,

> Youths who walk the streets at night are on the highroad to vice, for they speedily become acquainted with companions of both sexes who laugh at and decry everything that it is not disgraceful to engage in. Some of the poor girls in the early stages of their disgrace are young, light-hearted, and fresh-looking, and make in the eyes of their male admirers very desirable companions. But the more a youth gives way to vice, the more the desire for it grows upon him.[32]

By the late-Victorian period, urban night-clubs, open late at night to early morning, were increasingly common. They had a disreputable reputation as dens of vice, places of drinking, betting, dancing and sexual assignation. Provided those there were members, the police could not interfere. In London, by the 1890s, for the slightly better off, the Soho district predominated, though they could also be found round the Haymarket and West End. In the East End, reportedly foreign sailors were major clients. According to one Inland Revenue detective inspector, who had seen prosecutions of 114 London clubs, they were 'nearly all kept by foreigners'. In cities such as Swansea, Birmingham and Liverpool 'you can get as much liquor as you like for 3s 5d', and they provided facilities for smuggling tobacco and spirits.[33]

Victorian cities thus coupled shock value with popular appeal. The less respectable shared the reformers' interest in cultural zoning but perceived urban areas from a very different perspective, as places of pleasurable opportunity. For young immigrant workers, the bright lights and buzz of up-town life created leisure magnets. Towns drew in visitors bent on pleasure not only from the surrounding suburbs, but also from the rest of Britain, a form of vice tourism. The new barely-disguised sex directories for men about town or guidebooks such as Cruchley's *London in 1865: A Handbook for Strangers* or Charles Culliford Dickens's unconventional *Dickens's Dictionary of London* (1879) provided useful information for the respectable, but also tantalizing hints about where to go and what to look at. Respectable readers might guiltily fantasize about crossing these cultural and geographical divisions beyond their middle-class curtains.

Even at the start of the Victorian age London possessed what *The Times* called 'immoral localities' where people caught 'the germ of vice'.[34] Public and commercial spaces were well lit, but their sheer size and labyrinthine complexity meant that paradoxically they could be profoundly private places, full of strangers, creating excitement, mystery and escapism.[35] London's major attraction was the West End, with its huge theatres with enticing galleries and bars, restaurants, and new cosmopolitan and luxurious hotels such as the Ritz and the Savoy. The fashionable café culture of the Café Royal encouraged gambling games. The gentlemen's clubs of Pall Mall and St James's offered comfortable homo-social accommodation and comforts. In the early Victorian period, the Argyll was crowded with upmarket prostitutes, attracting wealthy men to its exclusive gallery, and clerks and tradesmen to its saloon. Its notoriety forced its closure in 1852 because it was supposedly 'the focus and complex of all metropolitan vice'. This forced girls onto the streets, so in 1854 it was reopened, because, according to the *Saturday Review*, it was 'on the whole ... better that the vicious population should be brought together than that it should be let loose on society'.[36] In the 1860s, one could find club-men and MPs dancing with fashionably-dressed prostitutes at the famous Holborn Casino, with its gilded interior and richly-decorated saloon.

Travelling to London to attend nationally significant events such as the Derby, the Boat Race or even the Great Exhibition provided excuses for other pleasures. There were well-known streets round the Strand where indecent books and pictures could be obtained. There were red-light areas for prostitution. The pleasure map of London stretched from Covent Garden to the Haymarket and beyond, a region referred to by reformers as 'idle and luxurious Clubland', filled with drinking and gambling places, entertainments and prostitutes.[37] The Haymarket was a gas-lit illuminated centre of bawdy night-life for upper-class gentlemen, a time when movement through London's disordered and vibrant streets provided a constantly-changing array of spectacle and performance, raucous laughter and novel excitements.[38] This complex geographical zoning of moral and immoral pleasures challenged the police who had to cope with a wide variety of nocturnal crime, different perceptions of its importance and many temptations to corruption.

Images of London dominated discourse, but all large cities offered similar attractions. Journalists such as Liverpool's Hugh Shimmin attempted urban moral improvement through their reports on 'low' leisure life.[39] But increasingly the 'fast youth' of other areas such as Glasgow's West End emulated London's unrespectable night life with its unprecedented variety of dangerous possibilities, where personal 'adventure' and self-creation could be pursued in an increasingly pluralized and therefore more anonymous cultural and commercially-focused modern leisure world.[40]

Privileged urban middle-class men could become strolling *flaneurs*, as much at home in the changing everyday life of the city as in private life, collecting and savouring experiences of constant change, making meaning through modern 'seeing' rather than participating in their varied excitements. They possessed sufficient wealth and power to form part of the spectacle while retaining a measure of control.[41] Some became seasoned and hedonistic urban travellers, enjoying bustle, excitement and a 'spree'. Clerks and medical students, 'swells' and 'gents', 'toffs', 'mashers' and 'cads' with flamboyant, rakish dress enjoyed the pleasures of sartorial elegance, consumption and dandyism. Some were middle class, others aped their appearance and mannerisms, confidently assuming counterfeit roles and displaying their masculinity, their fashionable clothing, looks and physical prowess. A 'swell' could easily be recognized by his extravagant, 'fashionable' taste in clothes, gloves and cane, his lazy manner and flouting of respectable manners and behaviour. His social background was less easy to identify. Popular magazines like *Ally Soper's Half Holiday* and audience behaviour in music halls and theatres showed that social roles and boundaries were becoming more fluid as the century wore on.

The late Victorians had a huge appetite for pleasure and sensation. The more radical or 'liberated' could be greedy, restless and uninhibited, responding with curiosity to publicity stunts and advertising, sensational stage shows, the exhibition of 'prodigies' (or 'freak shows') and films, sport and sexual notoriety.[42] Urban existence offered new possibilities for the dissemination of vice, new and exuberant cornucopias of pleasure. In parks and pleasure gardens, penny arcades and late-century department store shopping, scandal and novelty, people shared an appetite for sensation.[43]

The greater freedoms urban life offered meant that chance meetings could take place without any formal introduction in an expanding range of new contexts: the railway carriage or platform, the horse-drawn omnibus, the London Underground or the streets crowded with old and young men, women and children of all classes, occupations and identities. Sustained proximity offered more 'forward' young men or women the opportunity to strike up acquaintanceship, enjoy a fleeting urban flirtation, or exchange 'chaff'. Urban parks, intended to ennoble and dignify the minds of the people, draw them away from vice and provide respectable sites of public sociability, also offered privacy, peril and possibility. Their trees and bushes provided shelter for betting, homosexual meetings or for courting couples, while the upper and middle classes on horseback or in carriages could vicariously enjoy watching the lower classes at play.

For some, women's presence on the streets and in public places of entertainment caused enormous anxiety. By contrast, the volumes of diaries, notebooks and photographs of solicitor Arthur Munby (1828–1910), who worked for the Ecclesiastical Commission, showed a sustained fascination with women workers. As a young man he observed and exchanged glances with them and chatted to them whenever he could. He noted their occupations and interests.

Munby was solidly middle-class, educated at St Peter's School, York, and Trinity College, Cambridge. He was interested in literature and the arts, and his diaries regularly referred to his celebrity connections: Darwin and Dickens, Rosetti and Ruskin, Swinburne and Lord Salisbury. But it was conversations with street girls that led him, when aged twenty-five, to talk in May 1854 to a young maid-of-all-work, Hannah Cullwick. She was:

> a tall erect creature with a light firm step and noble bearing: her face had the features and expression of a high-born lady, though the complexion was rosy and rustic, and the blue eyes innocent and childlike; her bare arms and hands were large and strong, and ruddy from the shoulder to the finger tips: but they were beautifully formed'.[44]

He fell in love with and eventually married Hannah although he kept the marriage clandestine, and passed her off as a servant. Despite or because of their highly sexualized, fetishistic, sado-masochistic relationship, conducted often at a distance, they may never actually have had sex.[45]

Urban space also allowed males to satisfy their sexual desire for other men.[46] On streets or in parks, homosexuals could exchange complicit signals of recognition through movement, eye gaze, gesture, clothing and speech. The new iron urinals appearing in major cities from the late 1860s onwards were another potential meeting place. Piccadilly, Oxford Street and Wardour Street in Soho all became notorious for homosexual cruising in the 1890s, and cross-dressing male prostitutes could be found in Whitechapel and elsewhere.

Women, too, had to navigate the city landscape, meeting everyday life and its adventures and dangers. The city provided a backdrop to women of all social groups, some likewise in search of personal adventure and self-creation.[47] Walking, looking and greeting on the basis of mere appearance forced the emergence of new forms of female public behaviour and propriety. Rises in living standards gave young women increased income and increased leisure time. It became less easy to recognize social status. The dominance of the male gaze could be challenged, and bolder, and more audacious, unflinching looks returned. From the 1870s onwards, younger, respectable middle-class women began to visit the consumption-focused world of West End shopping streets, with their new goods and enticements to pleasurable impulse-buying, window-shopping and occasional shop-lifting.[48] New department stores, such as Barkers or Harrods, often modelled on Paris prototypes, in wealthy suburbs like Kensington, changed women's shopping habits. From the mid-1880s match girls, shop girls, secretaries and other women workers increasingly demanded their right to occupy urban public space. It became more and more difficult to distinguish between prostitutes who could afford fashionable middle-class clothing and appearance, and 'respectable' middle-class women. So the latter were subject to increased male sexual harassment, forcing them to speak out against unwelcome street 'annoyances' or 'impertinences'.[49]

But moving from the general, there were also specific locations linked to vice, though individual reformers varied in their views, whilst attitudes varied also over time and with location. Drinking, prostitution and gaming locations always caused concern, with regular statistical investigations. According to a statistical inquiry carried out by Leeds Town Council in 1838, it had 216 inns and 235 beer houses, 98 'dens of vice and infamy' tenanted by prostitutes, and two gambling houses.[50] The same year the *Bristol Mercury* targeted the 'beer shop and the pleasure fair' as forms of immorality attractive to the poor, and 'the tavern, the racecourse, the ball and the theatre' as 'about on a par' for the better off. Later in the century, Salvationist William Booth was zealous in denouncing such 'citadels of depravity' as music halls, dance halls, theatres, boxing rings and seaside resorts.[51]

Even shops were problematic. Some were covers for prostitution or, increasingly from the 1860s onwards, for the taking of bets. At Staleybridge Borough Court in 1872, a high street confectioner was reportedly found guilty of selling indelicately stamped cakes of boiled sugar, showing 'the figures of men and women in the most disgusting positions', which 'represented the most immoral ideas it is possible to conceive'. The local chief constable, giving evidence, admitted he had previously cautioned the prisoner about selling such goods, rather than immediately prosecuting. The mayor, in giving judgement, indicated his concern was largely that they were sold to children, telling the court that 'it was bad enough to sell such things to grown ups but to sell them to children was highly reprehensible'.[52]

Brothels, public houses, taverns and gin and beer houses, gambling 'hells' and betting houses are covered in subsequent chapters. Prostitution, for example, tended to be concentrated in particular red light areas. In London, the Society for the Suppression of Vice worked with clergy, vestrymen and others from the parishes of St James's, Westminster, St Martin-in-the-Fields and St Marylebone, to 'put down the open exhibition of street prostitution ... in the important areas of the Haymarket, Coventry Street, Regent Street, Portland Place and other adjacent localities', because it was carried on with no regard for public decency.[53]

As Britain became wealthier, ever more commercialized sites offered their enticements to consumers. By the 1880s, society viewed them with far more ambiguity: they were viewed as popular, yet also seen as problematical to the more respectable because they lacked order and decorum. London's more up-market West-End 'houses of assignation', for example, were variously described as 'haunts of amusement and pleasure' or 'gilded haunts of immorality'.

Specific locations of vice

Music halls and variety theatres

It was their content, performers and opportunities for sexual introduction that sometimes portrayed these as 'dens of vice' and avenues to moral destruction. The anonymous author of *Tempted London: Young Men*, writing in 1888, claimed that he had received 'the darkest account of the morality of the stage' even from theatrical managers, while 'actresses whose names are on everybody's mouths are notoriously impure'. The atmosphere of the music hall was 'replete with all that is noxious, demoralising, debilitating, destructive of energy and intelligence'. The halls were of a 'pernicious character', engendered distasteful 'looseness of behaviour and laxity of morals', rowdyness, misbehaviour, smoking and drinking, while songs were 'replete with double meaning, often descending to base indelicacy'.[54]

In the early Victorian period, London's West End song and supper clubs, with fascinating soubriquets such as the 'Cider Cellars' or the 'Cave of Harmony', attracted the wealthy. Gustave Doré and Blanchard Jerrold, writing in 1872, remembered them affectionately for their 'shameful song singing', mixing 'indecency and blasphemy', with an audience composed of MPs, university students and young bucks.[55]

The early provincial singing saloons and embryonic music halls in cities such as Bolton, Newcastle, Nottingham and Sheffield dated from the 1840s, following competition between beer houses for custom. By the 1850s, the theatres, especially the 'free and easies', two-penny theatres and long rooms for a young working-class audience, were being accused of featuring drunken performers and audience. London music halls such as the Eagle Tavern, with its Grecian saloon, ballroom, gardens and concert room, offered dancing, singing and drinking to couples and unattached young men and women looking for companionship, fun and entertainment. Reformers viewed many women there as 'common street walkers', a regular allegation levelled at the halls, and castigated young men as pursuing 'a career of vice', by adopting 'the slang and the vices of their betters'.[56] By the 1860s and 1870s, music halls had spread across the larger towns of Britain, with young middle-class males mixing in relaxed integrated escapist freedom with working-class patrons to watch singers, instrumentalists, clowns, comics, acrobats and dancers who were slowly becoming 'stars'.[57]

To anti-vice campaigners, theatres and music halls formed a vulgar, coarse and raucous entertainment industry, haunts of 'low-life', unfavourable to moral health. Early music halls were often linked to pubs, but later in the century, in Glasgow where concerned citizens complained, of the six halls mentioned in subsequent press coverage, only two sold alcohol, though pass-out tokens would have allowed drink during the intervals in neighbouring pubs.[58] Everywhere, rowdy and unrestrained behaviour in the darkened galleries, gangways and boxes attracted transgressors and annoyed reformers. Journalist James Greenwood saw the 1860s music halls he visited as 'unmitigated dens of vice', 'notorious sinks of vice and criminality', full of 'fast' young 'blades', sons of tradesmen, looking for 'unwholesome' entertainment.

Any lewdness, sensual performances, vile scenes or vicious sentiments caused offence. A critic of Manchester's Gaiety Theatre of Varieties in 1879 called it rather 'frowsty', with much 'indelicacy and broadness'. The *Illustrated Midland News*, covering the play *Milky White* in April 1870, observed one or two lines 'objectionable from their coarseness', which 'should be excised'.[59] Theatres and halls were increasingly regulated by local authorities attempting, often unavailingly, to maintain more propriety. The disreputable journal *Town Talk* gleefully reported on an 1878 judge and jury show in London's Leicester Square. The mock trial was 'full of smut', while 'glaring obscenities characterized the questions and answers'.[60] Even in the later 1880s, when content was more controlled, the halls were still portrayed as 'fortresses of Beelzebub'.[61] Between 1890 and 1892, inspectors representing the new London County Council made 1,200 visits to music halls to police behaviour, crowd and content. Immense efforts were made to make the halls respectable, and eradicate 'vulgar' content by more moralistic licensing authorities. In October 1892, of the applications to the London County Council Licensing Committee only 14 of 48 were granted, and two applications for music hall licences were refused on the grounds that the two public houses were haunts of vice. But music hall entrepreneurs had to balance such demands against those of their audiences, and the commercial imperatives of profitability.

Even after music hall content was cleaned up, popular performers like Marie Lloyd could deliver songs like *She'd Never Had Her Ticket Punched Before*, or *Oh, Mr Porter* with saucy innuendo for audiences and with total innocence for inspectors. Top performers were celebrities, and their well-publicized reputations and 'immoral' and 'impure' private lives, such as Marie Lloyd's three unsuccessful marriages, simply enhanced their fame.

By the 1890s, changes in taste, and more professional presentation, saw the halls increasingly defended by middle-class writers and essayists as respectable theatres for family entertainment. The social purity movement's attempt to close the promenade of the Empire Music Hall because of its prostitution was faced with virulent public disapproval, with its female supporters dubbed 'Prudes on Parade'.[62] London City Council's refusal to license the Empire until the promenade was removed was overturned by a higher court. Jerome K. Jerome and Eden Phillpotts' play *The Prude's*

Progress, which toured in 1895, ridiculed the pharisaic nature of one character who was a London county councillor and member of the National Vigilance Association. The same year, some newspapers gleefully satirized the actions of watch committees in other large towns: 'prurient prudes' in Cardiff, for example.[63] The largest London variety theatres attracted men in evening dress and fashionable ladies, employers and employees, wives and husbands to their well-funished seats and luxurious boxes. The highly successful chains founded by leading theatrical entrepreneurs like Horace E. Moss (1852–1912), from Lancashire, or South Shields-born Richard Thornton (1839–1922), gained widespread support. When the Bradford Empire opened in 1899, their Circuit Secretary announced that 'nothing will be seen or heard here that will raise a blush or put modesty to shame'. Yet despite reformist opposition rampant sexual display by prostitutes could still be found, and ambiguity, subversion and risqué entertainment were still popular. *Tableaux vivants*, for example, had women dressed in flesh-coloured body stockings and posing as nudes to represent famous gallery paintings, disguising titillating entertainment as high culture.

Pleasure grounds

These too were ambiguously viewed. Cremorne Gardens in Chelsea, London's chief pleasure ground, attracted pleasure seekers of all classes. Its towering elm trees, lawns and flower beds, kiosks, temples and feverishly-enjoyed dancing areas, illuminated by a thousand gas lights, and occasional firework displays, commemorated in Whistler's 'Nocturne in Black and Gold: the Falling Rocket' (1875), attracted up to 15,000 people a night, drinking, dancing and enjoying its spectacle. Darkness conveyed a special atmosphere. People could enjoy the excitement and the spectacle of fireworks and the flaring of the bright gas lights, but also the dangerous delights of anonymity and intimacy in the flickering shadows. By contrast there were more usually only 1,500 to 2,000 on fine summer evenings.

William Acton, searching for evidence of prostitution, visited Cremorne and found 'thoughtful, care-worn men and women' dancing. Acton, like other reformers, was confused by the manners and class identity of attendees, especially the number of middle-class males, suggesting that 'on and around that platform waltzed, strolled, and fed some thousand souls – perhaps seven hundred of them men of the upper and middle class, the remainder prostitutes more or less prononcées'. Of the latter's character he had 'little moral doubt'.[64]

Acton 'read' the women's occupation simply from their presence and appearance. Since he also believed that 'the intercourse of the sexes could hardly have been more reserved – *as a general rule*', that 'the younger portion of the company formed the dances, and enjoyed themselves after the manner of youth, but . . . without offence to the most fastidious eye or ear', whilst admitting that he himself was 'in quest of noise, disorder, debauchery, and bad manners', his reading was problematic. He accepted that the women there were generally quiet and modestly behaved, while 'pretty and quiet dressing was almost universal' and that it was open to the male visitors to invite attention and solicit acquaintance. But he still suggested that 'no gentlemanly proposition of the kind would have been rebuffed, no courteous offer of refreshment, possibly, declined'.

Cremorne was respectable enough to be generally supported by the magistracy, yet simultaneously attacked as morally corrupting, a public nuisance and a place that brought down house values. The local Vestry tried twice, unsuccessfully, to get magistrates to refuse its licences or introduce earlier closing. In 1871, however, following a campaign by Canon Cromwell, principal of St Mark's Training College, the Middlesex magistrates refused John Baum, the lessee, his music and dancing licences (though they were soon restored) at the largest meeting of magistrates that had assembled in the district, a clear indication of divided views.[65] Cromwell's petitions against Cremorne were met with coarse ribaldry and threatening letters from its supporters, but opposition continued. In 1877 Alfred Brandon, the minister of the Chelsea Baptist Chapel, attacked Cremorne as 'the nursery of every kind of vice'. Baum countered by suing for libel. Brandon's lawyers claimed that it was 'reasonable and proper criticism', purging society 'from courses which led to vice and immorality'. Although Baum won, the jury awarded token damages and crucially, not costs, forcing Baum to close.[66]

London's Crystal Palace was popular and more conventionally respectable, and attracted more working-class visitors. By contrast North Woolwich Pleasure Gardens was run by a series of music hall and theatrical impresarios. In the 1870s, it featured leading music hall and variety acts, alongside novel, curious and attractive events, such as a baby show, with 200 or more babies, which drew crowds of 20,000. Its supporters claimed that there was no impropriety in the gardens, but *Town Talk* claimed it was disreputable, full of 'vice' and 'low' clientele. Its correspondent reported in September 1879 that 'I accidentally came across a spectacle which almost froze the blood from my veins. I dare not describe what I saw'.[67]

Pleasure gardens across Britain offered similar promise, possibility, potential danger and problems, even though some deployed policemen to emphasize their public order. Birmingham had a series of such sites. Around 1870 the St Helena Gardens Music Hall and Pleasure Grounds had music and dancing as regular attractions. By the 1880s, Aston Lower Grounds put on a whole variety of day and evening entertainments, including athletics, bicycle and foot races, all associated with betting, despite notices prohibiting it, and occasional and desultory attempts to eject bookmakers by police and the lessee. There were concerts in its great hall, balloon ascents, electric lighting in the evenings, and occasional firework displays.[68] Manchester's Belle Vue Gardens and Pomona Pleasure Gardens offered similar facilities. Other gardens, such as Newcastle's suburban Jesmond Gardens, were places for pleasure and promenade, though according to the Tyneside music-hall performer, Joe Wilson, 'vile others', 'a slur an' disgrace to the gardens', spent their evening prowling about for individuals to prey upon, seduce and exploit.[69]

Fairs

Across Britain, customary events with leisure connections also attracted reformist complaints. Christmas, Easter and Whitsuntide, or carnivalesque occasions based on the church's year, especially fairs and wakes, were associated with conviviality, bawdiness and drunkenness. Respectable ratepayers found pleasure-seeking crowds exhibiting 'bad' behaviour and language, which was culturally and morally fearful and threatening, and linked to broader concerns about absenteeism, money improvidently 'wasted' on vicious pleasures, and the nefarious activities of pickpockets, prostitutes and others.

Urban customary and private fairs, supposedly for trade purposes, were common targets. Fairs specialized in locally-important commodities such as cattle, sheep, horses, cheese, geese or onions, and attracted large numbers of visitors. Annual hiring fairs for farm servants and agricultural labourers were also common, especially in northern England and Scotland, where they remained a vibrant part of local festival character, and commercial and social networking. The supposedly degrading and demoralizing mixing of the sexes and sense of freedom and abandonment after a year's living in at a farm gave hiring fairs a reputation for great drunkenness and profligacy.

Fairs attracted showmen, and the pleasure functions of fairs increased through the nineteenth century. At Sunderland, exchange of fairings, 'pottery, bazaars and stalls', 'gingerbread and candy', 'shows, swings, mountebanks, musicians and monkeys' were all listed as 'usual' attractions in 1849.[70] By the 1850s, some fairs were already being described as 'so-called pleasure fairs', and by the 1870s the term 'pleasure fairs' was in common usage. Often fairs continued as pleasure fairs when their original trade functions had disappeared or been taken over, as, for example, by auction markets for cattle. Wakefield stopped being a hiring fair in the early 1890s, as hiring agencies took over its role, but its pleasure fair continued. Pleasure fairs were described by opponents as 'saturnalias of vice'. At night, when business gave way to pleasure, their carnivalistic concomitants of gaudy colour, flamboyant lights, crowded drinking booths and pubs, circuses, freak shows, penny theatres, yelling showmen and boisterously raucous crowds offended and intimidated the more genteel, the rich, the respectable and religious.

There was no united anti-fair movement. The lurid vehemence levelled at fairs was often highly general and unspecific, unsubstantiated by direct observation or personal experience. A hyperbolic handbill issued by the

London Christian Instruction Society began by claiming that fairs promoted 'idleness', and thus restricted the earnings that would provide domestic comfort. Fairs were 'the haunts of vice' where 'abandoned women' waited for their prey. Fairs corrupted 'the morals of females, and lead on to seduction' in the 'dancing room, the drinking booth and the lewd shows'. Drunkenness was 'a common vice at the fair' and 'drunkenness leads to madness'. It ended by claiming that fairs led to 'felony' and so to 'the Jail!!! The Hulks!!! The Gallows!!!'.[71]

The disorderliness and boisterousness of the fairs in inner urban areas, their occupation of streets and blocking off of roads, their noise, bustle and commotion were all offensive. They threatened public order and property, obstructed daily business and restricted travel. In mid-Victorian East Yorkshire, the Church of England developed a powerful critique of hiring fairs,[72] yet attempts to replace hiring fairs with registers had little success. Their attractions were too deep-rooted.

The articulate, shrill and hostile comments regularly levelled against fairs, and the legal manoeuvrings attempting to suppress and abolish them, showed fairs were seen as problematic. Opponents' success in actually closing fairs is harder to assess. Some sixty fairs within a fifteen-mile radius of London's Charing Cross were closed down between 1750 and 1850, but there were complex and multifarious reasons for their disappearance. Some, such as London's Bartholomew, Smithfield or Greenwich fairs, were simply too close to urban centres. Urban expansion, limitations of space and increasingly higher costs were common reasons for fairs' demise.

Support for fairs crossed class boundaries. As Charles Pearson, Solicitor to the City of London reported in 1840, 'it is at all times difficult by law to put down the ancient customs and practices of the people'.[73] Attendance at fairs represented, at least for some, a key traditional 'right', and Whiggish notions of the people's freedoms led to some middle-class support for customary fairs. Attacks on fairs were presented as attacks on popular festivals and freedom, and on rights of time, the recreational calendar and labour. The fair also symbolized local identities of place, so affection and loyalty to the parish were also powerful. Such beliefs represented core Tory values, and notions of such rights did not disappear with modernity or industrialization.

The Fairs Act of 1871, which made provision for their abolition by the Secretary of State for the Home Department, following appropriate representations by local magistrates, or by the owner of the fair, claimed that certain of the fairs held in England and Wales were 'unnecessary, are the cause of grievous immorality, and are very injurious to the inhabitants of the towns in which such fairs are held'. However, the actual impact of the legislation was limited, although several larger Liberal provincial municipalities, including Birmingham, whose self-consciously modernizing leaders were Nonconformist and liberal in their attitudes, abolished their fairs in the 1870s. Underlying reasons were often economic. Opposition usually only succeeded when a fair was already in decline. Deliberate attempts to suppress a successful fair rarely succeeded, as fairs were often supported by a majority of inhabitants.

In Feltham in 1887, for example, the Commissioner of Police received a petition of 102 in favour of the abolition of its fair, supported by local magistrates, but 183 signed a counter-petition. The Commissioner noted that 'the abolition of the fair is a class question . . . it gives the Police trouble to keep order, and that while one class certainly enjoy it, its existence is the cause of annoyance to others'.[74] This oversimplified a complex debate. Stock dealers found fairs valuable. The tolls from fairs raised revenue for the locality. There were stall rents, local farmers could rent out land for grazing, and pub landlords and shopkeepers all gained increased custom, so many borough treasurers had a vested interest in keeping a fair going; by the 1880s, the police and Home Office were confident that order could be maintained and that the fairs were generally harmless. When there were anti-fair moves at Barnet in 1888, the local MPs, the Barnet Local Board, the East Barnet Valley Local Board, the Barnet Rural Sanitary Authority and the Public Vestry of Chipping Barnet all supported the fair's continuance.

Overall more urban fairs survived than were suppressed.[75] Many new fairs, self-consciously pleasurable, became symbols of modernity, using new technology such as film to attract custom. Birmingham's fair was soon resurrected as a pleasure fair. Hull had a pleasure fair from the late eighteenth century. Up to the 1850s, the local Poor Law guardians even celebrated it at the workhouse by giving plum pudding to paupers and pennies to children. Hull's fair moved site five times between 1835 and 1888 and the Corporation eventually laid out a permanent fair ground. Many fairs such as Nottingham's annual Goose Fair, Oxford's St Giles' Fair or Leicester's pleasure fair at Humberstone Gate evolved from their trading roots to become customary industrial holidays by 1901. In Yorkshire alone, Waddington's *List of Fairs, Feasts, Statutes and Rushbearings* still listed over 100 separate towns in the mid-1890s where fairs were actively celebrated, some occurring more than once each year.[76]

Horse-races

Race meetings, with their added concomitants of drinking, betting and gambling, places where risk and the risqué coincided, were also viewed ambiguously. Across Britain in the 1850s there were about one hundred flat racing courses and a smaller number of steeplechase courses. Nearly all county towns had an annual race meeting. Before the 1870s, when courses increasingly became enclosed, admission charges were limited to grandstand areas and vehicles. Attendance was free elsewhere and large numbers of booths, tents and stalls offered their wares and inducements. Huge crowds attended. Even in the 1840s, major meetings at Doncaster, Manchester,

Epsom and York attracted well over 100,000 spectators on race days. Small courses such as Rochdale could attract 8,000 or more.[77] Race meetings were major annual holiday events, built into the calendars of local industry, and often too into farm workers' contracts. Children would take time off school.

But race-horses were 'instruments of gambling' and there was clear potential for horses to be manipulated in the betting market, by owners, trainers, bookmakers and jockeys. In 1873 one aristocratic writer, Lord Henry Curzon, bitterly claimed that 'it would be a thousand times better for horseracing to cease, than that the racecourses of Great Britain should continue to be seminaries of swindling'.[78] Betting was a risky business, in which wealth, livelihood and reputation could easily be lost. Outsiders found its practices puzzling. Charles Dickens, for example, knew little of horses and disliked organized gambling. He ended his 1851 description of his visit to the Epsom Derby in *Household Words* still 'far from absolutely certain of the name of the winner'.[79] His visit to Doncaster during the September St Leger meeting, together with his friend Wilkie Collins, was later described in *The Lazy Tour of Two Idle Apprentices*. His alter ego, 'Mr Goodchild', portrayed ordinary betters as 'lunatics'. The professional bookmakers at Doncaster were, by contrast, 'keepers'. From the window of his 'expensive' lodging he observed 'the Lunatics, horse-mad, betting-mad, drunken-mad, vice-mad, and the designing Keepers always after them'.[80]

Meetings also featured other often illegal gaming activities. Early Victorian Ascot, for example, had up to ten gaming booths, containing roulette and hazard, though these disappeared as the upper classes retreated to new grandstands and paddock areas. Races, like fairs, attracted many other illegal and fraudulent gambling games to attract the gullible. For much of the century the thimble-rigging trick, involving three thimbles or shells and an apparently single pea, was the most common. All naïve spectators had to do was identify which thimble hid the pea to win their bet, after the three thimbles had been manipulated by sleight of hand, as indeed the naïve were being too. It was a game represented in the famous 1858 picture by William Powell Frith, 'Derby Day'. It was so common that folding tables were specially made to be quickly stowed away on the appearance of the police. Usually the men operated in small teams, anything up to perhaps six, with defined roles, some calculated to draw people into the fraud by encouraging them to bet or appearing to bet successfully themselves, others to turn heavy in case of trouble. Each annual fair or race-meeting brought new mug punters to fleece, innocents abroad. From around mid-century, the three-card trick (aka find the lady) which normally involved selecting the single queen amongst three face-down cards, grew more popular, usually involving four men working together to take people's money.

Temporary drinking booths of canvas, wood or even turf were erected at every meeting to cater for heavy drinking. In the 1860s in Manchester, during the three-day Whitsuntide races, when almost all factories closed, the *Free Lance* claimed that 'the people have gone to the races; the cabs have gone to the races ... and there is nothing and nobody left in town'. The Castle Irwell course was then described as 'a complete canvas city of public houses', one where 'the publican was ubiquitous' and 'it seems, indeed, to be taken for granted that all visitors to the races require a lot of something to drink and a little of something to eat'.[81] The races attracted thieves, occasional welshing bookmakers (failing to honour cash bets), counterfeiters, pickpockets and prostitutes.

So it was unsurprising that race meetings attracted social, economic, humanitarian and moral opposition. The respectable householders of Leith bitterly complained that their race meeting attracted 'vice and profligacy', and 'disgusting intemperance', but the town council were more concerned with the very significant revenue the races attracted and ignored their 1846 petition. Similar petitions in racing towns such as Doncaster, Chester and Ripon were likewise ignored.[82] The patronage of MPs and members of the House of Lords from across the country ensured that Parliament likewise protected race meetings.

The Paisley minister, Dr T. Houston, itemized racing's 'evils' as 'idleness', 'mis-spending of money', 'theft and dishonesty', 'Sabbath profanation', 'drunkenness', 'cruelty of animals', 'loss of life to riders' and 'gambling'.[83] At Chester, William Wilson, a Nonconformist, fought hard against 'the demoralising tendency' of the Roodee races in the 1860s, declaring:

> that short week has sown misery in a thousand breasts, has robbed many an inexperienced youth of his better principles, and many an unguarded female of her purity: has left many a parent to mourn over the victims of immorality, and has registered a thousand crimes ... Brawling, drunkenness, gambling, theft, fornication, suicide, and every vice denounced by the divine authority are invariably the results of the present racing system.[84]

In 1870, the Dean of Chester levelled much the same litany of accusations, complaining that 'each season seems to indicate an increasing tendency to fraud, obscenity, profanity and debauchery'.[85] But this was unavailing. Long-standing race-meetings rarely disappeared because of opposition, but rather, like fairs, largely only when economic circumstances changed.

The countryside

If opponents of vice saw cities and their commercialized leisure forms as 'the favourite seat of vice', then overcrowding in the countryside could lead to vice too. The respectable middle classes had limited direct experience of rural life and poverty. Some over-idealized rural life, while others were more negative, sometimes projecting their personal emotions on to their analysis. One country vicar, writing to *The Times* in 1858, described cottage rooms 'couched every night six, eight or even ten warm and throbbing bodies of different sexes whose ages vary up to 16, 17 or 18', in circumstances where 'the passions of nature are unnaturally forced into existence and unnaturally tempted into indulgence', and 'evil thoughts and prurient pleasures' emerged.[86] Conan Doyle's character, Sherlock Holmes, claimed that 'the lowest and vilest alleys in London do not present a more dreadful record of sin than does the smiling and beautiful countryside'.[87] Semi-rural mining districts such as those in South Wales, the North East or Lanarkshire, were often associated with negative images of dirtiness, and simplistic accounts of dens of vice, drunkenness and violence. Pit-row villages, with their marginal housing (despite the inner cleanliness of most pit cottages) and often poor sanitation, dominated by the power of coal-owners and their officials, were perceived as distinctive and disturbing. There lived dark demonic figures, a race apart with a shared identity, relatively isolated from middle-class society, living with coals and fumes. In the Northumberland and Durham coalfield, pubs were a focus of community life, despite bitter and persistent condemnation from miner Methodists and trade unionists. Gambling was highly pervasive, despite ongoing attempts to suppress it by local authorities.[88]

Vice on holiday

Early travel agents with temperance and religious backgrounds such as Thomas Cook, John Frane (who opened up the Scottish Highlands to tourism) or Sir Henry Lunn, whose creation of Cooperative Education Tours in 1893 was a first step towards the later Lunn Poly travel company, offered respectable, self-improving holidays for the middle classes. But British seaside and foreign travel, with their 'otherness' and distance from the pressures of domestic respectability also provided contexts in which behaviour could be linked to casual sex, gambling and heavy drinking. Holidays at the seaside had features of disreputable pleasure. A valuable safety valve, a legitimized escape from some of the more irksome constraints of respectability, they demonstrated the more frivolous side of even the mid-Victorian middle classes, and the vice-related attractions of earthy humour, excess drinking and sensual enjoyments.[89] For the working classes, excursions offered a change from work, to enjoy food, drink, dancing and raffish entertainment, in the less-restrained company of others often from the same neighbourhood. The Victorian seaside simultaneously compromised respectability and retained it, allowed individuals to slip in or out of disreputable guise. Victorian paintings and posters shed light on the way such places could be regarded as 'improper'. Local authorities were forced to balance control against recognition of their resorts' pleasure roles. Most resorts tried to retain a respectable image, with occasional moral panics over drunkenness and unseemly behaviour. Many introduced bathing regulations identifying separate bathing areas of the beach for men and women, the nature of swimming apparel, how close boatmen might approach, and at what age (usually ten) male children should stop swimming with their mothers. Most people were fully clothed whilst on the beach unless bathing. However, some unconstrained visitors and trippers indulged in excessive behaviour and defied convention. At Redcar in Yorkshire, for example, the annual visit of the Durham militia in the 1880s regularly featured drunkenness and naked bathing. Lacking bathing costumes and money to rent a bathing machine, the men regularly marched to the beach followed by a 'usual rabble of spectators of both sexes', and bathed nude, but more respectable complainants in their respectable lodging houses, watching the scene closely, were appalled at so much exposed flesh.[90]

Resorts always had overtones of sexual misbehaviour, with desire, requited or unrequited, a driving force. Flirtation was easier there, and new self-ascribed higher-status roles and identities could be assumed to aid seduction, unless most of the inland town went to the same place, when observant eyes might note misbehaviour. Prostitutes also frequented many resorts. At Blackpool, for example, prostitution was carefully ignored by police except for occasional low-key prosecutions, aimed at their more overt manifestations or in response to complaints. There were crusades against 'indecent prints' and obscene pictures in the 1880s, and against slot machines in the 1890s but by then most popular resorts had a more relaxed attitude to public morality.[91]

Notions of national identity saw 'otherness' in terms of foreign morality too. Trips abroad opened up new vistas of vice and hedonism. Travel to Venice, Paris and other foreign cities offered sensual or sexual adventure. Sex tourism, for both heterosexuals and homosexuals, was not new in the Victorian period. Sultry climates and British colonies provided a haven for travellers, searchers for the exotic, artists and poets. Some colonies gained fame as sites of sexual licence, although the relationships between colonialists and native populations varied widely in space and time, depending on local beliefs, norms and taboos. Isolated officials and merchants were almost expected to take local women as mistresses, while homosexual liaisons and scandals in the colonies surfaced regularly. Imperial expansion was linked in part to copulation and the keeping of concubines. Erotic imagination and sexual interaction served to mitigate the miseries and boredom of living singly overseas, and there was an enlarged field of opportunity for casual sex. The history of tourism and travel shows the sensuality and sexual promise of the Orient attracted the rich and the adventurer.[92]

And foreigners behaved in different, supposedly less moral ways. Contrasts were regularly drawn between the archetypical image of the stiff-upper-lipped Englishman and foreigners who were stereotyped as the 'over-sexed Oriental', or the 'impulsive', 'hot-blooded' Latin races, with their 'primitive' honour codes. The 'excitable Gauls' were a particular target of such fictional stereotypes. When *The Times* reported the acquittal of a married Frenchwoman after she shot her lover for being unfaithful in 1843, its headline 'French Morality' summed up the British view. As Wilkie Collins told Charles Dickens, 'the morality of England is firmly based on the immorality of France'.[93] In India, stronger images of the 'lascivious Indian' emerged during and after the 1857 rebellion, though the 'manly British' were also positively contrasted with the 'effeminate Bengali'.[94]

Conclusion

This chapter has shown the ways in which to certain groups in society, from social reformers and churchmen to the more respectable lower and middle classes, certain locations carried powerful and dangerous associations, full of vice and sin. Such places were felt to provide a cultural counterpoint and highly dangerous present or potential threat to church, chapel and the virtuous neighbourhood.

Some types of places were always associated with vice. It was the images of vice in Britain's urban slums which most dominated and stimulated anti-vice rhetoric and reformist efforts to develop help through slum visits and slum clearance. Alongside generalized criticisms of urban life and the leisure landscape, the Victorians developed more specific critiques of locations such as race-courses and pleasure grounds, theatres and music halls. Even the countryside was not immune from attack for its vices. With the ever-expanding rail network and steam ship services, visits to seaside resorts in Britain, foreign casinos and even the Victorian equivalents to foreign sex tourism began to emerge. Such locations were tempting. They offered excitement. They stimulated the mind, body and senses. Many locations offered opportunities for gambling, drinking and sexual pleasure. The next three chapters explore these three 'unholy vices', starting with the 'national evil', the 'demon drink'.

CHAPTER THREE

The Vice of Drunkenness

Even today, the role of drink in most people's everyday life is a matter of political and social debate. Likewise in the early 1870s, the problems of alcohol and drunkenness dominated the political agenda in Westminster corridors and across Great Britain. The 'drink question' and public house licensing provided newspaper headlines, while the Liberal government's 1872 Licensing Act was welcomed by some for its potentially 'beneficial' effects on public drunkenness. It restricted public house closing times to no later than midnight in large towns and 11 p.m. in country areas. Local magistrates had the power to shorten these hours. Some did. Boroughs could even choose to be 'dry', banning all alcohol. The Act also created an additional offence of simply being drunk in public.

Yet the extent of drunkenness at that time, whether legislative remedies would have any useful effect, and the general public mood, all proved difficult to assess. The Act was widely opposed and led to disturbances, demonstrations and even riots across the country by those condemning it as a 'tyrannous' system. Conservative newspapers printed editorials portraying it as a law with left the rich 'protected, privileged and undisturbed' while denying drink to the working classes.[1] The Liberal government was defeated in the 1874 election, a defeat the Prime Minister, Gladstone, described as having been 'born down in a torrent of gin and beer'.

Even for the historian, the results of the Act are ambiguous, once we start to examine figures at local level. This was where the elimination or toleration of drinking (and other vices) was addressed. So the police, the magistrates, the press and the courts were crucial in determining the local impact of such Acts. The debates at the time about the difficulties of reading inter-urban comparison statistics showed this clearly.[2] Following the Act, most towns showed an increase in arrests although this varied widely in its extent, some showed no change, and a tiny few showed a diminution. In 1874, Sheffield with a population of 239,947 had 1,112 drunkenness prosecutions, while Rochdale with its 64,000 population had nearly as many prosecutions (1,046), despite being only a quarter of the size. Rochdale's total had risen far more after 1872.

Were Rochdale and other towns where prosecutions rose becoming *more* drunken towns following the Act? Rochdale's Chief Constable, Samuel Stevens, who served the town between 1869 and 1881, was already a strong opponent of strong drink. He had taken drastic action to curb drunk and disorderly behaviour in the town, and closed some public houses even before 1872. So following the Act, his instructions to the force had changed. Previously the police as a rule had not arrested people for simple drunkenness, but only those who were drunk and disorderly or drunk and incapable. In his annual reports he made clear that drunks were now arrested even if not in a helpless condition and perfectly quiet. He argued that as a result midnight 'broils' were now less frequent and there was 'considerably less disorder in the streets at an earlier hour than formerly'. He blamed drunkenness on the ill-educated working classes of Rochdale, pointing out that 'of those prosecuted only 15 could read and write well'.[3] He suggested that Sheffield's figures were lower because the police there were less stringent in the exercise of their duties and making arrests.

Even within Rochdale, however, opinion was split about the Act and its effects. The Mayor, W.T. Shawcross, was opposed to the Act and saw the Alliance temperance reformers as fanatics. His judgements on the magistrates' bench reflected this. Another Rochdale resident, the Rev. W.N. Molesworth, was a strong supporter of the bill's principles and objects, and spoke at temperance meetings across Yorkshire. The local MP was ambiguous in his views.

Some believed the Act simply changed local drinking habits. In the late evening, after pubs shut, drinkers bought alcohol from off-licences and grocers, or went to private clubs, and there was much more private drinking with friends. Publicans set up working men's clubs. Others argued that economic factors impacted on drunkenness figures. At East Morley, the increase in drunkenness was blamed by the police on 'the largely increased rate of wages and diminution in the hours of labour' amongst the drinking working classes.[4]

Introduction

Right through the nineteenth century such debates over the vice of drunkenness divided Britain, bringing together issues ranging from social class and economics to cultural attitudes, politics, policing and religion. Many people enjoyed alcohol's pleasures yet it created binge drinking, disorderly behaviour and addiction. Some blamed drunkenness on societal failings, some wanted moral persuasion to reduce drunkenness, and some demanded total prohibition. The wrangles that it generated regularly figured in the making and breaking of governments, and it was an issue that divided opinion at local level in many British towns.

For many centuries, Britain's poor mainly drank ale and beer as thirst quenchers or for stamina. Water was often scarce, polluted and unsafe. The increased availability of cheap spirits, especially gin, led to more spirit drinking. Even so, when Victoria took the throne in 1837, alcohol was still not perceived as a major problem. All classes drank. Binge drinking was common even amongst the middling classes. Few worried about it. Gin palaces were popular in poorer areas. They lacked food and seating, but were sometimes provided with extravagant architecture to encourage sales.

But the use of alcohol, its evil or necessity, its pleasure or potential damnation, was increasingly problematic. Drink produced ambivalent responses even within the ruling groups and within Parliament.[5] It generated prolonged, heated and constantly refined debates. Most men drank. A sizeable minority did not. Women were less likely to drink than men, and played an important role in many church-related temperance movements. But women got drunk too, and in significant numbers. Yet legislation to reduce drinking risked adding to unemployment. It would put people from agricultural labourers and maltsters to brewers, barmaids and beer house landlords out of work.

Chapter outline

This chapter begins with a discussion of the ways in which drunkenness was portrayed as a vice by reformers. It then examines the changing popularity of drink. The discussion then moves to explore the ways in which reformers tried to deal with drink's problems, first stressing moderate drinking, then moving to persuade people to become teetotal and abandon alcohol altogether, and finally attempting to use political action to have drink banned. The role of the pub in offering facilities for drink is then considered, before assessing how much people drank across the Victorian period.

The vice of drunkenness and its consequences

Although many Britons enjoyed drink, Britain had a growing temperance movement. As society changed, apparently increased drinking assumed a challenge to traditional Christian ethics. Drunkenness affected social order. Initially moderate drinking was accepted for its social and sometimes wholesome effects, but respectable moderate drinkers were concerned about heavy drinking amongst the unrespectable working classes. Sobriety was associated with hard work, self-improvement and thrift. Drunkenness was associated with personal demoralization, domestic wretchedness through dissipation, ill-health and improvidence, as well as personal and social debasement.

Many reformers accepted that much drunkenness was generated by the dirt, disease and general environment of poverty-stricken urban life. But individuals could choose to be temperate. Excessive drinkers ('confirmed tipplers', 'inebriates' or 'sots') dominated temperance ideological imagery. Speeches, pamphlets and books reiterated stock complaints against drunkenness, the evils of Sunday drinking, intemperance and dissipation. Heavy drinking was a vice, a sin, a sign of individual moral failing and character weakness. Problems were blamed on alcohol and the weaknesses and personal deficiencies of drinkers. Therefore excessive drinking was a disease of the will. Such explanations helped people understand and locate the contradictions between drink's widespread availability in Britain, the increased demands for sobriety imposed by factors ranging from factory discipline to safe railway running, and the ways some constantly returned to drinking despite making solemn pledges.[6]

Intemperance

Intemperance in drinking terms meant different things to different people: drunkenness, or immoderate drinking, or any drinking whatsoever. Reformers were concerned about drunkenness, but their attacks on alcohol went further. Temperance leaflets blamed drink for damaged health, illness and premature death, crime, poverty, ruin of children and families, and many other ills of Britain's rapidly industrializing towns.

One businessman, a coach maker, giving evidence to an 1849 Select Committee, claimed pubs 'led men into the haunts of dissipation and vice'.[7] In 1852, it was claimed that intemperance was 'the monster evil of our day', the great producer of crime and misery'.[8] A London curate wrote to *The Times* in 1855 complaining that he had counted 170 leaving a single public house in his area, and that 'the results of this addiction to strong drink are poverty, wretchedness, prostitution, crime and vice of every description'.[9] In 1858, Glasgow temperance campaigner, Rev. W. Reid, saw drunkenness as Britain's national vice, because 'intemperance exceeds all other vices in the comprehensiveness of its devastations'.[10] In 1869, a Convocation of Canterbury committee concluded that intemperance was 'a terrible vice'.[11] In 1873, the Catholic Fr. Richardson saw 'the vice of drunkenness' as perhaps 'the most awful and fatal evil of modern times'. Some, he thought, had inherited their love of strong drink, but some drank to excess through 'imprudence and want of fortitude', or just enjoyed the 'companionship and conviviality' of the pub.[12]

In temperance discourse, the 'demon drink', that 'horrible fiend', was dangerous, 'a grievous curse', associated with dissipation, disease, destitution and dissolution. It caused 'frightful havoc', 'unspeakable agony and horror'. It was 'ghastly and hideous'. It affected health and reputation. It caused crime and poverty. The belief that drunkenness led to insanity was widely held, even within the medical profession. Doctors, priests and superintendents involved in mental asylums in industrial areas reported high proportions of drink-related insanity amongst inmates to various Royal Commissions. Doctors were uncertain about the exact medical relationships between addiction, drunkenness and insanity, and causality was linked to ideas of morality. Masters of Victorian workhouses sometimes likewise argued that most pauper inmates owed their poverty either directly or indirectly to drink.

By the later nineteenth century social reformers accepted the connection but linked it to other structural features in society.[13] Booth, for example, took drunkenness to be only one major cause of poverty. He claimed that in looking at over 1,600 cases of the 'very poor', in 14 per cent of cases their poverty was 'attributable to drink and thriftlessness', and 82 per cent of cases due to circumstances of questions of employment, while 4 per cent were just idle 'loafers'. For those who were simply 'poor', in 13 per cent of cases poverty was down to 'drink and thriftlessness'.[14]

The drunkard

Drink was portrayed as a major factor in crime and social disorder.[15] Women and children reliant on a heavy-drinking adult male could be badly treated, beaten, abused and malnourished. The Select Committee on the Married Women's Property Bill of 1867/8 believed that it was not uncommon for husbands to take their wives' earnings and spend them on drinking. Drink linked to pauperism and the poorhouse, to policemen and prison. To more outspoken reformers the alehouse led inevitably to the jailhouse. This was a perennial complaint from magistrates, albeit on highly impressionistic evidence, so the estimated strength of the association varied. One London magistrate in 1845 asserted that three-quarters of the persons in the prisons of the metropolis were there 'through the abominable vice of drinking'.[16] The House of Lords Committee considering the Acts for the sale of beer believed in 1850 that drunkenness was the main cause of crime, disorder and distress in Britain. Baron Martin at the Liverpool Assizes in 1867 believed that drunkenness seemed to be the source of nine-tenths of all crime.[17] Dealing with crime and distress had had to be paid for by respectable ratepayers.

Moreover, drink could be dangerously addictive, weakening and then destroying the 'higher', more moral portions of the personality and brain. Intoxication led to loss of self-control. Alcohol dependency could lead to fights, criminal behaviour, losing work, poverty, domestic abuse and other social evils, as well as illnesses such as alcoholic gastritis, pancreatitis and liver damage. Drink made rational men behave irrationally. People living near pubs had to cope with drink-related problems, impairing the life of the community.

So alcoholism was a social, moral and medical challenge. Only a few followed American practice by recognizing chronic alcoholism as an illness.[18] Samuel Pope, the Secretary of the United Kingdom Alliance, argued in 1856 that 'the appetite for drink ... unlike every other appetite ... is never satisfied. Indulgence is never followed by satiety, but by increased craving'.[19] The medical and legal recognition of addictive, uncontrollable drinking was novel even in the 1870s, when the British Medical Association and the National Association for the Promotion of Social Science began to develop treatments for alcoholics.[20] Earlier in the century, doctors had sometimes prescribed alcohol for a huge variety of ailments, some in quite staggering proportions. As the social role and status of the medical profession rose, public health concerns became more important, and the concept of disease became more widely understood. Chronic alcoholism was slowly accepted as a disease. In 1879, the government passed the Habitual Drunkards Act to facilitate the control and cure of addicts. The Act empowered local authorities to establish retreats, and defined an habitual drunkard as 'a person who, not being amenable to any jurisdiction in lunacy, is notwithstanding, by reason of habitual intemperate drinking of intoxicating liquor, at times dangerous to himself or herself or to others, or incapable of managing himself or herself or his or her affairs'. Drunkards, thought Dr Norman Kerr, the founder of the Society for the Study and Cure of Inebriety in 1884, should be hospitalized, not gaoled. The Society studied addiction and lobbied, unsuccessfully, for more retreats for the medical treatment of inebriates, but its initial membership of 232 dropped to 89 by 1899.

Alcohol could ruin lives, so the temperance movement could mobilize substantial public support. Distilled liquor, especially gin, rum and whiskey, made drunkenness easier and more likely. It produced more visible drunkards, whose personal demons, psychological and psychiatric problems, and complex psychosocial needs were distressingly evident. They could sometimes be heard and seen, dishevelled, abusive, shouting filth and lewdness, staggering or vomiting, roaming the streets or leaving public houses. Their bouts of excessive drinking offered visible evidence of alcohol's evils, to be exploited in reformist ideology and imagery.

In recent years, the historiography of modern drinking cultures has seen a growing interest in questions of gender in relation to public-house culture, and more emphasis on women drinkers in pubs. Older women going to the pub were freer than young women or women with young children, who were more vulnerable to taboos against women drinking, or allegations of sexual immorality and abusive or neglectful parenting. Drunken working-class women were more condemned than men, as drinking was considered to be especially unfeminine and contrary to expectations of working-class respectability. Women were regularly prosecuted for drunkenness, though less so than men. In London, 47 per cent of total prosecutions were of women in 1875, and 41 per cent in 1895. In Liverpool, the comparable figures were 26 and 24 per cent. George Sims, visiting London slum dwellers in the 1880s, accepted that the gin palaces, with their light and their glitter, were 'Heaven' compared to 'the Hell of their pestilent homes', and that drink gave them 'the Dutch courage to go on living', dulled their sense of shame, took the 'sharp edge from sorrow' and left the drinker 'in a fool's paradise'. But he was shocked to visit the home of Biddy, the most notorious 'drunkardess' in the neighbourhood. He described her:

> She is in bed, a dirty red flannel rag is wrapped about her shoulders, and her one arm is in a sling. She sits up in bed . . . and greets us in a gin and fog voice, slightly mellowed in the Irish brogue. Biddy had been charged at the police courts seventy-five times with being drunk, and she is therefore a celebrated character. She is scarcely sober now, though she has evidently had a shaking which would have sobered most people for a month. Her face is a mass of bruises and cuts, and every now and then a groan and a cry to certain saints in her calendar tell of aches and pains in the limbs concealed under the dirty blanket that covers the bed.[21]

She had been found blind drunk on the Saturday and was arrested, carried back on a stretcher, kicking, but the inspector had freed her the following day. Biddy had not been sober for five years. Her son had got into bad company and was in prison. In her wretched home she had 'taken to drink' to charm her sorrow away. Her rented rooms got dirtier, smaller and fouler. Her 'old man' took to drink through aggravation at her and now also got drunk every night.

Sims' narrative of Biddy's situation may well incorporate journalistic licence, but made clear that taken in excess, alcohol was a mind-altering drug, leading to possible addiction. In many towns about a third of what courts called 'habitual drunkards' were women. Some women came before the courts time after time.

Moreover, drunkenness impacted not only on both men and women, but also on all classes and all occupations, though temperance writers claimed that it was most commonly associated with the less educated, quoting figures that supported their case. Magistrate G.L. Fenwick, giving evidence to the House of Lords Select Committee in 1877, suggested it was quite remarkable how few educated persons were charged with drunkenness. He claimed some evidence that the vice was confined principally to the lowest groups in society. Liverpool figures from 1876 showed that of the 18,823 arrested that year for drunkenness, only 1.3 per cent could read and write well, while 35 per cent could do neither.

This argument was disingenuous. The middle classes were far more skilled in dealing with the police, avoiding arrest and drinking in safer contexts. Their drinking was largely invisible. Some recognized this. John Taylor, Vice-Chairman of the National Temperance Society, told the same Committee that drunkenness was increasing amongst the business classes and women.[22] Privately, drunkenness affected ladies, socially of spotless reputation, gentlemen of education, the titled, clergymen and lawyers, and even the lower middle class, the group most desperate to cling to respectability. Metropolitan Police records clearly showed that drunkenness was cross-class. Their figures in mid-century indicated the paradox that while skilled workers may have been keen members of temperance societies, bricklayers, masons, saddlers, carpenters, engineers, butchers, shopkeepers, tobacconists and bakers all had a higher than average chance of being arrested for drunkenness, as had some middle-class groups such as clerks or medical men.

Drunkenness statistics

Was such excessive drinking the vice of the few? And was it changing over time? This is difficult to say, given the problems of the statistics. Certainly drunkenness took much police time, especially at night. Between January and June 1852, for example, 80 per cent of all Cardiff Borough Police Court proceedings were for drunkenness. In Middlesbrough, drink-related cases amounted to about two-thirds of all offences in the 1850s and 1860s.

Drunkenness statistics were largely a function of policing and local temperance pressure, but the overall trend based on the Judicial Statistics for England and Wales is suggestive. Between 1857 and 1861 the average number of people proceeded against per 1,000 of population was 4.28. This then rose steadily to peak at 7.83 between 1872 and 1876. Some saw this as suggesting the temperance movement was failing. Others claimed it as a success in encouraging more arrests. Either explanation is possible. The trend thereafter was downward, reaching 5.84 between 1892 and 1896.

But figures varied with locality. Figures were particularly high in new towns. In Middlesbrough, in the five years centred on 1861, the drunkenness prosecution rate in the town was 19.9 per 1000 people. In Merthyr, between 1871 and 1873, the rate was nearly 14 per 1,000. Northern England had more drunkenness prosecutions, with Durham, Northumberland and Lancashire highest of all. In an 1894 survey, seaports from Birkenhead and Cardiff to Southampton and South Shields averaged 12.6 prosecutions per 1,000 people, topping the table of prosecutions. Even when such towns were excluded, mining counties such as Derbyshire and Glamorgan were still high, and London was also above the national average. Manufacturing towns such as Birmingham and Wolverhampton averaged 4.7. Pleasure resorts such as Bath or Ramsgate were lower, and agricultural counties had very few prosecutions, though in Northumberland, the high numbers of prosecutions in mining villages distorted the figures, and the northern rural areas had few prosecutions. Many towns and cities had areas that were especially notorious for drunkenness. In Middlesbrough, five streets usually contained about 40 per cent of all arrests.

Alcohol abuse killed. In 1849 in York, three men returned a single man, Richard Stout, to his room, collapsed in a wheelbarrow. He was 'much addicted to drink', especially gin, and died there.[23] But here again figures are difficult to interpret. The figures produced by the Registrar General of deaths in England and Wales due to delirium tremens and chronic alcoholism are bedevilled by medical problems of definition, where drunkenness triggered other diseases, and the significant fluctuation in the very small database. Over the period 1856 to 1865, for example, they averaged 4 per 100,000 of the population but varied annually from 3.3 to 5. As *The Times* admitted, such figures provided an 'uncertain conception' and a question 'impossible for the register books to reveal'.[24]

Local judicial statistics of cases of drunkenness and drunk and disorderly cases are problematic too, showing significant yearly variation. Figures responded to changes in magistrates' bench membership or senior police attitudes, or to local controls. In Liverpool, the bringing of beer houses under the control of magistrates in 1869 saw the number drop from 763 beer houses that year to 355 by 1872. The 1872 Licensing Act, which saw the introduction of licence endorsements for misconduct and stricter requirements for licence registration, had limited further effect.

By no means were all problematic drunkards arrested. Policemen rarely arrested drunks initially. Verbal abuse might be ignored. Benches were often lenient on a first offence, but hard on later ones. And figures could be manipulated. In Norwich the brewing interest and local magistrates were anxious to indicate to the Lords Select Committee on Intemperance that drink was unproblematic. In 1879, across 500 public houses only 100 people all year were convicted of being drunk and incapable.[25]

The temperance movement

Over the nineteenth century, powerful coalitions of reformers challenged the central role of alcohol, gaining support from leading opinion-formers. But reformers were divided; some relied on persuasion, others on coercion and legal sanctions. Some reformers accepted 'temperate' moderate alcohol intake, while others were strong supporters of total temperance. There was a fluctuating momentum to the campaign against alcohol.[26] There were periods of high enthusiasm, usually followed by quick periods of cooling off.

Early support for temperance and moderation

There was already increasing anxiety in Britain over drinking in the early decades of the nineteenth century, when the temperance movement was small and fairly middle-class in membership, trying to control and not prevent working-class drinking. The various small reform organizations believed in attacking 'excess' drinking by encouraging 'temperance' and 'moderation' by 'moral [per]suasion'. From the late 1820s the American temperance movement had some impact in Ireland and in ports such as Liverpool. Gin and other spirits, the 'distilled death and liquid damnation' increasingly available thanks to the retail supply revolution, largely came under attack.[27] A Beer Act of 1830, which encouraged the opening of pubs selling only beer, had unforeseen and potentially problematic consequences. It was politically popular since most people believed that beer was a necessity of life, and brought benefits to British agriculture. It removed the need for beer houses to get a justices' licence and replaced it with an excise licence, but it took away local restrictive controls, though local magistrates retained the power to annually license public houses and inns. Beer drinking quickly became cheaper and more widely available. Despite a Select Committee investigation of 1834 dominated by evangelicals convinced of the 'vice of intoxication', a further act of 1834 created a distinction between 'on' licences, costing three guineas, and 'off' licences, costing one guinea, selling beer for consumption 'off the premises'. Most anti-drink movements including the British and Foreign Bible Society, formed in 1804, London-based, though with strong support in Lancashire, Yorkshire and Cornwall, still had largely middle-class memberships, and aristocratic patrons and accepted moderate drinking of beer or wine by members.

Teetotalism persuasion

From the 1830s, the anti-drink movement became more aggressive. Harder-line reformers, especially in the north and Scotland, abandoned moderate temperance for a more radical position – total abstention. They argued that the 'dark, polluted, loathsome ranks of the drunken' were recruited from the mass of moderate drinkers. They measured success by the numbers of 'abandoned' drunkards 'emancipated' or 'reclaimed'. Self-improving working-class men assumed a leading role, to the dismay of moderates, who felt theirs was a more elevated movement. A leading advocate was Joseph Livesey (1794–1884), a Preston Baptist and a former handloom weaver who became a shrewd and affluent cheese factor and provision merchant.[28] He was a strong advocate of social and moral reform, a Sunday and adult school teacher. His attitude to drink's victims was compassionate, not judgemental. He believed that poverty, disease, squalor and high death rates in working-class areas like Preston were largely due to drink. Even moderate drinking led to the 'slippery slope' of eventual alcohol dependence. In 1832 he set up an abstinence movement to spread the doctrine of self-improvement. His followers signed a pledge to abstain from all alcohol. One ardent acolyte (a group described as 'apostles' in the 'Jerusalem' of Preston) supposedly coined the word 'teetotal' for total abstinence to signify their position.

Livesey became a newspaper editor, producing first the *Preston Temperance Advocate* (1834–7) and later the *Preston Guardian*, to promote his temperance ideals, arguing that 'teetotalism' was necessary to prevent appetite for alcohol, and eliminate addictive behaviour. His approach, relying on personal commitment to temperance, contrasted with the earlier reliance on leaders' social prestige. Sober teetotallers kept no drink. The most scrupulous would refuse to drink communion wine or take a medical prescription containing alcohol. Tea became the symbolic drink of morality and respectability.

In 1835, the *Preston Temperance Advocate* suggested that a teetotal order mutual benefit society might be formed. A new group, the Independent Order of Rechabites (a name based on an Old Testament reference to the sons of Rechab who would 'drink no wine') was formed in Salford. By August 1836, there were twenty-seven 'tents' or branches in the north west.

Teetotalism offended moderates but rapidly gathered momentum amongst the underprivileged working-class. It was dominated by skilled workmen, the more radical of the middle classes, and religious Nonconformists. Reclaiming drunkards rather than safeguarding the sober was an appealing approach. Some former drunkards proved desperate to atone for their drunken past. They enjoyed and felt exhilarated by the attention and their public appearances.

At first the teetotal movement advocated persuasion. Reformers believed the 'concentration of moral force' on temperance would focus attention on the problems and change public opinion and practice.[29] In 1842, moral 'suasionists' founded the National Temperance Society. This was followed in 1844 by the Scottish Temperance League.

Temperance and moral purity combined in the signed 'pledge' to abandon alcohol. Its exact form was vehemently debated. It became the 'cornerstone' of the movement, a symbol of commitment, a radical acceptance of new forms of spirituality and temperance habits. It symbolically renounced the blandishments of boozy companions and public house carousing. It provided an excuse for refusing drinks, a psychological crutch. It was a constant reminder not to break one's word. Pledges might be broken, men might fall from grace, but with true repentance, support and encouragement promises could be renewed.

Teetotallers believed that the Bible had ordained and commanded abstention, making it a criterion when accepting new members. In Wales, this led to deep conflicts within Independent chapels, because teetotalism became inextricably linked with Christianity. Moderation-supporting chapel ministers who felt that teetotalism was extreme, impractical and faddist, conflicted with Biblical teaching and encouraged bigotry and intolerance, found themselves targeted. They were subject to wild denunciations and bitter personal animosity, attacks in the press, libellous pamphlets, and calls for congregations to refuse to attend their services.

Pro- and anti-teetotallers batted the issue back and forth.[30] Moderation was popular with the middle classes and in the south of England, and many found teetotal fanaticism alienating. The upper classes, with a few exceptions, gave the new movement little support.[31] As time passed, self-made urban men increasingly dominated teetotalism's leadership, sacrificing wealth and wine cellars to the cause. Teetotal schools, lodging houses, shops, doctors and even insurance schemes and funeral parlours sprang up, creating a self-contained world for its followers.

But more beer houses led to a growth in beer consumption, and the House of Lords Committee into the Supply and Consumption of Beer in 1850 concluded that there had been little or no diminution in spirit drinking and that beer houses had simply further encouraged the drinking of beer. So from mid-century, those advocating total abstinence increasingly moved from persuasion to politics, demanding state intervention to enforce temperance by restricting public drink sales. Political debates increasingly focused on whether or not licensing should be replaced with total prohibition of all commercial liquor traffic, as the most ultra-temperance reformers demanded. They argued that the physical, moral and religious evils accompanying drink were sufficiently great to have the 'poison shops' closed.[32]

The Alliance prohibitionists

The apparent success of the introduction of the Maine Law in the USA banning *all* sales of intoxicants in 1846 led the Irish Quaker cotton manufacturer Nathaniel Card (1805–56) to hold an informal meeting in his Manchester house in July 1852. Leading temperance advocates in Manchester and Salford created a new movement, which in early 1853 took the name of the United Kingdom Alliance for the Suppression of the Traffic in all Intoxicating Liquors.[33] A General Council held its first meeting in October.

The Alliance had strong support in Lancashire, Yorkshire's West Riding, north-eastern coastal towns, Glasgow and Cardiff, especially from the elite working class and lower middle classes. Its financial support came largely from industrial manufacturers, often in textiles. The Alliance viewed the upper classes as corrupt and oppressive, actively encouraging drink by selling barley and boosting urban rents by building pubs. Under Alliance approaches, all sale of liquor in public houses and beer houses would be prohibited, though for political reasons the wine cellars of the wealthy would be initially unaffected. The target of the Alliance was the trade in liquor, which would change the drinking environment.

The strength of conviction and didactic seriousness of the Alliance ensured that temperance became an increasingly powerful social and political force, thanks to a combination of temperance propaganda and social and cultural changes. Drink was portrayed as the main 'social evil'. Initially, the Alliance concentrated on publicizing the principles of the movement and on exaggerating the strength of its popular support. In reality, its membership was not high. In 1858 it still only had 4,500 members. A grass-roots movement, it was ideologically democratic, but authoritarian about a ban. It quickly grew in strength and numbers. In 1860/1, Gladstone's Liberal government tried to move people away from public-house drinking by establishing off-licences for grocery and other shops to sell alcohol. They hoped to encourage more temperate drinking of beer at home, but with little success.

The more extreme Alliance temperance 'prohibitionist' supporters increasingly saw the teetotal 'persuaders' as barriers to the progress of their 'holy cause'. The persuaders responded by merging their earlier large organizations into a National Temperance League in 1856. Their different ideological views and differences in strategy created major controversy and this distracted the wider movement for some years.

Temperance was a single-issue movement, concentrating on educating individual MPs about temperance, hoping to force Parliament into action. Although the Alliance would have preferred a national ban, it quickly compromised to demand the introduction of what, given its repressive nature, it cleverly called the 'Permissive' Bill. This would allow local councils to impose a direct local veto on liquor shops, if called for by two-thirds of a ratepayer vote. It worked hard to convey the strength of its support, the urgency of reform, its financial power and the wealth of supporting argument for its case. It attracted Liberal support, and in 1869/70 the beer houses were brought back under the magistrate licensing system in the (vain) hope that licences would be refused.

But despite the work of its chief parliamentary representative, Sir Wilfred Lawson, its chief success came in 1872, when the drink question was seen as important once again, with a firmer Licensing Act prohibiting the sale of spirits to children under sixteen. It required the County Bench to confirm new licences, and deprived it of the power of giving new licences in opposition to local refusal. Public houses had to close at midnight in towns and 11 p.m. in the countryside. Paradoxically, the Alliance gave the Act little support. Lacking any sense of political realism, it could not compromise and accept half-measures by co-operating with powerful Liberal cabinet ministers. It vainly pinned its hopes on the passing of the Permissive Bill.

By 1872, the rival teetotal movement had almost collapsed. The teetotallers now pinned their hopes on the formation of children's Bands of Hope, rather than reclaiming their parents. Despite all their efforts, the evidence dismayingly suggested that drinking was still increasing. This retreat from a vice-ridden world dismayed Livesey. He felt that his movement had failed. Regretfully, he felt that 'the success of our early efforts has fallen ... short of our expectations and so much remains yet to be done'. He was also unhappy about the extent to which chapel and churchgoers dominated support.[34] The leading temperance advocates were aging: no longer *enfants terribles* but leading figures in urban society and politics. The movement turned inwards, no longer campaigning but further developing temperance organizations and building temperance halls.

The temperance movement tried moral persuasion once more in the late 1870s with the arrival from America of new approaches led by radical groups such as the Woman's Christian Temperance Union or the Good Templars, a working-class fraternal temperance society founded in the UK in 1868. Gospel Temperance linked temperance to revivalist religion, worrying less about the state and more about personal abstention. It received the support of both established and non-conformist churches. Millions briefly 'took the pledge' while publicans found more difficulty in convincing magistrates to provide licences.

Subsequently, several unsuccessful attempts were made to pressure Parliament to introduce prohibition. When the franchise was extended, reformers hoped that new voters would back temperance. They were wrong. The Liberal Party, which broadly supported temperance, was defeated in 1886. Temperance lacked the power to carry the mainstream. After successfully persuading the Liberal Party to adopt limited prohibition, reformers mounted further efforts. They recognized that any form of national prohibition lacked sufficient support, but allowing local authorities to choose a temperance position and refuse all licences still seemed a way forward. The last decade of the nineteenth century is widely recognized as a period when the management of public drinking became a heightened political concern in the UK. Regulatory questions over the discretion of licensing authorities, the design of public houses, the suppression of licences and the monetary value accrued by licensed properties appeared alongside increasing political pressure for local plebiscites on alcohol prohibition. The Liberals made local prohibition a part of its election programme in 1891, ensuring that in local elections, drink became an important issue.[35] In 1893 and 1895, a leading Liberal politician, Chancellor of the Exchequer William Harcourt, introduced government Local Veto bills for local option prohibition in England and Wales. Both bills had a clear class dimension, banning only public house and beer house drinking, not drinking in middle-class restaurants or private clubs or sales for off-premises consumption. But politicians disagreed on the issue of local control and licensing. The Bills were easily defeated. There was insufficient national taste for temperance. The Liberals were comprehensively defeated in the 1895 election and Harcourt was comprehensively defeated in his Derby seat.

The shock of defeat and recognition that their aims could not be achieved disintegrated the political prohibitionist movement. The movement declined. Moderate reformers once more dominated the debates, reframing the drink question as one related to social health and national efficiency, not private morality, and demanding a reduction in public house numbers. This inspired the Conservative government to create a Royal Commission on the Licensing

Laws, to deal with 'excessive drinking' by the working classes. This represented a particularly significant moment in British attempts to deal with the place of alcohol in a modern society, as efforts to *discipline* drinking became articulated through attempts to regulate drinking space. The licensing system tied the character and reputation of the licensee to a particular pub, and the correct concentration of licensed spaces represented one of the sticking points of the Commission. However, this concern with where pubs should be located was accompanied by questions about the management of circulation within pubs. A 'pub improvement' movement tried to regulate human movement through the provision of rational entertainments in comfortable pubs. Other temperance activists (such as Joseph Rowntree) insisted that rapid turnover and discomfort should be used to undermine pub attractions. By contrast, brewers wanted to use new pub designs to turn unpredictable circulation into pleasurable but profitable movement. All wanted to control drinking, and create a sense of secure space, but for different reasons. So the Commission carefully considered the design and layout of drinking establishments, their location within urban spaces, and their connections to neighbouring sites, addressing issues of access, visibility and movement. Attempts to control peoples' circulation within pubs became linked to the wider questions of social control and moral reform.

Dedicated teetotallers increasingly turned inward, socially isolated in the reassuring and safe haven of their drink-free subculture, and its temperance halls, temperance hotels and temperance societies. By the end of the nineteenth century the movement retained strong support only amongst the more evangelical groups in society.

The popularity of drink

Despite their efforts, even the most fervent of reformers recognized that drink appealed to a majority of adults. At the start of Victoria's reign, gin and brandy were already popular drinks and remained so for the poor for much of the century. Only Wales was predominantly a beer-drinking country. Drinking played powerful commercial, cultural, medicinal, nutritional, psychological and recreational roles in British life. Drink was found in town and country, home and work, and even in Anglican churches in the form of communion wine. Diaries show strong drink was part of the diet. In 1858, for example, the famous comic actor, John Harley, then seventy years old, described a fairly typical afternoon:

> Rehearsal at two, home to dinner at four, Roast beef, potato, biscuit, cheese, ale, port and sherry. Tea at seven ... Theatre at eight, saw Ellen on stage. Home at ten, supped at eleven, cold roast beef, biscuit, cheese, ale, gin and water. Read *Spectator* to Betsy. Bed at one.[36]

Drink was common in many homes for a whole range of reasons besides its taste. It was the panacea of the age. Spirits were believed to destroy worms, bring out measles and smallpox, restore depression, aid digestion, cure a cold or bowel complaint, improve sleep or help a confinement. Drinking accompanied key rites of passage. When a baby was born the doctor and neighbours drank to the happiness and recovery of the wife and the success of the child. Drink accompanied churching, christening and marriage. Early in the Victorian age, women might meet funeral attendants at the door with hot ale. Friends and relations returned to drink after the funeral.

For much of the century liquor was used as part of occupational identity. John Dunlop (1789–1868), a Greenock lawyer, philanthropist and prominent temperance reformer, wrote a survey of the cultural role of drinking in Great Britain in 1839.[37] His study demonstrated that alcoholic drink played a key role in sociability and hospitality, in the pub for travellers and for residents, but also in the workplace. He recorded a whole series of contexts where drinking was almost a compulsory part of working life. These included treating, paying for 'footings' at the start of apprenticeships, completing contract work, or learning a new skill. End of month pay weekends in iron works and mining were often given over to drunkenness. Builders celebrated laying the foundations of buildings with drink. In many heavy industries drink was perceived as a necessity to cope with the high temperatures, and was a source of strength and stamina, helping to dull fatigue. Foundry workers and forgemen could drink between eight and twenty-four pints of weak beer a shift. For many mid-nineteenth century pitmen and furnace men part of the contract was an alcohol allowance, while in the Midlands skilled artisans such as blacksmiths or engineers claimed them. In some areas and trades there was a heavy drinking artisan culture though this was becoming less common by the 1850s, as a more respectable culture began to replace publicly viewed behaviour amongst the labour aristocracy. Sailors took rum to counteract inclement weather. Henry Mayhew's 1850s study of the reasons for drinking alcohol given by stevedores employed in the Pool of London showed that many spent at least twelve shillings weekly on beer, porter or spirits to stimulate their work and quench the dust.[38] Sportsmen resorted to alcohol to aid stamina and courage. Drink literally gave them 'bottle'. Boxers were given a mixture of brandy and water. Jockeys might sip champagne.

Defenders of drink, while accepting its potential problems, argued for its cultural centrality, claiming that it was

> so deep, so ancient, so inveterate in the customs of our country, it winds itself round all our institutions and attaches itself to all our celebrations . . . Englishmen in general like a good fellow who is evidently drinking himself to death a good deal more than they do one who is rather more temperate and not quite so jolly.[39]

Giving evidence to a House of Lords Select Committee investigating intemperance in 1877, Professor Leon Levi argued that excessive drinking was 'natural' alongside any increase in wealth. He suggested that temperance figures were unreliable and that it was difficult to say how it should be regarded, asking, 'Is it a crime, or a vice, or extravagance or simple luxury?'[40]

Even policemen drank. Superintendents and chief constables constantly battled with its popularity amongst their forces and brought men up on drink-related charges, especially in the early Victorian period. At Salford, in the 1840s, the Minutes of the Watch Committee almost weekly revealed fines on constables for drinking on duty.[41]

In the 1840s, the medical profession still saw alcohol in moderate quantities as good for people. It was served in hospitals, workhouses and even public schools.[42] When elections relied on shows of hands and public polling, prospective MPs and their agents regularly bought and distributed alcohol to buy votes or to encourage rough treatment of opponents. In the South Durham election of 1841 at Darlington, the two Liberal candidates used the Sun Inn and the King's Head, and the Conservative candidate the Fleece Inn. During the election candidates gave their voters tickets for free 'refreshment' to be spent at the inns. John Bowes alone had election bills of over £4,000, much for such 'treating'.[43] In the 1860s, National Temperance League members were still denouncing 'the use of drink as an electioneering agent'. The Rev. Francis Close wrote a letter to the press arguing that 'Honourable gentlemen' were carried into Parliament 'on the turbid wave of national intoxication'.[44] Even after the Secret Ballot Act of 1872 treating by candidates only finally disappeared after the Corrupt Practices Act of 1883.

But it was the drinking amongst the unskilled working classes that reformers really targeted, even though moderate drinking remained popular amongst the wealthy and the middle classes. There was reluctance to acknowledge this. Indeed in 1856 *The Times* claimed that 'the educated classes of society have become extremely temperate, and it may almost be said that drunkenness is unknown amongst them'.[45] Middle-class drinking continued to be common, both inside and outside the home, in clubs and select hotels.

Such drinking was often social. One reason for the custom of women leaving the table was supposedly because of male drinking. West End clubs were popular upper-class drinking haunts. Gentlemen's clubs had servants, bedrooms and an air of quasi-domesticity with no female fingers wagging judgement. Organizations like the Jockey Club held meetings and drank in their own rooms. The Masters of Foxhounds had their annual dinner at Boodle's Club from the 1860s. There were similar opportunities for drinking for the middle classes. Quaker mill owners accumulated wine cellars so as to be able to entertain drinkers.[46] The diaries of Absalom Watkin, a self-made Manchester businessman, show his enjoyment of sherry and brandy, his wife's long-term problems through the

1860s with alcohol abuse, his daughter's heavy drinking, and the death of his son, a former mayor of Manchester, who regularly drank 'too much port'. One mid-century private drinking club in a Walsall hotel, composed of 'men of property and influence', began early in the evening and lasted till midnight, when members would stagger home 'with tottery legs and watery eyes'.[47] Public dinners offered generous corporate and public consumption of drink throughout the period – 'our powers we show by the number of bottles of wine we consume; our devotion is to our dinners', thought one observer.[48]

In September 1838, at a meal for some thirty wealthy men in Doncaster, 'the enlivening fluids began to flow around with equal spirit; the consistent and complimentary toasts were passed with zealous vigour, and the cheerful song was over and over again renewed with fresh and joyous energy'. A presentation of the Duke of Buckingham at Aylesbury in 1842, which praised him for his exertions on behalf of agriculture, included at least twelve toasts, interspersed with songs and speeches.[49] Toasting was a popular feature of most meetings of organizations from ratepayers' societies to sports clubs.

The American Nathaniel Hawthorne, a watchful observer of English characteristics, provided a description of the English middle classes in the 1880s enjoying the pleasures of alcohol at a London dinner. He claimed that 'they drank rather copiously, too, though wisely; for I observed that they seldom took Hock, and let the Champagne bubble slowly away out of the goblet, solacing themselves with Sherry, but tasting it warily before bestowing their final confidence'. After the meal, as in most formal dinners, 'a goodly group of decanters were set before the Mayor, who sent them forth on their outward voyage, full freighted with Port, Sherry, Madeira, and Claret'. A series of toasts followed, in honour of the great institutions and interests of the country, beginning with the conventional one to their 'gracious Sovereign'. The audience of 'stout middle-aged and elderly gentlemen, in the fullness of meat and drink, their ample and ruddy faces glistening with wine, perspiration, and enthusiasm' all joined in.[50]

Drinking was equally as common in the countryside. Many farmers provided a daily allowance of home-brewed ale, beer or perhaps cider. This could be as high as four pints or more, a provision especially common at peak working periods like harvest time. Sheepshearers likewise downed four or five pints a day. Farmers were often keen for farm workers to give it up in exchange for a 'beer money' addition. The resistance to this infringement of popular custom was sufficiently strong for it to continue well after the Truck Act of 1887 made the practice technically illegal, since farmers found its availability attracted labour. Where wages were low, as in North Oxfordshire in the 1880s, men would still go to the pub but slowly drink a single half pint of beer and make it last the evening.[51]

Up to and beyond the mid-Victorian period, sales of agricultural stock, farm implements, racing and breeding studs and so forth were accompanied by alcoholic refreshment. As in the case of auctions, it encouraged a certain lack of judgement and aided sales. One country vicar, writing to *The Times* in 1857, complained it was 'a source of great evil in our rural parishes'. He described the drink as of 'a very doubtful quality', calculated to 'stupefy the buyers' and improve sales, at the cost of 'the destruction of the moral feeling of many, both in the injury done to them and in the revolting scenes that follow'.[52]

Right through the period, heavy drinking was associated with fairs, race meetings, village feasts and wakes weeks and popular holidays such as Whitsuntide or Christmas. In Middlesbrough the festivities of Christmas 1858 and New Year 1859 gave rise to 'men in a beastly state of beer . . . half-puddled walking about in their every-day toggery and black faces . . . half-idiotic imbeciles, as they reeled along in all their glory' while 'there were assembled as vile a crew of roughs as ever escaped the inside of Deptford hulks'. As a consequence, parts of the town were 'bespattered with filthy ejections from overburdened stomachs' and 'bestial refuse met the eye at every turn, bearing the distinct testimony to the dregs of humanity which had been thereabouts.'[53]

The increased leisure time and real wages of the later nineteenth century added new opportunities. In South Wales, miners began spending Mabon's Day, a local holiday on the first Monday of each month, won in 1888 by William Abraham M.P. (Mabon), in 'dissipation and drunkenness'. According to one Merthyr inhabitant, 'a large number of workmen seemed bent on no other object than "swilling" themselves with beer'. At Newport workhouse, the inmates were allowed a few hours to visit friends and relatives on that day. According to the *Star of Gwent* it was 'a frequent sight to see them reeling back to the Workhouse intoxicated'.[54]

The pub

The central role of drinking places in everyday life has received only limited attention from historians. Yet public houses, selling spirits and beer, and centred on transport routes, and beer houses, usually in working-class urban areas, were major reformist targets. They were perceived as the cause and not the consequence of propensity to drink. They were 'the gates of hell', sinful places where innocent human beings accepted the temptations proffered by unscrupulous landlords and evil companions, and joined the legions of the corrupted. In 1850 a reporter for Chambers' *Edinburgh Journal* regaled his readers with a description of a Saturday evening in Manchester. Saturday night, he felt, brought out those who could only afford one night's drinking. Their appearance, he claimed, caused 'terror and astonishment' to 'respectable people', who had 'no idea' such people were living in the same town. There were, apparently, drunks everywhere. Around two or three 'gin palaces', he noted, a crowd of half-intoxicated people were collected, with 'noisy manners and coarse language'. On Deansgate he saw large streams of passers-by, and 'the greatest amount of drunkenness and profligacy'. Crowds of young and old, of both sexes, hovered around the spirit vaults, gin palaces and public houses.[55]

Such scenes were probably typical. There were far more pubs in Britain than churches, and the British spent more time there, so they attracted the bulk of reformist anger. In Walsall, for example, in the 1850s there were allegedly at least 200 public houses, inns and beer shops for its 26,000 people, but only twelve places of worship.[56] The number of places providing alcohol initially rose alongside population despite temperance efforts. In 1851, 60,579 premises had licences to sell beer and spirits, and there were 40,891 beer houses, with 37,598 selling beer on the premises and the rest off-licences.

The temperance organizations were able to use such statistics to point to some success in the later decades of the century. The number of pubs and beer houses in England and Wales peaked in 1869 and 1870. Per capita annual beer consumption peaked at 42.2 imperial gallons in 1876. Both figures then started to drop. The number of 'on' licences per 10,000 people in England and Wales was forty-nine in 1871, thirty-one in 1901.

The ratio of public houses to numbers of people was often used by reformers, but this distorted analysis, since places such as market towns, seaside resorts, ports or city centres like London's West End catered for visitors as well as locals. In the 1860s, Bradford had around 600 drinking places for a population of 140,000, Portsmouth, with its docks, nearly 900 pubs and beer houses for about 118,000 people, and Norwich, a county town and major market, had about 675 drinking places for a population of about 80,000. In 1899, London had one licensed house per 446 inhabitants, Manchester one per 180 inhabitants.[57]

Pubs were often clustered in particular urban areas, especially around markets, along main thoroughfares and near barracks and docks. County towns and cities always had substantial numbers of pubs. Pubs were spatially important and well-enough known to be used for direction-giving. London railway termini and Underground stations such as Angel, Elephant and Castle and Royal Oak were named after local pubs.

Drinking places had other social, cultural, recreational and economic functions beyond the selling of alcohol to pleasure seekers and thirsty travellers. They played a pivotal role in Victorian leisure and society by encouraging social cohesion, community and sociability. Moderate drinking liberated drinkers from domestic and work restraints and anxieties, and contributed to conversation, celebration and festivity. Pubs catered for basic human needs and the social exchange of news, goods and information. Like churches, they were free to enter, warm and well lit. They functioned as club, debating society, job centre, Masonic lodge and recreation room. The varying rituals of such organizations helped to confirm group membership and good fellowship. Most men spent at least part of their leisure time drinking in the pub.[58]

Pubs encouraged conviviality, a friendly fraternity of fellow drinkers. They functioned as recreational, meeting and communication centres.[59] They offered accommodation and lodging. In the first half of the nineteenth century, they still sometimes carried out administrative functions, such as the holding of inquests. They hosted auctions. The lack of attractive alternative public buildings meant that they became a meeting place for a whole variety of clubs. From the 1840s, the new railway inns housed both short-stay travellers and locals. In Sussex, for example, in the 1860s, local workmen as well as commercial travellers used the newly built Terminus pub in Seaford, and Liberals, Conservatives, Volunteer Corps and Friendly Societies held their annual dinners there.[60]

Meeting places that were alcohol-free were less attractive. Henry Solly (1813–1903) formed the Working Men's Club and Institute Union in 1862. He sought to help workers establish clubs or institutes where they could meet for conversation, leisure, business, and mental improvement without any intoxicating drinks. The prospectus argued that alcohol would be 'dangerous to the interests of these Societies' and 'earnestly' recommended its exclusion on prudential grounds. His attempts to keep his Union free from alcohol lasted just three years. Membership and revenue remained low until in 1865 he gave up trying to enforce restrictions.[61]

Early trade societies and trade unions also met in pubs, though increasingly radical activists emphasized sobriety and rational behaviour, and became influenced by temperance beliefs. The courts and lodges of some friendly societies, such as the Independent Order of Oddfellows or the Ancient Order of Foresters, which organized collective insurance against unemployment, illness or death, usually for skilled artisans, held their meetings regularly in pubs. They spent money not just on ceremonial paraphernalia but also on drinking and feasting. But excessive drinking was despised, and even in the early Victorian period some friendly societies, such as the Free Gardeners, fined 'any brother found in liquor' and expelled those guilty of a third offence.

Inns were sites of tradition, custom and popular culture. Customers were accustomed to their weekly cycle of predictable pleasures, meeting friends and enjoying drinks. Wages were sometimes paid there. In the north, some landlords acted as employment contractors. Wives and families attended Saturday pay days. The evening might then become a sociable family one, with drinking, eating and exuberant conviviality.

Workmen went into pubs in the hope of finding news of jobs. Tradesmen went there when they needed coins for change. Some pubs ran 'slate clubs', an early form of savings club. Pubs were centres for sport, news, games, entertainment, debate and discussion. Pubs displayed newspapers. One publican witness giving evidence to the 1849–50 Lords Committee into the Supply and Consumption of Beer claimed that,

All parties, from working men upwards, frequent my house. Journeymen workmen come in, bringing their bread and cheese, and they sit down and take their beer; then the tradesmen come, and see the daily papers at 11 o'clock in the morning, and in the afternoon and evening. We take in three papers a day.

He argued that his beer house was select and respectable. Disorderly characters took custom away.[62]

Rivalry between publicans competing for custom and business helped drive changes in popular urban pub culture.[63] Publicans became leading sporting entrepreneurs of the mid-Victorian age. Pigeon racers and other bird fanciers, gardeners, anglers, cyclists and bowls clubs all met there. Many pubs enclosed adjoining land and charged entrance fees for sports as varied as pigeon shooting, bowls, foot races, cycle races and rabbit coursing. Landlords encouraged competition because it generated trade. Landlords acted as stakeholders and patrons for local sportsmen, sponsoring events at enclosed grounds, recouping their investment by selling alcohol, charging admission and sometimes backing contestants. Sponsoring sporting events increased sales, given good weather. Afterwards losers would drown their sorrows. Winners spent their gains.

There were changes as well as continuity. Publicans were the entrepreneurs behind the early music halls, which grew out of public house free and easies in the 1850s and 1860s. When local legislation allowing licences for public performance of music and dancing was introduced in 1881, many towns introduced it. In Bradford, about two-thirds of publicans applied. National permissive legislation to do the same thing came under the 1890 Public Health Acts Amendment Act.

As betting grew more widely popular, many pubs became betting centres. Betting's increased popularity varied from region to region, though parts of Lancashire, Yorkshire, London and Birmingham were at the forefront. By the 1860s, pubs had become common bases for the taking of illegal cash bets. Results by electric telegraph began appearing in some 'sporting' pubs from the late 1860s. The publican Thomas Devereux, a leading north-eastern bookmaker from the early 1870s, purchased Stockton's White Hart Inn in 1878. After convictions for using the pub for betting, he put in a tenant, to avoid any chance of losing his licence. In 1882 he purchased the adjacent building and ran it as the Victoria Club, a notorious betting centre. The local police opposed renewal of his licence on the grounds that he 'was not a fit and proper person'. That Devereux was able to persuade the magistracy that he was entitled to a licence and was backed up by a series of testimonials from local politicians, military men and other 'respectable' people, indicates some Stockton magistrates took a different view.[64]

By the 1880s soccer and rugby teams often used public houses as changing rooms, committee rooms and venues for smoking concerts, while landlords and brewers were often leading investors in the new sports companies. One plaintive reformer wrote:

> The headquarters of the game are generally at a public house: the play-up cards in the hats of the partisans bear the name of some public house or hotel, players and patrons meet after the match in taproom, bar parlour or vault, then make a night of it as they discuss the details of the play and the prospects of the team. Committee rooms are at a licensed house; with the smaller clubs the dressing rooms are there too. The landlord lets his room without direct pay because the money spent in drink brings more than an adequate return.[65]

This close connection with the drinks trade led one Anglican vicar to declare in 1893 that 'football is a fascination of the devil and a twin sister of the drink system'.[66]

The drinking public constructed a cultural hierarchy of drinking places in terms of their appearance, facilities, quality of drinks and clientele. These ranged from the respectable inns for travellers and taverns for respectable casual drinkers, down to the ale house, gin shop and beer house for a lower-class clientele. Hotels and inns were often high status and frequented by clerks or the clearly middle class. In York for example, the two leading inns were the Black Swan and the York Tavern. These accommodated the wealthy during assizes and race weeks. The Black Swan's 1851 visitors' list during race weeks included Prince Henry of the Netherlands, and dukes, earls and other titled figures, as well as wealthy moneylenders, bookmakers and other less respectable figures. The York Tavern was even higher in status, a spacious inn owned by York Corporation. It functioned as a centre for race-meeting organization as well as accommodation, and also as a meeting place for the wealthy Freemason organization, as a centre for political news and for meetings of the York Apollo Club, as well as for the famous Gimcrack annual race dinner in the winter.[67]

Then there were handsomely-decorated 'respectable' public houses, ones used by the middle classes, in the leading thoroughfares. A mid-century example had costly carpets, mahogany furniture that was 'new and beautifully polished'. The seats were 'generally exquisitely soft and covered with crimson velvet' and the walls were 'ornamented with pictures and pier-glasses'. Clients, who were perhaps joint stock bank directors, city merchants or railway officials could be found drinking claret, port, whisky and wine.[68]

'Low' beer houses were at the bottom end of the scale. Though small, dingy, basic and poorly furnished, and sometimes doubling as brothels or 'houses of ill-fame', they furnished centres for community life and drink for those whose lives were often socially, emotionally or physically impoverished. Their light, brightness and relative space offered a huge attraction. Drinking there became associated with manliness and virility.

The temperance movement had some success in reducing the absolute number of drink outlets by the later nineteenth century. But by then the licensed trade was meeting the retailing challenges of urban life by upgrading the size, glamour and efficiency of pubs, making them a major visual attraction in the nocturnal townscape. Pubs were often more lit up than the surrounding streets. Some had long rows of elaborately engraved gas lanterns of wrought iron. Pub signs became bolder. Brewers got more adept at placing eye-catching advertisements for their beers and spirits. Plate-glass paned doors threw out their light into darkened streets, calling people in.

Pubs were deliberately made obvious to passers-by in other ways too. Many were on street corners. Almost all had several different doors, to encourage access. The average number of doors per pub in one 1897 sample was between three and four. It could be as many as fifteen.[69] Doors sometimes led into different compartments or sections. This allowed different social and cultural dynamics in different rooms and encouraged weekly rhythms of drinking rituals. It allowed landlords to practise price and social differentiation. Inside might be vaults, snugs, private bars, big public bars with deal-lined walls and sawdust-covered floors, or more select saloon bars. These were more richly furnished, perhaps with carpeted floors, decorated plasterwork, mahogany bar, mosaics, shining mirrors, a fire, or a brilliantly lit billiard room off the side. This attracted a continuous flow of free-spending customers.[70] Billiards became an increasingly popular game in public houses in the 1880s and 1890s, although only ten per cent of pubs had a table.

The major pub-building boom in the last two decades of Victoria's reign targeted the increasingly better-off working classes.[71] Brewers purchased pubs and improved or rebuilt them to costly, ornate and extravagant designs, using imported hardwoods, fine deeply-cut etched glass and stoneware. These new, highly-decorated pubs conveyed an air of sophistication, a sense of upward mobility, balancing refinement, respectability and overostentation. Incorporating large plate-glass or bow windows, gas lighting, gilded plaster, the hydraulic beer-engine and the island bar, the pub retained its position as a central feature of working-class life.[72]

Types of drink

What people drank varied. In poor areas cheap spirits were popular even in the 1870s. Some pubs brewed and sold their own beer, but the number of brewers in England and Wales dropped from its peak of 27,554 in 1830 as firms such as Charrington, Worthington and Bass increasingly 'tied' public houses to ensure themselves outlets. Porter, beer and stout were popular drinks in London and the south. In the north and Midlands, paler and brighter ales, increasingly brewed at Burton on Trent, were equally if not more popular. Bass's bottled India Pale Ale became a popular home table drink with the middle classes. Beer's alcoholic strength varied. Porter averaged 5.25 per cent alcohol at the breweries, but many publicans and beer house owners were reputed to adulterate it with water or small beer, to increase their profits.

When people drank

Pubs came alive on Friday, were most popular over the weekend and Monday and least used midweek. Up to the 1860s and sometimes beyond, many artisans, engineers, furniture makers and other skilled labourers, especially in places such as Sheffield, Birmingham or Stoke, took off 'St Monday' after Saturday payday and spent it drinking. For much of the century, Monday was more popular than Saturday amongst publicans as a day to offer commercial sporting events to increase custom. It only changed as Saturday afternoons became more commonly accepted as time free of work.[73]

For many workers Sunday was the main leisure time. The choice between church and sermon or the pub and a drink was often won by the latter. Religious moral reformers singled out Sunday opening for particular pressure, with some success. Sunday opening was limited from 1828, forcing closing during the times of divine service. Complaints then followed that churchgoers were seeing drunkenness en route. The Chairman of Middlesex Magistrates, for example, complained of 'the dreadful and disgusting scenes that presented themselves to the respectable families on the Sunday morning on their way to church'.[74]

Geographical variations

Reformers were more successful in getting Parliament to pass prohibitive legislation in the rest of Great Britain than in England. An Act first limited Scottish Sunday opening hours in 1848, and the Forbes-McKenzie Act of 1853, introduced by a Conservative MP, closed the public houses of Scotland on Sundays except to travellers. Irish pubs were shut on Sundays except in the largest cities in 1878. The measure was extended to Wales, with its many chapels and religious revivals, in 1881. In Wales there seems to have been broad public support, though shebeens (illegal drinking dens) became more common, and the Royal Commission of 1889–90 noted that while the restriction had increased sobriety in country districts, it had been largely evaded in Glamorgan's urban areas

In 1854, the Wilson Patten Act limited Sunday opening in England, shutting pubs between 2.30 and 6 p.m. and after 10.30 p.m. Rushed through Parliament, it proved difficult to enforce. Magistrates sometimes dismissed alleged opening hours offences, and in Norwich, for example, in 1866, the police had to admit in the Annual Report on Inns presented to the magistrates that despite their efforts, Sunday trading had gone on in several pubs during the year.[75]

How much did people drink?

What drink statistics we have indicate that the British drank a lot, especially spirits. Beer and other alcoholic drinks were the largest items of working-class expenditure after rent, well above meat and bread. A return of the Board of Trade estimated that 4,931,639 gallons of foreign spirits, 16,884,955 gallons of British-made spirits, 6,227,003 gallons of wine, and 16,543,781 barrels of beer were consumed in Great Britain in 1853 alone.[76]

How much individuals spent on drink was hard to calculate, though generally higher wages meant higher spending. The statistician Robert Dudley Baxter, in a paper read to the London Statistical Society in 1869, produced figures which distinguished between the 'temperate' urban labourer, spending from 2s to 2s 6d a week and the 'temperate' urban artisan spending from 4s 6d to 5s a week. Taking into account 'intemperate' expenditures by some, he calculated that the average weekly drink expenditure of a 'working-class family' would be just over 5s 9d. A special Committee of the British Association in 1882 estimated expenditure by a working-class 'family' as 6s 2d a week. At the end of the century, men in the most physically strenuous occupations, in the docks, sawmills, heavy engineering or mines, still spent 4s or more a week on their drinking, although so did painters and engineers.[77]

In 1898, Joseph Rowntree and Arthur Sherwell estimated 6s 5d a week for a working-class family. They argued that 'every endeavour has been made to exclude careless and unreliable returns'. Some researchers preferred to estimate the proportion of earnings spent on alcohol. Charles Booth believed that in London a quarter of working-class earnings went on drink. Rowntree estimated it was one-sixth of earnings in York.[78] Modern historians prefer estimates given in terms of expenditure on drink as a percentage of total consumer expenditure: perhaps 15 per cent of total expenditure in 1876, about 12 or 13 per cent of a higher total in the 1890s.[79]

In general, the evidence suggests that British drinkers' per capita annual consumption of alcohol rose until the 1870s and then declined slightly. Beer rather than spirit drinking was boosted by the Beer Act of 1830, but then declined slowly, perhaps because of low earnings and the impact of cyclical depressions in manufacturing industry, rather than the efforts of reformers. It reached 29.3 gallons annually per capita between 1855 and 1869. Beer drinking then rose, reaching 40.5 gallons annually between 1875 and 1879, encouraged by growth in real wages for many industrial workers, more surplus income and limited expansion of alternative commercial leisure. From 1880 beer drinking then started to decline slowly once again.[80]

Wine importation almost trebled between 1830 and 1870 before levelling off and then dropping slightly, as the Liberal governments tried to shift consumption in the direction of weaker alcohol and encourage temperance.

In the early Victorian period, gin was the most popular spirit drink. It was alluringly advertised and marketed. Names such as 'Best Cordial Gin' or 'Cream of the Valley' for the sweeter, heavier gins, decorative casks and specialized gin palaces, all helped spread its popularity from the 1830s. It became popular amongst the middle classes, especially for cordials and mixed drinks. The British imperial mission encouraged the drinking of dry gin and quinine tonic water in the tropics. Naval officers drank gin and angostura bitters. Rum was a more working-class drink. The wealthier often drank brandy or whisky, but as with other alcohol, consumption of spirits rose until the 1870s and then declined. Overall, between 1831 and 1931, spirit consumption per head per annum fell from 1.11 gallons to 0.22 gallons.[81]

Conclusion

Temperance was undoubtedly a powerful social and political force in Victorian Britain. It affected politics and shaped the beliefs of many religious organizations and social reformers. Even in 1901 reformers made unsubstantiated estimates of three million adult teetotallers in the United Kingdom. The temperance movement also extended women's role as key leaders of anti-drink sentiment, and temperance activity was one of the first ways in which women found a role in public life.

But the real difficulties it faced in achieving change meant that it did not succeed in eradicating drink, only in achieving a measure of control. Despite the energy of temperance advocates licensing legislation made little progress. Their success was far more limited than their public visibility implied, in part because the ideological differences between moral persuaders and prohibitionists were never resolved. The growing strength of teetotalism in Barrow, for example, in the late 1860s, saw a flurry of letters, attacking and defending the 'new religious sect'. Teetotallers denounced moderate Christian ministers. They were accused in turn of claiming 'that a man cannot be a Christian unless he is a teetotaller', of trying to 'strain [the Bible's] learning', and believing that 'the moderate drinker is worse than a drunkard'.[82]

By the last two decades of the century the British were drinking less. Clearly the various movements had contributed to changing attitudes, but other factors also aided their success. Alcohol had got relatively more expensive, and few reformers noted that for the working classes the amount drunk was closely related to price. Through the 1880s and early 1890s the price of drink failed to drop alongside prices of other consumer goods.[83] Demand may also have been due to changes in fashion, as people gained new leisure choices. Spending on food and drink alternatives sold by mineral water purveyors, teashops, ice-cream vendors and fish and chip shops rose. Improved amenities, more comfortable homes, the increased availability of a wide variety of consumer goods and services, from professional sport to the department store, and a decline in occupations involving heavy labour where drink was a necessity probably made some contribution to a relative decline in drinking. So did the growth in numbers of the professions and of clerks, the increased popularity of tea, the internal development of the police force, better standards of education, especially after Forster's Education Act of 1870, more involvement of men in political culture, and the expansion of Methodism into the coalfields. For all the noise that the temperance movement produced, it probably played a more peripheral role than often thought, since though it rallied the committed minority, it alienated the more moderate.

Despite the continued efforts of temperance movements by the end of the nineteenth century, drink remained a central part of much British culture. British breweries remained highly prosperous, incorporated as limited companies, and setting up 'tied' public houses to sell only their beers. And they had a well-organized National Trade Defence Fund to defend themselves against temperance opposition. Drink was still a divisive issue in British society. The attacks on it had succeeded only to a limited extent.

CHAPTER FOUR

Vice and Profligacy: Betting and Gaming

In March 1870 at Aintree, near Liverpool, the famous Grand National steeplechase had an exciting finish. A leading jockey, George Holman, riding The Doctor, just failed to win the race, despite being roared on by those in the crowd who had backed him. 'Hotspur', the reporter for the national daily, *The Telegraph*, described the severity of the finish as being so great that 'The Doctor's sides were fairly ripped up by the spurs'. Unusually for the time, when upper-class sports were largely immune from their attention, this prompted the National Society for the Prevention of Cruelty to Animals to bring a prosecution in Liverpool for excessive cruelty to the horse during the race. This was the first of its kind.

Betting on racing was very widely popular, and the Liverpool magistrates generally showed a clear bias in favour of racing and betting, so the RSPCA prosecutor was careful to begin by saying that this was *not* an attack on racing, a sport he described as 'our grand national pastime', and a 'noble' competition between horses and riders. He first cross-examined the journalist 'Hotspur', Henry Feist, who quickly backed away from his report's words, saying that it had contained a 'little sensation', a 'touch of spice', as his readers expected, and he merely meant to indicate the finish was 'severe'. But an Everton cab-driver, a police superintendent, two constables and a Kirkdale surgeon, all close to the race, confirmed that the horse had been unduly punished at the finish. Holman avoided giving evidence, but when the summons was delivered he had been heard to say that 'there was £30,000 we stood to win if I had been in first'. His words were used to show he was motivated by avarice.

In contrast, the defence claimed Holman was of good conduct and 'exceedingly humane'. A groom, a licensed victualler, a gentleman farmer, a merchant, a livery stable keeper, three veterinary surgeons and a butcher, attending the race from Liverpool and neighbouring counties, all denied that cruelty was inflicted on the horse. Some of these, however, had backed him, and the licensed victualler suggested that 'if he had been punished a little more' he would have won.[1]

The court was crowded and most of those present, described as 'sporting men', showed 'a strong manifestation of feeling' against the prosecution. When the bench, after a short discussion, dismissed the summons and allocated costs of £20 against the prosecution, there was 'a wild cheer'. The report was widely covered by the regional, national and Sunday press. In contrast to modern attitudes to animal cruelty, newspapers were largely non-judgemental.

This case study shows how far gambling occupied an ambiguous position. It was supported by many across the classes and was especially popular amongst men. The bench at Liverpool may well have shared such attitudes. As we can see, many of those giving evidence and attending the race came from the middle classes. All leading papers covered the race, which received detailed coverage in papers like *The Telegraph* with a literate middle-class readership. Indeed, horse-racing reports and racing tips were a press staple, but what was also suggested here by the prosecution was that racing could be represented as leading to temptation. The more hedonistic attractions of gambling risk and uncertainty challenged the respectable values of thrift, fairness and hard work. Money greased the market economy, but it could lead to a failure of morality and to greed, a wish to make money by whatever means seemed appropriate, whether by betting, cheating or losing control and going to extreme lengths to try to win.

Introduction

Clearly, gambling, like drinking, had wide social and cultural significance in Victorian society. Many novelists, such as Disraeli, Dickens, Eliot, Hardy, Moore, Thackeray and Trollope portrayed gambling negatively, not as a normal recreational activity but as addictive, a way of escaping urban problems by gamblers who lacked self-control. It was supposedly harmful, a contaminant of society, linked to crime, alcoholism or suicide.[2] Yet despite such moral condemnation it was commercially successful and widely popular across Britain. By the late nineteenth century, betting on horse-racing may well have been the most common pastime in Britain amongst adult men. It was highly resilient to the campaigns of moral reformers and to governmental legislation, even though the State steadily restricted public gambling opportunities, and tried to ensure gambling was confined to private gentlemen's clubs and horse race-courses. Indeed, gambling prospered and developed as a private commercial venture and bookmakers grew in number and their scale of operation, more in Great Britain than in any other contemporary country. Gambling was big business. In 1837, existing legislation against gaming was largely ineffectual, but in general attitudes towards gambling were largely shaped by beliefs stemming from the social class of those involved. It was perceived differently depending on who was actually taking part. So paradoxically the middle classes led the campaign against gambling, yet their entrepreneurs cashed in on gambling demands.

Chapter outline

This chapter begins by exploring the views of those reformers who saw almost all gambling as evil, a dangerous vice that caused economic, financial and psychological harm to individuals and families; a vice that was morally undesirable, creating wrong attitudes to work and to leisure time. Though accurate calculations of the social cost of gambling proved difficult, they argued that gambling harmed the wider community, bred idleness, and encouraged cheating and dishonesty.

Although some gambling activities such as horse-racing enjoyed cross-class appeal, specific class alignments developed in relation to gambling, creating gambling networks which were socially stratified. The upper classes had land, spare time and property, and substantial spare cash for high-stakes gambling. Credit was extended to them and there was an expectation that settling debts was a matter of honour. For the poor, bookmakers wanted cash in advance. So this chapter approaches gambling through the lens of social class, first exploring the upper-class gambling world, when excessive gambling was largely seen as an economic issue, of rich men choosing to waste their wealth and inheritance. At the start of Victoria's reign, social gambling and betting remained generally acceptable amongst the social elite, and such views retained support. The gambling of the rich was looked down on by the more respectable, but since the rich could afford it, there was rarely any attempt to challenge it through legislation. The gambling of the working classes, which was seen by reformers as both a moral and social problem, provides the central focus of the chapter. Working-class gambling, at least for those in that class not actively involved in church or political life, was increasingly pervasive over the period, helping to establish a leisure class identity. But working-class gambling was attacked and represented as deeply problematical to society and the individual. Figures were lacking, since ready-money off-course gambling was illegal, but indignant newspaper leader articles, prominent members of the Church of England and the Nonconformist churches, and social reformers all took a class approach. They might preach against upper-class betting but politically they targeted working-class cash gambling, attempting to reform and revivify the British. By the end of the century leading socialist politicians such as Ramsay MacDonald, Keir Hardie and John Burns were vehemently opposed to such betting too.

The final section focuses on middle-class gambling. This has been an area hitherto largely ignored by historians, since the Victorians themselves largely overlooked it, rarely giving it adverse publicity, in order to maintain an image of middle-class respectability and to support growing middle-class power, but as the case study shows, the middle classes were deeply involved.

General opposition to betting and gaming

In February 1844, in his evidence before the Select Committee on Statutes Against Gaming, one of the Senior Criminal Law Commissioners, Thomas Starkie, argued that while betting could be carried on imprudently 'to such an extent as to be a vice', a bet could be harmless, a matter of mere amusement. But when betting was excessive it became evil. It all depended whether such betting was affordable. So, he argued, 'the imprudence or the vice depends on a man's circumstances'. Another witness, the leading anti-gambling campaigner Robert Baxter, a Doncaster newspaper proprietor, believed that gambling was both 'fashionable', and 'indulged in by a very large and influential class'. It was rarely publicly noticed because carried out 'with a degree of privacy.'[3]

But as gambling grew more visible in the second half of the century, opposition grew. By the later 1880s, respectable public opinion believed that betting was growing in popularity amongst *all* classes of the community. This generated an intense anti-gambling campaign, not seen before, which was especially strong in north-west England, with the churches especially active, producing pamphlets and articles against both betting and gambling.

Anti-gamblers often misunderstood the nature, level and pleasures of gambling and betting. They commonly focused on more extreme examples of pathological, compulsively addictive gambling behaviour, though modern research suggests this applied only to between 1 and 2 per cent of the population.[4] Others assumed that individual gamblers inevitably lost, rather than the reality of gambling money being redistributed amongst those involved. Even so, their arguments resonated powerfully with the respectable middle classes with their belief in thrift. Lectures, speeches in Parliament, church sermons, pamphlets, articles and even novels increasingly stressed the 'deplorable vice of betting' or 'the vice of betting and gambling' in much the same way as they attacked drink as morally degrading, portraying gambling as a degenerative compulsion.[5]

Preachers combined two types of argument, moral and social, with particular emphasis on its supposed dishonest practices, heartless selfishness, demoralizing tendency, ruined families and desolated homes. For such arguments, betting was framed as an individual vice, a moral sin, while socially a problem gambler affected wider society. But there were also structural arguments attacking the commercial betting industry, with bookmakers a particular target.

Moral arguments

Anti-gamblers pointed to the 'immoral attitudes' gambling sustained and encouraged. It was a sin. Gambling was harmful, breeding covetousness and idleness, and encouraging dreams of vast wealth rather than industrious work. Reliance on chance rather than rationality to determine income and fortune flew in the face of the capitalist work ethic. Winnings were unearned, threatening Victorian society's economic basis. Wealth was only legitimate if received by gift, exchange of goods or work. Gambling took money without giving a good or service in return. It created nothing of social value and was a waste of individual effort. Some even attacked Stock Exchange gambling as springing from the same motives.

Social arguments

Gambling was portrayed as dangerous, causing serious financial and psychological harm or loss of jobs. Though only a minority of men or women spent any more than they could reasonably afford, anti-gamblers claimed that 'poverty and vice invariably are promoted'.[6] Gambling was a wrecker of lives: a destroyer of homes and families, a bringer of destitution. It brought misery to the family. Adult gamblers seriously neglected their children, and there was an increased risk of anger and destructive violence after losses, especially from pathological gamblers. Gambling damaged financial security, family relationships and physical and emotional health. Wages used for gambling were improvidently squandered instead of saving money or purchasing something economically or socially useful. Headlines such as 'Suicide through Losses on the Derby' reminded people of the personal harm excessive betting could cause.

Moreover, addictive gambling behaviour was seen as linked to criminality. The anti-gambling campaigner Lord Hawke, in his evidence to a House of Lords Select Committee on Betting in 1901, cited criminal court evidence of 80 suicides, 321 embezzlements and 191 bankruptcies allegedly due to betting. However, his arguments were based on fraudsters' mitigation pleas and in most cases the situation was more complex. Quite often, for example, bankrupts had only turned to betting when already in financial trouble.

Other arguments

Towards the end of the century, when industrial competition from the USA and Germany was increasing, betting was further attacked on the grounds that it would distract workers from production and make businesses less efficient than those of Britain's competitors. In early 1890, the same year that the Wesleyan Conference issued its first Declaration on Gambling, the National Anti-Gambling League was formed. It had the ultimate objective of totally abolishing all forms of 'the terrible vice', the 'gambling fever', the 'curse of the age'. It adopted a strenuous and totally uncompromising approach to the reformation of England's gambling behaviour, attacking it as non-productive, irrational, anti-social in its relationships, over-reliant on luck and a poor way of transferring property. It lobbied the Home Office regularly and by the beginning of the twentieth century was gaining support.

Scapegoating those in the gambling industry, especially bookmakers

Whilst moral reformers were opposed to people gambling amongst themselves, their most venomous language was directed at its commercial organizers: the owners of gambling and betting rooms; gambling tipsters and promoters; and most especially the bookmakers who literally 'made a book' on specific sporting events, offering ante-post odds (well before the event) as money came in, or starting-price odds based on last-minute bets.

Bookmakers offered a betting market where those who wanted a bet could find odds on an event. To anti-gamblers, however, betting men were 'the drones of society', who 'have not done a single thing to enrich the world's store of physical and mental comforts'.[7] Bookmakers were 'an army of social parasites' or 'blood-suckers', grasping rogues preying upon fools: 'ill-favoured spiders', 'a devil going about seeking whom he may devour', 'greedy scum' or 'harpies', devouring predators exploiting innocent punters. They were anti-Christian, satanic evil incarnate: 'devils', 'fiends', 'demons in human form'. Street and course bookmakers had to be noticed to attract custom, but their physical appearance too attracted negative comment. Some were 'corpulent' or 'obese', implying greed and gluttony. They were 'jewellery-bedecked', 'loud-voiced', 'over-flamboyant', 'drunken', 'lascivious', and 'cigar-smoking'.

So bookmakers were simultaneously stereotypical villains and the capitalist business entrepreneurs of a commercial, profit-focused gambling market, providing another example of the contradictions and moral ambivalences surrounding the demands of the betting world. Bookmakers were portrayed, maligned and caricatured in the light of anti-gambling preoccupations.[8] Their self-perceptions and those of many customers were much more positive, and they often projected a more respectable image, even if that was sometimes self-serving.

The richer credit bookmakers, often operating from fixed bases, and on the race-course, were men of real substance. Joseph Pickersgill (c. 1849–1920), a course bookmaker, familiarly known as 'Honest Joe', described as 'a cultured man' with 'the instincts of a gentleman', died with a fortune of £745,459, a modern multi-millionaire.[9] Successful bookmakers were figures of significance, attracting some respect and admiration in working-class communities. They increasingly presented themselves as respectable, cultivating an image of honest dealing and of living by a code of sporting honour, 'decent fellers' who gave support to regular customers on occasion and sometimes generously donated to local charities, churches and schools. Even opponents accepted that they 'settled up' betting debts. Bookmakers could not afford to be dishonest lest they lost custom. They had a vested interest in being 'straight'.

By contrast, ordinary street bookmakers were in stronger competition for resources and custom. Some bookmakers in the 1870s and 1880s, for example, were part of a more criminal business subculture that involved them in turf wars, business rivalry, bad debts, violent behaviour, street fights against other bookmakers or aggressive customers, obscene language and drunkenness.[10] At this level there was a more ambivalent relationship between bookmakers and their customers: supported for the services they provided but also potentially dangerous 'hard' men, defending territory, maintaining status and alert for attempts at fraud.

The upper-class gambling world

Prevalence of gaming

Though there were eighteenth-century laws trying to control the incidence of upper-class gaming and minimize its financial impact when carried to excess, gaming remained widely popular in 1837. Royalty, politicians and the more raffish and rakish amongst Britain's landed and leisured social elite enjoyed it. It offered an exciting mode of conspicuous consumption, a fashionably pleasant way of passing their increased leisure time. Gambling offered relief from boredom. It had a distracting, escapist appeal. It could temporarily be all-consuming, generating intense anxiety, excitement and increased heartbeat. This might be covered up with assumed indifference, although particularly for those from a Protestant background it mixed guilt with its pleasures. Some, often intensely religious, like the 5th Earl of Grafton, avoided it utterly.

Playing games of pure chance like dice and lotteries, gambling games requiring skill such as billiards, whist and other card games, or betting on horse-races, boxing and other sporting events, provided a common social bond for many of the aristocracy and land-owning gentry, armed forces officers, Members of Parliament and others who made up this class. Any interpersonal wagers made publicly, sometimes recorded in personal pocket-sized betting books, were settled after the event, as a matter of honour, though there were always defaulters. Newspapers reported the changing betting odds and prices on future sporting events. Gambling arguably stimulated the British economy as substantial amounts of money and goods changed hands.

In the early Victorian age, table games such as even/odd/rouge/noir, card games of various sorts, such as faro or baccarat, where the banker had an edge, or dice games like hazard, were common in the all-male contexts of London's elite gaming houses around St James's and Westminster. These gaming houses, elite commercial capitalistic enterprises, were sometimes described with powerful symbolism by opponents as 'hells' or 'pandemoniums', and their owners and associates 'hellites'. Gaming was even more popular at the well-patronized private political gentlemen's clubs such as Boodle's, the Cocoa Tree or White's. These attracted the aristocracy and gentry, leading politicians and law-makers, and so were safe from prosecution, even though all gaming clubs and private houses where gaming parties were regularly held were unlawful. Crockford's Club, established in 1828 by a fishmonger's son, was the most fashionable place to gamble. By 1838, according to an article in *Fraser's Magazine*, 'half the legislators of the country', including the Duke of Wellington, were members, and were supplied with champagne while they were encouraged to lose.[11]

For many men and for some women amongst the aristocratic and gentry groups, gaming formed a key part of elite sociability. So gaming also took place in their country and town houses, at hunting lodges, at spas and during race meetings, as a diversion whilst enjoying other leisure forms. Many aristocratic women enjoyed it: visiting each other's houses to play card games for guineas, or getting their partners to place bets for them at race meetings.

During the mid-nineteenth century, the pressures of respectability, more working-class interest and involvement, turf dishonesty and dislike of high-stakes plunging temporarily reduced those aspects of upper-class gambling which attracted anti-aristocratic and anti-corruption rhetoric. Excessive gaming became less fashionable, but gaming continued, albeit more discreetly. In the British army, gambling debts, previously merely a matter of honour, were increasingly viewed as a disciplinary offence. Involvement rose again from the 1860s, stimulated by the young Prince of Wales and his set. For most involved their expenditure was moderate, and the amount of gaming was decreasing, but there was some limited increase in high-stakes gaming at some upper-class West End clubs in the last quarter of the century. This was largely due to the increased popularity of baccarat, introduced from the French casino resorts. Very occasional police raids on the respectable, upper-class clubs in the later nineteenth century still bagged high-status members though their names seldom surfaced. Popular imagination still perceived clubs as places where aristocratic fortunes could be lost. After a raid on the Field Club in 1889, reported in the press under headings such as 'High Class Gambling' or 'Society Gambling', its proprietor pleaded guilty. He paid a fine of £500, keeping his grateful upper-class clients out of court. No action could be taken against them or negative publicity given once a guilty plea had been proffered.

The rich also found gambling opportunities on their vacations. Continental inland watering places such as Baden, Ems, Homburg,

Wiesbaden or Aix had a far more relaxed attitude to gaming, and quickly added casinos and private clubs with roulette, baccarat and other games to existing health facilities, attracting women as well as men.[12] High-stakes gaming there was popular with the Prince of Wales. Seaside casinos at Monte Carlo, Boulogne or Nice soon became major visitor attractions, despite gambling's French illegality. However, the later nineteenth century saw most European countries turn against gambling houses. There was an International Association for the Suppression of the Gaming Tables of Monte Carlo at this time.

Horse-racing

Alongside gaming there was also substantial wagering on sporting activities. Whilst there was some upper-class betting interest in sports such as hare-coursing and pugilism, it was horse-racing that provided the major upper-class sports betting context. In the late 1830s, nearly a third of all dukes, marquises and earls subscribed to the *Racing Calendar*. Major urban race meetings such as Ascot or Epsom often offered gaming facilities too, with canvas marquees, gaming tables and equipment to cater for demand. Doncaster's St Leger meeting offered hazard as well as betting at its Subscription Rooms and the Mansion House, perfectly safe from prosecution as the local governing elite either joined in or turned a blind eye.[13] Earlier in the century on-course betting rings were literally rings of betters clustered together. Later spatial railed-off betting rings appeared on courses.

A minority of upper-class 'turfites' (followers of racing, 'the turf'), viewed racing as a betting battleground. Even early in Victoria's reign there was sufficient betting market on future races to allow fluid groups of race-horse owners, their trainers, jockeys and hangers on, secretly associated with commissioners and bookmakers, to offer odds and make bets on their own or others' horses. They did this at Tattersall's Rooms, London's most select betting venue, as well as other London gentlemen's clubs or northern betting centres like Manchester's Post Office Hotel or the Waterloo in Liverpool. They sought to outwit other confederacies and delude and exploit the general betting public. Those more interested in betting extended their associations with leading bookmakers into other select betting clubs. In 1860, London's Victoria Club opened its doors, with a socially-mixed membership paying six guineas annual subscription. The even more exclusive Turf Club opened in 1876. Up to the 1860s such betting rooms still saw the staking of some large amounts, sometimes pushing expenditure too high for upper-class incomes to bear. But by the 1870s this was becoming rare, thanks to the publicity given to some rash high-stakes plunging, better information about horses' condition, fewer chances to manipulate betting odds and more control over credit betting in the betting clubs.

Betting's problems: heavy losses by a reckless rich minority

Some gamblers lacked the intellect and personal qualities to control their gambling. A tiny minority became pathological gamblers, or demonstrated compulsively destructive behaviour. Usually they eventually lost estate lands, wealth and reputation. In 1855, Frank Villiers, a Jockey Club steward, had to flee to France, owing £100,000 due to his betting losses. Other upper-class gamblers, including John Stanley and Lord Maidstone, followed later that decade. A major 1860s scandal concerned young Lord Henry Hastings, weak, foolish, attractive and amusing, with a reputation as a compulsive and self-destructive gambler, drunkard and womanizer. He ran off with Lady Paget, the fiancée of wealthy young Lincolnshire landowner, Harry Chaplin, a leading race-horse owner. Hastings extended his rivalry with Chaplin to racing. In 1866, Hastings had a very successful year with his own horses, despite often foolishly accepting poor market odds, but in 1867 he laid heavily against Chaplin's horse, Hermit, a leading contender for the Epsom Derby. It won. Hastings lost an estimated £120,000, with more than £10,000 owed to Chaplin. Hastings then tried to recoup his losses with increasingly desperate plunges. His debts mounted. He sold his Scottish estates for £300,000. He sold his hunters, hounds and most of his racing stable. Yet he still owed £40,000 as the racing season ended. He maintained a semblance of solvency, continuing to bet and race his remaining horses. He soon fell into the hands of the money-lenders. His best horses were manipulated in the market for their benefit, not his. The press were moralistic, mocking and merciless. He died a few months later, at the age of twenty-six, broken in health and financially ruined. In 1870, the 6th Duke of Newcastle went bankrupt, having lost around £200,000 as the result of his racing activities, while in the same decade Sir Vincent Hynde Cotton, of Madingley Hall, Cambridge, lost his estate through gambling, and ended up working as a coachman.[14]

Gaming scandals and cheating

It was the young, inexperienced and foolish, the weak or unknowing amongst upper-class gamblers who most recklessly gambled their dynastic fortunes. They were rarely successful, chasing losses and failing to understand odds or keep records of their gambling. Weakness or vulnerability was manipulated by the rapacious at the race-course, in gentlemen's clubs and at country house parties. Some 'gentlemen' kept themselves by clever gambling, making it their main income, partly through legitimate skills, but sometimes through sleight-of-hand, confidence tricks and collusion. There were regular allegations that 'men of very high rank and standing in society' who lacked money were paid by some clubs to decoy 'opulent young men' into playing.[15] Others just cheated. Where possible such behaviour was covered up and kept within upper-class circles so as not to damage people's reputation. Only very occasionally were the gullible able to fight back. In 1842, for example, four members of the nobility brought an action to recover their losses at the Minor St James Club House, arguing that the gaming there had been grossly unfair, and received £3,508.

Such rare cases of gambling excess reaching the press become 'shocking', 'scandalous' narratives exploited by anti-gambling groups. In 1837, for example, Lord de Ros, wealthy, of good position and reportedly a very good whist player, was privately accused of cheating at the notorious Graham's Club in St James's Street, London, marking cards and reversing a cut when he was the dealer. This was conduct of 'the meanest and most degraded description', but nothing was done publicly initially. Rumours reached *The Satirist*, which published them. His upper-class accusers then went public. They suggested that they had been initially anxious to suppress any public report because of their personal feelings and the injury that would be inflicted upon upper-class 'society' by the exposure of a person of his rank and station. When de Ros brought a very widely-publicized prosecution for slander against one of his accusers it was revealed that there had been suspicions about his play for six years. Some had avoided playing with him. Others, equally suspicious, sought gain by partnering him. He lost the case, the jury retiring for only about fifteen minutes.[16] Disgraced, de Ros and his family left the country.

Royal gambling, especially by Edward, Prince of Wales at hunting, shooting and racing house parties, helped to legitimate both gaming and betting on horse-races amongst the elite 'fast set' surrounding him. In 1890, however, gambling scandal touched him after he stayed with a *nouveau riche* shipping magnate, Arthur Wilson, during the St Leger Race Week. On the Tuesday, the Prince suggested a game of baccarat, using his own counters, and acted as banker. The Wilson family had no gaming background, but Wilson's son, Arthur, watching, decided that Sir William Cumming, rich, arrogant, good-looking and a Scots Guards Lieutenant-Colonel, was cheating, adding counters surreptitiously to potentially winning hands. Others of his family and a neighbour, watched too. Eventually they informed others of the Prince's party, who told the Prince, who had not noticed any cheating. The unanimous views of the Wilson family swayed him, although Cumming vehemently denied the accusation. Cumming was pressured into signing a document swearing to refrain from gambling, tantamount to a confession, under the threat of otherwise being warned off the turf by the Jockey Club. The scandal soon leaked out, and MPs, clergy, the media and others were outraged at the scandal. This forced Cumming to sue the Wilsons for slander, seeking £5,000 damages. Leading advocates on both sides did their best to influence the court's decision. Though it went against Cumming, he may well have been innocent, but the scandal picked up on the antagonistic concerns of respectable society about the Prince of Wales and the card-playing and racing lifestyle of his group.[17]

Betting scandals and cheating

By the early years of Victoria's reign, bare-knuckle pugilism was gaining a particularly unsavory reputation for its violence and organized 'crosses', dishonest attempts to fix results for betting purposes. Horse-racing, despite its followers' attempts to portray it as the sport of kings, also had corruptive elements, including some of the upper classes. Some Jockey Club members had always manipulated the odds of their race-horses in the betting market to suit their betting books, and so profit, rather than to run their horses 'fairly'.[18] Betting was often perceived as morally corrupting and its consequences carried dangers for the naïve better. Racing insiders could profit through a variety of morally-dishonest tactics to control betting odds or race results. Inducing corrupt jockeys to hold horses back, bribing stable boys to find out how horses' trials had gone, or spreading false rumours about chances were all strategies that helped gamblers. Rich race-horse owners sometimes withdrew their horses if they could not get the odds they wanted, even if that meant others lost their money. They might even gain more by its failure by secretly betting against it beforehand. Where a horse was secretly sent out to lose a race, the owner gained because his horse would be handicapped with less weight to carry for a later race, and have more chance to win. In 1887, internal Club divisions surfaced about the propriety of such behaviour when a senior member of the Club, Sir George Chetwynd, was accused by another member, Lord Durham, during a speech at York, of running his stable in a way that was fraudulent, sometimes holding his horses back for financial gain. Chetwynd, a close friend of the Prince of Wales, chose to sue for damages. There was insufficient evidence to prove Lord Durham's case, but despite Chetwynd's apparent cool, calm and confident answers, it soon became clear that he and his jockey were involved in what seemed highly irregular and suspicious financial entanglements. The jury gave judgement in his favour but for only the very significant minimum damages of a farthing (0.1p).[19]

Opposition to upper-class gambling

The early nineteenth century saw many anti-gambling tracts aimed at upper-class gaming, all arguing that it was a dreadful vice. Sermons, tracts and political pamphlets attacked upper-class gambling as a dreadful and immoral vice that placed Britain in grave peril, threatening religious faith, trade, government and domestic life. Throughout the nineteenth century, attacks on upper-class gambling usually focused on its malign effects and provided accounts of those who had wagered too heavily, with consequent loss of estates, financial ruin and even suicide. As the century wore on, the middle classes increasingly viewed upper-class gambling as decadent, symbolic of an out-of-touch and out-dated social order. More populist, often Liberal

Party-supporting newspapers argued that the working classes could not be expected to refrain from gambling when the upper classes showed such a poor example, arguing that the humble imitated the vices of the rich. As the *Leeds Mercury* argued on 29 May 1856, 'the upper classes of society set in this respect a very bad example to the humbler classes'.

Lloyd's Weekly Newspaper in 1874 fulminated on the 'national vice of betting of which persons in the highest social position show the most flagrant examples' and which produced 'more social evils in this country than any other cause' and affected 'all ranks in society from the peer to the stable boy'.[20] *Reynolds's News* targeted upper-class gambling remorselessly. In 1877, for example, it claimed:

> The vice of gambling is remorselessly on the increase . . . Simply may it be referred to the contaminating example of the upper orders of the State. When a nation maintains a class of the community who have naught to do for a living, but who are necessarily, from their position, addicted to luxury and self- indulgence, the country can expect nothing but evil results.[21]

It also targeted betting laws themselves, arguing that they bore down only on the workers and not the upper-class lawmakers.[22] It complained at the 'hypocrisy' of an English justice that allowed the 'aristocratic and middle class gamblers of the West End clubs to be let off by the magistrates'. It claimed that 'more damage is done by dabbling and gambling in stocks and shares than in betting. The only difference is that one is held to be respectable', and suggested that 'the money lost on betting . . . is merely child's play in comparison with that lost in card playing in West-end clubs [or] on the Stock Exchange'.[23]

In the 1890s, the Prince of Wales became a target for hysterical anti-gamblers and anti-royalists, with MPs, the press and members of the church joining in. The London Baptist Association in 1891 passed a motion deploring the increase in gambling, 'especially amongst the upper classes' and its 'effect on the morals of the whole community', pointing up the recent 'revelations in connection with the Prince'.[24] The Bishop of London deplored the reckless gambling of some of the wealthy classes. As the *Westminster Gazette* pointed out in 1894, 'where leaders in society are affected by the mania, it is not surprising that younger people should give themselves up to the folly'.[25]

Policing and governmental responses

Given that upper-class gambling was not likely to cause social unrest or revolution, there was little active policing of upper-class gaming in the first years of Victoria's reign. Parliament had a relative lack of concern with the gaming habits of the upper classes, but in 1844 it appointed a Select Committee to investigate gaming in more detail, especially the extent to which existing legislation was being evaded, why the police had such a poor record on the suppression of gaming houses, and what if any amendments should be made to the laws.

This forced London's Commissioner of Police, Sir Richard Mayne, into temporary action. He sent 345 London policemen to launch a coordinated crackdown on seventeen gaming houses, mostly around Piccadilly, Regent Street and Albemarle Street. Some managers were clearly tipped off: only eighty people were found, and very little money was seized, except for one 'hell' where £3,014 was discovered.

The Select Committee on the Gaming Laws quickly concluded that the anti-gaming laws were ineffectual. It attempted to allay public concerns, defending upper-class gambling, whilst suggesting that only the poor needed protection. But it also took the *laissez-faire* attitude that governments should not be controlling how people spent their money, and so they should not be punished for gaming. Nor should the courts be wasting their time adjudicating betting disputes, though cheating should continue to be punished as a crime of obtaining money by false pretences. The 1845 Gaming Act was a significant watershed, which provided that all wagering contracts and gambling debts should be unenforceable through the courts, attempting to curb betting by increasing the risks, though tacitly implying that the wealthy upper classes, bound by the honour code, would always pay up: the triumph of hope over experience. Its primary concern was to reduce the legal actions over gambling debts cluttering up the courts, but it was also viewed as having moral purpose. But its effect was to increase the numbers of ready money betting offices in major cities.

In the later nineteenth century, there were only occasional attempts to address high-stakes gambling. A judge's decision in an 1884 case that the playing of baccarat in a club was unlawful had only a brief effect. The upper classes seemed to be immune from the law, which appeared chaotic, ineffective, and rarely enforced.

Working-class gambling

The prevalence of gambling

Demonstrating confidence in one's assessment and judgement of one's own or others' skills by risking a 'friendly' cash wager or a betting-related challenge had long, deep roots in working-class life. Some wagers risked all a man had. Many individual sports such as rowing and sculling, pugilism (prize-fighting), pedestrianism (foot-racing), fishing, pigeon-racing, dog-racing, quoits, bowling, wrestling and billiards all attracted challengers, patrons and a betting market. At all of these irregularly-held occasions, such wagering offered excitement, heightened tensions and added to sociability, while inside knowledge helped successful betting. Initially, many gambling events had access free to all: racing on moors and heaths, rowing watched from riversides, and foot-races on public roads. By the 1850s, publican entrepreneurs were already creating enclosed grounds beside their public houses to run a variety of sporting events. They charged admission and attracted drinking and betting custom, though anti-gambling magistrates would sometimes succeed in getting them closed. By the 1880s, dog handicaps had become more popular than pedestrian events at some tracks. It was easier to attract entries and there was slightly less corruption, although dogs could still be held back. In some northern towns a hundred or more dogs might be entered for a prize of £10 to £20. In 1899, an Oldham competition offering £25 attracted 240 dogs running in sixty heats.[26]

But luck and chance played a significant role in working-class culture. So other gambling activities, more reliant on chance, offered significant attractions. In pubs, dominoes, dice games, quoits and cards were significant social betting activities. Police rarely interfered.[27] For the urban poor, boys and young men, especially those casually employed, a group described by one Alnwick journalist as 'young undergraduates in the school of vice', coin-gambling games were popular.[28] They offered excitement, sociability and competition for low stakes. The coin game pitch and toss was particularly common in northern England, especially in coal and iron-stone mining areas like South Northumberland or Cleveland. It was played outside on public thoroughfares, streets and highways and recreational areas. It took place irregularly throughout the year, weather-dependent, mainly early on Saturday evening (after pay day) or Sunday, to the offence of churchgoers. Crowds of a hundred or more often assembled to watch. One preacher at Burnley in 1882 described the 'sin' of 'groups of men and boys, their garments fluttering in rags, and their minds as dark as Hottentots, playing at pitch and toss for pennies and halfpennies'.[29] Uncomprehending middle-class magistrates and reformers perceived a deprived, dissolute and delinquent adolescent culture, a symptom of wider crises of morality.[30] Its deep roots in tradition, support in local communities and its determined resilience made it hard for the police to defeat despite the regular complaints of lack of action. Organized systems of scouts could spot even disguised 'polis' a long way off. Prosecutions and fines had little effect. In South Northumberland, annual prosecution numbers increased steadily from twenty-two in 1872 to 307 by 1913, covering offenders from eleven-year-olds to men in their fifties, some with a long history of offences.[31]

Betting on horse-racing

The expansion of the racing industry and the growth of horse-race betting as a main working-class betting interest were due to several factors. These included the rise in real wages, a shorter industrial working week from the 1870s, changing patterns of leisure spending, wider newspaper circulation providing results and training information, increased rates of literacy and the development of the electric telegraph which from the late 1860s allowed rapid transfer of betting information.[32]

This form of betting has attracted substantial historical study and its main lines of development are clear.[33] Betting was far more common in working-class life than its opponents wished to admit. Those scholars who turned their attention to working-class gambling in the late 1970s suggested it first became widespread in the 1880s.[34] Recent research, however, convincingly suggests a more gradual build up over a longer period. By the end of the century, as real wages grew and hours of work modestly reduced, there may have been three million betting regularly, and many others having a more occasional flutter. Street betting was so widespread that by 1896 the *Liverpool Review* claimed that 'there is no sane man in Liverpool who does not believe that betting is indulged in daily ... by all sorts and conditions of people. From the merchant prince to the casual labourer, and from office clerks to shoe blacks, betting has its thousands and tens of thousands of devotees'.[35]

Accurate estimates of numbers involved prove impossible. The variations in police prosecutions, for example, which show London, Manchester and Liverpool as having particularly high rates, may simply reflect differential pressure from anti-gamblers. Rural areas, offering only limited opportunities to bet, still largely relied on postal betting or a runner in a local public house collecting bets.

Skilled artisans and young men were the betters who dominated prosecutions everywhere. These were the two groups likely to have some excess of income over committed expenditure. The evidence of betting slips, whilst not reliable, is consistent in indicating that the normal stake was moderate, between sixpence and a shilling, rarely as much as half a crown. There was little evidence of excessive expenditure and much of self-restraint. Most gambled only what they could afford. Only a tiny minority gambled compulsively, often exhibiting sensation-seeking, impulsive and risky behaviour. For most, once real wages increased, money spent on bets often rose alongside an increase in savings, perhaps for holidays or burial clubs.[36]

What was also clear was that some betting was regular, for small amounts, and had rational and intellectual elements based on gaining and assessing information, the form, other racing statistics and risks. For most of those involved, it was socially and culturally significant as an expression of modest and moderate leisure expenditure, carefully self-regulated. Indeed, working-class gambling has been described by one leading historian of gambling as 'a moderate, economistic and expressive form of regulation', perceived and used 'as a form of self-help'.[37] It was rarely irresponsible, passive or foolishly impetuous, though certainly some purely trusted to luck. Amongst the working classes the excitement of a win at good odds provided a lump sum it was hard to save for. It supplemented income, allowed a rare treat, or took household items out of pawn. Most of those who backed horses were male, but there is scattered evidence of women betting from the 1860s if not before, though some may have been placing bets for men. By the 1890s, however, there was public concern over working-class women's betting, and claims that it had been increasing in recent years. Observers throughout Britain noted women in the crowds frequenting betting streets and open spaces, and girls betting in factories.[38] Working-class cash betting, right across urban Britain, had become a local underground 'black' economy, controlled by the community, not the police or government.

Support for betting in working-class life

Though gambling was widely popular, ideological attempts to justify and legitimate it publicly were rare. Gambling was a culturally-contested activity. Support for gambling could be discerned far more by being involved in the activity rather than making speeches, writing about it or defending it in other ways. The cultural challenge to anti-gambling rhetoric faced its powerful discourses somewhat uneasily. It was not possible to make gambling respectable. Nevertheless, gambling's defenders tried to fit gambling more closely into the cultural values, expectations and beliefs of the British.

Across the country, many people, perhaps most, did not see betting as inherently evil. It was argued that gambling was impossible to stop. It was part of human nature. Attempts to introduce legislation against betting and gaming were met by arguments that while legislation against such admitted vices was morally laudable, such action attacked civil liberties, and that the combination of 'desire for gain and a speculating tendency' and temperamental need by some for 'stimulation and excitement' rendered legislation ineffective.[39] Its benefits in terms of employment, revenue and entertainment spin-offs were pointed out. The sporting press represented the anti-gamblers as obsessive religious zealots, attacking a traditional and pleasurable amusement that did little harm. Anti-gamblers were dismissed as 'cranks' or 'puritans', against all pleasure. The *Illustrated Sporting News* described them as 'faddists' who because they did not enjoy gambling themselves, 'hate to see anyone else do so'.[40]

As betting became more widespread, an ongoing, sustainable feature of working-class lives, the Sunday newspapers, who catered for a predominantly lower-middle class and proletariat readership, began to develop a new form of argument in betting's support, more in tune with their readership. Even in the 1850s, they were read by at least one adult in twenty. Their circulation rose alongside literacy rates. *The People* had reached 360,000 in 1890. In 1896, *Lloyd's Weekly Newspaper* became the first newspaper in Britain to reach sales of over a million. By then both papers devoted between 40 and 50 per cent of their sports coverage to racing, especially to commentary on recent races, betting tips and race predictions. They tried to justify and support the cultural practice of gambling by suggesting that working-class betting was 'a fact of life', attempting to lend it legitimacy and presenting it as a 'respectable' recreation. They portrayed working-class betting as a mere leisure activity, a harmless form of amusement. They even suggested that working-class gamblers were more virtuous than rich and greedy 'speculators' for profit, the stockbrokers on the Exchange, race-horse owners, dishonest touts or bookmakers.

Commercial support for working-class betting: bookmakers

There had been working-class bookmakers taking bets for the upper-class racing market in Tattersalls, race meetings and elsewhere even at the start of the nineteenth century, paralleling the growth of entrepreneurship in wider society and in capitalist culture. But by the 1840s, there was already sufficient urban working- and middle-class demand to create a betting market on future races. What were termed 'low list houses', 'betting offices' or 'betting houses' began to emerge in London, York, Manchester, Liverpool and elsewhere. Manchester's police returns of the late 1840s and the 1850s show customers were largely working class, often from the textile mills.[41] The term 'office' helped confer legitimacy, and signalled a business function in a society driven by commercial imperatives. They displayed hand-written betting lists of odds on forthcoming races and earlier racing results. They entered cash bets in ledgers, paying winners after the race. Some used press advertisements, others displayed signs, an indication of tacit social acceptance, though there were risks of fraud. One 'listman' from Old Millgate, Manchester, absconded with an estimated £1,000 to £1,500, taken over three weeks largely on the forthcoming Aintree races.[42]

In large towns, list houses were soon to be found in large numbers, and though made illegal in 1853, after a few symbolic prosecutions, especially from 1858 to 1859, they were largely left alone. Newcastle-upon-Tyne had an estimated forty or fifty 'betting houses', mainly in pubs, by 1861. Liverpool's public houses gained a reputation as 'resorts for betting men' while betting houses were 'a large and growing nuisance', and 'more numerous [than] generally supposed'. They were socially ranked, used by males from a wide variety of occupations, yet remained aloof from prosecution.[43] When police tried to prosecute innkeepers there the magistrate Robert Gladstone, the less-famous brother of William Gladstone, then Chancellor of the Exchequer, said that if the upper classes could gamble without prosecution, then 'what justice was there ... in not giving the same privilege to other classes', and forced the police to withdraw their prosecution.[44] By the early 1870s, even towns like Chester, where the betting market was smaller, had, as opponents admitted, 'local bookmen' who would take a bet from 'inexperienced youths of all classes ... tradesmen as well as their assistants and shopboys [and] the labouring and artisan class', and lay off excess money by sending it to 'betting firms in London'.[45]

As betting demand grew from the 1870s, less wealthy bookmakers became predominantly street-based, although public houses continued to be used, alongside shops such as newsagents or tobacconists where large numbers entered and helped to conceal bookmaker offices. Street bookmakers had their own territories, or beats, just like policemen. Quaysides, parks or crowded streets all provided cover from police surveillance, and made it easy to receive bets or escape pursuit. As business expanded, factories, businesses, shipyards and other industries often had agents collecting bets on behalf of bookmakers, and 'bookies' runners' delivering money and betting slips to the bookmaker on a regular basis. Rural betters could send money and bets by post to bookmakers' offices.

Locations where a bet could be placed had become very extensive by 1901. Street betting continued, but bets were still placed with bookmakers or their associated 'runners' in many public houses, even though publicans were anxious not to lose their licence, and so took care to display notices banning betting, even when tacitly condoning it. Bets could also be placed in railway bookstalls, beer houses, butchers, baker and tobacconists' shops, with milkmen and with agents in larger workplaces, despite spasmodic police action.

Media support for gambling

Working- and middle-class betting spread in large part due to the constant stream of information from the sporting press from the 1850s onwards. The *Racing Times* (1851) and *Sporting Life* (1859) sold for only a penny and came out initially twice weekly. Other cheap competitors followed, providing more democratized access to racing information.[46] By 1870, leading papers such *The Sportsman* or Manchester's *Sporting Chronicle* provided the 'sporting intelligence' about jockeys, training, conditions, horse health and previous form, the going on the course, the state of the odds and racing predictions ('tips') to help readers rationalize their bets and improve their chances. In 1880, *Sporting Life* alone sold 300,000 copies a week, and became a daily in 1883. By 1895, the three leading racing papers all had circulations in excess of 300,000 for each issue.

In the 1870s, racing news began to be a regular feature of most regional daily papers, and when in the 1870s the *Manchester Evening News* began printing the day's racing results it increased its circulation by 500 per cent. Many newspapers gained revenue by including advertisements for tipping and postal betting services.

This flow of information eventually allowed bookmakers to introduce starting prices, based on the odds on the course that the leading sporting papers later reported, first for their postal credit customers and then for everyone, from the mid-1860s. These published starting prices boosted betting further. These were seen by punters as fairer; taking starting prices stopped manipulation of earlier ante-post prices by the dishonest. Starting prices induced more people to wait to bet until just before the event, ensuring there was less chance of manipulating the betting market. Almost all newspapers supported betting by accepting advertisements relating to betting products and services: sweepstakes, list bookmakers, tipsters (sometimes ironically given the religious title 'prophets') and postal betting and equipment for bookmakers.

As football attracted larger working-class crowds in the late 1880s, some northern newspapers began running competitions offering weekly prizes to purchasers completing the most accurate list of soccer match forecast results. In the 1890s, as leagues provided more regular fixture lists, some bookmakers copied this approach, often issuing their own lists of matches and then later coupons. This was technically illegal, given that they collected stake money at grounds and from their agents round about.

Specialist books appeared too. A carefully anonymous legal 'Gentleman' wrote the pamphlet *The Laws of Betting or Betting Legalised: A Clear Summary of the Acts and Guide to Investors* (1874).[47] Other guides explained how 'investors' could make money through betting. As betting grew in scale, it increasingly became seen as a commercial opportunity. It offered profits and income. It relied on technological innovations such as the telegraph, the railways and printing presses. It had the same commercial ethics that characterized capitalist enterprises such as trade in ironstone or cotton, or the buying and selling of books. More ironically, for many gamblers it mirrored the claimed rational values and approaches of its critics in relying on information and reason. The language of advertisements, with its linkage to the world of the money-market via references to 'commission agents', 'turf speculation', 'profits', 'offices', 'investment', 'clients' and 'investors', or 'the science' of 'betting systems' was the language of business. 'Remittances' were to be 'invested' according 'to instructions', in the 'best market at the lowest quotations'. 'Price-currents' were to be 'forwarded'. Betters saw themselves as sporting gentlemen, using rational, careful and calculative approaches to investment.[48]

Gambling problems

Fair play in gambling depended on the honesty of the parties involved. For much working-class betting there was an element of risk beyond the bet itself. Bookmakers were problematical, were not always to be trusted and could disappear without paying out. Sporting contests could be lost deliberately since competitors, from a background of little education, low wages and risky jobs, could sometimes be tempted to make more money by losing, betting against themselves through betting commissioners, or being bribed to lose by bookmakers. The English Football Association, the Amateur Athletic Association and other sports bodies were very aware that betting involvement might corrupt sportsmen, lead them to lose deliberately and potentially affect result reliability. But this was hard to stop completely. When supporters backed their man, team or animal they wanted to know that the sport was 'on the square', that their bets had a fair chance of being won.

For those opposed to gambling, it was its visibility on the streets that offended. Pitch and toss, for example, played on the street when respectable families were going to Sunday church, was a source of constant complaint. Betting with bookmakers on the street rather than surreptitiously in public houses caught the attention of reformers. It drew crowds and blocked pavements. In Manchester, tradesmen were already complaining of this by 1859.[49] The language of the 'betting nuisance' of working-class street betting, or, much more commonly 'the betting evil', reflected a growing moral panic amongst reformers. Thereafter there were regular anti-betting letters from the righteous, rarer indignant articles from journalists and very occasional long leader columns from anti-gambling newspaper editors, such as those found in the *Manchester Guardian*, one of the few papers to refuse to print racing results, on the issue of street betting.

Policing, local authority and governmental responses to gambling

The growing numbers of list houses in London in the early 1850s created anxiety amongst those who felt working-class recreational betting needed control. Letters to the London press expressed concern, especially about their attraction to the young. The government acted. The 1853 Betting Houses Act made it illegal in England and Wales for people to assemble in one place other than on race-courses to place cash bets, on pain of a £100 fine, although credit betting for the wealthy remained legal. In his introductory speech the Attorney-General painted a grim picture of servants, apprentices and workmen tempted into betting, betting 'their few shillings' and then supposedly finally 'drawn into robbing their masters and employers'. The 'attendant vices' of corruption of the young and betting's links to criminality and criminal urban subcultures were a 'mischief' that was 'perfectly notorious'.[50] Parliament responded quickly and the Act was passed without debate.

The Act's effects were limited. Although magistrates continued ritually to announce their keenness to put down the 'betting menace', the Act was enforced only very spasmodically, although 1869 saw a short-lived moral panic with prosecutions in Sheffield, Manchester, London, Liverpool, Newcastle and elsewhere, and questions in Parliament. In all cases the magistrates claimed to be intent on putting the 'houses' down. Meanwhile postal commission bookmakers set up in Glasgow or Edinburgh where legislation did not apply and advertised in British papers that they would receive postal order cash bets.

The government responded once again with a Prevention of Gaming (Scotland) Act in 1869 which allowed the imprisonment of those found with 'professional implements' of gambling, and a tightened up but still ineffectual Suppression of Betting Houses Act of 1874. It tried to restrain street betting, to prohibit the publication or distribution of material relating to methods of betting banned by the 1853 Act by placard, handbill, card or advertisement inducing people to bet, and to make the 1853 Betting Houses Act apply to Scotland. This simply forced some (but not all) of those postal bookmaker offices taking cash to relocate again. This time they moved offshore to the French coast or the Netherlands, whence they could send representatives to take ready-money bets at the leading race meetings, whilst maintaining their British letter and telegraph business. Other Scottish offices maintained the fiction of merely being legal credit bookmakers. When postal services became more reliable foreign lottery tickets became popular from the 1870s onwards, widely advertised in the press, technically illegal and opposed by the Home Office, but providing a financial revenue stream for the General Post Office and for newspapers.

So there were divided views in Parliament. Tory governments were particularly unwilling to act. Even the Liberals realized that if they acted on gambling they were likely to offend a large number of voters and so were cautious in terms of law-making. The large numbers of Catholic lotteries attracted complaints motivated by religious protestant sectarianism, but promoters were often based in southern Ireland. So this, too, was difficult politically.

Though there were police prosecutions of public house landlords for allowing betting, few lost their licences as a result. There was much uncertainty surrounding the law, and there were institutional and operational divisions between the police, who had responsibility for enforcing the law, and the Home Office. There were also major problems of interpretation and implementation. Gambling law was regularly attacked both in the press and by members of the public as 'class legislation', attacking only working-class betting. Legislation was piecemeal, full of anomalies and contradictions.

One strategy used by local authorities opposed to street betting was to encourage local police to prosecute bookmakers and betters for pavement obstruction. Bylaws against street betting were becoming more common by the 1880s but it was only in the mid-1890s that many London councils like West Ham began to introduce them. The police rarely prosecuted unless pressured by reformers, an indication that despite the Acts betting was not generally regarded as a vice. Policing needed public consent. Even the Metropolitan Police, whose figures were the highest of any town or city, still seemingly recognized that the laws were almost unenforceable. The laws were unpopular and there was widespread evasion. They made only sporadic efforts at enforcement, usually only in response to respectable complaints and expressions of outrage. By the late nineteenth century, it is clear that many policemen were unwilling to act. They looked the other way. Others colluded with bookmakers for financial benefit.[51] In Liverpool, a leading betting centre, there were only twelve convictions for betting and gaming in 1894. In 1898, in Middlesbrough, the police patrolled the local 'betting ground', not to make arrests for betting, but to see that good order was maintained there.[52]

Middle-class gambling

Support for gambling

Middle-class gambling had a far lower public profile than that of the wealthy, and has received little academic attention. The press gave it reluctant coverage, and middle-class men shunned publicity. To interfere with middle-class gambling clearly appeared to be an undue interference with personal freedom. Some middle-class men enjoyed gaming, but with the wider availability of cheap newspapers and rapid telegraph communication, betting on future horse races provided a more common leisure interest. This spread downwards within the middle class as young, unmarried clerks and others found themselves with some spare money to risk. By the late 1860s, it could be claimed that 'in these days, particularly amongst what may be called the lower middle-classes, to bet is the rule and not to bet is the exception'.[53] As the *Worcester Journal* of 18 May 1889 pointed out, 'there is a very large middle-class element and of the blame for all kinds of gambling this class must bear a very heavy proportion'. In the late nineteenth century there was a widespread belief that gambling was increasing amongst the middle classes. A committee of the Church of England's Convocation of Canterbury argued that 'amongst the middle classes ... there was *undoubtedly* [my italics] a large increase in gambling and betting'.[54]

Prevalence of gaming

It was largely in London that 'common' gaming houses initially attracted significant middle-class custom, especially in Covent Garden and the East End. In 1838, there were already about twenty-five of these with some staying open all day as well as much of the night.[55] The main gambling games played were hazard, whist and piquet. Roulette tables were also available.

Such gaming was illegal but was hard to prosecute. The police were reluctant to act, despite their knowledge of such clubs, and raids were spasmodic. Almost all gaming houses had barred windows and solid, metal-plated doors which had to be broken down, giving the players more time to conceal evidence; codes of signals alerted the players. There were also ways of escape across roofs or through tunnels. It was common knowledge that some police officers were in the pay of proprietors and could provide warning.[56] It was, thought one newspaper editor, 'next to an impossibility to procure sufficient proof'.[57] Anti-gambling magistrates might still convict, but other magistrates, more supportive of gaming, sometimes discharged the defendants. Convictions depended very much on the distribution of legal power in the community.

Certainly the few named defendants in police raids on 'common gaming houses' were usually middle-class. One near Wormwood Scrubs, in 1869, for example, bagged a clockmaker, interpreter, commercial traveller, chronometer finisher, tailor, provision dealer, cabinet maker, coffee-house keeper, printer, cattle dealer and two commission agents.[58] A raid on the Adelphi Club in a middle-class area of London, in 1889, also identified a large middle-class involvement. By then throughout the country there were many similar premises offering smaller-scale gaming facilities, and in 1898 Ashton's *History of Gambling in England* claimed that they abounded, 'thanks to the laxity of the law with regard to so-called clubs'.[59]

Betting on horse-racing and other sports

Informal middle-class wagering could be found in many sports from pugilism (bare-knuckle boxing) and golf to cricket, which regularly attracted betting on grounds before and during the game up to and beyond the 1860s, although thereafter its growing association with Britishness and amateurism diminished its presence. Football seems to have attracted informal wagers by those in the stadium. Greyhound-coursing attracted betting too, with the Waterloo Cup, established in 1836 at Altcar, and named after a Liverpool public house, the key event for leading owners, mostly middle and upper class.[60]

But horse-racing was the most popular male middle-class betting activity. Middle-class papers such as *The Times* and *Morning Post*, regional papers such as the *York Herald* and the *Yorkshire Gazette*, and the sporting paper *Bell's Life in London* were already giving substantial space to horse-race betting information well before 1837. This has rarely been a theme explored by historians, since it seldom surfaced in contemporary anti-gambling material. The middle classes provided strong support for horse-racing through their contribution to race funds, race-course share ownership and organization, office-holding in the industry, and race-horse ownership, though some raced their race-horses under assumed names to maintain respectability.[61] From Newcastle and Newmarket to Doncaster and Derby, middle-class town councillors were happy to support their traditional race-meetings for their economic benefits and to ignore local objectors. When Doncaster's vicar, the Rev. Dr Vaughan, wrote to the Town Council in 1869 complaining at their encouragement of races which he saw as accompanied by 'social and moral evils' and the encouragement of 'indolent vice and reckless venture', the Council meeting ruled that no notice should be taken of his letter and ironically pointed out that the income from the races aided the town and allowed grants for charitable and religious objects, including a contribution of £10,000 for the parish church.[62] Some deflected arguments against betting by pointing to the speculation daily taking place on the London Stock Exchange, or the various commodity exchanges elsewhere. These could be offered as industrial and commercial parallels to gambling. An 1854 *Times* editorial, whilst opposed to gambling, accepted that the English were 'the most gambling company in the world, and our mercantile classes the worst in speculation'.[63]

Middle-class men (and their wives and families) could be found at meetings, usually in the grandstand, in substantial numbers. A dominant press image was of women getting attendant men to place bets for them. In the 1850s, attendees of Shrewsbury races included a wine merchant, a law stationer, a commission bookmaker, the Jockey Club's secretary and banker, a rentier, a surgeon, a saddler and a farmer. At Liverpool's summer Aintree meeting there were 'earls, viscounts, noble lords, honourable captains, gallant admirals, members of Parliament, magistrates, aldermen, town councillors, merchants, brokers, publicans, business men of every grade'.[64]

Middle-class betting took place on and off the course, in betting rooms and clubs, with commission agents on credit, or via postal cash bookmakers.[65] In 1847, *Bell's Life*, then claiming 27,000 readers, generally included between twenty and thirty advertisements from London and regional commission agents aimed at 'country' betters offering to take bets at then current odds.[66] By the 1870s, legal credit bookmakers, whose customers usually needed a bank recommendation and a salary, were operating in many towns across the country. Customers included merchants and industrialists, members of professions like lawyers or doctors, tradesmen, shopkeepers and clerks. Most middle-class gentlemen's clubs provided facilities too, since there too the law could not interfere.

From the 1870s, the middle classes could also use the betting clubs opened by wealthier bookmakers, receiving racing information on tape machines via the telegraph, and later the telephone. Some clubs demanded introductions and election for members, and annual subscriptions, indicating a largely middle-class membership. In Manchester there were increasing numbers of betting clubs in the 1870s and early 1880s, though in 1885 the police used 170 men in a major raid, arresting over 200, while Liverpool had over twenty clubs by 1887.[67] Provincial clubs such as Stockton's Victoria Club (1881) or Nottingham's Victoria Club (1882) were often named after London's leading betting clubs. The press in such areas regularly reproved the police for failing to take action against what were seen as almost 'approved' or 'authorized' clubs, despite the law. Such action was rare.

While many magistrates were opposed to betting, others were consistently reluctant to convict, dismissed cases or issued minimal fines, revealing tacit acceptance of its practices. In Sheffield, opponents felt that 'magistrates, mayors, aldermen and constables' all ignored the street crowds of all ages and both genders betting their shillings and half crowns on races.[68] Sometimes magistrates insisted on observing the letter of the law, and pointed out a weakness in the police case to allow the case to lapse. Minimal fines were commonplace. When in 1869 an informer summonsed a number of leading bookmakers for having offices at Ascot to take bets on the meeting, the five magistrates were 'unanimous' in giving only a 'nominal' penalty.[69]

The increasing popularity of sweepstakes

The 1823 Lotteries Act and other prohibitive laws against public and private lotteries likewise always had only limited effect. For those trusting to pure chance and the remote dream of drawing the ticket containing the name of the winning horse and gaining a huge win for a small stake, an alternative form of betting, the sweepstake, was already growing in popularity as early as the 1840s. Many newspapers contained advertisements from sweepstake organizers, their competitions based on leading horse races. A few were fraudulent but most simply commercial enterprises. From the 1850s, occasional social gambling on these 'sweeps' was becoming part of much home and office life, even though technically illegal. By the 1880s, the 'Derby sweep' on the Epsom horserace was an institution in most banks, insurance offices and warehouses, especially in the south of England. There was social pressure to take part. Indeed the Stock Exchange sweep on the Derby, begun in 1882, charged brokers a £100 a ticket, and had substantial prizes, though almost everybody would 'draw a blank'. The other major office sweep was the Oxford versus Cambridge Boat Race.

Consequences and problems

Substantial gambling losses amongst the middle classes occasionally surfaced. In December 1838, for example, *The Times* contained an appeal on behalf of a widow 'of exemplary character' and four orphans, reduced to want because her husband Samuel Mumford, a 'respectable' young man from Stansted, had become addicted to 'the vice of gambling', neglected his business and lost his property. He had left his family in destitution and committed suicide. The widow now 'earnestly and respectfully' entreated donations to maintain herself and her children. Such tragic tales were not uncommon, and whilst this story may have been untrue, a confidence trick, such moralistic narratives drew charity and sympathy for the victims of middle-class male gambling.[70]

In terms of gaming, reports of middle-class involvement more commonly only surfaced when they themselves were cheated, rather than their active cheating. In 1858, for example, John Sidebottom, in his late twenties, a member of a large Manchester-based cotton-manufacturing firm, lost £25,000 playing with crooked dice at the Berkeley Club. When he began to lose again he became suspicious and stopped a further cheque, and took the men concerned to court.[71]

Middle-class betting scandals likewise surfaced rarely. One of the most publicized was the 1855 press coverage of the life of medical doctor William Palmer (1824–56) which became a salutary and sensational example of gambling's dangers. He was born into a wealthy family but his was a tragic tale of 'vice and profligacy', illicit sex and risking all to back his and others' race-horses for far more than he could afford. It was a melancholy melodrama ending in the highly suspicious death of a friend. The press painted a fanciful picture of his disreputable medical student life.[72] He became an indulgent church-attending husband, but also an increasingly heavy gambler, owning and running race-horses, attending race-meetings from Newcastle to Brighton. He was soon in heavy debt. He was a philanderer, who fathered two illegitimate children, one on his wife's maid. The modern clinical recognition of links between pathological addiction to reckless gambling and compulsive sexual behaviour perhaps offers an explanation, although he appears to have tried to avoid excessive drinking.[73] He heavily insured the life of his wife and brother, who both soon died. The insurance company refused to pay the second claim. By November 1855 Palmer owed £11,000 he could not pay. When his racing partner, John Cook, died after dining with him, and Palmer was understood to have purchased strychnine shortly before, he was accused of murder. His lifestyle ensured that press and prosecution blackened his name still further with hints at up to fifteen poisonings. As a doctor he had attended dying family and friends to whom he owed money. Despite lack of any conclusive post-mortem poison indications, strong circumstantial evidence pointed to his guilt. Deliberately sensationalized detailed press reports covered his trial. Several books were published almost immediately afterwards.[74] He was hanged outside Stafford jail, watched by a curious crowd of over 30,000, attracted by his celebrity and his unrespectable lifestyle.

Far more usual were reports of white-collar cases of fraud where clerks or other middle-class employees robbed employers to feed their betting habit or where employers went bankrupt through betting. These were gleefully seized on as evidence of betting's corruptive nature. According to *Lloyd's Weekly Newspaper*, in 1865, the betting young man 'neglects his business or profession . . . losses lead him into temptation and he embezzles'.[75]

Policing and governmental responses to middle-class gambling

These were limited. Because middle-class betting was largely socially invisible, legal on the race-course and on credit and carried out off-course by telegraph and post rather than with street bookmakers, it was not of major concern to police, the Home Office or to the government. However, Lord Palmerston's Gaming Houses Act of 1854 was directed in part at middle-class gaming, and imposed penalties on owners and occupiers of 'reputed gaming houses'. It explicitly made such middle-class 'common' gaming houses illegal and increased police powers of entry and search. It also proscribed cheating, and provided that all gaming and wagering contracts would henceforth be unenforceable by law.

Nevertheless, many continued clandestinely, sometimes enjoying a measure of tacit protection from the police. The gentlemen's clubs in London continued to have little hindrance. The Metropolitan Police and Home Office showed limited interest in London's middle-class gambling clubs, pursuing a policy of what the press described as 'masterly inactivity', so that they experienced long periods of immunity from prosecution. Generally, middle-class gaming and betting was very limited in terms of police regulatory activity.

Conclusion

The anti-gambling groups were numerically small, but had power, passion and elite position, enjoying privileged access to magistrates and Parliament. To them, gambling was a vice, attacked on moral and social grounds, while the commercial industry that catered for its seductive influences and destructive tendencies, especially bookmakers and those running gaming rooms, was seen as especially evil. Despite this, gambling proved very resilient to opposition, whether from moral and social campaigners, police or government. Governmental legislation, including the 1845 Gaming Act and the 1853 Betting Houses Act and its 1874 follow-up proved ineffective, as did local authority by-laws to control street gambling. The laws against gaming houses and bookmakers were only occasionally enforced.

Although class prejudice continued to be a consistent element in gambling legislation through the Victorian period and beyond, gambling and betting could be found across all classes and in many different forms. Gaming and betting on racing amongst the middle and upper classes was usually just an exciting aspect of their leisure experience, though a few gambled to excess and bankrupted themselves. Some families suffered through betting. A few faced ruination. Working-class gambling was viewed far more unsympathetically by the legislature because of its detrimental social impact and because the working and industrious community could least afford it. But alongside the rise in working-class real incomes in the second half of the century, off-course betting on horse-racing, and other opportunities for betting became a major leisure interest for many in this class. It attracted regular complaints. However, despite the extreme views and wild exaggerations of the moralist anti-gambling lobbies, few working people gambled compulsively, and there was little firm evidence of any link between working-class gambling and extreme poverty.

By the end of the century, gambling was a regular occurrence in the lives of a majority of the British population, generally accepted, despite the illegality of many of its forms but the tensions remained unresolved. Many religious and respectable reformers still believed that gambling was a growing and dangerous vice. In less observantly religious families, the belief that betting was a longstanding and pleasurable sporting tradition and also a commercial activity was often deeply culturally embedded. Its attractions had ensured its self-sustaining growth, popularity and acceptance amongst the working classes as standards of living rose. So the laws against gambling were generally, indeed almost invariably, ignored or disregarded.

CHAPTER FIVE

Sexuality, Pornography and Prostitution

While drink and gambling might harm individuals and families, it was 'sexual vices' that offered the greatest potential threat to Victorian society. Sex within marriage was always respectable, though wider popular morality often tacitly accepted premarital sexual activity in the context of a clearly established courtship relationship and promise of marriage. Many other sexual activities challenged gender-specific cultural anxieties about relationships, patriarchal practices of domination and control, or conventional respectable life.

Here as elsewhere the focus was often on working-class vices. Middle-class sexual vices usually remained less publicized. A Manchester example illustrates this well. John Potter (1815–58), educated at Edinburgh University, ran a large wholesale drapers' merchant's firm in Manchester, and became an alderman in 1845. He was clearly popular amongst the Manchester electorate, and was mayor there three times. He was a Deputy Lieutenant of the County Palatine and his status was further recognized when he was knighted by Queen Victoria in 1851 and elected as a Liberal MP for Manchester in 1857.

But how respectable was he? Friedrich Engels, the German socialist writer, who privately lived in Manchester in an unmarried sexual relationship with the working-class radical Mary Burns, took a sceptical view. Commenting to a friend on Potter's election, he suggested he was

> a great hunter after prostitutes ... and is especially intimate with the celebrated Miss Chester (alias Polly Evans), whom he has twice got pregnant, and to whose legal expenses he contributed £50 when she appeared at the Liverpool Assizes... [He is] popular with the prostitutes, cab drivers, publicans, street arabs [homeless street urchins] and the less respectable elements amongst the citizenry. When he was Mayor the prostitutes experienced a respite from police harassment'.[1]

Who was this Miss Chester? She was well known in Manchester as an upmarket brothel *madame*. In 1852, when she was aged twenty-four and the keeper of a disreputable house in Major Street, she was charged at Liverpool Assizes, along with another girl of twenty-six, with inducing an abortion. Even then she was able to find two sureties of £100, and retain a costly 'eminent council'. Both women were acquitted.[2] Presumably Potter had helped with expenses. Much of what we know about her comes from her book *Memoirs of Madame Chester of Manchester* (undated but c. 1868), though it is a stock exemplar of the genre and so needs to be sceptically read. Despite her occupation, its content was never explicit about sexual matters, but covered her leisure and social life of balls, theatres, dinner parties and so on. She described herself leaving home at fifteen and living with a young officer and then moving to Manchester, and spending some time in France, London and elsewhere, while often kept by rich men.

Her memoirs suggest that many of her clients, and those of her 'girls', were the 'respectable' upper and middle class: rich Manchester merchants, 'first-class gentlemen' (some titled), 'swells', the 'son of a very rich cotton lord', a Manchester restaurant owner, someone in 'the upholstery business', and a number of 'officers', often enjoying her company, playing cards, spending money freely, and drinking heavily at her premises. Many were described as being the 'worse for liquor', 'fuddled' or 'palatic drunk' when there.

Despite her occupation, her clientele seems to have largely protected her from prosecution and she was known to be on good terms with the police. Her only major court appearance was in 1868 when she was still running an upmarket brothel and night-club. One of her customers, William Taylor, a respectable well-off wool merchant, carrying on business in Birmingham, Bradford and elsewhere, appears to have tried to avoid paying her for the 'facilities' offered by giving her only a half of a £50 Bank of England note, borrowing £10 and later leaving without paying up. After some weeks he went back with a local police inspector, demanding the £50 half-note back, after finding his bank would not reimburse him for its 'loss'. He appears to have hoped that the threat of court action would make her hand it over, but the police inspector merely tried to mediate. Taylor prosecuted her in Birmingham, not Manchester, to have it returned. Chester again employed a QC though she was portrayed as a 'prostitute', running a 'house of ill-fame', who had been 'driven to a course of wickedness and vice'. Even so the jury did not believe Taylor, and found for her. But because they believed the money was 'for carrying on debauchery and for immoral purposes' the financial charges she made were unlawful, so she received no money, while Taylor did not receive the note and paid costs.[3]

This case study of John Potter, Friedrich Engels, William Taylor and Miss Chester sheds light on the less respectable side of Victorian middle-class sexual life, but for many Victorians sexuality was far more problematic. Respectable people perceived the dangers and temptations, demoralization and debauchery of sexuality everywhere: in the overcrowded slums where males and females slept together; in Yorkshire pits where naked miners slaved alongside working-class women; in London where newly-arrived girls were trapped into prostitution; even in the dormitories of public schools.

The Victorian age was simultaneously obsessed with virginity, purity and sexual promiscuity. There was widespread fear and negative attitudes towards sexual issues such as adultery, bigamy, and prostitution. These could stem from the dictates of evangelical religion, possible marriage to the wrong person, the costly economic consequences of raising children, or the medical dangers associated with pregnancy and childbirth. They might be associated with the calamitous social problems of illegitimacy, the threat of syphilis and other contagious sexual diseases, or the sheer power of overwhelming desire. Both men and women could feel shame, guilt, embarrassment, sexual threat and anxiety. As a consequence discretion or disapproval meant that most people avoided discussion of the topic in respectable contexts.

Chapter outline

For these more respectable groups in Victorian society, sex and vice were closely connected. So this chapter begins with a chronological overview of the topic. This is followed by discussion of the way sexual topics were addressed in the print media, and the ways these were affected by themes of class and gender. Some of the main areas perceived as sexual vices are next explored in turn: premarital sex and adultery, the 'great social evil' of prostitution, sexually-transmitted diseases, pornography, masturbation, and same-sex relationships.

Chronology

Many historians recognize a series of different chronologies, changes and continuities relating to Victorian sexuality. The age is too long for simple summing up, with attitudes to sexuality in a state of flux. What limited consensus there is suggests an initial period of fairly general moral restraint, often with a current of anti-sensuality, peaking between 1830 and 1850. This drew on evangelical protestant sermonizing and secular rationalists wanting more masculine 'self-control', exercised through conscience, continence and chastity. Such views surfaced in a variety of contemporary discourse. Female sexual desire became viewed as problematical and sexuality generally became more suspect. Initially, legislation was limited and uneven. An 1839 Metropolitan Police Act prohibited the 'common prostitute' from soliciting 'to the annoyance of inhabitants or passengers' and in 1847 similar legislation was applied to places outside London. A Bill for the more Effectual Suppression of Brothels and of Trading in Seduction and Prostitution was introduced into the Lords in 1842 by the evangelical Bishop of Exeter. It failed. The Earl of Oxford and other evangelical reformers gained an Act for the Protection of Women in 1849. Its impact was minimal. A series of Disorderly Houses Acts enabled local authorities to prosecute brothels for disturbing the peace. The 1857 Matrimonial Causes Act enabled couples to obtain a divorce through civil proceedings, but women divorced on the grounds of adultery had no legal right to their children.

Victorian attitudes to sexual morality were sometimes linked to the control of family size.[4] In the 1840s, the extension of wage labour which had created more better-off and independent young people was linked to early marriage, generally high birth rates and very large families. Children were a social and financial responsibility; a burden and not a benefit, until they were old enough to earn money. Limiting fertility and delaying marriage until a family could be supported became a lifestyle choice, especially for middle-class males. Some sought their sexual pleasure in other contexts. The 1860s were briefly more 'permissive' though still attracting concern. The mid-Victorian era simultaneously saw a high valuation given to marriage, home and children, and the huge popularity of sensation novels featuring passionate women. Moralism and male scientific investigation began to produce ideas of orthodox human sexuality based on a combination of medical/biological and social ideas, with men sometimes portrayed as 'naturally' polygamous. Moralists often saw male sexuality as an almost irresistible force, though such 'dangerous sexualities' needed to be checked. Restrictions on female sexual autonomy and choice were severe. Men asserted what was acceptable and attempted to control women's sexuality. In one admittedly very rare case, Dr Baker Brown, a former President of the Medical Society of London, gained temporary notoriety in 1858 for what we now call female genital mutilation. He treated his patients with hysteria by the drastic measure of removing the clitoris, sometimes without their full knowledge and consent.

Thereafter concerns and conflicts grew. The 1870s saw a temporary flight from middle-class domesticity, with more men marrying later or not at all.[5] Some men 'kept themselves pure'. Others found temptation too attractive, whilst maintaining a long engagement to a respectable girl. For most Victorians direct control of conception without loss of sexual pleasure was unknown. Couples in all classes increasingly chose to limit and plan family size, partly within a culture of more regular abstinence, and perhaps more eroticized anticipation. A significant proportion of middle-class men remained bachelors, becoming prime customers for urban sexual entertainments. The rise of feminism and women's rights led to campaigning against the notorious Contagious Diseases Acts that attempted to deal with sexually transmitted disease and its effects especially in the armed services. Evangelical Christians attacked sexual licence amongst young men.

Modern historians, from Foucault onwards, have argued for an 'explosion' of changes in sexual attitudes and in public and private ways of talking about and dealing with sexual issues around 1880, peaking more openly by the 1890s.[6] Legal, cultural and moral concerns attracted widespread interest. With more application of science to study of sex the medical and legal professions, reformers, educators, women's organizations, Nonconformist Christians and other anti-vice groups, were all keen to construct and impose their own sexual and moral behavioural 'norms'. Evolutionary ideas of male sexuality as a biological imperative were challenged by those who claimed that the civilizing process should enable them to transcend animal instincts. In the late 1880s, there was a female-dominated Social Purity campaign against sexual double standards and patriarchal assumptions about morality, and for male as well as female celibacy outside marriage. Campaigners raised renewed concern about prostitution and young girls, theatrical indecency and publicly-displayed images of naked women. They also attacked male prostitution in the cities and the schoolboy relationships found in the public schools.

The Criminal Law Amendment Act of 1885 for 'the protection of women and girls, the suppression of brothels and other purposes' was one result. An amendment made acts of gross indecency between males whether committed in public or private a misdemeanour liable to imprisonment for upto two years. This and the trial of Oscar Wilde in 1895 were key stages in making homosexual relations and intimate friendship between men 'unmanly' and illegal.[7] Those behaving differently, whether homosexuals or masturbators, could be defined as 'impure', deviant or pathological, upsetting heterosexual bourgeois morality and social order.

In late Victorian Britain, individual sexuality was perceived as a vexing social problem, partly as a result of debates about women's social, legal, political and economic position, a widening of male suffrage, and an increasingly powerful middle class keen to assert its respectable values. Respectable moral pressures may be one reason that over the Victorian age, the proportion of illegitimate births declined, though this is debated.

Sex and the print media

The period is particularly complex, because although there were powerful behavioural codes, constraining what was and what was not accepted as proper to discuss in print, these spread across and within classes, and varied with time, place and context. There was always a certain amount of boundary negotiation. Victorian mores and discourse allowed for rigidity or fluidity, complexity and contradiction. There were regular flurries of moral panic and condemnation, often followed by decreasing interest in the topic. On the one hand, sex was portrayed as problematic, linked to female subordination or sexual fears. On the other, it formed part of commercial leisure, personal relationships or socializing in new social spaces.

For what people did or said, current context was all. The novelist Mary Ann Evans (George Eliot), for example, constructed her models of female sexuality in the context of dominant Victorian social norms. Her novels were famous for their high moral tone, but she also lived openly with her lover, George Lewes. His wife had had children by three other men, which he had accepted, so he could not divorce. It caused the couple scandal and heartache.

Charles Dickens's books extolled the virtues of pure-minded domesticity. He even attacked G.M.W. Reynolds' mildly erotic sensation novels as pandering to 'the basest passions of the lowest natures'. Yet he disliked his wife's constant pregnancy and consequent increase in size. The couple separated shortly after she discovered Dickens's affair with the much younger actress Ellen Ternan, whom he pursued round the country, before setting her up in a small house in Slough, which he took under a false name to conceal the relationship when she left the stage to be with him.[8] She accompanied him when visiting France, but not to America where he felt press publicity might damage his reputation. Here again, Dickens's behaviour was tailored to context.

Some Victorians certainly *were* factually uninformed, hugely embarrassed or emotionally frigid about sexual matters, or addressed the topic through cautious reticence and modesty, giving little of their private lives away. But the period also saw the introduction of 'modern' conceptualizations of sex and active female sexuality, presenting sexuality in multiple ways. Apparently moral writings, for example, were sometimes heavy with erotic subtext, hidden desire and sexual preoccupation. Sensational newspaper sexual scandal reports showed how the Victorians imagined sexuality and sexual transgressions, as well as indicating what could and what could not easily be talked about.[9] By the 1870s, even respectable newspapers were being attacked for defiling their columns 'with matters which cannot but be injurious to public morality and destructive of public virtue'.[10] Sometimes sexual temptations were indirectly discussed through another issue. In 1868, the *Daily Telegraph* received 281 letters, largely from young lower middle-class men, clerks and tradesmen, about the difficulties they faced in working away from family social support or affection. Some had deferred marriage while awaiting sufficient money (perhaps £150 to £300 per annum) and position to maintain a wife in the standard of domestic life similar to that of their parents. Many letters described the sexual 'temptations of immorality' while they waited.[11] Later, in 1888, it ran a series on 'Is marriage a failure?' and got over 27,000 letters in ten weeks.

Some newspapers, such as the *Illustrated Police News* (from 1864) provided tabloid-like salacious coverage of the law-court details of crime and vice. Even respectable newspaper editors, by the 1880s, were well aware that publicly supporting virtue, yet simultaneously providing detailed and increasingly sensational descriptions of the vices they fought, such as child prostitution, sold large numbers of newspapers. The resulting debates over how much to report, and the relationship between press coverage and respectable public morality, were explored in the columns of leading national newspapers. Scientific biomedical and socio-scientific publications such as the *British Medical Journal* and *The Lancet* saw sex as a legitimate subject for research and discussion, while popular songs and bawdy poems were full of sexual innuendo.

But there was strong opposition to providing sexual information to the wider public, even on contraceptive knowledge and methods, as the famous obscenity trial of Annie Besant and Charles Bradlaugh for publishing a sixpenny 'indecent, lewd, filthy, bawdy, and obscene' book on the subject in 1877 made clear.[12] Such actions protected masculine privilege, and protected public morals while limiting legal intervention. Around mid-century, for example, there were widespread press and medical complaints about the 'disgraceful' inclusion in many papers of 'defiling', immoral and 'obscene' advertisements from publishers for materials variously called 'Silent Friend', 'Vital Regenerators' or 'Guides to Manhood'. These covered guidance on topics such as impotence (for which many newspapers advertised pills 'to restore youthful vigour'), sexually transmitted diseases or masturbation, and provided explicit physiological engravings of 'the organs of generation'. The Silent Friend's advertisements, which even featured in *The Times*, claimed it to be the 'greatest medical work of the age' on 'youthful indiscretions and consequent impediments to marriage'. It contained 'a prescription, known as the preventative lotion, preventing the possibility of contamination.'[13] The 'vile nature of the traffic', regard for public welfare, decency and honour supposedly demanded that such advertisements be stopped. Yet such material had been around since at least the 1830s and continued to be sold throughout the century.

Study of Victorian popular fiction, social analysts, newspapers, periodicals or medical texts all show that unrespectable sexual topics were constantly conjectured about, though it is impossible to say how far such discussion permeated private conversation. They show that sex was considered problematic and dangerous, especially but not solely for women, whose moral welfare and modesty were perceived as vital. But loving relationships or other emotional ties, sexual fulfilment within an affectionate companionate marriage and mutual pleasure through sex were also often valued.

Discussion of many dimensions of sexual activity was linked to the language of vice. The uncomfortable 'prevalence of vice' in large towns was a key issue, and sensationalist reporting brought its 'corruption', 'depravity', 'dreadful iniquity', 'atrocious crimes', 'frightful excesses' 'abominable sin' and demoralizing nature to the attention of respectable readers. Sex outside marriage, described as 'fornication', was a major target. For the more evangelical priesthood it was 'the lowest form of sexual irregularity', a 'sin against nature'. Sexual 'indecency', 'impurity', and the vicious offences of 'libertinism' were all likewise high-profile, much-discussed sources of anxiety. In 1865 Henry Butter wrote a book aimed at young men, *Is the Pleasure worth the Penalty: A Common-Sense View of the Leading Vice of the Age*, subtitled, *What's the Harm in Fornication?* It told his readers that fornication, like other vices, was progressive in its nature. Just as drink led to habitual drunkenness and delirium tremens, fornication too carried its punishments: adultery, divorce, illegitimate children, 'virulent' and 'loathsome' sexual diseases, madness, debilitation or death. Anyone professing Christianity should recognize its wicked folly, abstain from lascivious acts, practices, and unchaste thoughts and perform 'mental quarantine'. Sermons in the 1870s and 1880s used the Biblical New Testament narrative of the woman taken in adultery to argue that fornication was the 'leading vice', even if less seen, because it was concealed with 'cunning'.[14]

Class and gender

Victorian society was patriarchal, and class and gender strongly influenced public attitudes to sexual 'vices'.[15] Respectable Victorians often believed that illicit sexual vices were much more prevalent amongst the poorer working classes than elsewhere, thanks to their supposed 'lax morality', not least that of groups such as costermongers or factory girls.[16] They felt girls' public behaviour was shocking, though they failed to acknowledge the lack of access to domestic privacy in working-class life; foregrounding low-status female working-class wrong-doing did not offend or frighten middle-class women.

Equally, there were other stereotypes such as the upper-class debaucher. Respectable men were supposed to be good providers and chivalrous defenders of women's virtue and naïvely believed to be most unlikely to exploit vulnerable women. By contrast upper and upper-middle 'gentlemen' or sons of the newly-rich commercial business group were regularly represented in newspapers, melodrama and fictional literature as libertine seducers of working-class girls and female domestic servants. They were portrayed as predators, roués and perpetrators of sexual harassment, and supposedly the group that kept prostitutes in business.[17] In Dickens's *David Copperfield* (1850), pretty little Emily was seduced and ruined by the 'gentleman' Steerforth. In Eliot's *Silas Marner* (1861), Molly Farren, a barmaid, contracted marriage secretly with Godfrey, the squire's eldest son, but when she was pregnant he failed to acknowledge her. She turned to drink and laudanum and died in the snow. In another of Eliot's novels, *Adam Bede* (1859), Hetty Sorrel, a beautiful but naïve, vain and pleasure-loving country girl, was seduced by young squire Captain Arthur Donnithorne, who had little intention of marrying her. Following the birth of his child she abandoned the baby in a field and was tried and found guilty of infanticide. In Hardy's *Tess of the d'Urbervilles: A Pure Woman Faithfully Presented* (1891), Tess, from a poor village family, was seduced by libertine Alec d'Urberville, a gentleman, and her life from then on spiralled downwards. Hardy pointed up the sexual double standard, to which Tess falls victim. As the book's title indicates, Tess was portrayed as being a truly good woman, but despised by society after losing her virginity before marriage.

Another dominant image was that of the 'kept' woman, the adulterous mistress or lover kept in accommodation elsewhere often while the man lived with his wife. In the way Victorian artists, journalists and novelists portrayed this, one dominant motif was one of power, with better-off males taking advantage of their social position to seduce poorer females, though there was often some sympathy, and the suggestion of possible redemption for such girls. It was the upper classes which were often blamed. To one correspondent to *Reynolds's News* in 1886 squires and lords were 'a rapacious caste who look upon no social sin and no scandal as disgraceful as long as they can plunder the people'. The paper gleefully reported any 'astounding revelations on the lives and vices of the wealthy'.[18]

Such class-based stereotypes need to be treated with caution. The records of the London Foundling Hospital in the years from 1840 to 1870 contained many deeply poignant letters and statements from mothers of babies, their neighbours and relatives, employers and lovers. Many of the girls had been in domestic service or employment, and they usually claimed to have been seduced and abandoned. This was sometimes by the wealthy, or employers and their sons, but sometimes too by men from a similar social background.[19]

More generally, however, the double standard ensured that blame for sexual 'vice' fell on women rather than men. Breach of promise cases, for example, show that for some men, once a woman agreed to sex, she failed to be virtuous and chaste and so lost all respect and 'character', while they did not. It was the women who were viewed as 'defiled', and would 'attract disgrace'. Like prostitutes they were often (mis)represented as purely passive victims. Their sexual history would be scrutinized, men got off scot free. The Divorce Law of 1857 laid down that male adultery was not a matrimonial crime unless exacerbated by other offences, while female adultery on its own was sufficient reason for divorce. Male writers sometimes portrayed respectable women as devoted domestic angels, moral and virtuous, passive and powerless, and above all pure, untainted by physical desire. Even George Eliot, in *Adam Bede*, portrayed her 'good' female character, the fervent Methodist preacher Dinah Morris, as completely pure, unselfish, modest, and unfailingly generous and sympathetic. Much male medical science believed that men were passionate, driven by the social and psychic forces of their sex drive, while women were basically without much sexual feeling.

In Victorian sources terms such as 'fallen' women, 'wayward' girls, or 'deviants' were all used as metaphors suggesting transgression and movement away from the 'right' and 'normal', respectable, Godly way, and falling into temptation and vice, and yielding their chastity. 'Fallen' identities were varied, and were often the result of abuse or sexual exploitation. A parliamentary Select Committee enquiring into venereal disease in 1867, for example, felt that prostitutes and other 'fallen women' 'for the most part were victims of seduction'.[20]

The term fallen sometimes included any woman engaging in non-married sex, but usually one either visibly unmarried and pregnant, living with a man out of wedlock, a mother of illegitimate children, or engaged in prostitution, though occasionally women alcoholics, delinquently working-class or over-sexually responsive women were included too. For women, marriage was a key indication of respectability. 'Living in sin' was frowned upon, though becoming more common.[21] As town populations grew, their greater anonymity made single women socially and economically more vulnerable. The previous networks of support from extended families and kinship groups when relationships failed or difficulties occurred were less powerful. Family opposition or class differences might put pressure on young men not to marry. Pregnant servants usually lost their jobs. Shamed parents might throw a girl out, as her pregnancy attracted social censure, humiliation and often shame. Getting financial support from the child's father was hard, and the resulting economic and social difficulties were so grave that many women handed over their babies to foundling hospitals and orphanages, or in real desperation committed infanticide. Fallen women represented a moral contagion, and daughters might be hidden away when unmarried and pregnant to remove them from the gaze of respectable society.

Yet the fallen state involved strange inconsistencies and many paradoxes.[22] Girls seduced in promise of marriage, or 'respectable' girls who had made one slip often got a substantial amount of sympathy from judges, juries, or foundling hospital governors and matrons. Novelists such as Dickens and Hardy also showed sympathy for their plight. On the other hand, rape trials were rarely mounted, unless the woman was respectable, was raped by a clearly 'bestial' working-class man, or violence was clearly used. Guilty verdicts were rare. Victorian middle-class male jurors were obsessed by 'false' accusations, especially when it was the domestic servant or employee who accused the 'respectable' gentleman.

Prostitutes were demonized and victimized, yet had more freedom than wives to control what they did with their bodies. They could sell sexual favours commercially, and for a few women there might be at least temporary upward mobility. Prostitution was a leisured and profitable occupation for a few. It improved their circumstances and aided family finances.

So press images were ambiguous. Writers were restricted by the expectations of their middle-class respectable readers so had to be condemnatory, even sometimes implying that loss of virtue suggested moral corruption. But simultaneously they wanted to elicit sympathy and sentiment, so such women were often presented as remorseful and unthreatening to the respectable, while both paintings and novels were also often full of pathos. Rather than condemning 'fallen women' the reader or viewer was often left feeling sympathy and pity for their plight, and blaming the seducer.

Pre-marital sex and adultery

Despite secular and religious reformers' idealization of chastity, and attempts to establish overt social pressures to support it, 'irregular' sexual activity was not uncommon. There were long-established and customary courtship norms, with premarital sex as a commitment indicator in longer-term relationships, often following professions of love and proposals of marriage. There is ample evidence that many couples anticipated marriage, or married once a baby was on the way. The ratio of illegitimate births was relatively low, especially in urban areas, and highest in rural counties like Norfolk and Hereford.[23] Though disapproved of, in breach of promise cases a woman who had sexual intercourse only with her fiancée was considered a victim. It made little or no difference in the setting of damages.[24] In England about 25 per cent of such cases had involved sex between the couple. In working-class London the figure was certainly higher, with female servants, for example, more concerned about pregnancy in practical rather than prudish ways, and aware of the dangers of deception and insincerity.[25] Couples often waited many months, making love infrequently, in hastily improvised conditions, perhaps after parents had gone to bed, in stables or out of doors. Finding time and places to be alone was often difficult. In one 1886 breach of promise case, Mary Wilkinson claimed that after telling her family he wished to be engaged to her, and a courtship of over a year, William Hampson first had sex with her in a railway carriage between Manchester and Leigh.[26]

Any sexual activity outside marriage was seen by the respectable as wrong. On the subject of sex, St Paul's teaching had always been clear. His first letter to the Corinthians stated that 'neither fornicators nor adulterers ... shall possess the Kingdom of God'.[27] All the Christian churches were alert to encourage a purer attitude. In the Church of England, for example, the Church Discipline Act enabled bishops to set up commissions to accuse clergy who 'offended under the laws ecclesiastical' by being 'guilty of the foul crimes of fornication, adultery, incontinence and immoral conduct' with named women, 'thereby bringing great scandal on the Church'.

The press always demonstrated a perverse fascination with such cases, providing detailed reports. In 1852, for example, an ecclesiastical court tried the Rev. Dr Thompson, vicar of Kington near Hereford, for adultery, having kept and harboured in his vicarage, over two years, Harriet Blinkes, a married woman who was 'notoriously lewd and unchaste'. The case was covered not just in Hereford, but across the provincial and national press.[28] Some married men kept mistresses, but divorce was difficult. Newspapers reported divorce cases citing adultery, on the ground of public interest, but were often criticized as simply 'parading before the public all the prurient details ... the publicity it gives to sexual vice ... the impurity which it suggests'.[29] In 1886, the Liberal politician Charles Dilke (1843–1911) was disgraced and lost his ministerial post following the divorce-case revelations of an extra-marital affair, though despite moralist opposition he was re-elected in 1892. In 1891, the Irish Nationalist MP Charles Stewart Parnell lost his seat. He had had a long-standing affair with Kitty O'Shea, the wife of another Irish MP, but the husband sued for divorce, and the Roman Catholic Church attacked Parnell.[30]

The great social evil: prostitution

Feminist historians have been prominent in what has been a significant body of work on Victorian prostitution in recent years, with detailed studies of locations such as London, York, urban Scotland and Ireland. Much has focused on reformist campaigns to control or abolish it. But there is also material on its organization, making clearer how women came to work as prostitutes, and the extent of desperation, exploitation and false promises and difficult living conditions faced by women exploiting their bodies as commodities. Literary and cultural studies have explored the ways it was constructed within Victorian society.[31] Definitions of prostitution were rarely clear-cut. For some it was a brief stage. Some women moved from unrespectable prostitution into respectable marriage. Ill health, addictions and lack of financial and other resources meant some never left the profession to lead more stable lives.

Prostitution or 'whoring' was perceived by most of British society as a female 'vice' yet a fact of life in a male-dominated society. In the Victorian age attitudes to prostitution were complex and usually moralistic. Some tried to ignore the way it entwined with urban culture. Many others viewed the prostitute as a necessary evil needed to cope with male sexual urges. In 1869, W.A.L. Lecky argued that as 'the supreme type of vice, she is ultimately the most efficient guardian of virtue. But for her, the unchallenged purity of countless happy homes would be polluted'.[32]

From the 1830s, there was increasingly concern about public order and prostitution's visibly flagrant brothel and street manifestations in urban areas, offering social as well as moral contagion, with their 'gross' language and 'great indecency' of *public* behaviour. Only a few publications focused on prostitution between 1800 and 1840, but as it became perceived as a pressing social problem, books and articles proliferated rapidly. Prostitution was too easily seen by the respectable. It simultaneously repelled and fascinated, weighing heavily on the respectable conscience, even if others turned to it. Reformers deliberately publicized it, demanding stricter legislative action. They promoted a sustained cultural campaign of intimidation in their sermons and letters of complaint to the press. Prostitution was socially and culturally constructed under the banner headline of 'The Great Social Evil'. It was eroticized and demonized, represented as a depraved and dangerous element in society, a sexual economy that should be driven underground, made publicly invisible.

In the expanding urban economies and widespread population growth of the 1850s, opposition to the 'circulating harlotry' of the streets gathered further momentum. Its freedom from social (and male) control attracted enraged complaint, condemnation, attempts at legislation and reform movements. Prostitutes were scapegoated into an outcast identity and lifestyle, called 'harlots', 'Jezebels', 'dirty persons', 'shameless women of abandoned character', 'women living loose lives' or 'whores', and projected as social pariahs, 'fallen women', utterly demoralized and abandoned, satisfying the 'demand for vice', different from 'normal' women. But other less negative words were sometimes used for them: 'streetwalkers', 'painted nymphs', 'free companions', 'nymphs of the pave', 'unfortunates', 'females of a certain description', frail sisters', 'the sisterhood', 'wrens', 'Cyprians', 'Hecates' or 'soiled doves'. With rising real wages, some prostitutes could enjoy a measure of economic and personal independence until loss of looks or disease took their toll, by soliciting in increasingly popular commercial leisure locations like the music halls as well as the streets, creating a moral panic.

In theory the police had legal powers to control prostitution, though these were generally used when prostitution became a particular problem and a temporary focus of local public and religious condemnation. Urban police orders often instructed constables to ignore prostitutes if they were not disorderly or being 'indecent'. Arrest figures, largely focused only on street prostitution, are a poor indication of numbers involved, varying with location, reformist activity and patterns of policing. Many prostitutes worked the streets, but brothels were less targeted, as were London's West End establishments offering erotic massages to their customers at the end of the century. There was a decline in convictions after 1885 but this could have been due to successes of social purity activists, a lack of police activity, or to the action of local authorities in shifting prostitution into specific areas away from middle-class view. As in the twentieth century, police relationships with prostitutes, brothel madams and others were complex, with allegations of corruption and the payment of bribes. One letter to *The Times* in 1847, for example, claimed that

> It is also well known that as poor women may be either persecuted or tolerated at the will of any individual policeman, many unprincipled fellows amongst them seem to regard drink and gratuitous favours from these poor creatures as regular perquisites of office.[33]

London was reputed to have huge numbers of prostitutes, and certainly places such as Piccadilly, the Haymarket or the Radcliffe Highway by the Thames were notorious. When Frenchwoman Flora Tristan visited the capital in 1839 she overcame her 'repugnance' and investigated, finding its streets 'full of them'. One evening she and two male friends walked around Waterloo Road, through a neighbourhood 'almost entirely inhabited by prostitution and people who live off prostitution'. She watched girls heading over the bridge to the public buildings, theatres, taverns and gin-houses of the West End, 'where they ply their trade all through the night and return home between eight and nine in the morning'. Later she visited a 'fashionable' gin palace, where prostitutes paraded in their finery, and watched the behaviour of 'young noblemen', 'very honourable members of Parliament' and others, plying women with drink.[34] Through the 1850s, there was a widespread belief that 'shameless' and open displays of street prostitution were carried on 'to an extent tolerated in no other capital or city of the civilised world'.[35]

For the Victorian male, prostitutes were a focus of encounter and fantasy, mixing elements of attraction, threat and degradation. Historians know more about the women involved than their potential clients. Reformers sometimes stressed upper-class patrons, though given the numbers of women supposedly involved it is clear that a much broader cross-section of male society was involved, with police prosecutions identifying middle-class and aristocratic men alongside a majority from the working classes. The Bishop of Manchester believed in 1872, in a speech on 'The Vices of the Age', that customers included not only 'many wealthy merchants' but also 'married men, churchwardens, deacons of congregations'.[36]

The numbers involved in prostitution were always unclear. Police figures show amazing disparities, suggesting widespread under-reportage. In 1863, for example, the respectable cathedral city of Durham (population c. 14,000) supposedly had seventy-four prostitutes while Salford (population c. 103,000) had only 100 and Rochdale (population c. 138,000) had 125. Reformers exaggerated figures, not least because they often misidentified working-class women's social behaviour in leisure areas in the evenings after work, classifying it as showing 'disgusting exhibitions of vice'. Any woman living outside conventional morality or indulging in casual sex might be so stigmatized, and prostitution could be part-time: casual or intermittent as a temporary career move to raise money or seasonal. It was often a relatively short life-cycle choice for working-class women, many of whom were orphaned or from backgrounds with little family support, and choosing prostitution rather than the poorhouse. Census returns coupled with police records show that at least some prostitutes moved location regularly trying to avoid notice. Leticia Farrell, for example, described as 'a prostitute of the lowest kind', had various convictions in the Accrington, Blackburn, Preston, Burnley (Lancashire), Belfast (Ireland), Kendal (Westmorland) and York areas, sometimes soliciting, as when she committed 'an indecent act on Blakeley Moor', sometimes drunk, and often stealing from her customers.[37]

And there was a continuum of prostitution, as social surveys showed, with a continuing *demi-monde* of courtesans at the top, living under the protection of fashionable gentlemen in superior accommodation, to be seen riding or in carriages in Hyde Park or Rotten Row in London. Famous examples, such as Catherine Walters (aka Skittles), mistress of the Prince of Wales, in her tightly-cut riding habit, were popular London figures, 'pretty horse-breakers', painted and sketched by artists, especially during the 1860s. Just as today, there were foreign prostitutes too. In the late 1850s, complaints were particularly exercised by the (un-English) behaviour of 'the great number of foreign prostitutes' systematically imported into the country, by 'base, filthy and filthy-living men'. Estimates suggested there were perhaps 200 foreign prostitutes, mostly from France, but also from Hamburg and Belgium, whose 'open and disgusting indecencies and practices . . . give cause of gross public offence.'[38] London still had colonies of French prostitutes in the 1880s.

Available figures must be treated with great caution. *Prostitution in London*, an alarmist pamphlet written in 1839 by Dr Michael Ryan, compared it unfavourably with Paris and New York to underscore the need for reform. He felt that 'licentiousness, as well as other vices' had rapidly increased, and suggested that there were 80,000 prostitutes in London alone, a figure far higher than police estimates of 8,000 or so. Soon afterwards, a Scottish former house-surgeon produced an enquiry into the extent, causes and consequences of prostitution in Edinburgh, asserting confidently that the city had about 800 full-time prostitutes and a further 1,160 part-timers.[39] In the 1880s, *The Lancet* medical journal also estimated that there were approximately 80,000 prostitutes in London, about 3 per cent of the population, while in Newcastle a survey concerned about the problems of drunkenness, 'vice and social riot' in 1883 claimed the town had at least a hundred brothels.[40]

When brothels, sometimes described as 'disorderly houses', 'houses of ill-fame', 'immoral houses' or 'bawdy houses', were targeted by local purity campaigns in the 1890s, this usually just resulted in relocation. A Liverpool campaign simply found, according to one letter to the press, that Liverpool 'cleanse[d] its house at the expense of its neighbours . . . Birkenhead here is just swarming with them, like flies in a sugar basin'.[41]

There has been much research into campaigns to prevent or reform prostitution and the 'rescue work' carried out. Many reformers understood that some girls entered prostitution 'through necessitous circumstances'. They were sometimes single mothers, 'unfortunate women', exploited by men, taken advantage of in a period before reliable contraception. They attracted pity as much as obloquy. Stronger criticism after mid-century was levelled at the men who patronized them. Prostitutes were constructed as victims, often not entirely 'dead to shame' and trying to preserve their 'womanly modesty' in the face of male lust. Feminist propaganda was still constrained by an extremely limited vocabulary, constructed around the theme of female victimization. Defences of prostitutes as women who were not yet 'dead to shame', and still had 'womanly modesty', were common.

Future Prime Minister W.E. Gladstone was one of many who voluntarily patrolled at night to try to keep women from a 'life of vice', and lead them to a 'decent' life. Recent detailed study of his diary suggests that his intentions were good, and he genuinely saw it as a Christian duty. When he talked to attractive prostitutes he found them smart and stimulating, which he recognized as threatening his spiritual health. The diary implies that he may have had some limited physical encounter. More certainly he turned to private self-flagellation, painfully subduing his feelings of guilt, to remain self-controlled in his Christian path.[42]

Churches ran relief organizations. Many charity organizations were created: penitentiaries, reformatories, houses of mercy and associations such as the Ladies' Association for the Care of Friendless Girls (which had 106 English branches in 1885 taking in 'wayward girls'), the Church Penitentiary Association, the Homes for Hope, or the London Society for the Protection of Young Females and Prevention of Juvenile Prostitution. These rescue homes were used by relatively few women, often as temporary refuges. Even after two years of 'repent and reform experience', many girls returned to their earlier life-style.[43]

In the 1870s, a relatively small number of generally young British girls had been induced to go to Brussels, the Netherlands and France and ended up working in the state-regulated and supervised brothels there. This was apparently well known to the Home Office, Foreign Office and British police. But early in 1880, Alfred Dyer, a Quaker purity campaigner, heard that a young English girl was kept against her will in a licensed brothel in Brussels. Working with Brussels Quakers, he organized her return to London. In echoes of more recent trafficking, his enquiries suggested that some English girls claimed to have been entrapped under false pretences with offers of bar work, shipped overseas and forcibly detained in Brussels and Antwerp brothels. In debt for board and lodging, and threatened with personal violence, they were ignored by the Belgian vice police. An investigation by the Belgian authorities denied this, but Dyer felt this was a cover-up, a 'sham', a 'judicial farce', linked to foreign police corruption.[44] The British press sensationalized the story, picking up the anti-European issue of 'foreign vice', 'foreign lust', 'slavery' and false entrapment with further unsubstantiated allegations of 'little children, English girls of from ten to fourteen years', kidnapped and sold, to be sexually exploited by 'wealthy men who are able to pay large sums of money for the sacrifice of these innocents'.[45] Dyer's further investigations suggested that up to twenty procurers had been at work in Britain since the mid-1860s.

The government responded with a House of Lords Select Committee to investigate the law relating to the protection of young girls. Despite suggestions from a London CID officer and the British consul in Brussels that the girls there were not naïve, knew the situation and were leading a 'doubtful' or 'loose' life before they went, the government initially decided to tighten the law.[46] The Bill struggled, however, attracting limited support even in the Cabinet. The House of Lords was opposed to legislation, with one noble Lord arguing that since 'few of their Lordships . . . had not, when young men, been guilty of immorality', legislation was not necessary.

When a softened Bill also failed in May 1885, purity campaigners decided to pick up on three emotive aspects, those of child abuse, prostitution and aristocratic licentiousness, to change attitudes. Until 1875, sexual intercourse with a twelve-year-old had been legal, but then the Offences Against the Person Act raised the age of consent to thirteen.

There were high-class London brothels that catered for men prepared to pay large sums for young supposedly virginal and 'clean' girls. On 6 July 1885, the *Pall Mall Gazette* published a detailed account of the purchase of a thirteen-year-old girl, Lily, from her parents, by a female brothel-keeper for a sovereign. Her virginity was checked. She had been passed on to a procuress for £5, and taken to a London brothel. There she had been chloroformed and raped by a purchaser. Presented under the headline 'The Maiden Tribute of Modern Babylon', the story was largely invented by the paper's editor, W.T. Stead, who had deliberately purchased Lily from her parents to prove that what he called 'white slavery', the abduction, sale and organized rape of young English virgins, was possible. In fact the girl was transferred to the care of the Salvation Army. The article's Old Testament references to Babylonian temple prostitution would have been recognized by many readers. The melodramatic article referred to a supposedly 'vast tribute' of girls, who were 'literally killed and made away with – living sacrifices slain in the service of vice'. Stead's reports covered 'the loathsome abnormalities of sexual vice', the sexual exploitation of children and 'unnatural crimes' in lurid detail.

Its impact was immediate and powerful across Britain, rocking society to its foundations. The paper received many letters complaining of the publication of such 'horrible details', 'damnably pernicious' and 'prurient' material while others urged him to 'go on . . . in the good work'. Stead, though threatened with prosecution, drew out the story with further 'revelations' over the next few days, graphically describing how innocent children were decoyed into prostitution by trickery, the corruption of officials who turned a blind eye to the trade, and the wealthy old men for whom it catered.

Under pressure, the government responded with the Criminal Law Amendment Act, which raised the age of consent for girls to sixteen, made sexual assaults on girls younger than thirteen a crime and on girls between thirteen and sixteen a misdemeanour, as well as taking a tougher stand on soliciting.

Another result of Stead's articles was the formation of the National Vigilance Association in August 1885 'for the enforcement and improvement of the laws for the repression of criminal vice and public immorality'. It was an important and significant reform player and lobbied Parliament effectively for many years. It absorbed several older societies, and enjoyed widespread support across Britain with regional branches. Its main objective initially was to protect young women and girls from sexual exploitation. It went on to pursue repressive campaigns against French pornography (including Zola and Flaubert), birth control information, immoral or indecent advertising of any sort, postcards, music-hall content and prostitution, encouraging private prosecutions and passing on complaints to supportive police officers. Even the nude in art was targeted as a threat 'to public morals'. The 1889 Indecent Advertisements Act, passed in part thanks to their lobbying, banned any advertising relating to 'any complaint or infirmity arising from or relating to sexual intercourse'.

Sexually transmitted diseases

Fornication spread sexually transmitted diseases, especially syphilis and gonorrhoea.[47] The topic, often described as 'the social disease' was rarely talked about or addressed in print. It was shameful and distressing. It could be passed on to partner and children. Treatment was difficult, and often ineffective and painful, masking rather than curing symptoms. Asking one's doctor for help was not easy. By the 1860s, possibly 10 per cent of the population suffered. Various 'celebrated balsamic pills' for 'venereal eruptions', concentrated 'detersive essences', or perhaps Perry's 'purifying specific pills' could be purchased through the post. Some saw it as God's punishment for fornication, 'the natural retribution of sexual vice'.[48] Others argued that offering a cure would 'have a pernicious effect on public morality and weaken self-restraint'.[49] Ordinary hospitals would only treat syphilis in out-patient clinics, though the Lock Hospitals in London, Edinburgh and elsewhere specialized in treating women with aggravated forms of sexual disease.

Many of those infected were prostitutes, who were often unfairly blamed as the main source of infection rather than men. By the 1850s there was widespread social concern over the rapid spread of gonorrhoea and syphilis. *The Lancet*, for example, carried editorials on 'Prostitution – the need for its reform' (7 November 1857) and on 'Prostitution: Its Medical Aspects' (20 February 1858), the latter focusing on venereal disease and its impact on the British Army in military areas. Problems were emerging not just in southern England and Ireland but across the Empire, from Gibraltar to India or Australia. Soldiers and sailors were discouraged from marriage or homosexual relationships, British society would not accept licensed brothels or the issue of condoms to military personnel, and prostitution was seen as a necessary sexual solution.

But a substantial proportion of men were infected and unfit for service, so venereal disease was undermining the strength of the armed forces. This was a politically powerful argument. Following a Parliamentary Committee in 1862 to inquire into venereal disease, a Contagious Diseases Act was passed in 1864, the first of three statutes providing for the sanitary inspection of prostitutes in specific military areas. Annual Statistical, Sanitary and Medical Reports of the Army Medical Department and Statistical Reports on the Health of the Royal Navy kept the need to shield men from venereal disease before Parliament. A further parliamentary Committee inquired into the Pathology and Treatment of Venereal Disease with a View to Diminish its Injurious Effects on the Army and Navy in 1867–8.[50]

At first sight, the Acts seemed sensible attempts at regulation. Police were given powers to arrest any apparent prostitutes in specific naval ports and army towns. Those arrested were subjected to compulsory medical examination testing for venereal disease. If infected they would be confined in a Lock Hospital, initially for up to three months, later for a year, to provide a cure. There were even suggestions that the Acts might be extended to Britain's civilian populations, but they rapidly attracted opposition.

For organizations like the Methodists, the Acts were criticized as condoning and encouraging and *de facto* legalizing an abhorrent vice. Others, however, opposed the Acts on human rights grounds. The Acts were directed only at women, who were regarded as already 'fallen'. Compulsory examination of the soldiers and sailors who spread the disease was rejected by Parliament as a solution. So the Acts were one-sided, scapegoating women in general and depriving some of liberty. Any virtuous respectable 'decent' woman speaking to a man could be humiliatingly arrested. Police action was arbitrary, capricious and uncertain and open to bribery.

An anti-contagious diseases movement grew rapidly, led by campaigners like Josephine Butler, who argued that male lust was to blame. It offered genteel middle-class women the chance of social activism, speaking publicly on what had been regarded as an improper area for women to discuss. This signalled a change in women's role, challenging the idea that women occupied a 'separate sphere'. Men, they argued, were 'the main causes both of the vice and its dreaded consequences for public vice'. Men created the demand. Women just sold their sexual services, and there was a class bias, singling out working-class women. The Acts merely drove prostitution underground, away from police eyes. It also made women reluctant to seek help. The movement encouraged better social hygiene as one solution, while debating how far men should be blamed, and how prostitution should be treated. The Congress of the British and Continental Federation for the Abolition of the State Regulation of Vice in 1883, for example, wanted equal morality and equal justice between the sexes but no official recognition of prostitution as a trade. The campaigns were drawn out, but were eventually successful, forcing first the Acts' suspension and then repeal in 1886.

Obscenity and pornography

Victorian sexual pleasure separate from reproduction was, largely for male readers, found in the availability of pornography, a key part of the expanding network of sexual discourse and consumer culture. Middle-class Victorians were resourceful in creating loopholes in the demands of sexual respectability. Fantasy was one escape, reading, writing and imagining sexual pleasures, especially their heterosexual forms. So for example, it was quite acceptable for the literate and classically-educated to purchase Restoration poems, the works of classical authors such as Petronius, or bawdy French verse fables from bookshops. Even Gladstone read such material.[51]

What counted as pornography reflected and affected the Victorians' imagination.[52] Museums, art galleries or dealers' rooms were deemed appropriate forums to reveal male and female nudity in a Classical content to their respectable and educated middle-class clientele. There visitors could observe, interpret and enjoy works of high art nudity despite what was often a clearly erotic subtext. Wealthy businessmen often purchased it. The English painter William Etty (1787–1849) carved out a respectable reputation for his powerful nude paintings of women in poses from Classical antiquity, carefully chosen to provide moral messages. In respectable art discourse, the artistic nude was acceptable, nakedness was not. His subject matter was prestigious but raised issues about sexuality, desire and public morality. Ernest Normand's *Pygmalion and Galatea*, painted in 1866, and showing a part-clothed Galatea, like Shaw's later play embodied fantasies about the perfect female, sexual temptation and men's desire for and control of women. Even less-respectable magazines were able to avoid legal constraints by illustrating their pages with carefully-selected reproductions of Classical nudity and 'high art'. These could also be reproduced in shop windows and in advertising. Towards the century's end, the Art Nouveau movement included the controversial artist Aubrey Beardsley (1872–98), a daring critic of sexual conventions, whose drawings of men and women were often explicitly erotic. He drew on Japanese erotic art and English pornography, history and mythology, and sought to shock. He was rumoured to have slept with his sister, and was adopted by Wilde, who claimed he had 'made' him. Beardsley's drawings offered challenging new notions of masculinity and femininity. His women were intelligent, actively sexual beings, at a time when women were finding new roles, and popular journals and magazines began publishing stories and articles about the supposedly formidable viragos, the 'New Women' who instead of staying at home, rode bicycles, smoked, let their hair down, looked down on men and even demanded votes or a university education.

But contemporary poses or even Classical nudes sold in the 1890s in postcard form to the working classes were a different matter. Pornographic material, with its intense awareness of the sexual body, had long been widespread, though following the 1837 Vagrancy Act display of obscene materials in windows or elsewhere in public led to trial. Such material was profitable. Political radicals and Chartists sometimes used sales of erotica to subsidize their political campaigns and pamphlets. The Victorian pornography industry became a flourishing part of the emergent consumer culture and rise in literacy, responding to demand, with constantly changing definitions and meanings.[53]

In the early Victorian period the Society for the Suppression of Vice attacked this 'most pernicious traffic' in 'obscene' material, organizing prosecutions, effecting the seizure of prints, pictures and books, or stopping importations of supposedly 'dangerous' material from France.[54] Its prime focus was on book displays and on London pornographic booksellers like William Dugdale (1800–68) based in Holywell Street, famous for its trestles of cheap, respectable and unrespectable books and prints, its displays and advertisements for obscene materials and its 'warehouses of vice' that circulated them across London and beyond.[55]

The rise of this mass print culture caused new anxieties that what was described as 'obscene' and 'pornographic' material would be made available to the working classes rather than to those of sufficient education and social status who could control their passions. The cheap, mass-produced and widely-sold material celebrating sensual pleasures and the pursuit of varied forms of lovemaking was attacked as degenerate, particularly poisoning the minds of the young (of both sexes) and pandering to the tastes of the corrupt old. Victorian doctors saw addiction to pornography as encouraging lust and having debilitating effects on the body, and suggested that the young, many women and the growingly literate working classes would not be able to distinguish between fact and fiction

By about 1849, Dugdale was a leading pornographer who ironically used the imprint 'The Society of Vice' for some of his expensive limited editions of obscene works. Unsurprisingly, he became a particular reformist target, regularly prosecuted and sentenced to prison, once, in 1851, for two years. Rumours of influential contacts in high places and of preferential deals struck during his trials reflected a widespread belief his material had a following amongst the supposedly respectable and permeated all levels of society. The adverse publicity his prosecutions generated helped the introduction of the Obscene Publications Act in September 1857 dealing with pictorial and literary pornography, which implied it was already found everywhere (at least in London). Obscenity, which had lacked legal definition, was legally defined in an 1868 test case as 'material tending to deprave and corrupt those whose minds are open to such immoral influences and into whose hands a publication of this sort might fall'.

The writers of the books he sold are less well known. Much material is anonymous (or written by authors with names like 'Ramrod') and undated. Captain Edward Sellon (1818–66), whose books included *The New Epicurianism: Or The Delights of Sex Facetiously and Philosophically Considered, in Graphic Letters Addressed to Young Ladies of Quality* (1865), and *The New Ladies' Tickler or The Adventures of Lady Lovesport and the Audacious Harry* (1866), was born to a fairly wealthy family and well-educated. He served in the Indian Army from 1834 to 1843, reaching the rank of captain, experiencing a variety of what he called 'amorous adventures', sleeping with prostitutes, native women and officers' wives. He acquired a taste for young girls, aged about twelve or thirteen, while there. Reckless, immature and immoral, he was a convivial raconteur, generally popular and enjoyed strong drink. Returning to England he married what he supposed to be a young heiress, but the estate proved to be mortgaged. Initially, family money enabled him to keep a mistress and spend time philandering in London, returning to his wife only rarely, though they had four children. But money soon ran out, and he supported himself in jobs such as coach-driving and fencing instruction. He worked at a girls' private school in Hampshire, where he got involved in further sexual scandal. To avoid prosecution he returned to London, where he turned to writing pornography, but he appears to have been becoming increasingly depressed, and in April 1866, he shot himself in his hotel room in Piccadilly.[56]

His unfinished autobiography, published after his death, ostensibly describes his early life and sexual encounters as a teenager, into his twenties and beyond. Explicit and candid, he wrote frankly about a variety of sexual topics, from infidelity and prostitution to cross-cultural and cross-class sexual practices. His material often focused on the visual as well as on sexual acts themselves.

> Imagine a skin white as alabaster, a slender waist, a Spanish back with a delicious fall to it, over which meandered her waving golden hair ... a bottom the largest, the most dimpled and the whitest I have ever beheld, supported on thighs so rounded, so symmetrically proportioned, so altogether ravishingly exquisite that an angel of light could not have withstood such temptation. I stooped down and buried my face in those hills of snow, then rising up, I slipped with ease into her mossy grotto, and at it we went again. She jutted her bum out to meet my thrusts, she stretched out first one leg then the other, passed her hand between her legs and felt my wand as it went in and out ... and soon brought down another sweet shower. 'Oh you're a man! A man!' she said, 'more charming by far than M----. He shall have me no more, sweet boy-faced fellow. I am thine for ever.' And she fell fainting on the bed.[57]

Pornographic texts varied in their themes, picking up on gender, class, age, race and even religion, with some violently anti-Catholic pornographic material. Much of such literature was misogynistic and degrading, sensually selfish, largely presenting images of women's bodies and responses as erotic object of the male gaze and of male sexual conquest and domination of the submissive female. There was material voiced from a female perspective, written supposedly by liberated titled ladies, parlour maids or even elderly ladies remembering their earlier sexual initiation, but whether these were actually written by women is not known. Some texts acknowledged active female sexual agency and egalitarian sex between men and women.

Wish-fulfilment accounts describing sexual encounters across the generational barriers were quite common, most often older men's encounters with sexually-libidinous young schoolgirls or between a young boy and older women, as in James Reddie's *The Adventures of a Schoolboy* (1866), and including troilism, bondage and group sex without shame. Pornography entwined with class with encounters across its barriers, most usually male erotic encounters with attractive titled women, or lower races and classes. In such contexts, the formal social proprieties were often observed, including correct forms of address. In an Imperial age, the photographs brought back to Britain of naked or semi-naked Africans could be represented as interesting because scientific, anthropological and educational, or as implicitly sexual and so filthy, dependent on context, while lustful Turks represented the Ottoman Empire.

Sex with prostitutes was another perennial feature. For the middle classes, working-class prostitutes were sometimes the central spectacle of their encounters and fantasies, simultaneously repudiated and desired, attractive yet dangerously degraded and threatening.[58] The material in *My Secret Life*, by 'Walter', published from 1888 onwards, and generally regarded as partly fiction but sometimes based on his own experiences and those of acquaintances, describes sexual experiences largely but not always consensual. These were occasionally with partners of his own class, but more usually prostitutes, servants and working-class women. Themes such as voyeurism or sado-masochism also occur. The various underground novels, short stories and verse serialized in *The Pearl*, probably the leading erotic publication of the period between 1879 and 1881, had titles such as 'Lady Pokingham, or They All Do It', 'The Sultan's Reverie' and 'Miss Coote's Confession'. A substantial minority of male heterosexual pornography described anal sex with women, which may have been a way of avoiding contraception.

The English obsession with masochistic flagellation, linked to public schools and sexual dislocation also featured.[59] To the French, it was 'le vice Anglais'. The poet Swinburne, for example, had a well-known predilection for this. This long-standing tradition of sado-masochistic and flagellation pornography continued with texts such as George Stock's *The Romance of Chastisement* (1870). Lesbian sex was also occasionally described.

How widely such material was circulated is unclear. There were elite collectors such as the London textile trader, Henry Spenser Ashbee (1834–1900), who possessed thousands of volumes of erotica, and was part of a wider group of intellectuals and 'gentlemen' personally and privately interested in such material, claiming it as a function of their cultural superiority. There was a much larger mass audience for the cheaper books produced.[60] Between 1834 and 1880, the Society for the Suppression of Vice alone seized over 380,000 obscene prints and photographs, 80,000 books and pamphlets and five tons of other material – this was just a small proportion of the material sold. This mass audience have been argued to be largely male 'artisans, clerks, army and naval officers, students, journalists, professionals, businessmen, government officials'.[61] The debates leading up to the Obscene Publications Act, however, suggest that such publications were also sometimes consumed and viewed by women.[62]

London was certainly a centre of the international erotic picture trade up to the 1860s. The Metropolitan Police 'obscene publications' Squad (formed in 1863) and the Customs Consolidation Act of 1876 which empowered them to seize 'indecent or obscene' photos, as well as prints and books, then began to have some effect, especially at the cheaper end of the market, while the National Vigilance Association was also very active.

Simultaneously, however, technological change in photography created a new mass market for mainly soft-porn, 'lewd and indecent' and 'disgusting' photographs, sold across Britain, largely by local photography shops, but also regularly cautiously hawked on the streets, selling in huge amounts. As early as 1874, a police raid on the houses of Pimlico photographer Henry Hayler produced 130,248 obscene photos, many of young children (including his two young sons), and letters from customers across Europe and America.[63] Some photographers attempted to avoid the law by advertising 'studies for artists' use', 'half draped and undraped' supplied to customers only following an assurance that they were only required for artistic purposes. The 1880s saw a market for translations of French novels, described by moralists as 'the foreign literature of vice', with little protest from the press.

Masturbation

The 'destructive' practice of what the Victorians often described as 'the solitary vice', 'solitary indulgence' or 'Onanism' was often portrayed as damaging vital physical and mental health. According to some medical authorities it created sickness and debility, and perhaps even insanity. The inherent dangers of the vice, they thought, included 'complete collapse of body and mind', 'premature breakdown amongst young men', and feelings of 'hopelessness and degradation'. According to one physician's advertisements in the 1840s, it led to 'loss of virility, dorsal consumption and many other disorders which often renders life an unvaried scene of despondency'.[64] It could leave a person withdrawn, weak-minded and self-mutilating.

In the second half of the century, fear of masturbation became more obsessive as socially conservative medical discourse became ever-clearer and more certain about its medical dangers. It became categorized by many as an aberrant pathology. The Commissioners in Lunacy regularly provided an analysis of the causes of insanity in England and Wales. In 1879, it included 1,862 cases caused through 'intemperance in drink', 104 through 'sexual intemperance', 82 through venereal disease, and 149 through 'self-abuse (sexual)', though the basis of such figures is unclear. It was concluded that excessive sexual 'expenditure' of the 'life force' and lack of self-control could make a person feeble, flabby and pale. In 1881, the *British Medical Journal* editorial discussed it, though very carefully and with little detail. It was supposedly 'a grave social problem', a dangerous 'form of vice'. Medical journal discourses about masturbation even found their way into the construction of characters in mainstream and pornographic Victorian fiction.[65]

Alongside the medical concerns were moral fears: those of it becoming a first step on the way to immoral sexual behaviour, the keeping of mistresses or going with prostitutes. From the 1880s onwards, there was also the growing fear of it leading to homosexuality. It was presented as an issue relating only to boys and young men (though female masturbation is suggested in Victorian pornography), part of the wider sexuality of Victorian discourse. It was treated with fear and loathing. Parents, educators, doctors and religious leaders were all alerted to stamp out any traces of child sexuality. This involved constant surveillance and a very wide array of preventative and corrective measures, including a device invented by a doctor which used electric shock treatment, inflicted on a sleeping boy's penis upon erection.

Masturbation, together with homosexuality, was a particular concern in public schools, with pubescent pupils, living closely together in dormitories. The 'purifying' of public schools was one objective of the National Vigilance Association. Public school head masters over the last four decades of the century set out to inculcate better discipline in their schools. They used the cult of athleticism to create models of manliness and masculinity which they hoped would distract boys from 'vile' practices. Chapel worship and strenuous games such as rugby supposedly provided a form of 'muscular Christianity' which could ensure that boys were rarely 'idle' enough to find time for them.

Same-sex relationships

In recent years there has been a growing body of historiographical work on the development of urban gay subcultures.[66] In Victorian thought, vice and homosexual activity were linked though its nature varied with changing understandings of sex, gender and identity and people's constantly debated sense of what was 'normal'. Heterosexuality was held to be normal *and* natural. For example, any form of anal intercourse with male, female or animal was called sodomy. Until 1861, this technically carried the death penalty, and afterwards carried a term of imprisonment. Between 1800 and 1835 eighty men were hanged for this, but those prosecuted and imprisoned for sodomy and other homosexual offences were most often those artisans and servants belonging to an urban, largely working-class sodomy culture.[67]

The law largely ignored other social groups, though any sexual activity in public was frowned upon.

By the 1840s, however, there was a wider sense amongst respectable moral reformers that any public homosexual behaviour associated with the upper-class elite was unacceptable. But to publicize this, instigate police investigations, and let the public knew how widespread such 'vices' were would create scandal.

So a variety of transgressive sexualities, including lesbian, gay, bisexual and transgender roles, often continued to surface, side by side with heterosexual life. Male cross-dressing, for example, experienced quite diverse receptions. In one notorious 1870 case, a male couple who had been using West End shops, hotels, theatres and other commercial leisure facilities for about three years without complaint while wearing women's clothing were arrested and charged with conspiring to commit an unnatural offence. Widely reported, the trial details indicated that there was little outrage, and the bulk of those members of the public inside and outside the courtroom were supportive. Apparently 'some of the assembled mass cheered them, some hissed and some clapped their hands'. They were found not guilty.[68]

Male homosexuality was rarely talked about directly. It was a 'mute sin', one of 'filthy and disgusting nature' and for some time occasional trials still focused on the gay working classes, while newspaper reports were carefully coy in discussing this 'nameless crime', the 'unnatural offence' or 'depravity' with very limited detail, describing the evidence as 'unfit for publication'. Reports employed an obscure vocabulary drawing on street slang through Classical and religious references to medical jargon: 'mollies', 'poofs', 'ganymedes', 'chestnut gatherers', 'Mary Annes', 'sodomites', 'pederasts', 'inverts', 'androphiles' or 'parisexuals'. In the 1890s, they were even called 'Uranians', a word used by writer and social reformer Edward Carpenter (1844–1929) in 1899, when he was living with a younger male partner. It stemmed from the gay German writer Karl Heinrich Ulrichs, who 'outed' himself in front of 500 German Jurists in 1867.[69]

As such categorizations and identities evolved, the word homosexual was coined in the late 1860s and little used initially, but had become part of normal usage by the 1880s. The concept was a complex one. Ideas associated with it might include romantic love, various forms of sexuality, financial arrangements, or merely a need for homo-social intimacy. Through the 1860s middle- and upper-class same-sex unions were still generally tolerated so long as they were carried out discreetly and secretly, but by the 1870s they were becoming increasingly visible but tolerated only on the margins of society, though prosecutions were still few.[70]

The increase in overt homosexual behaviour was especially but not exclusively amongst the intelligentsia. Writers such as Algernon Swinburne, Walter Pater, J.A. Symonds and Oscar Browning and some university dons promoted 'Greek' or Platonic relationships.[71] This slowly helped create a more distinct gay subculture, as did a counter-cultural defiance of the moral teachings of the reformers, which made the forbidden more alluring, and the extended bachelorhood of some middle-class males.

While largely clandestine owing to laws prohibiting 'indecency' in public, homosexuals were able to exploit the availability of the new public toilets, erected in an attempt to stop public urinating in the streets and impose more respectable behaviour, for 'cottaging' purposes. They hung around for short, anonymous sexual acts in the cubicles, often in well-established locations, after exchanging coded looks and behaviours. This offered scope for encounters between males of different classes and ages.

But under pressure from moralists, the police made efforts to stop this, treating men as criminals, and sometimes using entrapment tactics to make arrests. Sometimes too, unwanted propositions, or deliberate attempts at extortion, also led to prosecutions. The men accused appeared to be part of the mainstream in occupational terms, often lower middle class or workers. Newspaper details, however, were limited and imprecise, since activities were of 'a disgusting nature, quite unfit for print'. The trial process marginalized the men's voice, though some reports imply touching or masturbation rather than penetration.[72] Barracks were also notoriously a pick-up place, while there were notorious male brothels near London's Regent's Park and elsewhere.

Increasingly, homosexuality was being redefined by mainstream discourse as evil and diseased, a source of moral contagion to the young, effeminate and not masculine, languid and lazy instead of industrious. It was a threat to the supposed purity of British life. At the same time some scientists and doctors were beginning to develop news structures of understanding, arguing that homosexuality was inborn, and so natural in some men.

For much of the century male non-sodomy homosexual activities were technically legal though 'sodomy' possessed a sufficiently broad and vague definition that almost all homosexual activity was risky. But in 1885 the moralist Liberal MP, Henry Labouchère, introduced a last-minute clause into the Criminal Law Amendment Act that made 'gross indecency' – any kind of homosexual activity between men – a criminal misdemeanour, and this was soon applied to private consensual acts. This created a clearer homosexuality identity and affected ideas of heterosexual manliness and thereafter there was growing police activity. To an extent, since the better off and the intellectual classes had easier access to privacy, they could largely avoid persecution.

But 1889–90 saw the exposure of a house in London's Cleveland Street, one of many male brothels frequented by rich and middle-class men, reportedly including 'a number of aristocrats', allegedly including Prince Victor Albert. They were 'slumming' with often part-time working-class male prostitutes, often below sixteen, many working simultaneously as telegraph boys for the Post Office. The case attracted huge publicity right across the country. It was a 'scandal', 'indescribable and loathsome', reflecting on 'society' and its morals, and sparked a wave of homophobia.[73]

The trials of Oscar Wilde, playwright and poseur, for gross indecency in 1895 were further stages in making both homosexual relations and intimate friendship between men 'unmanly'. Wilde was reckless and self-destructive, addicted to young working-class male prostitutes. On 18 February 1895, the Marquess of Queensberry, the father of Wilde's young, petulant and sexually-voracious lover, Lord Alfred Douglas, left his calling card at Wilde's club inscribed: 'For Oscar Wilde, posing sodomite'. Douglas was no innocent. He was enjoying life in Algiers with a handsome fourteen-year-old boy. Wilde sued for libel but the attempt backfired. He lost the case and was tried for sodomy.

The trials attracted bigoted Victorian press denunciations of homosexuality led by traditionalists in Parliament, police and the churches, and discussed openly, repeatedly and publicly. For the *Methodist Times* it showed that 'wickedness in west London has reached depths of audacious depravity unparalleled since the days of the declining Roman Empire'.[74] Wilde soon realized he was 'feasting with panthers'. He attempted a defence of what he called 'the love that dare not speak its name' by rationalizing his behaviour using notions of Platonic 'Greek love', the devotion of an older man for a youngster, which was supposedly noble, ennobling, celibate and spiritual, not based on lust. His speech was greeted with riotous applause from the supportive galleries, but Judge Wills sentenced him to two years hard labour, saying it was the worst case he had ever tried. Even so, despite the public furore, representations of same-sex desire in late Victorian aesthetic contexts continued, and were tolerated as long as they kept away from overt visibility.

In clear contrast, the language of vice was rarely applied to lesbian relationships, though they were clearly known about, and described in pornography, while the terms 'lesbian' and 'Sapphic' came slowly into literary use, often being represented as an especially repulsive/seductive French vice. It has been argued to be probably more widespread than sometimes thought, though there is very limited first-hand source material, and it has proved hard to distinguish it from female friendship.[75] Some joint female authors such as Edith Somerville and Violet Martin (aka Somerville and Ross) shared passionate, companionate and nourishing relationships without attracting innuendo. Usually women were singled out, victimized, but here women were exempted from the legal sanctions that applied to men.

Conclusion

In large part it was anxieties about specific aspects of male sexuality that dominated Victorian thought. Sexuality was a field of simultaneous debate, fascination and concern. Art, medicine and literature all responded to such concerns. There was certainly some Puritanism and repression. Prostitution, pornography and masturbation were rarely discussed in much detail. The later years of the period saw homosexuality becoming more publicly visible, and simultaneously less tolerated. Much of this was about power, power of men over women, of policing over prostitution, over the young by the old, and of respectable thought over unrespectable pleasures and vices. But there were a variety of attitudes even to topics such as prostitution or pregnancy outside marriage, where there was growing understanding and sympathy for the women involved. In terms of their attitudes to sexual 'vices', the Victorians cannot be simply stereotyped.

CHAPTER SIX

From Vice to Virtue

The battle against vice was fought at a number of levels, yet without committed, hard-working men and women to support it, and strategies in place to advance their cause in the face of hostility, it could never have succeeded. A good illustrative example of a key figure is provided by Catherine Booth (nee Mumford) (1829–90), the wife of William Booth, the founder of the Salvation Army. Sadly, she is now perhaps less well-known than her husband, yet at the time she was widely admired as a social reformer and champion of women's rights. She was also a dominant force in the movement, described as its 'Mother', responsible for many of its innovations and strategies to gain support.[1] She was the daughter of Methodist parents, a keen student of the Bible and a deep theological thinker. Her abhorrence of drink developed when her father, a carriage-maker and preacher, broke his pledge, lost his faith and became a drunkard. Raised in Nottingham, at the age of twelve she had already become the secretary of a Juvenile Temperance Society. She met William at the Brixton Wesleyan Methodist Church in 1852. She was forceful, with strong opinions, and encouraged William to pledge total abstinence from alcohol and to preach against it on the streets. They married in 1855 and she inspired her husband to become a full-time touring evangelist. Though she suffered poor health and had eight children, she was quickly active in preaching and proselytizing (from 1860), social work and letter writing. She was an exceptionally eloquent orator, better than her husband. Her speeches were often described as stirring, challenging and magnificent, and she could deal well with hecklers. When they set up Christian mission stations in London's East End, the couple used musical instruments and songs, flags and symbols, to attract audiences to their outdoor tent meetings, whilst making strong speeches against prostitution and strong drink. They also warned against tobacco, over-fine clothing, wealth, hurtful reading and dangerous acquaintances. They gained support despite attracting hostility and derision from brothel owners, pub landlords and hostile members of the public, who sometimes threw mud, liquor or rotten eggs at them.

When the Booths jointly set up the Salvation Army in 1878, Catherine continued to play a key role in defining issues and matters of belief. In an imperialist age, the organization's rhetoric, structure and paraphernalia were strongly military, for both men and women, in the battle against vice. She wrote tracts on temperance for the Temperance Society, and was a strong supporter of the growing purity movement, with strong views on the age of consent for girls. She gave great encouragement to the preaching contributions of women members, the group the press described as the 'Hallelujah Lasses'. She was particularly adept in preaching to and gaining financial support from wealthy patrons, and also travelled abroad, to France and Switzerland, to preach and spread the movement. In Britain, she was hugely popular in reform circles. She achieved great spiritual results and attracted converts, especially amongst the alcoholics, prostitutes and the 'undeserving' poor. According to one former drunkard and professional pugilist who was converted, it was 'a way that lays hold of drunkards and thieves, and makes them sober and honest and clean and happy, and teaches them to love and fear God'.[2] She contributed significantly to the movement's newspaper *The War Cry*, lobbied MPs and conducted many public meetings throughout the 1880s, mainly in London, in temperance halls, before breast cancer cut short her career.

Chapter outline

This chapter explores some of the internal dynamics of the anti-vice movements, and picks up many of the issues the case study above raises. It first covers the backgrounds of some leading reformers, their varying motivations, the contexts in which they associated, and the formation of the various organizations and societies who provided direction, influence and action. It then turns to the various initiatives and strategies which they used to assist their success: preaching and communicating with supporters, educational activities to put key messages across to the wider public (and to children in particular), rescue activity, the offering of alternatives such as temperance hotels, public demonstrations of support, lobbying and pressure group politics. This latter led to a range of successful legislation, as earlier chapters have shown. So this chapter concludes with an assessment of the extent of their success.

The reformers

Reformers were often acutely attuned to the social and moral ills of British society, and so concerted action against vice by small groups of reformers could become a major agent of change. Those involved in the fight to create better social order to their communities and the wider world came from a variety of backgrounds. Evangelicals, churchmen, social workers, journalists, politicians, aristocrats, philanthropists, industrialists, feminists and others all tried to call the attention of the public and Parliament to the social and moral problems of vice. They sought to create a better, morally and socially improved, Britain. Yet leading activists needed strong moral courage. They faced public abuse, or accusations of being hypocritical and acting for selfish and corrupt motives. Most were impressive – sincere, virtuous and committed, spending time, effort and money in campaigning. They were highly motivated, purposeful, pious, public-spirited and serious, leading by personal example. Many reformers were skilled networkers and competent speakers. Their political and social activities often gained them public recognition and responsible positions. Significant numbers were active across a wide range of reformist and humanitarian activities.[3] They were often progressive thinkers. Their voices were raised loud in opposition to vicious behaviours. Their views impacted on legislation. They could, however, also be dogmatic, obsessive, over-rigorous and so intolerant that they were unable to compromise with others of different views.

Anti-vice leaders came from all classes, and varied in age and gender. Vice was highly politicized, and many supported the Liberal Party, but attacks on vice came from across the political spectrum. Many fought several vices simultaneously. John Edge, one of the more moderate temperance reformers, for example, was also active in addressing feminine behaviour. He wrote *Female Virtue: Its Enemies and Friends* in 1841 for the London Society for the Protection of Young Females.

Despite the divisions within the religious world, many ministers of religion played leading roles. A Catholic temperance movement led by Father Mathew of Cork called Catholics across Britain to abstinence around mid-century, but in general Catholics were less active against gambling. More Church of England leaders supported temperance than total abstinence, but later in the century Rev. E. Lyttelton and others were strong supporters of social purity. Evangelicals were particularly key supporters of temperance, but the more literal biblical interpretations of more radical religious dissenters, such as Methodists, Wesleyans, Quakers or Baptists, often led them to action against all the major Victorian vices.

There were a few upper-class activists like Sir Walter Trevelyan, the progressive agriculturalist, who became the first president of the UK Alliance, or Lady Henry Somerset, the President of the British Women's Temperance Association in 1890. Other wealthy landowners helped in other ways, perhaps refusing to renew racing leases or closing down public houses on their estates.

Civic leaders and industrialists were important too. Titus Salt, the textile baron, an ardent Congregationalist and temperance reform campaigner, combined religious motives and practical industrial, economic and social reasons in attempting to fight the vices of his mill-workers. He supplied them with good housing, sanitation and amenities in Saltaire, near Bradford.

Workers he employed were expected to be sober and God-fearing, punctual and hard-working. He banned smoking, betting and swearing. Public drunkenness and violence were virtually unknown in his streets.[4]

In York, the Quaker Rowntree family, which included cocoa, chocolate and sweet manufacturers as well as professionals in education and the law, attacked vice on an even wider canvas. They were involved in various social and moral reform movements, in Sabbath and adult school work, in fighting immorality and seeking to reform society.[5] They were active temperance advocates. The Rowntree factory rules attempted to enforce 'appropriate' moral behaviour amongst its girl and women workers. Joseph Rowntree (1836–1925) believed that understanding the underlying causes of vice, evil and weakness would help change society. He was a social innovator supporting many radical and reforming causes, co-writing *The Temperance Question and Social Reform* in 1899. He was also appalled by gambling and saw it as one of the great scourges of society.[6] Seebohm Rowntree (1871–1954) carried out his own survey into poverty in York in the 1890s, published as *Poverty, a Study of Town Life* in 1901.[7] Primary poverty, he argued, was where a family did not earn enough to obtain even the minimum necessities. Families suffering from secondary poverty had sufficient earnings, but 'wasted' money on vices such as alcohol. They were preyed on 'by the publican and the bookmaker' to escape 'the monotony of their work and environment'.[8] Like his father, Seebohm was a committed and active member of the Liberal Party. He strongly opposed gambling and produced *Betting and Gambling: A National Evil* (1905).

There were members of the professional middle classes too, from doctors, teachers in more prestigious schools and university professors to clerks. Dr Frederick Lees (1815–97), from Leeds, a celebrated philosopher, orator and author, worked for teetotalism tirelessly. The Wesleyan Thomas Halliday Barker (1818–89) was a clerk and then an accountant, before becoming a hardworking administrator for the UK Alliance from about 1853. John Gulland, a Scottish lawyer, was secretary of the National Anti-gambling League in the 1890s. He was succeeded by John Hawke, a member of Lloyd's, the insurance organization and a former vice-president of a local Liberal association. He disingenuously portrayed the League as 'entirely unfettered by political or religious views', claiming members from all parties and both Houses of Parliament.[9]

Some politicians played an active role in supporting active anti-vice movements. Anti-temperance MP Sir Wilfred Lawson (1829–1906), another Liberal, was President of the Alliance from 1879, and its wittily humorous chief advocate in Parliament. Another supporter was Thomas Palmer Whittaker (1850–1919), businessman and newspaper editor, who became a Liberal MP in 1892.

There were also social campaigners with working-class roots. There was an explicit high moral tone and respect for self-improvement to be found in Chartism and Owenism, and later in areas of working-class organizations like the trades unions. So several leaders were self-educated self-improvers, like Joseph Livesey (see Chapter 3). George Williams (1821–1905), after a supposedly 'careless, thoughtless, godless, swearing' adolescence as a draper's assistant became a devout Christian and founded the Young Men's Christian Association in 1844, to save young shop-workers and help them find friendship, form good habits, resist worldly temptations and become good citizens.

Working-class socialist leaders regularly stressed the links between drink, poverty and crime. They often combined secular and religious arguments.[10] William Lovett, a cabinet-maker famous as the Methodist secretary of the London Working Men's Association, attacked racing, gambling and drinking and self-interested and incompetent aristocrats. In the coalfields of Northumberland and Durham, Primitive Methodist preachers used their rhetorical skills, confidence and moral weight to attack mine owners for exploiting drink as an agent of control. They saw gambling as parasitic upon the miners, arguing that moral improvement would improve their material circumstances.[11] Key leaders of the Social Democratic Federation and the Independent Labour Party in the 1880s and 1890s, such as James Keir Hardy, Ben Tillett and Tom Mann, were teetotallers. They saw drink and gambling as problematic, holding back mining families from better lives.

Some articulate, better-off women escaped domesticity and became involved in anti-vice societies, charity work, temperance organizations and fund-raising, especially later in the century. Mrs Clara Lucas Balfour (1809–78) was a celebrated woman temperance lecturer and writer. Elizabeth Ann Lewis (1849–1924), wife of a wealthy coachbuilder, worked with Blackburn's Band of Hope. She was a key figure in a teetotal mission, a 'Blue Ribbon Army', which she introduced to Blackburn in 1882. Female purity movement leaders such as Ellice Hopkins (1836–1904) were often devout churchgoers, anxious to cleanse society, challenge sexual double standards and improve morality and pre-marital male chastity.[12] Josephine Butler (1828–1906), born into a leading northern Liberal landed family, was a philanthropist, writer, educational and social reformer, and passionate orator. She took up women's rights issues in Liverpool in the later 1860s, and became a vociferous figure in the campaign against sex trafficking, child prostitution and military-endorsed brothels. Their arguments forced churches to engage more directly in discussions of sex and promoted more public and religious discourse on sexuality.

The wide, cross-class mix of backgrounds from which reformers came was important. This range of gender, class and experience allowed them to vary their approach. It also meant they could address a range of audiences, using different language registers and different forms of argument depending on the context. Having articulate women in the movement was a key factor, at times providing a more specific female view of issues. This helped the media to pick up anti-vice arguments and disseminate them across Britain.

Motivations for reform

It was always easier in an avowedly Christian country, to defend virtue and attack vice, but to fully understand the motives and momentum underpinning the Victorian anti-vice campaigns we need to set them in the wider context of social change and the growth of national and international temperance culture.

The early nineteenth-century social change in cultural values was part of a 'civilizing movement'. It saw urban elites providing more 'rational recreations' for the urban poor.[13] Puritans had always feared the people's pleasures, and fear of social unrest remained a potent force, but in the early decades of Victoria's reign many more felt concerned about moral decay. Their concerns stemmed in part from rapid change, population growth, urbanization, industrialization, geographical mobility, social protest and the growing commercialization of 'modernity'. There were demands for more self-discipline, self-regulation and self-control to shape civic behaviour, public decency and moral atmosphere.

Such ideas and invocations spoke powerfully to the emotions of respectable people. They would improve people's lives. They would make for a better, more rational and caring community. The reformer Henry Vincent, for example, in an 1858 speech, saw human life as experiencing increasingly dangerous 'sensual' temptations, ever-increasing numbers of the dangerous 'masses' and more mobility and 'excitement'. He felt that every district now contained a large number of young men who were

> living lives so rude and profligate, vulgar and illiterate, but we must say of them that they are tainting themselves rather for a life of vice, or folly and of ignorance than for a life of domestic virtue.[14]

British society was becoming more democratic and wealthier. Increased real wages, free time and choice changed patterns of leisure consumption. Traditional means of regulation and control weakened. This created contexts in which drinking or gambling to excess and religious apathy became more common. Narratives about vice and its evils, which portrayed vice and virtue as monolithic moralities, helped people make sense of a changing world.

One perceived solution to social problems was 'moral [per]suasion', moderation and a more 'temperate' approach. The 'self', rather than the state, should change. Temperance became associated with the governing of personal desire: self-regulation, not just of alcohol intake but of anything that required the abandonment of self-control and morality.[15] Temperance symbolized moral progress towards a future Britain in control of its own destiny and salvation. Losing control was an invitation to the problematic pleasures of excessive sensual gratification, whether through drink, gambling or carnality. This unholy trinity caused growing concern. The real and imaginary anxieties they generated meant that the debates about them became compelling social issues.

One response was the contemporary spiritual revival, which had a major impact on discourse and ideology, even on non-church attenders.[16] Religious faith and Christian duty were major motivators of urban reformers who censured 'idleness' and the hedonistic and morally questionable vices associated with secular sites of mass leisure. They wished to make Britain more moral.[17] It was, for some of them, a 'battle' for Christianity itself, a battle against sin, Satan, and the unbeliever, calling sinners to repentance and redemption.[18] It was sometimes a 'crusade', a religious image exploited to unite reformers under a single banner, as in the Church of England Temperance Society's *Young Crusader's Hymn and Song Book* (1894). From an individualist and moralistic perspective, the collective pleasures of drink and gambling appeared alien.

In Victorian Britain, Christianity still had widespread support. In some places between 40 and 50 per cent of the population attended churches on Census Sunday 1851. There were significant regional variations and local factors, with attendance weakest in the low-status industrial towns of England's north and Midlands. There was also a clear link between religion and class. Working-class districts within cities saw lower church attendance. Despite a widespread sense that church and chapel doctrines were not to be taken literally, Nonconformity rose in its social power and influence post-1851. It peaked in the late nineteenth century. The middle classes were the most regular church attenders.

As in America, Protestant Christianity dominated the attack against disreputability, vice and rough behaviour. It possessed multiple organizations, reformist committees and societies, and a deeply-felt sense of moral absolutes and discipline. But variations in sectarian attitudes make it less clear whether reformers largely shaped their respectable identities within the context of submission to religion's ethical demands or selectively exploited sacred texts as ideologies of justification. Non-Christian minorities established in Britain, including Judaism and Islam, also taught that the 'great sins' of gambling and drinking were greater than any benefit offered. Opponents of vice worked hard to extend their power and create support for a much improved moral order and authority, and a more reformist British leisure culture. They mixed constantly with like-minded individuals. They received regular confirmation of their beliefs and apparent evidence of support.

Secularists and followers of the Enlightenment movement were also keen to place their respectable credentials behind the campaign for moral reform and social improvement. Social control, attempts to forge new social norms and a new social consensus and the social consciences of the wealthy all played a part. The middle classes tried to assert moral superiority over the 'undeserving' working classes and the more hedonistic upper classes, and attempted to improve their characters.

Civic leaders demonstrated their prestige, increased status or gained votes by fighting vice. They stressed civic progress through hard work, thrift, and rationality. Some of the wealthy created a compensatory rhetoric of stewardship.[19] For governments, restrictions on drinking hours or control of venereal disease in port areas appeared socially beneficial. For industrialists, a well-behaved and moral workforce literally paid dividends, increasing production and business effectiveness. Vice undermined profit margins and was antagonistic to industrial and national progress.

So the anti-vice movement attracted followers with a range of motivations, often evangelical and Christian, but also sometimes secularist or from other faiths. Many were deeply concerned with the impact of the social changes which Britain was experiencing, and felt attacks on vice promised moral reform and the social, economic and cultural improvement of the working classes.

The formation of anti-vice organizations

The extraordinary networking skill of reformers in creating reform movements and voluntary associations was a vital factor in their success. Lone individuals could do little to fight the vast tide of vice. They had to join together to mobilize reform, maintain momentum and achieve their aims. Associations, clubs and societies were vital. The patterns by which individual effort turned to the formation of societies, which then in turn expanded and created an impression of much action, were broadly similar. Quite often an individual would begin by organizing a conference or meeting to address a previously publicized issue and then get wider opposition together.

W.T. Stead, the editor whose articles provided impetus to the political campaign against child prostitution in the 1880s, provides a useful example of the shift from individual effort to organizational creation. Stead arranged conferences to recruit support. Then he organized a Vigilance Association of London to ensure the enforcement of legislation by government and the police. The Association's members distrusted the willingness of the Home Office to enforce the law, and thought a vigilant public could ensure action. The far older Society for the Suppression of Vice handed over its limited funding (c. £50), and merged when the Vigilance Association became the National Vigilance Association (NVA) in August 1885. This had a broader purity agenda: 'the enforcement and improvement of the laws for the repression of criminal vice and public immorality'.

Following a prestigious late-August conference and London rally, further associations, such as the Minors' Protection Society, rapidly followed. The NVA provided purity speakers and set up chastity leagues, stimulated many new vigilance committees, and encouraged existing organizations to affiliate. Press coverage conveyed the impression of a major national movement. It created registries of members and institutions. Its General Council consisted of delegates from the affiliated groups and other appointed members. By 1888, 300 local committees had affiliated. Expansion forced a move to regional sub-organizations: Sunderland and the north east, Manchester and the northern counties, Birmingham and the Midland counties, Bristol and the south western counties, and South Wales and Monmouthshire.[20]

Its Executive Committee created subcommittees to deal with organizational and financial matters concerned with preventive, legal, parliamentary and municipal issues. Its legal subcommittee handled about 200 cases annually against sellers of obscene wares, rapists, homosexuals and brothel keepers. NVA branches all over the country sent and received information about such vices and relayed them to police forces.

Stead's approach was fairly typical of the reformist organizions which had proliferated from the 1830s onwards, if not before, and were a key feature of Victorian society more generally. Their unity provided strength, a 'concentration of moral force', and provided a sense of community and identity.[21] These local and national societies shaped and dominated discourse and debate, thanks to their vigour, their participative levels and their collective organization. Though they addressed different vices the strategies and tactics the various groups involved adopted were very similar, and the membership of different anti-vice groups often overlapped. Lacking a consistent definition, each society's membership operated and acted on particular and often quite limited views of the focus and nature of vice.

Being society members made people feel good, part of a wider group with shared ideals. Society membership, like religion, formed a kind of social cement and provided recognition. Others looked up to them. They felt admired. Membership offered education, friends, support and sometimes even jobs. Opposition to vice could be worn as a badge of status. Reports of meetings often suggested this element of self-satisfied display. When the City and North of London Auxilliary Society for the Suppression of Intemperance held its fifth meeting in 1841, the report described it as 'orderly and well conducted'. The audience were 'highly pleased' at its passing of resolutions. This the journalist inferred, suggested 'a strong appearance of ostentation in this sturdy sobriety'.[22]

Reformers often felt more comfortable sharing class, gender, religious or political affiliation, and even occupational backgrounds, so movements often formed separate associations even when sharing aims, creating a plethora of organizations with very similar titles. This did not help their cause. In terms of temperance, for example, there was a Roman Catholic total abstinence organization, the League of the Cross, founded in 1873. English physicians supporting total abstinence and more research formed the British Medical Temperance Association in 1876. The British Women's Temperance Association was founded in Newcastle the same year. There was even an Army Temperance Association in 1895.

These voluntary associations, whether focused on temperance or social purity, were dedicated to repressing, censoring or eradicating immorality and imposing their own norms, values and behaviours. Some entertained millennarian hopes of creating a vice-free world. Yet similarities could be superficial, with very different sets of expectations and social aspirations. Some societies were uncompromising, extremely radical and single-minded, almost fanatical, in their opposition to particular vices. The Independent Order of Good Templars, founded in New York in 1851 and widespread across the USA, was brought to England in 1868. It proved especially popular in strongly Protestant, Calvinist areas of Scotland. It was associated with sectarian, economic and social discrimination. Membership was secret, with elaborate rituals, and involved a comprehensive, lifelong abstinence pledge.[23]

But all such organizations faced the reformist equivalent of the product cycle. They innovated, quickly became popular, but then lost momentum, began to stagnate and decline, losing membership and subscriptions. This could be due to factionalism and internal dissention, achievement of some limited objective, or simply becoming temporarily unfashionable. In Scotland, for example, in September 1838, forty-one delegates, representing thirty societies, met in Glasgow and formed the Scottish Temperance Union. With a rapid growth of support, in June 1839 Eastern and Western Scottish Temperance Unions were formed, with headquarters in Edinburgh and Glasgow respectively. The movement peaked in 1842 with a revivalist surge across Scotland, but then declined. In 1844 the Eastern Union became extinct, and the Western Union was dissolved in 1847.

Organizations might then attempt a relaunch, reinvigorating themselves by merging with other societies. The British and Foreign Society for the Suppression of Intemperance, for example, was strong at the start of Victoria's reign. Leading figures such as Lord Stanhope and Sir C.E. Smith addressed annual meetings. The Society was positively reported, as were the speeches, which claimed that the 'cause of temperance was ... making rapid progress throughout the kingdom of Great Britain'.[24] But by 1842 funds were 'not in a flourishing condition' and the room for the meeting was 'not well filled'. This forced the Society to seek a union with the New British and Foreign Temperance Society, whose membership was also in decline.[25] The Church of England Temperance Society, founded in 1862 and rooted in Anglo-Catholicism, tried to overcome the problems of schism by having different sections for abstainers (more often working-class) and more moderate often middle-class drinkers. It also retained 'most friendly relations' with Nonconformists in the National Temperance League and the UK Alliance.[26]

Anti-vice organizations were more successful when they could combine to form a national movement, as in the case of opposition to gambling. Anti-gambling public meetings began appearing more commonly in the 1880s, often introduced under the auspices of Nonconformist churches, or Christian endeavour unions. Both were alarmed at the spread of working-class street betting. The National Anti-Gambling League was formed in 1889.[27] It had some smaller branches scattered across the country, although the heart of its support was in the north. It soon had major branches in London, York, Manchester, north-eastern England and Scotland, and granted membership to subgroups of existing social and religious organizations.

Anti-vice organizations were central to providing unity, but many struggled to maintain direction and support over time. Reasons included internal divisions, restrictions on membership, rivalries with other organizations, and constant proliferation, flowering and then becoming unfashionable. But where an over-arching national organization incorporated a number of existing organizations, its voice became louder, as in the case of the National Anti-Gambling Association.

Their strategies – using the media

The anti-vice societies were pressure groups whose three main purposes of communication aimed to inspire, educate and integrate their followers into a larger body. They communicated via formal meetings, reports in the press and through direct mailing. Reform movements recognized the importance of 'spin' and coverage in the more supportive of the mainstream regional and national press. So they worked hard to ensure meetings, speeches, sermons, and other reform events were well covered, but where editorial support for reform affected media circulation and profits this might be curtailed. In dealing with betting for example, Nonconformist editors could potentially restrict the availability of betting information by refusing to print results, but even papers controlled by Quaker families were usually forced, reluctantly and with great embarrassment, to provide a full results service, even while their editorial columns fulminated against betting.[28] The *Northern Echo*, associated with the Darlington Pease family, set its typeface firmly against racing results and reports in the 1870s, but it resumed the printing of results in the 1880s, as did other Liberal anti-gambling newspapers such as the *Leeds Mercury* and *Manchester Guardian*.

To reach a wider audience, reformers regularly wrote letters to the press. Charles Kingsley, clergyman author of *The Water Babies*, was sufficiently concerned about the wickedness of gambling amongst Chester's young men to write letters to the local paper in 1871. These were addressed to the young 'fools' who gambled, some of whom were 'sons of merchants and manufacturers, as well of squires and noblemen'.[29]

Many reform organizations, however, communicated more directly with their membership in print form. Most members of moral movements were literate, keen on education and always interested in receiving magazines and weekly journals, some with competitions. In 1837, for example, the British and Foreign Society for the Suppression of Intemperance offered a prize of £100 for the 'best essay on the mischief, vice and folly of intemperance'.[30] Material emphasized specific vices, their dangers and the possible consequences of an immodest act, a single drink or bet. The benefits of a respectable, virtuous life were constantly stressed. Such material helped to create imagined communities of readers sharing experiences and attitudes.

For the temperance movement, early newspapers included a *Weekly Journal of the New British and Foreign Bible Society* between 1839 and 1841 but this was not able to sustain its readership. *The British Temperance Advocate*, the mouthpiece of the British Association for the Promotion of Temperance, was initially produced in Douglas, Isle of Man in 1839, to avoid stamp tax and United Kingdom postal regulations, and claimed a circulation of about 10,000. Even the travel entrepreneur Thomas Cook briefly ran a newspaper, the *Anti-Smoker and Progressive Temperance Reformer*.

By the 1850s there was a very substantial temperance newspaper and periodical press. Wales, for example, had fourteen different Welsh language temperance journals. A penny journal of moral and social reform, the *Alliance News,* was printed in Manchester from 1855. The *Weekly Record*, from the National Temperance League, was first printed in London in 1856. In Scotland, the *Scottish Temperance League Journal* emerged in 1857. The *Church of England Temperance Magazine*, later the *Temperance Chronicle*, came out in 1862. In 1860–1 the three main weekly temperance newspapers had a combined circulation of 25,000. The first successful temperance journal aimed at a female readership was the *White Ribbon*, from the National British Women's Temperance Association, in 1897. Temperance periodicals were issued by national, regional and even very small local organizations, though few local temperance newspapers lasted more than a decade. Derby's *Temperance Bells* (1890–1940s) was a rare exception. They were often heavily serious if not turgid, but could include songs, stories, puzzles, poems and images. Readers could write in and enter competitions, helping to create feelings of participation and membership.

It was the 1870s before a purity press emerged. *The Pioneer*, the organ of the Social Purity Association and the Moral Reform Union, was launched in 1887. An anti-gambling press began only in the 1890s, centred on the twice-yearly *Bulletin* of the National Anti-Gambling League. The *Bulletin* documented its activities, including public meetings, lectures and sermons, the forming of local branches, pledges, petitions and subscription lists, and the reprinting of any relevant anti-gambling material from the regional and national press. Contents also included lists of harm done to families by betting, crimes caused by it, analysis of the inaccuracy of betting tips, and quotes from public figures denouncing betting.

Most printed material was, like the reform movements themselves, serious in tone and approach, and was also used to reach outside audiences, especially as literacy rates rose. But in a less literate outside world, more useful dramatic, visual ways of presenting the reformers' case in print were surprisingly less commonly used. Humour was often lacking, although the 'Hopeful' series of Sunday school dialogues in the 1880s and 1890s claimed to be 'humorous and interesting'. Temperance cartoons too tended towards the serious.

Books, pamphlets, periodicals, tracts and sermon texts were another common means of getting the anti-vice message across, though only the more literate could read them. These also provided arguments and ideas for preachers, parents and members to use. The British Library still contains well over 2,000 books devoted to the Victorian temperance causes. The UK Alliance used its funds to support a National Temperance Publication Depot which produced substantial numbers of temperance publications between 1880 and 1895. The Church of England Temperance Society had its own publication depot which began modestly in the late 1860s, and slowly expanded over the next decades, before a major expansion in the 1890s. Most anti-vice organizations devoted at least some of their subscriptions to the printing of relevant material. This included guidance about setting up branches, notes for teachers, courses of instruction, sermons and readings. The Church of England Purity Society published a series of 'Papers for Men' in the mid-1880s.

Written material was supported by evidence collected largely from Parliamentary Commissions and the press. Persuasion took different approaches. Sometimes campaigners presented moral arguments drawing on Christian biblical principles. Sometimes they appealed to enlightened self-interest, arguing that vice wasted money and resources, and its abandonment would mean material gain and the purchase of other, more essential commodities: better food, clothing, help for children, or days out. Sometimes they focused on health reasons, based on medical authorities, experiments and statistics, as on the threat of alcohol to family and wider society. Death, disease and injury were all linked to inebriation. Water had always been a powerful temperance image and as fresh water was made more widely publicly available by local authorities, temperance reformers reminded people of its use as a replacement for beer.

So reformists attempted both to restrict media information of the 'wrong' type, such as betting results and tips, and ensure coverage of their activities in the mainstream press through reports and letters. They also communicated with supporters through a range of printed material, including newspapers, journals, magazines, books, pamphlets, periodicals, tracts and sermon texts. They provided information and educative material and tried to bring together those who were already literate, serious-minded and supportive of the movements' aims.

Other forms of outreach to followers and wider audiences

Ecclesiastical, educational and moral voluntary agencies of reform believed that the broader public needed to be effectively persuaded or *re-educated* to accept intellectual and moral progress and enlightenment, pointing up the consequences of bad actions or suggesting that vice problems were increasing. So printed media provided only one approach.

Preaching from the pulpit or at public meetings against drink or gambling was perennially common. The Alliance held 2,539 meetings in England and Wales in 1873, but usually in areas of existing strength. Public meetings, where the converted addressed the unconverted, were often more common in the earlier, enthusiastically proselytizing stages of a campaign, before organizations turned to consolidation. They soon realized that the unconverted were difficult targets so meetings were carefully organized, with rows of seats, and speakers, including reformed drunks or gamblers, giving witness to enthusiastic and already committed audiences. Wherever possible they were held in well-known buildings, such as Exeter Hall or Manchester's Free Trade Hall. They were chaired by high-status figures, such as aristocrats, local mayors or bishops. These men suppressed (as far as possible) any dissenting voices. Saving drunkards was an aim, but drunks disrupted meetings, so a visitor to a temperance hall might well see someone a little the worse for drink immediately ordered out even though he belonged to that class which ought to have been allowed to hear statements the lecturer had to give in favour of total abstinence.[31]

Speakers were carefully chosen but varied in their approach. A few were entertaining, might sing or dance as well as speak, dress eccentrically, use fluent, colloquial, witty or humorous language. Others were more serious, didactic, listing facts and statistics. They firmed up the faith of the wavering and half-hearted in congregations or attracted the curious or just bored passers-by. Well-known preachers always attracted crowds.

Early vice moralists focused on individual failings, casting people's actions as proof of their sins or moral weakness. Sometimes they used reformed sinners to show the possibility of moral change. These were recruited in meetings, usually at a point when they recognized their addiction and weakness, or identified empathetically with reformed sinners on the platform. Most addicts had usually used vices initially to satisfy deeply-felt emotional needs. This was often eventually at the cost of uncontrolled spending, concealing and lying about their behaviour, bankruptcy, relationship breakdown and illness. So those who had found strategies to help them change their behaviour would release their pain, tell others of *their* sins, reshaping their story for maximum impact and turn respectable, creating a new persona, status and way of life. Robert Carr of Castleford, West Yorkshire, who began preaching in the later 1860s, was a reformed drunkard. He came forward on the circuit of reform chapels to regale listeners with vivid tales of his previous drunken degradations, and eventual conversion, moral transformation and salvation. Carr began preaching in West Yorkshire in the later 1860s on the subject of 'Drunkenness, Moderation and Sobriety'. In 1873 he wrote a short autobiography of his 'misspent life'. Drink had taken away his morality and sense. It led him to quarrelling and fighting, defrauding former friends, and into gaming and betting on horses. He put his craving for strong drink above the needs of his wife and children. His suffering and misery had only ended when he found Jesus.[32] Such former drunkards and gamblers probably exaggerated their excesses. *The Life of Jane Johnson*, a Salvation Army member, published in Leeds in 1883, proclaimed her 'the champion drunkard of the world'.

Not all were well received. Their addresses were at times incoherent, highly inappropriate or poorly delivered, and could 'do much to put temperance into contempt' with a 'contemptuously laughing audience'. Some more intelligent citizens were probably unimpressed and contemptuous of their advocacy, seeing the supposed lifestyle changes as superficial, covering up continued weaknesses in character. For others, the accounts were simply embarrassing. Indeed, some came to scoff.[33] But some preachers were successful, even if their claims were inflated by self-interest.

Visual material, either printed on posters or on banners, also had an impact. The anti-vice movement, in its public manifestations, was probably more strongly sustained by its images and symbols than by its ideology. It certainly relied heavily on symbolism, often religious in origin, and thus on people's ability to interpret it. Such examples included female figures representing knowledge, temperance (always shown as a woman) trampling on the snake of evil, the sword and olive branch of justice and peace, carrying of a shield against evil vice, or St George and the Dragon.

Anti-vice societies organized opposition largely though the work of their secretaries and the employment of professional or semi-professional agents. Secretaries had to be enthusiastic and highly active, writing regular letters to the press as well as managing society affairs. Some organized local plebiscites, canvasses or petitions, which generally indicated an overwhelming majority in favour of reform. This was unsurprising since questions tended to be framed in a leading, prejudicial way, offered few alternatives, and were restricted to householders and those attending places of worship.

Such approaches were typical of the movement. A committee of the Convocation of the Province of Canterbury, for example, headed by the Archdeacon of Coventry, a leading temperance campaigner, which sent out inquiries into the extent of intemperance in 1868, asked extremely leading questions. These began by focusing on 'the extent of the evil', and 'probable causes'. They then explored the impact of intemperate habits on 'morality and attendances on the ordinances of religion', 'domestic happiness and comfort', 'education of working classes', the 'health of the population', and 'crime, pauperism, lunacy and attendant expenses on the community at large'. Next they probed the 'special influence for evil of traffic in intoxicating liquor on Sundays or late hours on other days', and the 'general influence of the liquor traffic on the vigilance and fidelity of the public'. Finally, they turned to the exploration of possible remedies.[34]

The British and Foreign Temperance Society had ten semi-professional agents as early as 1835. The later UK Alliance divided the country into districts supervised by agents, but they were often side-tracked from addressing vice directly and used for other practical business such as collecting subscriptions, sending begging letters to patrons or pushing publication purchase. Revenue and high status subscribers indicated potential power, so most societies publicized their subscription lists if they were sufficiently impressive. Cash was spent on publicity. Agents' preaching was increasingly confined to chapel, church or hall, and to those already numbered amongst the faithful. It helped to marshal those who were already opposed to vice.

Preaching, however, could not be heard by and could not convert the already vicious. Few brave souls visited pubs or racecourses to directly confront unconverted sinners, and attempt preaching. The Baptist F.B. Meyer, who had preached against Leicester races in local chapels in 1882, tried unsuccessfully to address the Leicester race crowd in 1883. He escaped unmolested with some difficulty.[35] Giving out short tracts to the public was little easier. At Manchester races in 1838, a Primitive Methodist group addressed the crowd and distributed leaflets, denouncing the sinfulness and folly of the day. Most leaflets ended up littered on the course.[36]

Attracting children

As adults often proved obdurately difficult to save from sin, reform organizations increasingly targeted children, believing they could more easily be recruited to the cause and socialized into better moral behaviour. The British League of Juvenile Abstainers, a temperance example, aimed at children, was founded in Edinburgh in 1847 by John Hope (1807–93), a philanthropist and wealthy lawyer. Between October 1846 and June 1850 he spent £3,043 on the movement, whose members had to abstain from alcoholic drinks, tobacco and opium, and study the Bible. Outings to botanical gardens or the zoo were organized to encourage membership, and built up bonds of loyalty and goodwill.

In England, the Band of Hope, also founded in 1847, was associated with Baptist and Methodist churches, mission halls, Sabbath schools and temperance societies, sometimes holding mid-week evening meetings. It made itself attractive with occasional picnics and parades, hymns, addresses, recitations, slides, competitions, music and prayers for children.[37] By 1860, there were 160 Bands of Hope in London alone. In 1864, a UK Band of Hope Union was formed. By 1871, Manchester alone had 161 societies. Edinburgh Union had had thirty-five Bands of Hope in 1878. By 1901, Britain had more than 28,000 societies with a total membership of more than 3.5 million children.

Sunday schools also played a pivotal role. They attracted children from both urban and rural backgrounds. In 1888, roughly three out of four British children attended. They were attracted for a variety of reasons:

their basic literacy and moral instruction; the predominantly working-class teachers; the prospect of respectable recreations in the form of free galas, processions, excursions, sports or prizes; or pressure from parents who either wished their children to be brought up as Christians or perhaps just wanted their home free of its children for a short while. Membership was certainly impressively high but absenteeism and poor teaching definitely affected outcomes. Few children continued their support into adulthood. Sunday schools were in part an agent of social control and partly working-class encouragement of honesty, self-improvement and respect for others. They helped publicize anti-vice campaigns throughout the century. Sunday school pupils regularly pledged to abhor drink, and by the 1880s children were being induced to sign a witnessed pledge against gambling as well. One of many such, in 1887, read:

> Believing Gambling, Betting on Horses etc., to be a sin against God and a great curse to men, I hereby pledge myself, in Christ's strength, to abstain from this evil in every form, and to do my utmost to save others from it.[38]

Children's material was carefully structured. There were brightly-coloured certificates of membership, or of merit, and long-service certificates. There were badges and medals, including a 'holdfast' bar for each year of membership and attendance attached to the Band of Hope medal or a special badge of honour for reciting, essay writing or good conduct, or for officers. Badge of Hope pledges combined Christian symbols and pictures of children.

Rescue activity

Preaching, rallies, meetings, tract distribution, publications and counter-attractions had some impact, but the more committed reformers wanted to do more than attempt cultural change from the outside. They wanted more positive action, to 'save' people from vice. The image of rescue, 'salvation' from vice was a symbolic and extremely powerful metaphor in reformist rhetoric, even when such 'rescue' might have unpleasant consequences for individuals, such as the police efforts to impose the harsh restrictions of the Contagious Diseases Act which supposedly 'rescued' the various young prostitutes they arrested 'from vice'. Reformatory and industrial schools for girls supposedly saved them from a life of vice and crime, especially from mid-century. Aiming to rid society from the curse of prostitution through prevention, the Ladies' Association for the Care of Friendless Girls had 106 branches across England by 1885, while Catholic Ireland had its Magdalene Asylums. There was an assumption, embodied in the title of the Church Penitentiary Association, that those 'rescued' should demonstrate penitence, though women attended for a range of reasons, perhaps just escaping a harsh winter.

Some reformers spent time and effort entering slums and courts, providing charity and trying to change the morality of the working class by missionary and domestic visiting. They hoped to sustain a vibrant and significant minority religious subculture in the slums, although feverish activity and public vindications concealed a very limited impact.[39] Church elders and Sunday school teachers were already establishing active city missions in Glasgow, Chester, Coventry, Leeds and elsewhere by the 1840s, teaching morality and self-improvement. Churches ran relief programmes, and wealthy benefactors set up educational schemes, such as the Ragged Schools, which were praised for allowing pupils to be 'rescued from vice and misery'.[40]

Both sexes were involved. In 1841, for example, a Miss Macarthy applied to the secretary of the Tract Society with connections to the Wesleyan Chapel in London's City Road to become a 'distributor' in the slums. Later she founded a school, provided children's dinners, organized class meetings, weekly services and agencies for relieving want and instructed 'the ignorant' in the 'way of life'.[41] The Hon. Maude Stanley (1833–1915), another practical reformer, daughter of the politician Edward Stanley, devoted a significant amount of time to social work in the early 1870s as a district visitor around London's Five Dials. Shocked at the way youngsters played cards, gambled and behaved, she involved a local shoemaker and postman as teachers and helpers, and made contact with young men and girls in the streets, courtyards and alleys. She set up a refuge, developing Sunday schools, night classes and a club. Her Sunday afternoon class began when she invited four boys to come, those brought others, and from that time to August, she had 'a varying number of from eight to twenty-five every Sunday'.[42]

Offering better alternatives

To keep people away from temptation and the malign consequences of vice, another strategy was to offer alternative pleasures and distractions, more 'rational recreations'.

Church attendance was voluntary, but offered social friendships and recreations as well as spiritual and moral guidance. Evangelizing and respectable church activities for young men and women increased from the 1860s onwards and by the century's end recreational activities included dances, tea parties, singing classes, excursions, socials, and even amateur dramatics as well as a variety of sports.

The local authority and philanthropic provision of parks, libraries, reading rooms, museums, and art galleries illustrate similar attempts to civilize urban populations and offer more rational alternatives to rougher forms of working-class leisure. Bradford councillors at mid-century listed the church, the chapel, the concert hall, the library and the park, and 'a large public hall' as helping 'draw the working classes from those dens of vice to which they were tempted to resort'. They accepted that 'dark, uncleansed, un-watered, uncomfortable homes' needed improvement too.[43] The Poor Man's Friend Society in 1841 aimed to address pauperism, immorality, vice and intemperance by providing gardens and allotments for the poor. The paradox was that while many of these 'rational recreations' aimed to make the working classes more respectable, many ended up being socially exclusive, restricted to the middle classes. Those recreations which were more sedate, ordered and morally safe were also sometimes less widely appealing.

More specific secular counter-attractions were created. Cocoa houses, temperance refreshment rooms and hotels, mechanics' institutes and even the first working-men's clubs provided alternatives to the public house. Temperance catering firms grew up to service them.[44] The National Temperance League even created a Temperance Building Society and a Temperance Provident Institution to try to firm up support, while the London Temperance Hospital in 1873 did not use alcohol in its treatment.

The mass rally for big crowds led by a leading populist preacher was another common tactic, one particularly exploited by the temperance movement. There were regular temperance rallies across Britain from the 1840s. 'Gospel' temperance rallies were imported from the USA in early 1881, when the American evangelist and 'reformed rum-seller' Francis Murphy came over to extend his 'Blue Ribbon' Temperance campaign, so-called because of the blue ribbon badge presented to each person who signed the total abstinence pledge. Murphy first began preaching in northern England and Scotland. In Scotland, the Dundee hand-loom weaver and poet William McGonagall wrote, with more enthusiasm than talent:

All hail to Mr Murphy, he is a hero brave
That has crossed the mighty Atlantic wave
For what purpose let me pause and think
I answer, to warn the people not to taste strong drink
And I'm sure if they take his advice, they never will rue
The day they joined the Blue Ribbon Army in the year 1882.

Murphy extended his campaign to Manchester, Dublin and Norwich, where he was drawn through the streets in a carriage with four horses, supported by scarlet-clad outriders, in a procession with banners, flags and massed bands, parading along streets where bottles hung from windows as a symbolic representation of their occupants' temperance beliefs. Over 30,000 people welcomed him. Over the 1880s, about a million people signed the pledge and wore the blue ribbon.

These big rallies in support of temperance or purity helped to demonstrate the movements' support to a wider public. Major rallies were well-orchestrated, and like all popular protest marches of the time full of symbol, sound and visual imagery, with brass bands and music from tambourines, drums and fifes. A purity march might have white roses for purity, young women clad in virginal white and banners with slogans such as 'War on Vice', 'Shame, Shame, Horror', or 'Men. Protect the Women of England'. Rechabite marchers might wear collars, aprons or sashes and carry regalia.

In an age when brass bands, classical and church music all attracted substantial interest, reformers used music to attract converts and promote their cause. John Guest's *Musical Entertainer: Songs and Ballads for Penny Readings and Temperance Entertainments* (1876) provided material for temperance entertainments. Songs, anthems, hymns, cantatas, part songs and marches were enthusiastically penned by reformers. In the 1890s, the best and most popular temperance hymns were collected into *Hoyle's Hymns and Songs for Temperance Societies and Bands of Hope.*

Reaching a music-hall audience was a far more difficult task. Even so, a few performers included songs about the adverse effects of drink, such as *The Poor Drunkard's Child* (1880) or *Please Sell No More Drink to My Father* (1889). Penned by music-hall journeymen writers, they were created to appeal to the emotions and sympathies of a working-class audience. *The Good Templar's Happy Home* (1883) described the happiness of a wife whose husband had taken the pledge. The song, written from the wife's point of view, praised her husband as keeping away from the pub, faithful, no longer swearing, attending to his books, while the children now had clothes.[45] On Tyneside, Joe Wilson, a workman turned entertainer, was hugely popular on the local entertainment circuit in the 1860s, but his personal experience of the problems of drink led him to an increasingly positive emphasis on temperance in later songs, though at the expense of their popularity. The temperance movement also developed new forms of theatrical literature and performance, both professional mainstream and amateur theatricals, to help spread their message.[46] A classic example of such melodrama was *The Trial of Sir Jasper: A Temperance Tale in Verse*, about a greedy brewer, caring little that he condemned the families of drunkards to poverty and death.[47] In Glasgow, the Abstainers' Union organized very popular Saturday night concerts from the 1850s, with professional music hall entertainers and international opera stars.

Young women in work and with money were portrayed as particularly at risk. Some were undesirably financially independent, supposedly frivolous spenders, flirtatious or sexually precocious, over-influenced by peers. For such individuals, various girls' clubs, such as the Snowdrop Bands, the Girls' Friendly Society, and the YWCA, offered more rational forms of respectable leisure, aiming to develop better habits of self-reliance and independence.[48] For those out of work, places like the Trewint Industrial Home in Hackney in the late 1860s housed 'thirty girls over fifteen years of age ... restrained from vice, to which they had been exposed by being without situations'.[49] Boys' clubs likewise offered respectable counter-attractions for potentially disruptive lads. Some organizations, such as the Young Men's Improvement Societies, had a religious bias, others such as the Boys' Brigade, a more military one, but both acted as an alternative focal point for loyalties.

Sunday school excursions could function to take children away from temptations, and were prominent in attempting to keep children and adults away from the races, and their associated drinking and gambling. Thomas Cook's first temperance excursion in 1846 was a Sunday school counter-attraction to a Leicester race meeting.[50] Anti-race protesters, including individual Sunday schools, Sunday School Unions, and temperance organizations, arranged their own processions or created alternative festivals. At Newcastle-upon-Tyne, children from the various Sunday schools processed through the town en route for their trips, excursions and picnics, often led by fife and flute bands. After 1881, the various Newcastle and northern counties' temperance organizations offered a two-day Temperance Festival as a race-day alternative, with band contests, kite flying, bicycle races, football games, military sports, children's games and foot racing. Like the races, the Festival offered contests and competitions, and like the races too it had, by 1883, stands, twenty-four large marquees, a long range of tents, tables and stalls.[51]

Such alternatives were costly, and by the end of the nineteenth century most had almost ceased. Rail excursions and galas had to be underwritten and sometimes lost money, especially if the weather was bad. It was also becoming clear that the policy of offering alternatives was often ineffective in the longer term.

Pressure groups politics

Politically-aware campaigners soon recognized that their power could be increased and their crusade made much more effective by pressuring the police, magistrates, newspapers, circulating libraries, various government agencies and even Parliament itself. Effort was needed to *legally* prohibit or curtail vice, with fewer pubs, better police supervision of all drinking places and suppression of all gambling and brothels.

So the police and magistrates were urged to further action against prostitution, drunkards, the many forms of street betting or other sinful behaviour via letters and sermons. Some came from concerned locals, others from society officials, demanding results, more successful prosecutions and a stop to law breaking. There were also attempts to get senior officers appointed who would be more active against vice.

Certainly prosecutions of public house and beer house landlords varied according to changing police and magisterial attitudes. In Norwich, for example, between 1836 and 1851, convictions of landlords of public houses and beer houses averaged 2.3 annually, until the arrival of a new superintendent increased the figure dramatically. The figure rose to 25.8 convictions a year between 1853 and 1859.

Pressing magistrates to introduce local bylaws was another common tactic. The increasingly common introduction of bylaws concerned with street obstruction from the mid-1870s reflects the response of anti-gambling magistrates and police to an apparent increase in betting. Manchester, for example, passed a bylaw in 1875 that defined any three or more persons assembled together for the purpose of betting as obstructing the street.[52] Following the Municipal Corporations Act of 1882 several authorities, led by Wolverhampton, introduced a more specific local bylaw to deal with street betting. Usually it asserted that 'no person shall frequent or use any public place, on behalf of himself or any other person, for the purpose of wagering or agreeing to bet or wager with any person, or paying or receiving or settling bets'. Offences were subject to a fine not exceeding £5.

There were also attempts to stop the publication of 'inappropriate material'. Like recent animal-rights movement supporters, a minority of purity activists pressured writers through visits to their homes, overt surveillance, public proclamations and warnings and threatening letters. Pressure was put on circulating libraries not to stock such material. As public libraries were founded, sympathetic librarians were encouraged, sometimes by reformist local councillors, to black out racing results before putting papers on display.[53] This was relatively ineffective, and had fairly symbolic impact. Public houses, for example, might provide such material to draw people in. Friends might share the cost.

Anti-vice reformers saw pressuring governments and getting legislation passed as the most effective way of combating vice, improving morality and effecting change. The preaching, letter writing, lobbying, offering of alternative recreations and other actions were all tactical moves in this wider battle. So all the major organizations lobbied Parliament, put pressure on Members of Parliament and ensured that they came before Select Committees and Royal Commissions to provide 'evidence' for inquiries. The temperance movement was extremely good at employing such lobbyist tactics. When in 1849 and 1850 the Select Committee of the House of Lords considered the Acts for the sale of beer they received a series of petitions from municipal bodies, boards of guardians, magistrates, congregations, all addressing the 'evils' of existing legislation. From 1860 onwards, during any Parliamentary sessions relating to drink, the Alliance employed an agent to provide background briefings to friendly MPs. High-status deputations put pressure on Cabinet ministers and forced policy utterances. In 1869, the Beer House Licensing System Amendment Association worked extremely hard just to ensure that municipal organizations petitioned in favour of a change in the licensing of beerhouses. A deputation led by the Archbishop of Canterbury met with the Home Secretary and Prime Minister Gladstone to ask government to support the National Association for Promoting Amendments in the Laws Relating to the Liquor Traffic. The Archbishop claimed it was 'representative of all classes in the community and the religious views of all denominations'.[54] In support of the Permissive Bill of 1869, 4,000 petitions, with nearly 800,000 signatures, reached Parliament. In 1872 signatures totalled 1,388,075.

When one set of arguments failed to work, lobbyists would shift to another to manipulate the terms of discourse for political advantage and influence policy. So, for example, purity activists used the rhetoric of eugenics and medicine and the supposed feeblemindedness of some prostitutes to persuade politicians to enact legislation on sexual matters, deliberately shifting the debate to one in terms of science.

The Alliance and National Anti-Gambling League spent much time debating whether they should put up candidates themselves or put pressure on existing candidates at elections, when every vote counted, giving them 'test questions' about their attitude to temperance or gambling. When no candidate supported temperance, Liberal candidates could be blackmailed by threats of abstention or switching votes. The Alliance even employed a full-time electoral organizing secretary, J.S. Owen, at a salary of £200 per annum. Not everyone supported this form of pressure. In 1863, *The Times*, for example, called it 'unscrupulous terrorism'.[55]

How successful were they?

The experiences of anti-vice reformers were intensely social, self-confirming and mutually reinforcing. People with whom they associated at home, church or work generally agreed with them. They constantly found the evidence of evil they sought in the public world around them, and this shaped and structured their understanding, which they then wrote and talked about; association was a key feature of the movement.

Association and lobbying brought a measure of success. In part, it came through national impact and legislative changes relating to topics such as temperance, but there were also successes at local level, where action was able to remove temptations to vice, the closing down of public houses, stopping of drink sales or the cessation of race meetings.

Many urban parks had bylaws that forbade the selling, buying or drinking of alcohol. At Albert Park, in Middlesbrough, for example, a bylaw of 1868 read 'No intoxicating beverages of any kind shall be sold or vended within the boundaries of the said park'.[56] Country landlords with closed villages on their estate, or paternalistic employers who provided workers' housing, such as Titus Salt at Saltaire, could ensure public houses were banned. More select seaside residential and commuter resorts took care to limit drinking, and ensure prostitution was kept out. At Coatham in the North Riding of Yorkshire, a seaside resort developed in the 1860s by the Newcomen family, devout Anglicans, the housing was carefully controlled and there were firm restrictions on the building of licensed premises. No beer houses were allowed, only one public house and one hotel.[57] In one of their closed villages nearby, there was no pub.

There was some very limited success in controlling race meetings, especially round London. At the Kingsbury racecourse in London, which had seven meetings a year by 1869, magistrates tried to control it and close it down in 1877 by refusing licences to publicans.[58] When this failed to close it, a Glasgow MP, described by his opponents as a dour, sport-hating Sabbatarian Scot, successfully brought in an Act that required all racecourses with ten miles of Charing Cross to be licensed by local magistrates, and this ensured its closure, as it did several others.[59]

But more generally, racing was difficult to stop, given its strong support not just from the upper classes but also substantial sections of the middle class, so in traditional racing towns, external attempts at race closure were usually unsuccessful. Gambling faced similar problems. In a gambling example, when Hawke became leader of the National Anti-Gambling League in 1893, he promoted the wider use of anti-betting bylaws and took action against newspapers that encouraged betting. He also attempted organized prosecutions of racecourses such as Newmarket and Northampton, some bookmakers, postal betting and betting clubs. He attacked leading owners like then-Prime Minister Lord Rosebery. These prosecutions had little success, suggesting that the judiciary were unwilling to support such moves in the face of the legal ambiguities involved, and because the races at Epsom, Doncaster or Newmarket, for example, were all firmly supported by the local authorities.

Reformers had more chance of success where a race was newly established. At Halifax, a new enclosed course was set out in 1878 at a cost of nearly £40,000, initially attracting crowds of about 20,000, but a Congregationalist pastor, the vicar of Halifax and a number of local councillors, including the mayor, strongly opposed, and in 1879 they brought successful prosecutions for minor offences against the race company, although fines were small. Opposition to the races from local industrialists was strong enough to ensure that workmen were not able to absent themselves from work with impunity, and the meeting closed in 1884.[60]

Reformers tried to impose their values on the wider community by politically dominating watch committees and magistracies, though this was tempered by their concern not to overspend on police budgets. Because economy was a major concern exhortation often replaced real action. Magistrates had a range of views, some for example, being wealthy brewers. So they often adopted a *laissez-faire* approach. Through the 1840s and 1850s various petitions and deputations from London wards, local vestries and clergymen to the City of London or to the Home Office, complained that the Police Commissioner and magistrates were reluctant to act with regard to prostitution, but they received little satisfaction.[61]

Reformist goals also concealed tension. They wanted state controls, such as restrictions on the sale of alcohol or the banning of betting at sports events. Yet they also stressed individual choice and self-control. They felt able to combine these views partly because they believed that legislation would provide a very rapid solution. Their own ability to recognize but govern their passions and desires led them to believe that this constraint was equally possible for all. It was a Utopian vision of social and emotional life that was practically problematical.

The temporary alliances between reformist Christians and secularists battling against vice did not stop each trying to demonstrate superior moral credentials. By 1851, when Matthew Arnold wrote his 'Dover Beach', with its images of the 'Sea of Faith', once 'at the full', now experiencing a 'melancholy, long, withdrawing roar', while 'on a darkling plain, swept with confused alarms of struggle and flight ... ignorant armies clash by night', the Christian faiths were having to meet the challenges of increased secularism. The power of the churches and biblical teachings was lessening. There was growing estrangement between leisure and religion. Commercial leisure forms such as horse racing, music halls or publican-organized sports became increasingly popular. All this limited political success.

Conclusion

Despite the efforts of campaigners and their ability to form organizations and societies to provide direction and action, the tangible results of their actions were relatively limited. There was some impact on legislation, especially in terms of drink, less so in terms of sexual vice and gambling. Yet the movements' efforts do appear to have had other, less obvious, but significant impacts. Both Liberal and Conservative governments felt sufficiently threatened by the constant pressure of the campaigners not to attempt any liberalization of the laws with respect to these areas. The cumulative effect of the constant barrage of publicity ensured some effect on wider British attitudes. The anti-vice movements offered an alternative and more moral reformist culture. This certainly attracted a proportion of the British population. The Sunday schools and Bands of Hope attracted children. Rescue activity helped some women, and the anti-vice message more generally was life-changing to some, though the data does not permit any assessment of actual numbers. Its moral and social messages also linked to the ideology of Victorian respectability and it is this to which the final chapter turns.

CHAPTER SEVEN

Vice and Respectability

Respectability had significant cultural power in Victorian society, but then as now, its potency was such that criminals and fraudsters were able to trade on its representations to exploit the naïve and gullible. One widely-circulated mid-century news story described one whole family who made their money by doing so.[1] Mr Kaggs, a former butler to a nobleman, had eloped with and married the nobleman's daughter, who was immediately cut off from any inheritance by her father. Thereafter they traded on Kaggs' own eminently 'respectable' appearance and on his wife's knowledge of society to defraud charitable wealthy ladies. Their daughter, Bessie, who was described as being interesting, slim and elegant, with fine white hands and soft voice, dressed shabbily 'but not too shabbily', played a key role. She called on the houses of targeted women and politely described her father as a poor lieutenant, wounded at Barossa in the service of his country, and now on a bed of sickness and unable to support his family. She sought a little help. A visit would be arranged to his sick room. When this was due, the family would retire to the garret of their house, which would appear clean but uncomfortable. Mr Kaggs would lie in bed, with a white handkerchief with a family crest carefully left on the counterpane. There would be a military newspaper and a large family Bible nearby. His wife would be propped up with pillows on an armchair. When the visitor arrived, the parents, with refined voices, would speak little, but sound distressed. Bessie did most of the talking, explaining their sad tale. Money was nearly always proffered. If a basket of poultry, meat, food and dainties was also provided, Bessie would clinch the deception by ostentatiously sharing with her parents anything that had not been cut, but putting aside anything cut, or partial, which she said should be 'for poor beggars'.

What is significant here is how various signs of respectability were so ruthlessly exploited for financial gain: gentlemanly and professional status (claiming to be a lieutenant, possessing an aristocratic family crest), literacy and education (the newspaper), polite speech, religious faith (the family Bible), clean and neat clothing and house, respect for parents and family, and even charitable giving. Gender, occupation, location, appearance and status played off each other to shape the deception.

Introduction

This term 'respectability' was already being applied to social behaviour in the eighteenth century, and was coming into more common use by the early nineteenth century.[2] It was a significant watchword in everyday social conversation and in print. It was the most 'respectable' who were most opposed to vice, though 'respectability' was always (like 'vice') a fluid and slippery concept, and never a cultural absolute. It was sometimes merely used as a way of describing supposed 'middle-class Victorian values', but was often far more complex.

Late twentieth-century politicians, such as Margaret Thatcher, often used the call to bring back 'respectable Victorian values' as shorthand for a supposed more moral time, now regrettably passed. For many leading historians since the 1970s, respectability has been a significant way of summing up and characterizing the Victorian age. It was a period that supposedly saw the rise of 'respectable society' *par excellence*, creating a sense of social cohesion. Many Victorian lives were certainly shaped by the quest for personal and public respectability, though respectability could be partial and vulnerable to self-indulgence and affluence.[3]

Chapter outline

This chapter explores the relationship between vice and respectability. It revisits some of the discourses surrounding vice found in earlier chapters, such as gender, religion and location, and uses them in an exploration of respectability's important social and cultural role, and the ways the term was commonly employed. It could apply to the maintenance of appearances, to behaviour and clothing or to specific actions. It could be a role to be played, so though rules for behaviour were sometimes linked to perceived motives, motives themselves could be constructed as part of the role-playing. Respectability was always dependent on context. One key context was that of class grouping so this is next examined, before we turn to the importance of respectability to social life. Respectability often paid, and its loss had consequences played out in the theme of ruined lives, another subject borrowed from vice discourse. As we have already seen, locational contexts varied in their respectability, as did the time and day when an action took place. The generational life-cycle affected respectability, and adolescents and young unmarried men in particular often behaved less respectably. Views of respectable behaviour often varied with age. Next to be explored is religion, which played a key role in transmitting ideas of respectability, despite faith's

The importance of respectability

In the early nineteenth century, industrialization and urbanization transformed some aspects of popular leisure, and some traditional less respectable customary activities like bull-baiting and cock-fighting were generally abandoned or driven underground. But simultaneously commercial leisure and its attractions were beginning to modify developing notions of rational recreations and respectable pleasures. New and more modern leisure forms emerged, such as the increasingly syndicate-run music halls and theatres, popular seaside resorts like Blackpool, association football, rugby, tennis or golf, enclosed sports grounds, cycling and the beginnings of film. These were ambiguous in terms of respectability but enjoyed dramatic increases in popularity. Early academic studies of leisure placed heavy emphasis on such changes, though revisionist thinking has demonstrated the many continuities, and argued that changes were often protracted and uneven and less revolutionary than used to be thought.[4] Even in the new forms of commercial leisure there were important continuities in terms of the persistent appeal of hedonism and people's stress on pleasure, even when these were described as vices. Drink and the pub continued to be staple pleasures and though drink consumption peaked in the 1870s, it stayed high. Gambling had become a major industry by the century's end.

So the social and political forces at work in Victorian society and its leisure were often shaped by and in their turn shaped cultural struggles over respectability and vice. Middle-class respectability, dominant around mid-century, was still powerful in 1901. Through this period, some people within the middle classes and more respectable working classes sought to distinguish themselves from the more disreputable 'fast set' amongst the aristocracy, whom in other ways they sought to emulate, and the unrespectable working classes from whom some of them had sprung.

For many in this group, loss of respectability could mean loss of cultural and economic capital, but to be effective, respectability had to be recognized and accepted by others. Few people were completely respectable all the time. Few people were totally addicted to vice's pleasures. Most people tried to appear respectable where possible, but could occasionally be tempted. So the strictness of the observation of respectability varied with individuals and with contexts. Respectability was therefore most powerful in relation to the home, religious contexts and the workplace, where pressure from spouse and family, clergy and employers could be wielded, and only a little weaker in relation to the neighbours. In many businesses, respectability was highly valued, and employers constantly stressed the dangers posed by drink, gambling and illicit sex. The idealized Victorian middle-class home represented a private refuge from the morally ambiguous and dangerous world, and was struggling to reform its morals and manners. Respectable recreations were enjoyable, but were interpreted as a physical re-creation of the body, discharged for the sake of one's family and employers. They should be 'rational', confined and defined in terms of their respectability, following rules of propriety, and undertaken only when work had been completed, neither morally corrupting nor recklessly extravagant. For some people, respectability was powerful and all pervasive. They had strong feelings of disgust at vice and sin. It felt natural to oppose both. Reminders of the vice that surrounded them merely helped to maintain social order and a strong moral boundary. Some canonical scholarly writers, critics and diary writers of the period, such as Elizabeth Eastlake (1809–93) or Henry Crabb Robinson (1775–1867), were very reluctant to reveal matters considered 'private' and aspects of the self in their substantial diaries. Robinson, for example, resorted to shorthand when he recorded scandal and gossip. They willingly lived up to their self-constructed cultural codes of respectability, and tried to shape them publicly.

But the debates that the various vices generated suggest that respectability was a continually-contested term, incorporating contradictions and developing unevenly in relation to different leisure lives. It was subject to multiple, diverse and individual interpretations, negotiations and exchanges. Respectable middle-class views could potentially be repressive and manipulative in leisure contexts, and succeeded against unfashionable targets such as cock-fighting, but they struggled much more when confronted by the great triumvirate of gambling, drinking and sex, which were often enjoyed with companions. Individuals might embrace respectability in one context, yet simultaneously resist it in another. Reading was a respectable activity, but the many sensational novels written by women authors for female readers often focused on mature, intelligent and charming yet sexually aroused women, who tried to conceal their deeper feelings from men. Individuals could be obsessed with hearing about and passing on gossip about their neighbours' scandals, yet cling to respectability to avoid being the target of gossip themselves.

In pre-Victorian times, respectability was a device which emphasized middle-class moral superiority over the working classes. Increasingly, through the nineteenth century, members of the working classes were encouraged to join this 'respectable' group. For some of the poor, and for much of the lower middle-classes, being respectable helped to keep up self-respect in difficult circumstances, and boosted public reputation too. Yet whilst many accepted respectable values in principle, they also shaped and modified them to their own ends. So respectability had multiple dimensions linked in complex ways. It could be a type of social identity. It could also be social and material status, a form of cultural capital or self-assertion, a personal or moral attribute, or something perceived through behaviour, appearance, clothing and specific actions.

Reformers needed unrespectable pleasures to act as a counter-point to make their own lives feel worthwhile. They needed their twin other, the 'roughs' and disreputable individuals whom vice supposedly attracted. Respectability was a powerful ideology. It reinforced social status. It aided cultural power. So respectability and un-respectability needed each other. They were linked in complex, subtle and reciprocal combination. Reformers needed to challenge disreputable pleasures, and the dissolute and unrespectable 'others' who enjoyed them, to help justify their authority, and keep the 'roughs' in place. Their arguments were strengthened if these pleasures, and the transgressors who enjoyed them, could be portrayed as marginal and deviant individuals, not those occupying what might be seen as the centre ground. Respectability was central to the cultural ordering of life, and ideas of respectability were forged out of conduct perceived as damagingly problematic.[5]

The appearance of respectability

In part, respectability was a matter of moral character, self-control and reputation. To have respectability was to be respected, held in esteem or be the recipient of 'respectful' addresses and requests. Respectable could therefore be applied not just to men, but, for example, to newspapers and journals, to married women, families or inhabitants of a town. In applying for a job, 'good character' was required. Respectability was associated in Victorian texts with terms like 'serious', 'sober', 'responsible', 'steady', 'trustworthy', 'intelligent', 'grave', 'quiet' and 'attentive'. It had gradations, so one could be 'more', or 'highly' or 'eminently' respectable. Categories such as appearance, behaviour, membership of a particular denomination, or one's professional, commercial or industrial status, all provided clues to assess levels of respectability.

The respectability of Victorian society was often one of surface trappings, of appearance, so it could be merely a façade, shaky and under strain. Its conventions varied from group to group, from place to place and from context to context. There were significant differences between public rhetoric and private Victorian practice, and compromises to be made in terms of behaviour and private thoughts. Many people aspired to public respectability and the avoidance of any association with vice, but 'respectable' meant very different things to aristocratic grandees, the upper-class 'fast' set, Methodist ministers, struggling clerks or better-off artisans. The morality and behaviour of the respectable working classes was not that of the respectable middle classes. They had different leisure lives and very different incomes.

Sometimes respectability applied to visual features, with appropriate clothing, sufficient dwelling space to avoid overcrowding, personal cleanliness and posture used merely as a simple way of pigeon-holing people who did not appear 'rough'. A clean-looking appearance supposedly indicated social worthiness. The commonly-used term 'respectable-looking' summed up this view. Policemen on the beat, faced with making discretionary choices about policing, often chose to target those whom they believed 'needed to be arrested'. Such definitions often overlooked those otherwise appearing respectable, and policemen much more commonly arrested those appearing to be deviant in some way. Once they were arrested, those prisoners who appeared respectable, maintained decorum and were 'respectably dressed' were more likely to get bail.

Clothing demonstrated gentility, but clothing, like beards, had to be related to fashion and generation. Respectable middle-class men in the 1840s were clean-shaven, with side whiskers. Wealthy men with beards were dissipated, cranks, revolutionaries or perhaps artists. By the 1860s, though, distinguished men had luxuriant beards, a mark of eminence and authority, and only the older generation saw them as disreputable. Moustaches and beards became widely popular until the 1890s, when they fell from fashion and to be clean-shaven again became a mark of respectable modernity. The right sort of domestic environment likewise provided respectability. By the later nineteenth century, symbols such as piano ownership, improving newspapers, a garden or a domestic servant carried heavy cultural meaning. Speech could be respectable, showing propriety and decorum.

At home, at church and at work, respectability often paid economically and in terms of cultural capital, the non-financial social assets that promoted social mobility helped gain a better job, public office, or involvement in charitable affairs. It required an unsullied reputation in the community, and conformity to respectable public behaviour. Those who were respectable had more chance of gaining credit, finding opportunities for their children or obtaining better-quality housing.

Respectability was exploited by moral reformers, who elevated respectable attitudes and characteristics above other concerns. By claiming and dominating the moral high ground, they consistently presented respectability as a simple monolith to which (supposedly) almost everyone (or at least all 'right-thinking' people) subscribed. This allowed respectability to be widely claimed in the press and other discourse as a characteristic Victorian value. Unsurprisingly too, complex processes of narrative logic, contradictions, and ostentatious omissions aided such arguments.[6] Temperance and respectability, for example, were sometimes, but not always, presented as going hand in hand.

Reformers were active in widely-admired cultural institutions from town councils and Boards of Health to the magistracy and charitable groups. Churches, chapels and sometimes the Liberal Party all provided the networks of shared beliefs, lifestyles and support they needed. Social networks linked to these played a key role, encouraging courtship, marriage and family advancement within 'decent' communities. For members of such groups, any fall from grace and respectability threatened them, their family and community. Appearances were a matter of the highest social and personal importance. Some Nonconformist churches expelled members who sinned. The Bible Christian Church was one of several who made teetotalism a condition of communion. Benefit Societies' rules sometimes expected members to process to divine service and dine together at some unlicensed building.

Respectability, class and occupation

Many historians have found the notion that the discourses surrounding vice and respectability worked to cement forms of social distinction a persuasive one. Sometimes it has been claimed that 'the cult of respectability belonged principally to the middle classes (and especially to a lower middle class anxious to distinguish itself from the working classes)'.[7] It helped provide coherence and moral integrity. Respectability, in the sense of the aspiration to be a 'gentleman', was a criterion of class. The middle classes claimed that certain of their 'respectable' attitudes and habits were characteristic values of the English.[8] Behind such beliefs were often unacknowledged fears of the possibility of losing economic and cultural power. Respectability was simultaneously a demonstration of social mobility, since people could aspire to or rise into respectability or fall from it.

The term 'respectable' was widely used. There was usually an assumption that everyone else understood it. The Victorians themselves sometimes used 'the respectable classes' or 'respectable society' as synonyms for those above the masses, and the word often preceded nouns such as 'gentlemen' or 'tradesmen'. Decency here was related to the ability to spend money. The editor of *Golf Illustrated* in 1900, for example, discussing the eligibility of players for golf tournaments, who needed to be members of a 'recognized golf club', suggested that the meaning of 'recognized' could be summed up 'in the word "respectable" '.[9] Henry Mayhew found that London costermongers saw 'respectable' people as 'pretty tidy off for money', 'growing rich', 'mostly well-dressed', and usually 'church-goers'.[10] For the Bishop of Manchester, in 1870, the respectable class was 'the well-to-do class, who live in good houses and have got the advantage and privilege of good homes'.[11] In 1892, respectability was ironically summed up as being linked to wealth, education and appearance:

It's having money in the Bank,
It's being a personage of rank,
It's having spent three years at College,
With great or little gain of knowledge,
It's going to Church twice on Sunday,
And keeping in with Mrs Grundy,

It's clothes well cut, and shiny hat,
And faultless boots, and nice cravat,
It may be Law, or Church, or Ale,
Or Trade, on a sufficient scale.[12]

Juries, witnesses, chairmen of meetings, audiences, corporations, businesses and firms or tradesmen could all be 'respectable'. Clergymen, dissenting ministers, rectors, vicars, or Free Churchmen in Scotland might be 'eminently respectable'. The prefix 'respectable' was applied to professional men like attorneys, chemists, solicitors or medical practitioners. It encompassed merchants and industrialists but also vendors and dealers, tradesmen and shopkeepers, managers and clerks, and farmers. Even though brewers produced beer, they usually sought status, and were always amongst the respectable mercantile aristocracy of the country, found in Parliament and in leading public roles in towns and cities.[13] To be respectable could simply signal financial stability. Tradesmen, clerks, and others had to furnish credentials as to their respectability to obtain a loan.

Yet respectability among the lower middle and skilled working classes, whose consciousness of precarious status has been assumed to make them most strongly identified with the concept, was often interpreted differently. For the lower middle classes, marginal men and women, shop and office workers, teachers and others desperate to reach true middle-class status, conservative in temperament and politics, respectability provided a lifeline. It kept them above the vulgar, while their 'salary' distinguished them from the better-off skilled workers who often had better incomes but spent them differently. They were perhaps keenest to maintain the trappings of respectability, however defined, especially in manner, dress and associations.[14] Their situation was brilliantly satirized in the 1892 novel by George and Weedon Grossmith, *Diary of a Nobody*, which focused on the staid, accident-prone lower-middle-class clerk Charles Pooter and his wife Carrie, desperate for respectability, and their petty vanities and ambitions.

Better-off Victorians talked about 'the respectable poor', though they judged this largely by appearance and respectful behaviour, the surface indications of having accepted middle-class respectable values. If workers appeared respectable and took up rational recreations, activities the middle classes stressed, which they hoped would encourage better time and money management, and be a distraction from the pub, they began to become 'the deserving poor'.

The nature of working-class respectability and how far it followed middle-class models proves difficult to assess. There was certainly a social distinction within working-class society between the 'rough' and the 'respectable', though since people socialized across such divisions and sometimes moved from one to the other as life chances changed this was never fixed. Some historians have seen such working-class respectability as an attempt to impose respectability by the middle classes. This formed part of a cultural and religious attempt to remould older rougher working-class values, and these required negotiation.[15] Studies demonstrate that by the late nineteenth century many ordinary workers in towns like York found respectability a core value. Living in a 'respectable' street, in a neat tidy home, had positive effects on their communities, provided them with self-discipline and self-restraint and earned local respect. For those who aspired to retain an implicitly Christian morality and self-discipline, and wanted to appear worthy and reputable in the community, respectability could provide a strategy to help cope with the social and economic challenges and uncertainties of change. Significantly, such research suggests that moderate drinking or the occasional bet were not perceived in these communities as threatening their respectability.[16]

Victorian newspaper job advertisements from middle-class employers often demanded a 'respectable' person, especially those in domestic service as nurses, laundresses, housekeepers, governesses or other servants, or as workers such as apprentices. 'Respectable' references were also sought. Domestic servants may have transmitted 'respectable' values when returning to their families.

In part, the ethic of respectability could bind members of different classes together. Respectability then became not a distinction between classes but a distinction alongside class, between individuals and groups located on a continuum of respectability and un-respectability. For some people in the working-class community, respectability was not an externally-imposed, filtered-down version of middle-class respectability, which could be actively rejected, ignored, negotiated or accepted. Instead it was adopted and adapted by the working classes for their own purposes. So it stemmed from working-class culture itself, though meanings were even more fluid, variable and constantly redefined. Sometimes respectability conveyed strong impressions of class pride and independence.

Cultural divisions within the working class meant that appearing respectable rather than 'rough' could keep a man in a job, and so provide a safeguard against insecurity or unemployment.[17] Membership of a friendly society could indicate self-help, respectability and moderation.[18] So could payment into a burial club. For women, in its strongest form respectability meant fiercely defending privacy and the avoidance of borrowing or participating in gossip, though this could limit wider social networks of friendship and exchange.[19] Studies of urban areas such as Leicester have argued that a distinctively collectivist version of respectability, by no means deferential towards the middle classes, was becoming an increasingly important part of working-class life and consciousness in the later nineteenth century.[20]

Historians have also increasingly recognized that respectability could become a role to be played, the calculated maintenance of a respectable front, to be assumed or abandoned as context demanded.[21] Oscar Wilde's play, *The Importance of Being Earnest*, for example, has many characters who appear to have another less respectable life involving the pursuit of pleasure beneath the conventional surface appearance of Victorian correctness, propriety and respectability. Respectability had multiple representations. Especially in urban contexts, individuals and groups found it possible to adopt, discard or modify them according to social context and cultural preference. This may have applied particularly to skilled workers, but more generally the role-playing aspects of people's identities were important, especially when in the company of those in other social groups.[22] A worker, for example, could assume a respectable role in particular situations, for a variety of reasons, such as material gain, to get overtime or to gain promotion. The workers for whom respectability was a regular and consistent way of life were probably a relatively small minority.[23] Likewise, for middle-class men exploring London's delights, street life could be simply a 'performance', a carefully chosen 'presentation of the self', rather than just demonstrating one's status.[24] In certain contexts the middle classes could also choose between conflicting social norms of behaviour, perhaps to be respectably restrained, tactful and courteous, or un-respectably outgoing and exuberant.[25]

The consequences of loss of respectability

The importance of displaying respectable behaviour can be seen in all sorts of contexts, and its potential loss had weight. Resultant shame could be public or private, judged by the law's dictates, the norms of society or those of their acquaintance. Public disclosure of a major fall from respectability, such as a court appearance or a divorce, could be calamitous. Respectable ladies avoided mixing with those offering possible contamination. Most people tried to conceal their private shame from the public. Gerard Manley Hopkins, for example, helped to keep his homosexuality private by becoming a Jesuit and writing his poems mainly about nature.

So for many Victorians the inculcation of potential remorse and guilt helped to ensure 'proper' control and behaviour. Where potential indiscretion might be exposed, there were powerful internal fears of potential labelling, ridicule, disapproval or stigmatism. The loss of respectability could be due to many reasons, and not all were in a person's control: debt and bankruptcy, suicide in the family, addiction to drink or drugs, a son with 'unnatural desires', a pregnant daughter or an adulterous affair. The weight of such feelings could haunt the family. The heroine of Thomas Hardy's *Tess of the d'Urbervilles*, for example, after her rape and subsequent pregnancy is described as having 'conventional' feelings of guilt, self-doubt and shame when walking through the cornfield with her baby, even though being blameless. She felt she was 'a figure of Guilt walking through the halls of Innocence'.

Even in the reporting of suicide, the extent to which the victim had lived a morally sound or morally deviant life attracted compassion or condemnation, and contributing factors such as mental illness and harsh socio-economic conditions were less stressed. So where a suicide had left a family unprovided for, judgements were especially harsh where the person concerned had lost his money through gambling, whilst heavy drinking before committing suicide also distorted reports. Suicide notes, especially from women, often showed a similar moral judgement on themselves.[26]

Further social constraints could be exercised through the policing network of disapproving gossip, which demonstrated the current consensus of what was socially acceptable, even if such boundaries were redrawn over time. To avoid any loss of respectability, some homes became fortresses of privacy. Pervasive street networks of formal and informal surveillance over expected behaviour helped socialize younger community members into similar ways of thinking. Police, municipal authorities and even park-keepers could also be expected to reinforce these behavioural expectations, and to challenge any manifestation of vice. This created an impression that respectable behaviour was 'normal', that there was social consensus on the issue.

Sermons and talks regularly stressed the theme of 'ruined lives' and their causes, especially after mid-century, emphasizing that the decay of virtue would rapidly be followed by downfall. For young men, it was the potential 'fall from respectable position', thanks to 'drinking, gaming, the excitements of the theatre, the racecourse and [other] temptations' that was most dangerous.[27]

The gender double standard ensured that men often escaped the full consequences of sexual sins, but women who were seduced, 'fell' or became pregnant, were 'ruined young ladies', sometimes abandoned by their families, cast away in shame. For traditionalists, women literally embodied family honour. A woman's shame was that of the husband and parents. As earlier chapters showed, Victorian society cold-shouldered women's sexual sins, and their families shared in their disgrace. For many Victorian women, others' fates confirmed their own successful negotiation of the narrow path of virtue. They understood that lust and physical attraction were often transitory, and the possible consequences were bitter: loss of purity, virtue and innocence; poverty; regret, shame and self-reproach.

A revealing 1895 example of traditional male attitudes was demonstrated when a well-educated Socialist 34-year-old woman, an architect's daughter from Battersea, wanted to demonstrate her disapproval of current marriage laws by living with her railway clerk boyfriend instead of marrying. She was only prepared to change her surname or live abroad with him. After her concerned parents failed to persuade her otherwise, her outraged father had her medically examined. A leading insanity specialist immediately signed emergency commitment papers under the Lunacy Act, because the woman could not see that her plans meant 'utter ruin' and 'social suicide'. Her brain 'had been turned by Socialist meetings and writings'. She was forced into a carriage by her father and brothers, bound with rope, and locked up in the Roehampton Priory Institution. She was only released after appeal to the Commissioners of Lunacy, who pronounced her 'foolish' but perfectly sane.[28]

The records of foundling hospitals and paternity suits or the case histories in Victorian Magdalene asylums, penitentiaries or refuges, where women were kept from tainting respectable society, often showed women's tragic stories. Even in that context, a calculus of respectability was often applied by the committees assessing the women who applied for a place. At the London Foundling Hospital, the women had to apply detailed information about themselves and the context of their relationships. Those in 'respectable' positions, in previously stable relationships, with an initial promise of marriage, and from more affluent districts, gained more credit. Those who had support from affluent and respectable individuals, especially employers or family members, improved their chances of winning over the committee.[29] Those women applying successfully to leave their child at the Foundling Hospital presented themselves in their applications and interviews as 'disgraced' yet with a worthy 'respectable' character, and as shamed and humiliated by men who had failed to carry out their promises. Giving up their baby was the only way to continue a life of respectable virtue. The importance of respectability meant that some of the girls' parents abandoned their daughters, leaving them to face the difficult choices alone, though others gave them more support and tried to preserve their reputation.

Novelists explored the theme of such moral ruin regularly, and artists, whose own personal lives were sometimes disreputable, painted pictures illustrating its consequences too. Richard Redgrave's *The Outcast* (1851) showed a frightened young girl and her illegitimate child thrown out by an intransigent father, immune to the pleading of his wife and other children. Augustus Egg's triptych *Past and Present* (1858) told the story of the discovery and disastrous outcome of a wife's adultery. John Roddam Stanhope's *Thoughts of the Past* (1859) showed a kept mistress, whose lover's glove and walking stick lie on the floor. She looks ruefully or sorrowfully towards the Thames, which suggests the literary convention of the 'ruined' prostitute drowning herself. This echoed stories and poems such as Thomas Hood's 1844 poem, 'The Bridge of Sighs', with its themes of beauty, sin, scorn, and heavy hints of a young woman's shameful 'evil behaviour', 'slips' and unmarried pregnancy before her suicide, which left her 'past all dishonour'. Her body was pulled from the filthy, polluted Thames, itself a metaphor for urban depravity, vice and weak morality.

But not all took this view. In Thomas Hardy's poem, 'The Ruined Maid', written in 1866 but only published in 1901, a prostitute talking to a friend described herself as 'ruined' in each refrain, but only with very heavy irony. Having become a rich man's mistress, she seemingly had no regrets for being 'ruined'. She showed her friend her fine clothing, her jewellery, and demonstrated the polished speech that made her 'look like a real lady'. As she boastfully pointed out, 'that's how we dress when we're ruined'.

The men involved usually suffered less. Indeed having a 'reputation' with women could gain admiration from others. As one newspaper editor put it, 'vice, unless it is shameless, excludes no gentleman from the society of ladies'.[30] Middle-class men might keep a mistress or visit prostitutes, and this was tacitly understood. Married women would still be happy to offer hospitality. Even accusations of rape or sexual indecency committed by respectable men on working-class women were looked on sceptically as perhaps motivated by blackmail. In April 1870, for example, after a six-day trial, John Jackson, the married rector of Ledbury, living in a household with family, tutor and several servants, was found guilty by the Dean of Arches of adultery with his cook and systematic indecency with another servant, with the suggestion of similar offences with previous servants. Not all believed in his guilt. *The Times*, *The Spectator* and some in the local community were sceptical of the evidence. Others may have ironically celebrated his misbehaviour. Either way, when Jackson went back to Ledbury he was met at the station by more than 1,000 people who escorted his carriage through the streets, which were decorated with bunting.[31]

But eventually there could be an impact even for men. Then as today, MPs like Parnell might have to resign following a scandal, and romantic novels often ensured men got their come-uppance. In Mrs Edward Kennard's *Morals of the Midlands: A Sporting Tale* (1899), Rory McGregor, who hunted, shot and rode splendidly, but belonged to a Midland hunting set, a 'light-hearted, roistering sporting crew' with lax morals, enjoyed liaisons and flirtations. His aunt offered Rory a legacy if he married Rhoda Markham, the book's conventional, moral and religious heroine, a woman committed to the sanctity of marriage. He did so, to her delight, and they had a child. But Rory continued his 'fast' life, thought Rhoda had 'peculiar old-fashioned ideas', and began an affair. He left Rhoda to live with Daisy, who had pursued him for some time, but this finally brought down the weight of societal disapprobation. He lost his income and was forced to work as an agent for a horse dealer at 'only' £100 a year. Daisy left him and respectable morality triumphed when Rory returned to Rhoda.

So keeping up a respectable façade could be vital. The fatal blunder in social life was the 'unpardonable' or 'unforgivable' sin and disgrace of 'being found out', the latter a phrase echoing across Victorian discourse. It was regularly stressed as the century's greatest commandment, the 'eleventh'. This was viewed as the one that should be observed most carefully. If position in the world and the respect of friends was important, it could not be transgressed without consequences.

Many saw it as a virtue to aspire to maintain the complex social coding of external respectability even if they fell short in their private life. They might be censorious of others, even if they recognized their own shortcomings and felt guilty. Many in unconventional sexual relationships, gay couples or extra-marital relationships tried to maintain the appearance and manners of respectability and good conduct even when actually transgressing morality, and often agonized over their failure to observe conventions.

The relationship between Mary Evans (George Eliot) and George Henry Lewes, a married man who had earlier condoned his wife's affair, provides a useful example of the complex relationship between sexual desire, married love and respectability. A scandal first broke in literary London after the couple eloped together to Germany. One supporter of the *Edinburgh Review* wondered if Evans was insane, for the act seemed like mental aberration. The writer believed that Lewes was justified in leaving his wife but not in making Miss Evans his mistress. There was widespread debate about whether the man or woman was most to blame.[32]

The couple, however, seem to have used their time away to think through their own relationship as lovers, companions and writers, and reconceptualize their understandings of respectable ideology and companionate marriage. On their return to England, the couple observed a conventional domestic monogamous relationship out of wedlock, and the relationship grew over time. By the 1860s, Evans was signing her letters Mrs Lewes, an indication of the importance that respectable marriage held for her. But she had suffered for her earlier actions with exclusion from the normal social life of literary London for at least a decade. Her family disapproved of her lifestyle, indeed her brother broke off all contact. Personally, she reflected an earnest morality in her novels, and the couple regulated published standards of sexual propriety in their editorship of the *Westminster Review*. Morals were lax in Lewes' literary circle. Another of her friends, John Chapman, shared a house with his wife and mistress, and seems to have had a short affair with Eliot in 1851. In 1867, however, they were introduced to Princess Louise, the daughter of Queen Victoria, who was a fan of the novels, and this confirmed Mary's renewed respectability.[33]

The Victorians understood the rules well enough to break them when they really wished, and there were cultural contexts and certain life-cycle stages where respectability had a less powerful hold, and debates were less firmly fought. In terms of class, the relationship between affluence and attitude was certainly not always clear. Few in the middle classes subscribed to the code of respectability at *all* times, though for some, a highly-vocal minority, it was all-encompassing.[34] Some novelists, writers, poets, painters and sculptors were already living a model of privately unrespectable life by the mid-Victorian period, though the number was not large. They often scorned private property, had a degree of sexual license and were often anti-religious and left-leaning. Journalists, publicans, credit bookmakers or even police detectives could be on the margins of respectability, with appropriate incomes and social position but linked morally through their work to elements of vice. An extensive biographical dictionary of Liverpool's merchants acknowledged that the class contained 'gamblers, profligates [and] infatuated lovers of sport'.[35] Not all employers lived exemplary lives; there could be major differences between the standards that they expected from their workforce, on pain of sacking, and their private behaviour in relation to sex, gambling or drink.

Some occupations figured in the press, then as today, because public opinion expected those workers to behave in particularly respectable ways, and where they were discovered not doing so, press coverage followed. Reports on vicars, priests, doctors and other professionals fall into this category, most often when sexual crimes occurred, while 'a too sociable temperament, and excessive fondness for society' led several vicars and priests to be 'caught by alcohol'.[36]

In reality, offences against respectability were more likely where work took men away from home. Jobs where patterns of work took men away, as with those with irregular working hours, were difficult to reconcile with respectable domestic life. Businessmen in London or other large cities were able to enjoy its anonymity. Everywhere, commercial travellers were likely to at least occasionally and opportunistically break the monotony and boredom of hotel life by living a heavy-drinking or sexually predatory existence, unregulated and anonymous.[37] They often thrived on conviviality and the establishment of 'connections'. The agent of one Stratford Brewery, Edward Pole, increased his sales by regularly attending race-meetings and fairs in the Midlands. When his relationship with his employers soured and they prosecuted him for 'non-accounting', they used his attendance to try to discredit him, but the jury found in his favour.[38] Those in the drink trade or involved in commercial leisure often enjoyed betting and drinking, seemingly with little effect on their respectability in terms of obtaining senior community positions on local authorities, Boards of Health or committees. Writers and artists often suffered the further disreputable challenge of irregular income. Much of the work done by women, in a generally patriarchal society, was seen by its very existence as unrespectable. Women working as barmaids, actresses and music hall artistes, and successful well-off female athletes or swimmers, for example, were often portrayed as women with questionable reputations.[39]

Place, time and respectability

As we have seen in Chapter 2, the hold of respectability was weak in some locational contexts. The anonymity of large urban areas and the range of pleasures on offer opened up multiple leisure opportunities and identities. Different social and cultural locations allowed people to reflect on the contextual meanings of respectability and problematize them. Going 'up' to London provided opportunities for provincial business and professional men to indulge in activities they might publically shun at home. The liminal nature of locations such as the seaside, the music hall, clubs and pubs, the racecourse and fair made them particularly attractive venues. In part, their respectability depended on clientele. So the theatres and music halls became more respectable if sufficient numbers of the apparently respectable attended. In 1865, *Lloyd's Weekly Newspaper* defended them, suggesting that there were 'very righteous people' visiting the halls and theatres, and that people needed fun. There was 'a moral as well as a physical gain in a hearty laugh'.[40] London's Bedford Music Hall was seen as having 'one of the most respectable audiences which we have ever seen in a building devoted to variety entertainments'.[41] Music halls always had significant numbers of middle-class patrons, and theatres experienced an expansion in the second half of the century, catering more for middle-class families, so the 1895 attacks by purity groups on London music halls were ridiculed by some newspapers across Britain. The *Cheshire Observer* said the attacks were merely the 'voice of the prude' and the 'hysterical sisterhood', and that the police testified to the respectability of those frequenting the halls.[42]

Whilst all public houses might be clearly defined as sinful places by temperance preachers, newspapers, police reports and social surveys regularly represented them as running along a continuum of respectability, sometimes attracting 'highly respectable' patrons. There were supposedly hundreds of 'respectable houses' even in London's East End, and this very common phrase, alongside similar ones such as 'a quiet, well-conducted and respectable house' can be regularly found applied to pubs across Britain. Landlords too could be 'worthy and respected'.

Select holiday resorts maintained a respectable front, with a substantial middle-class family clientele, though attempts to make them more respectable were often resisted by groups of locals. The seaside offered a legitimate safety valve from some of respectability's constraints. Roles could be assumed, new identities masqueraded, and more hedonistic pleasures occasionally enjoyed, with no loss of respectability back home.[43] Research into racing and its associated betting has also clearly demonstrated the extensive involvement of the 'respectable' middle classes.[44]

Respectable attempts to improve social space could rebound. The new public parks and the new public toilets erected in an attempt to stop public urinating in the streets, as part of an attempt to impose more respectable behaviour, soon found less respectable uses. Parks were used by courting couples and bookmakers. Toilets found a new use by homosexuals for 'cottaging' purposes.

If place was important in determining the extent of respectable or unrespectable behaviour, so too was time, though this has been less explored by historians. It seems clear that behavioural codes impacted differentially at different times of day, different times of the year and at different points during the week. Unrespectable behaviour was often found at night, cloaked in darkness, hidden from respectable view. Specific celebratory times of year, such as the wakes weeks in the Black Country or Lancashire, the Whitsuntide holidays, or the anti-Catholic Guy Fawkes celebrations in Lewes and elsewhere in November, were all times when everyday respectable constraints might be cast aside. There was even some ambivalence about Sunday itself, since people were not at work. The Sabbatarian debates over the 'right' use of Sundays and the unrespectable material found in Sunday newspapers illustrate the respectable concerns. For much of the Victorian period, especially in small workshops and amongst the self-employed, there was significant use of absenteeism on what was called ironically 'St Monday', taken as an extension of Sunday time off for often unrespectable activity by some workers. Such examples all illustrate the point that we need to do more to tease out this area and the stakes involved in the debates over behaviour.

Generation and respectability

One major thrust of respectability was generational, discouraging middle-class youths from more sinful pleasures. Respectable behaviour was related to age and generation, and the passing of the generations, from child-rearing and schooling, and the transition to adulthood, marriage and family life, to 'maturity' and old age. Less respectable behaviour was more common at certain times in the life cycle, especially amongst pupils and teenagers, younger unmarried males, and older men whose families had grown up.

The dilemmas of respectability varied with, or in defiance of, this aging process. Equally, older people in the 1830s, for example, carried forward attitudes and values from their Georgian upbringing. Some of the rising generation of the 1890s introduced novel conceptions of what constituted acceptable lifestyles and behaviour at their social level, as, for example, in the modernism, effete sophistication and self-indulgence of some literary and artistic figures. The lifetime experiences of individuals and the primacy of generation still need much more consideration too.

The young were always at risk. Public schools, for example, could exemplify the vices as well as the virtues of Victorian life. Adolescence was a crucial period for puberty and sexual identification, but sometimes associated in the closed context of the public school, where public expression of sexuality was more common, with increased sexual appetite, violence, brutality and sadism.[45] As Major Dumbarton, a character in a book by the British humourist and short story writer Hector Hugh Munro, better known by his pen name Saki, was later to point out, such experiences could be highly damaging. When his female companion was wondering how a child might become depraved and vicious, Dumbarton remarked, 'Goodness gracious, you've got to educate him first. You can't expect a boy to be vicious till he's been to a good school'.[46]

The actual motives lying behind anti-vice rhetoric about the moral corruption of children are particularly difficult to assess. In part such rhetoric was symbolic, in part moralistic and in part an attempt to control working-class behaviour. The Offences against the Person Amendment Act of 1875, which raised the age of consent from twelve to thirteen and imposed severe penalties on those seducing or abducting young women without their parents' consent, was motivated in part to safeguard the welfare of wealthy heiresses. In some cases too, the rhetoric of morality may have reflected concerns amongst middle-class parents that their own children could fall prey to vice and ultimately live in disgrace rather than replicate or exceed their parents' social position. Once the young could read there were the dangerous so-called penny dreadfuls and 'bloods'. These penny part serials and cheap weekly periodicals were melodramatic and exciting, containing escapist adventure stories often featuring the battle against evil and vice, and were read widely by literate and semi-literate adolescents, even those from respectable homes.[47]

The young unmarried male was a powerful image and major concern. He enjoyed more free time than his elders, and often applied himself more to play than to his work.[48] Life was sometimes selfish and debauched, as young men sowed their wild oats. They could spend their time in clubs, music halls and similar contexts. Away from home, opportunities for such behaviour were certainly wider, and descriptions of university and military student behaviour then, as now, suggest a more hedonistic life style, more frivolous, more idle and more immoral. London students of law and medicine stood out even by the 1850s with visits to brothels, abuse of policemen and riotous behaviour.[49] Medical students, gifted in terms of birth and education, were notorious for recklessness, lawlessness and caddish 'unmanliness'. *Town Talk* suggested that 'their jokes are practical and brutal, their carouses, sottish and degrading'.[50] For many university students, Oxford and Cambridge were not rich hothouses of intellectualism, but places for pleasurable play. The 1852 Royal Commission to inquire into the State, Discipline, Studies and Revenues of the University and Colleges of Oxford noted the extravagance and dissipated habits of students, and was told that the 'openings to vice' were 'the bane of the system', thanks to the opportunities for 'fornication, wine, cards and betting'.[51] The mid-Victorian Disciplinary Books kept by the Senior and Junior Deans of St John's College, Cambridge, for example, contain regular references to 'disorderly' parties, noisy games and singing, 'intoxicated and riotous behaviour', other forms of self-indulgent hedonism, and to students staying out all night despite the curfew, which indicated some students' general disregard for respectable behaviour.[52]

The slightly older unmarried male was simultaneously one of the more powerful images and his potentially unconstrained behaviour one of the more major concerns in mid-Victorian literature. Young middle-class men were always a notoriously unstable group. In moral strictures on their behaviour they supposedly enjoyed more free time than their elders, and applied themselves more to pleasure than to business. In most large towns there was a flourishing unrespectable nightlife. In Liverpool, for example, the dances and supper rooms were frequented by the young and artless, 'well-dressed men, men of standing, the sons of merchant princes' who frequented prostitutes there and 'tipped their hats to them on Lord Street in the face of day'.⁵³ Young working-class women, earning but unmarried, spent much leisure time enjoying themselves prior to marriage.

The combined influences of workplace, domestic situation and reduced per capita income provided few opportunities for less respectable leisure during the years of childrearing for both sexes, but in middle age, some men at the pinnacle of respectability were still keen to prick the bubble of potential pretension and smug hypocrisy by less respectable pleasure: dangerous desires, excitement not enlightenment. Older men, for example, could be seen in music-hall audiences, enjoying drink at home or in the public house, patronizing prostitutes or attending race meetings. The cumulative impact of the dominant respectable rhetoric meant that such action was often accompanied by guilt, while some provided personal narratives of shame in their diaries.

Religion and respectability

Organized Christianity certainly dominated the attack against disreputability, vice and rough behaviour. Respectable parishioners often clustered together, gaining strength from association, living in the same neighbourhoods, going to the same churches and sharing leisure and work contexts. These self-sustaining cultural contexts allowed the respectable to talk and listen to others who apparently shared the same values and beliefs. Here they could enjoy the services, tea parties, bazaars, talks, lantern lectures, picnics, drama and choral societies, sewing circles, concerts and other activities that cemented and celebrated their shared moral standards. They could display their respectable credentials, clothes, houses and lives, congratulating themselves and each other, and demonstrating their disapproval of the 'sins' and 'evils' of disreputable life. While those with a strong religious faith were less likely to be attracted to more sinful pleasures, the place of a guilty conscience in shaping attitudes to leisure has also still to be really explored.

Yet despite their praiseworthy moral framework and set of purposes that advocated social duty above self-interest, and sacrifice above profit, the wider British public were not always grateful to experience campaigners' advice. What was regularly clear was that, as a Belfast newspaper admitted, 'the moral reformers met with a very strenuous opposition when engaged in their laudable work'.⁵⁴

Attitudes varied considerably even within Christianity. Protestant nonconformity was always in the vanguard of proposed moral and cultural reform, but there seemed to be a sliding scale of respectability within it. Roman Catholicism, with its notions of mortal and venial sins, appeared to be more open in its acknowledgement of human frailties. Quakers and Unitarians had to contend with the respectability deficit implied by their heterodox beliefs, while the pro-temperance actions of the Salvation Army regularly came under attack from supposedly more respectable groups, some from within Christianity. A famous example of this came in Basingstoke, when a few Salvationists arrived in September 1880, marching up and down the streets on Sundays, singing hymns and preaching temperance. They had the support of the local newspaper, Nonconformist churches and various teetotal societies, and built up support, but the town of 6,700 had at least fifty pubs in 1881 and three breweries, so they were opposed by the Conservative drink lobby and those concerned about possible loss of jobs or by the noise of their Sunday demonstrations. Over the next six months, there were verbal and physical attacks on the Salvationists and their supporters by a group self-styled the 'Massaganians'. The local paper dismissed them merely as a mob of roughs but the issue divided the council, the magistracy and local churches. The town was split. Some leading figures marched with the Salvationists, others supported the Massaganians. The local vicar organized a Home Office petition to have the Salvation Army cease their parades, while a counter-petition came from the Congregational Church.

The situation came to a head on Sunday 27 March 1881, when the Salvation Army morning march was followed by a large crowd, drowning out the band with rough music and waving the Union Jack as a counter to the Salvation Army flag. In the afternoon, up to 3,000 people assembled outside the Salvation Army headquarters to demonstrate. The Riot Act was read and the streets were cleared only with difficulty by the police with military help. Those later convicted of affray or obstruction by Liberal magistrates received short prison sentences. After release, they were banqueted at the Basingstoke corn exchange. Interference with marches continued but when individuals were arrested they were merely bound over. The issue became the central focus of the September municipal elections, when a Tory, Church of England and Massaganian alliance was victorious.[55]

Gender and respectability

Gender divisions often lay at the heart of debates over respectability, though until recently there has been more focus on male cultural life and the workplace than on Victorian female identity. Here, too, respectability varied with context.

Men were expected to be the heads of households. Even for the scientist Charles Darwin, patriarchal sexual respectability was supposedly entirely natural and one of the main prerequisites for evolutionary progress. The entrepreneurial and professional middle classes and the evangelical movement represented women as carriers of social and religious virtue.[56]

For much of the period, there was male pressure on women, and most especially middle-class women, forcing them from the public into the private domestic sphere, and into more respectable ways of thinking and behaving. Women were expected to assume the 'sacred duty' of maintaining the virtuous home and raising children to embrace middle-class values and practices.[57] In mainstream male discourse, any frank enjoyment by women of leisure was often associated with other, even more sinful pleasures.

In the Victorian home it was often women's role to construct and maintain the respectable reputation of the family. Respectability here was concerned more with what others thought.[58] 'What would the neighbours think?' was a key question. It was judgemental gossip and rumour, social networks and exchange that created a family's reputation in the home, street and neighbourhood. Criteria were multiple, complex and varied. How a woman spent her housekeeping, the cleanliness and tidiness of her house, how the children were brought up, behaved and educated, and the way the husband was managed might all be subject to scrutiny. Her family was meant to be a sanctuary that helped to preserve, reinforce and perpetuate moral, religious and respectable values.

Respectability was the social imperative that reined women in. They were expected to maintain the appearance of virtue, the embodiment of the respectable ideal. Being a little straight-laced, showing fortitude and discipline, helped reputation. So did attributes such as submissiveness, modesty, self-sacrifice, patience and altruism. To William Acton (1813–75), the outspoken moral campaigner and medical doctor, well-known for his beliefs that women were generally sexually uninterested, that vanity, greed, love of fine clothing, or distress and hunger drove women to prostitution, the ideal woman was:

> An English wife and mother, kind, considerate, self-sacrificing and sensible, so pure-hearted as to be utterly ignorant of and averse to any sensual indulgence, but so unselfishly attached to the man she loves, as to be willing to give up her own wishes and feelings for his sake.[59]

Women's reputation was more easily threatened, and sensual desires were definitely to be contained or concealed. Sexual misconduct by a woman was often portrayed as deviant and unnatural, a fascinating yet repelling anomaly. It was often harshly judged. In many Victorian novels, 'fallen' female characters such as Nancy in Dickens's *Oliver Twist* (1837), sexually exploited by men, might have inner nobility, but they were still stigmatized, and they were conventionally removed from the novel through their death. 'Fallen women' in novels nearly always 'fell' from an initial highly respectable state.

Not all women subscribed at all times to such values, and accepted their imposition, however. Research on the ways gender was ideologically constructed has suggested that respectable middle-class values could be deeply contested.[60] Barmaids, music hall artistes or actresses often found their own self-identity as respectable under challenge, negotiating over their role with male managers or customers, though marriage, especially to a male higher in status, made a significant difference.

Towards the end of the century, traditional prescribed gender roles were perceived to be breaking down, facilitating a mood of cultural insecurity. Older generations thought Britain was degenerating into 'sexual anarchy' and longed for a return to stricter definitions of gender where men and women continued to be fixed in their separate spheres.[61] There were heated debates over attempts by the new department stores like Whiteley's in Bayswater to open refreshment rooms which could serve alcohol to customers. Whiteley argued that his women customers were respectable, and it was safer for them to have a drink and perhaps a biscuit in his store. The local paper's editor worried that the rooms might attract women 'dressed as ladies' who would make it 'a place of assignation' and that they might also make respectable women into drunkards.[62]

Women taking part in sport found themselves under moral opprobrium from male stereotypical ideals of female personal conduct, but it could be liberating. Cycling, for example, was attacked as an indecent practice, but it gave women who could afford bicycles freedom to explore their environment more widely. Middle-class women who began playing golf or tennis also faced initial opposition, but increasingly these became acceptable social activities. But at times women could actually exploit men's notions of double standards. In horse racing, for example, women often got men to place bets for them, perhaps receiving the winnings in the form of a pair of gloves, but not having to pay out on a losing bet. In the case of mixed sports, women could get away with behaviour which etiquette forbade to the middle-class male. The numerous accusations of female cheating at mixed sports suggest that whilst women were apparently placed on pedestals as public paragons of virtue, they could get away with cheating more easily. On the respectable middle-class croquet ground, for example, some women were able to jettison their passive role and dominate or indeed humiliate men, mixing flirting with tantrums, wrangling and vociferous argument.[63] Indeed, in 1893 Lewis Carroll plaintively claimed that 'croquet is demoralising society. Ladies are beginning to cheat at it terribly, and if they are found out, they only laugh and call it fun'.[64]

For men, less respectable recreations were much more likely to be found in an all-male context, but the clubs where such activities took place often retained respectability. The Victoria Club, the Turf Club, and the Junior Tattersalls Club in London, or the Waterloo, Camden and Grosvenor Clubs in Liverpool, were only a few of the many men-only clubs with their betting, billiard-playing and bookmaking membership scattered across the face of urban Britain. Most major race-meetings had their homo-social race clubs, of which the Jockey Club and Bibury Club in England, the Dublin Turf Club, and the Royal Caledonian Hunt Club in Scotland were the most socially elite and respectable. Many of the rugby, harrier and other more middle-class sports clubs likewise had a close relationship with drinking and other pleasures.

Legislation

Throughout the Victorian period, reformists of many persuasions attempted to change society through legislation, though in practice the legislature was often reluctant to act, and internal divisions within parties remained important. Liberal governments were generally far more likely than Conservative administrations to respond to reformist pressures. The debates were about how far Victorian society could be made respectable, and in whose image. Governments agonized about how far respectability could be *imposed* through legislation, and whether it was better to press for reform at national level, or start with local reforms and build up impetus.

Like others in the Victorian market place, reformers were trying to purvey a product, the rational and moral life that they themselves found attractive and wanted others to share. Vice was a commercial product too, so its commodities – strong drink, prostitutes' bodies or betting facilities, for example – had commercial similarities to cotton or coal. They had to be affordable, and environmental factors and technological changes influenced demand and supply. Vice was a hedonistic, culturally-powerful consumer product purchased across the classes, and there was, very clearly, a substantial market demand, one growing with increased leisure time and rising real wages. Drink, for example, to reformers a major vice, was also a major industry. So it became increasingly difficult to adversely categorize brewers and publicans, who fed the demand for drink, as unrespectable, especially when they became wealthy or became active in Conservative politics. So they were defended. One Liverpool vicar, for example, preached against 'teetotal bigotry and tyranny', arguing that it was 'anti-freedom' and set on moral coercion, and represented the 'twisted judgement' of a 'faction'.[65]

There were conflicts and debates between supporters of social morality and possible state intervention on the one hand and the imperatives of market economics and *laissez-faire* capitalism on the other. Some put principle before profits, but many of the middle class held brewery investments. This created a dilemma for the British state and law makers about whether or how to control the supply issues that lay at the heart of the vice business.

So attacks on vice incorporated a challenge to the central tenet of Victorian capitalist society, the power of free market forces. Legislation to make the main vices illegal attacked commercial capitalism, people's rights to earn money and consumers' personal rights: the rights of prostitutes and their clients, sellers of alcohol, bookmakers and others. And when there appeared to be successes, such as the fall in per capita consumption of alcohol in late Victorian England, the extent of a clear link with legislation was questionable.

But even when legislation *was* passed, some magistrates were reluctant to act in terms of refusing pub licences or sentencing illegal street bookmakers, pitch and toss participants and other gamblers. For the police, who could only act with the consent of the populations they supervised, prosecutions often took place on a ritualistic occasional basis unless pressured by adverse press coverage or the work of anti-gambling associations, purity campaigns and the like. Police and magistrates largely ignored middle-class drinking and gambling, addressing them largely when they uncomfortably intruded into cross-class spaces or received press publicity and complaints.

Conclusion

Respectability was less monolithic than it appeared. Victorian society was increasingly more governable as the century wore on but the thesis of the 'rise of respectable society' was true only in part. Reformers had some success in making respectability a major ideological force in public and domestic contexts. By the end of the century there was more moderation and restraint being shown by workers and their families, although the relative impacts of other factors such as the 1872 Education Act, reformist activity, factory discipline and other factors on this are impossible to assess accurately. There was some success in introducing legislation to control aspects of drink, gambling and sex, as earlier chapters have indicated. Reformers themselves often provided good role models, usually educated, thrifty, continent, serious and happy to defer present gratification for future gain.

Though vociferously active, they were a small group in society. In 1988, a leading historian of Victorian respectability estimated that 'the puritan-evangelical blueprint of family conduct was adopted in its entirety by no more than a small minority of the middle classes'.[66] Because respectable reform's leading figures, especially industrialists, merchants and professionals, possessed cultural capital as well as moral and religious zeal, they were able to make their voices heard regularly across the media, even if the wider population did not necessarily share their beliefs. At certain times, in certain contexts, they certainly had a very significant impact. Many people found that respectability could be highly useful, and common-sense survival strategies could give the appearance of respectability by fitting with local expectations.

While the appearance of respectability was certainly important, Victorians had multiple identities and could employ ruses and stratagems to easily move in or out of respectable or unrespectable roles. Here again, it has been suggested that it was not possible to infer that 'normal or majority middle-class behaviour actually conformed' to full respectability, and that the persistence of its propaganda suggests less the triumph of its ideal, but rather 'the persistence of large numbers of regenerates happily sampling the pleasures and amusements of the world'.[67] Victorians were far more complex and multi-faceted than has at times been recognized. Reformers erroneously conflated the respectable acts that individuals carried out with more permanent respectable identities. In general the impact on human behaviour in certain leisure contexts, especially in terms of three key leisure practices of drink, gambling and sexual behaviour, was less than reformers hoped.

Epilogue

As this book has shown, Victorian society was divided over vice. Some people wanted to impose the most strenuous moral standards on public life; some tried and failed to live up to their good intentions about drink, gambling or sexual relationships but wanted others to be better behaved; and others, for a whole variety of reasons, ignored societal strictures, and were attracted to pleasure, aestheticism and decadence. Undoubtedly, the key vices and their adverse societal, community, family and personal impacts appalled many Victorians. Yet others found that behaviour associated with vice offered amusement and sensation, pleasure and commercial profit.

Why were the Victorian campaigns against vice only successful in part?

One major reason was that the actual numbers of active adult reformers were relatively small, smaller than many Victorians realized. Figures for the adult membership of their many societies and organizations were rarely high, and membership overlapped, inflating figures. Reformers were often misled about their numerical strength because they met and mixed with others like themselves. Funding for reform movements was always limited. Most organizations were over-dependent on a few rich subscribers.

The anti-vice campaign groups were divided amongst themselves. Motivations varied: fear, Christian duty or social reform. There was an absence of solidarity. Initiatives by different organizations were often incompatible. Most organizations experienced personality clashes and internal divisions about their mission, tactics and strategies. Some tried to contain vice, others tried indoctrination and education, others legal abolition. Once well established, societies often lacked real impetus and direction. Organizational reports eulogized any successes and downplayed failure. Reports were rarely rigorous, and their allegations largely depended on anecdotal rather than carefully-gathered, sifted and analysed evidence and research data.

Reformers were not always able to live up to their high ideals. This laid themselves open to the charges of self-interest and hypocrisy. Even Sunday papers such as *Reynolds's Newspaper* or the *News of the World*, which strongly pursued an editorial morality of individual betterment and outrage at the wickedness of the privileged, were also happy to print salacious, sensational and pleasurable details of crimes and court cases for their bourgeois readers. Reformers also found that their efforts sometimes simply gave the oil of publicity to the fires of vice. The more they attempted to repress it, the more others desired to break free of constraints and sought sensation. The scandalous stories and terrifying tales meant to inculcate respectable, decent behaviour sometimes advertised and incited possible disobedience to such behavioural norms. It was probably for that reason that some of the leading preachers of the Victorian age avoided talking about vice at all. They found they were more effective when they focused positively on Christ's teaching rather than, more negatively, on the vices and sins of the modern world.

Reformers' apparent vocal fanaticism and feelings of moral superiority often alienated their support, making the strength of their principled and idealist convictions into a weakness. They were often negative and actively combative, inflexible and unrealistic, attacking their opponents virulently, and shouting them down, trying to deter them from public statement of their views. To more extreme reformers anyone who was not a friend was an enemy to be publicly attacked. They failed to recognize that theirs were minority causes, and that shrillness and self-righteousness could antagonize people. They over-estimated the perceived importance of their cause.

Their arguments were much less strong than they appeared. Reformers rightfully recognized that addictions and cravings for sex, alcohol or gambling were harmful to the individual, family and Victorian society. But when they regularly conveyed the impression that they believed such vices in moderation *inevitably* led to excess this alienated many potential supporters. Most people knew better. Reformers were also prone to focus their attacks upon those marginal groups in Victorian society whose vices were most noticeable. They did not realize that many other men and women across all social classes perceived themselves as sharing many of the universal values of 'respectability' and sought moral improvement, but at the same time were adopting a policy of moderation in their approach to 'vices' such as drink.

All this meant that the Victorian drive to improve the well-being of society, and tackle the problems created by leisure activities linked to vice had only limited success. For all their sound and fury, in many leisure contexts the impact of anti-vice movements was far stronger on public rhetoric than on private practice. Reformist rhetoric was constantly reiterated, which sometimes convinced reformers that their beliefs appeared to have general public acceptance. Below the surface, change in behaviour was difficult, since many vices had a level of private toleration or acceptance. Preachers who moved outside reformist communities to address the wider public about drink experienced regular attacks, the breaking up of meetings and injunctions.

Drink, in particular, even though to reformers amongst the major vices, was widely popular. Relatively few respectable people knowingly met with those who were addicted to it. Addicts remained largely invisible not least because wives, husbands or children of addicts often attempted to conceal their shameful problems. The drink trade was powerful, and lobbied Parliament almost as often as the temperance movement. Most if not all prime ministers drank. There was often strong, overt political and social support for gambling and drinking at local and national level. Because moral reformers were most often associated with the Liberal Party, their causes increasingly became a partisan, party-political issue. The Tory Party was less keen on restrictions and legal measures relating to moral issues, despite some internal divisions. Brewers and publicans, most often Tory, exercised great influence in local politics. In 1850, for example, a Welsh correspondent told the *Morning Chronicle* that in Merthyr and Dowlais 1 in every 3.5 voters was a publican or beer-keeper.[1] Brewers and publicans, especially when they became wealthy and active in politics, contributed to the party in terms of funding, and could call on political support and votes from their many customers.

The British landed aristocracy still retained power and influence at the end of the century, and many of them found the views of radical Nonconformity about temperance quite alien. Many members of the state church, the Church of England, did not support temperance.

Such factors combined to ensure that the anti-vice groups' attempts to impose a more virtuous morality were met by strategies of resistance, some tacit, and some active. Opponents, then as now, picked up on political philosophies such as those of John Stuart Mill (1806–73). In his book *On Liberty* (1859), Mill stressed individual rights: citizenship, liberty and freedom of thought. He opposed the coercive forces of reformist moralism and challenged the claims of the state to impose controls on leisure life, unless there was definite harm to others. In discussing fornication and gambling, Mill took the view that there were arguments on both sides, though he made some distinction between public and private acts. He believed that people could choose to do harm to themselves through vice if they chose, without punishment. Governments had no need to punish vice. In general, the market was the final arbiter. He also argued that there was a potentially intolerant 'tyranny of the majority' in imposing a democratic vote.

So reformers sometimes found themselves satirized and ridiculed, and their Puritanism, preaching and views were scoffed at. Through the century, their sermons were described as 'cant' or 'false religion', their motives 'misguided'. They were 'kill-joys' or 'misled fanatics',[2] or dismissed as meddling do-gooders, trying to impose their own overbearing morality, and threatening the choice and liberty of others.

Was the Victorian age different in its battle over vice?

In terms of its respectability and attitudes to vice, the Victorian age was certainly very special, if not unique. It differed significantly from both the Georgian century preceding it and the twentieth century that followed. For example, the statistics relating to forms of disreputability such as alcohol abuse, theft or illegitimacy were relatively high at the beginning of the nineteenth century. They fell noticeably during the course of the Victorian period, though illegitimacy remained high in remote rural counties like Westmorland and Cumberland (which, paradoxically, also had high levels of religious observance). They reached their lowest in the years immediately before the First World War, when family life still centred round ceremonies of respectability, and gender politics still tended to be based on a gender double standard. The growing affluence of the working classes saw further incremental increases in respectability amongst the more religious.

However, the last years of the nineteenth century and the early years of the twentieth also showed the first indications of being a moral turning point. The middle classes were increasingly embracing a wider, more hedonistic notion of fun. The hypocritical and snobbish elements of middle-class respectability had been satirized as early as 1855, if not before, in William Thackeray's *The Newcomes: Memoirs of a Most Respectable Family* (1855). Parliament's hypocrisies were emphasized by the *North-Eastern Daily Gazette* in 1883 in the headline 'Pharisaical Respectability'.[3] By the 1890s there were further signs of a reaction. An 1891 editorial in the *Glasgow Herald* suggested that respectability was almost becoming seen as a 'crime', ironically suggesting that 'Respectables are in for it with a vengeance', and that 'the gallant but small and martyred body of Respectables' face the onslaught of 'the tyrant Disrespectability'.[4] By 1897, the paper noted an increased 'revolt against respectability' and more frankness in speech.[5] The same year, Geoffrey Mortimer's *The Blight of Respectability* (1897) attacked respectability as simply a mark of gentility, suggesting it was 'a shoddy God', 'a canker', 'a fell disease' and 'a contagion'. *Reynolds's Newspaper*, which greeted the book with approval, suggested that

> much of the dreariness and consequent discontent manifest on every side of this country arises from our flagrant respectability. Now the word 'respectable' means 'worthy of respect' but curiously enough, few of the respectable people are entitled to much consideration.[6]

Increasingly too, letter writers were growing more confident in suggesting that the reformist movement had far less support than it appeared. One writer, for example, discussing 'Purity and Prudery' argued that the purity movement represented 'the fanatical zeal of a handful', an 'insignificant minority' during a brief 'wave of Puritanism'.

> It is the case of the minority seeking to rule over the majority and that is wrong in principle, and opposed to all sense of justice and expediency . . . our boasted freedom is no more than a farce and a name.[7]

After 1914, the moral order shifted at a slow and more or less steady pace alongside the decline of organized religion, until the mid-1950s. Each era had a slightly different view of acceptable and unacceptable, anti-social behaviour, peculiar to the age, as contexts changed. People had constantly to debate the categories which were socially constructed. The following decades saw a more rapid shift, perceived by at least one historian as 'the death of moral Britain'.[8] Many Britons were still largely sober during the inter-war years, but after the 1960s, gambling, different sexual attitudes and heavy drinking became more respectable amongst a larger majority of the population. This impacted increasingly on policy makers and their philosophical assumptions, with a shift from moralism to the liberal reforms of the 1960s onwards. For neo-conservative historians, this has been interpreted as a shift from Victorian 'virtues', those defined patterns of public and private behaviour such as respectability, orderliness, hard work, self-reliance and deferral of gratification, to the vaguer concept of 'values'.[9]

In sum

Throughout the Victorian period and beyond, vices such as gambling and drink offered fun, excitement, sociability and a form of social cement. They sometimes enjoyed cross-class support, shared values and interests. They offered commercial profits. Their potentially harmful consequences for individuals, family and society were overlooked by some. So they could appeal not just to the supposedly rough, but also at times to the supposedly respectable. Adverse consequences were strongly emphasized and at times perhaps even over-emphasized by others. But although the reformist arguments gained wide publicity and thus appeared powerful, it is clear that they were far less effective than they appeared, certainly in terms of impacting on people's private lives. Vice was on the frontier of debates over legitimate and illegitimate leisure, but in the battle between the moralists and the commercial and private world of vice, neither side was able to win the war.

NOTES

Introduction

1. Richard Symanski, *The Immoral Landscape: Female Prostitution in Western Societies* (Toronto: Butterworth, 1981).
2. Commission on the Sanitary Condition of the Labouring Population: Report on Scotland, 1842 (008), p. 190.
3. General Board of Health Report on the Epidemics of Cholera in 1848 and 1849, 1850 (1173–5), Appendix, p. 33.
4. F.M.L. Thompson, *The Rise of Respectable Society: A Social History of Victorian Britain 1830–1900* (London: Fontana, 1988).
5. M.J.D. Roberts, *Making English Morals: Voluntary Association and Moral Reform in England 1787–1886* (Cambridge: Cambridge University Press, 2004).
6. Fergus Linnane, *London, The Wicked City: A Thousand Years of Vice in the Capital* (London: Robson Books, 2007); Catherine Arnold, *City of Sin: London and its Vices* (London: Simon and Schuster, 2010).
7. For example, Judith R. Walkowitz, *City of Dreadful Delight: Narratives of Sexual Danger in Late-Victorian London* (London: Virago Press, 1992); Lynda Nead, *Victorian Babylon: People, Streets and Images in Nineteenth Century London* (New Haven: Yale University Press, 2000); Margaret Harkness, *In Darkest London* (Cambridge: Black Apollo Press, 2003); Simon Joyce, *Capital Offences: Geographies of Class and Crime in Victorian London* (Charlottesville: University of Virginia Press, 2003); Seth Koven, *Slumming: Sexual and Social Politics in Victorian London* (Princeton: Princeton University Press, 2004).
8. For example, Peter Andersson, *Street Life in Late Victorian London: The Constable and the Crowd* (London: Palgrave, 2013).
9. John K. Walton and Alastair Wilcox (eds), *Low Life and Moral Improvement in Mid-Victorian England: Liverpool Through the Journalism of Hugh Shimmin* (Leicester: Leicester University Press, 1991); Andy Croll, *Civilizing the Urban: Popular Culture and Public Space, Merthyr c. 1870–1914* (Cardiff: University of Wales Press, 2000).
10. John Greenaway, *Drink and British Politics since 1830: A Study in Policy-Making* (Basingstoke, 2003); James Nicholls, *The Politics of Alcohol: A History of the Drink Question in England* (Manchester: Manchester University Press, 2009).

11 A.E. Dingle, *The Campaign for Prohibition in Victorian England* (London: Croom Helm, 1980); Lilian L. Shiman, *The Crusade Against Drink in Victorian England* (Basingstoke: Macmillan, 1988).

12 John Burnett, *Liquid Pleasures: A Social History of Drinks in Modern Britain* (London: Routledge, 1999); Rod Phillips, *Alcohol: A History* (Chapel Hill: University of North Carolina Press, 2014).

13 For example, Mark Girouard, *Victorian Pubs* (London: Studio Vista, 1975); Richard Tames, *The Victorian Public House* (Princes Risborough: Shire, 2003); Paul Jennings, *The Local: A History of the English Pub* (London: The History Press, 2011).

14 For example, R.L. Williams, *Drink and Society in Victorian Wales c. 1820–1895* (Cardiff: University of Wales Press, 1989).

15 David Dixon, *From Prohibition to Regulation: Bookmaking, Anti-Gambling and the Law* (Oxford: Clarendon Press, 1991); David Miers, *Regulating Commercial Gambling: Past, Present and Future* (Oxford: Oxford University Press, 2004).

16 Mark Clapson, *A Bit of a Flutter: Popular Gambling and English Society c. 1823–1961* (Manchester: Manchester University Press, 1992); Roger Munting, *An Economic and Social History of Gambling in Britain and the USA* (Manchester: Manchester University Press, 1996).

17 For example, Carl Chinn, *Better Betting with a Decent Feller: Betting and the British Working Class 1750–1990* (Hemel Hempstead: Harvester, 1991); Mike Huggins, *Flat Racing and British Society 1790–1914: A Social and Economic History* (London: Frank Cass, 2000).

18 For example, Lucy Bland, *Banishing the Beast: English Feminism and Sexual Morality 1885–1914* (London: Penguin, 1995).

19 Paula Bartley, *Prostitution: Prevention and Reform in England 1860–1914* (London: Routledge, 1999); Maria Luddy, *Prostitution and Irish Society, 1800–1940* (Cambridge: Cambridge University Press, 2007).

20 For example, Tom Winnifrith, *Fallen Women in the Nineteenth Century Novel* (London: Macmillan, 1994); Diane Mason, *The Secret Vice: Masturbation in Victorian Fiction and Medical Culture* (Manchester: Manchester University Press, 2008).

21 For example, Matt Cook, *London and the Culture of Homosexuality 1885–1914* (Cambridge: Cambridge University Press, 2003).

22 Peter Gay, *The Bourgeois Experience: Victoria to Freud Vol. I: Education of the Senses* (Oxford: Oxford University Press, 1984).

23 For example, Michael Mason, *The Making of Victorian Sexuality* (Oxford: Oxford University Press, 1994); Michael Mason, *The Making of Victorian Sexual Attitudes* (Oxford: Oxford University Press, 1994). Lesley A. Hall, *Sex, Gender and Social Change in Britain Since 1880* (London: Macmillan, 2000).

24 Allan Harty, *A Concentration of Moral Force: the Temperance Movement in Sunderland, 1830 to 1853* (Sunderland: University of Sunderland Press, 2004).

25 Geoffrey Best, *Mid-Victorian Britain, 1851–1875* (London: Fontana, 1971).
26 For example, Gowan Dawson, *Darwin, Literature, and Victorian Respectability* (New York: Cambridge University Press, 2007); C.W. Master, *The Respectability of Late Victorian Workers: A Case Study of York, 1867–1914* (Newcastle: Cambridge Scholars Publishing, 2010).

Chapter 1: The Language of Vice

1 Peter Gay, *Schnitzler's Century: The Making of Middle-Class Culture, 1815–1914* (London: W.W. Norton, 2001).
2 See for example, *The Times*, 16 June 1860.
3 Dan Cruickshank, *The Secret History of Georgian London: How the Wages of Sin Shaped the Capital* (London: Random House, 2010).
4 Vic Gatrell, *City of Laughter: Sex and Satire in Eighteenth Century London* (London: Atlantic Books, 2006); Ben Wilson, *Decency and Disorder: The Age of Cant 1789–1837* (London: Faber and Faber, 2007); Boyd Hilton, *The Age of Atonement: The Influence of Evangelism on Social and Economic Thought 1750–1865* (Oxford: Clarendon Press, 1988).
5 Donald Grey, 'Early Victorian Scandalous Journalism: Renton Nicholson's "The Town" (1837–42)', in J. Shallock and M. Wolff (eds), *The Victorian Periodical Press: Samplings and Soundings* (Leicester: Leicester University Press, 1982), pp. 317–32.
6 See Roy Porter and Lesley Hall, *The Facts of Life: The Creation of Sexual Knowledge in Britain 1750–1950* (London: Yale University Press, 1995), pp. 278 ff. for discussion of how texts were read.
7 Evidence of Mr Tufnell, Poor Law Commissioners Annual Report, 1841 (327), p. 145.
8 *The Times*, 17 May 1865; Alan Metcalfe, *Leisure and Recreation in a Victorian Mining Community* (London: Routledge, 2006), p. 70.
9 Matthew Hilton, *Smoking in British Popular Culture 1800–2000: Perfect Pleasures* (Manchester: Manchester University Press, 2000), pp. 60-82; *Freeman's Journal*, 15 September 1884.
10 *Southern Reporter*, 6 April 1871.
11 Departmental Committee to Inquire into the Jurisdiction of Metropolitan Police Magistrates 1900 (Vol. 374), evidence of Sir C. Elliott Q. 861.
12 Inquiry into the laws relating to patronage, simony etc. 1874 (289). Special Committee of the House of Lords, p.58.
13 The Riverside Visitor (Thomas Wright), *Pinch of Poverty* (London: Isbister and Co., 1892), p. 148.
14 Anon., *Memorials of Dean Close* (London: George Rivers, 1885), p.78.
15 Francis Close, 'Lecture on The Dangerous Classes', delivered 11 April 1850.
16 Francis Close, *On the Evil Consequences of Attending the Racecourse* (Cheltenham: privately published, 1827).

17 Address of the Very Reverend the Dean of Carlisle to Glasgow Abstainers (Glasgow: Glasgow Scottish Temperance League, 1861).
18 Francis Close, *Tobacco: Its Influences, Physical, Moral and Religious*, sermon at Carlisle, 1859.
19 H. Shimmen, *Liverpool Life: Its Pleasures, Practices and Pastimes* (Liverpool: Egerton Smith and Co., 1856), pp. v–vi.
20 Anon., *Tempted London: Young Men* (London: Hodder and Stoughton, 1888), pp. 237–50.
21 *The Times*, 28 March 1856.
22 *The Free Lance*, 16 June 1867.
23 *The Star*, 23 February 1858
24 *Town Talk*, 28 June 1879.
25 Tony Collins and Wray Vamplew, *Mud, Sweat and Beers: A Cultural History of Sport and Alcohol* (Oxford: Berg, 2002), p. 2.
26 2nd Report of the Select Committee on the Regulation of Public Houses, Hotels, Beer Shops etc, 1852/3 (855), Appendix 2.
27 B.J. Davey, *Lawless and Immoral: Policing a Country Town 1838–1857* (Leicester: Leicester University Press, 1983).
28 F. Richardson, *The Crusade* (London: R. Washbourne, 1873), p. 26.
29 National Archives, Home Office files HO45/6608: Street prostitution 1857–8.
30 National Archives: Home Office files HO45/9666/A45364: Complaint re immoral conduct and lack of police action on Clapham Common.
31 A.G. Swinburne, 'Dolores', stanza 9, in *Poems and Ballads* (London: J.C. Hotten, 1866).
32 Thomas L. Reed, *The Transforming Draught: Jekyll and Hyde, Robert Louis Stevenson and the Victorian Alcohol Debate* (Jefferson, NC: McFarland, 2006).
33 Parliamentary Papers, Commission of Inquiry into Charities in England and Wales 1840 (219), paragraph vi.
34 *The Times*, 12 November, 1847.
35 Roger Adelson, *Mark Sykes: Portrait of an Amateur* (London: Jonathan Cape, 1975), p. 67.
36 Niall Ferguson, *Civilisation: The West and the Rest* (London: Penguin, 2012).
37 Rev. Charles Girdlestone, 'Rich and Poor', in Viscount Ingestre (ed.), *Meliora or Better Times to Come* (London: J.W. Parker and Co., 1852), p. 21.
38 *Northern Echo*, 15 July 1885.
39 Rev. W. Reid, *Our National Vice* (Glasgow: Scottish Temperance League, 1858), p. 15.
40 Emelyne Godfrey, *Femininity, Crime and Self-defence in Victorian Literature and Society* (Basingstoke: Palgrave Macmillan, 2012), p. 23.
41 *Cleveland News*, 27 January 1883.
42 *The Times*, 6 January 1872.

43 For a useful survey of moral reform movements see M.J.D. Roberts, *Making English Morals: Voluntary Association and Moral Reform in England 1787–1886* (Cambridge: Cambridge University Press, 2004).
44 Patrick Joyce, *Work, Society and Politics. The Culture of the Factory in Later Victorian England* (London: Harvester Press, 1980).
45 Stefan Petrow, *Policing Morals: The Metropolitan Police and the Home Office 1870–1914* (Oxford: Oxford University Press, 1994).

Chapter 2: The Spatial Dimension of Vice

1 The visibility and relationship to social space of moral crusades against prostitution has been well analysed by Richard Symanski, *The Immoral Landscape: Female Prostitution in Western Societies* (Toronto: Butterworths, 1981); see also Phil Hubbard, 'Sexuality, Immorality and the City: Red-light Districts and the Marginalisation of Street Prostitutes', *Gender, Place and Culture*, 5, 1, 1998, pp. 55–72.
2 Andy Croll, 'Street Disorder, Surveillance and Shame: Regulating Behaviour in the Public Spaces of the Late Victorian British Town', *Social History*, 24, 3, 1999, pp. 250–68.
3 'Dwellings of the Poor in Bethnal Green', *Illustrated London News*, 24 October 1863.
4 Peter Andersson, *Streetlife in Late Victorian London: The Constable and the Crowd* (Basingstoke: Palgrave Macmillan, 2013), Ch. 2.
5 Fergus Linnane, *London's Underworld: Three Centuries of Vice and Crime* (London: Anova, 2004).
6 David W. Bartlett, *London by Day and Night* (New York: Hurst and Co., 1852), pp. 18–20.
7 Judith R. Walkowitz, *City of Dreadful Delight: Narratives of Sexual Danger in Late-Victorian London* (London: Virago Press, 1992).
8 *Ainsworth's Magazine*, Vol. 6, November 1844, p. 377.
9 *The Times*, 26 September 1856; Nigel Green, *Tough Times and Grisly Crimes* (Newcastle: Nigel Green Media, 2006), p. 77.
10 Henry Mayhew, 'Labour and the Poor 1849–50; Letter XXX', *Morning Chronicle*, 29 January 1850.
11 Henry Vigar Harris, *London at Midnight* (London: General Publishing Co., 1885), pp. 10–12.
12 Howard J. Goldsmid, *Dottings of a Dosser* (London: T. Fisher Unwin, 1886), pp. 9–10.
13 *East London Observer*, 10 October 1857.
14 Henry Colman, *European Life and Manners* (1845), quoted in Asa Briggs, *Victorian Cities* (Harmondsworth: Penguin, 1968), p 116.
15 Daniel Joseph Kirwan, *Palace and Hovel or Phases of London Life* (1870; London: Abelard Schuman, 1963).

16 J.E. Mercer, 'The Condition of Life in Angel Meadow', *Transactions of the Manchester Statistical Society 1896–7*, pp. 159–73; Annual Meeting Report, 1868, p. 5, quoted in Paula Bartley, *Prostitution: Prevention and Reform 1860–1914* (London: Routledge, 2000), p. 3.
17 *Hull Packet*, 28 July 1871.
18 Andy Croll, *Civilising the Urban: Popular Culture and Public Space in Merthyr c. 1870–1914* (Cardiff: University of Wales Press, 2000).
19 David Taylor, 'The Frontier Revisited: Thrift and Fellowship in the New Industrial Town c. 1830–1914', in A.J. Pollard (ed.), *Middlesbrough: Town and Community 1830–1950* (Stroud: Sutton Publishing, 1996), p. 83.
20 William Booth, *In Darkest England and The Way Out* (London: Salvation Army, 1890), pp. 15, 56, 157–9, 180.
21 Beatrice Webb, *My Apprenticeship* (1926: Cambridge: Cambridge University Press, 1979), p 321.
22 Jerry White, *London in the Nineteenth Century: A Human Awful Wonder of God* (London: Jonathan Cape, 2007).
23 David W. Bartlett, *London by Day and Night* (New York: Hurst and Co., 1852), p. 126.
24 Drew Gray, *London's Shadows: The Dark Side of the Victorian City* (London: Continuum, 2010).
25 M. Hewitt, 'The Travails of Domestic Visiting: Manchester 1830–1870', *Historical Research* 71, 175, 1998, pp. 196–227.
26 This section on visits draws on Seth Coven, *Slumming: Sexual and Social Politics in Victorian London* (Princeton: Princeton University Press, 2004).
27 Margaret Harkness, *In Darkest London* (Cambridge: Black Apollo Press, 2003); Jack London, *The People of the Abyss* (London: Nelson and Co., 1903).
28 Ellen Ross (ed.), *Slum Travelers: Ladies and London Poverty, 1860–1920* (Berkeley, CA: University of California Press, 2007).
29 House of Commons Commission on the Sanitary Condition of the Labouring Population of Great Britain 1842 (006), pp. 63, 197.
30 *Pall Mall Gazette*, 28 November 1883; William Knox, *Industrial Nation: Work, Culture and Society in Scotland, 1800–present* (Edinburgh: Edinburgh University Press, 1999), p. 94.
31 *Birmingham Daily Mail*, 31 May 1871; *North British Daily Mail*, 27 December 1870, quoted in Douglas A. Read, 'Playing and Praying' in *Cambridge Urban History of Britain, Vol. 3* (Cambridge University Press, 2000), p. 782.
32 Anon., *Tempted London: Young Men* (London: Hodder and Stoughton, 1888), pp. 247–8.
33 *Edinburgh Evening News*, 18 December 1896.
34 *The Times*, 22 August 1838.
35 According to Lynda Nead, *Victorian Babylon: People, Streets and Images in Nineteenth Century London* (New Haven: Yale University Press, 2000). London could be seen as the Babylon of the Apocalypse.

36 *Saturday Review*, 1 October 1853.
37 Arthur Sherwell, *Life in West London: A Study and A Contrast: Volume 3* (London: Methuen, 1897), p. 137.
38 Peter Bailey, *Popular Culture and Performance in the Victorian City* (Cambridge: Cambridge University Press, 1998).
39 John K. Walton and Alastair Wilcox (eds), *Low Life and Moral Improvement in Mid-Victorian England: Liverpool Through the Journalism of Hugh Shimmin* (Leicester: Leicester University Press, 1991).
40 Walkowitz, *City of Dreadful Delight,* p. 11; M.A. Simpson, 'The West End of Glasgow, 1830–1914', in M.A. Simpson and T.H. Lloyd, *Middle Class Housing in Britain* (Newton Abbott: David and Charles, 1977), pp. 44–85.
41 W. Benjamin, *Charles Baudelaire: A Lyric Poet in the Age of High Capitalism* (London; New Left Books, 1976), pp. 35–66. See also K. Tester (ed.), *The Flaneur* (London: Routledge, 1994); Vanessa R. Schwartz, *Spectacular Realities: Early Mass Culture in Fin-de-Siècle Paris* (Berkeley: University of California Press, 1998).
42 See for example, Matthew Sweet, *Inventing the Victorians* (London: Faber and Faber, 2001).
43 Michael Diamond, *Victorian Sensation or The Spectacular, the Shocking and the Scandalous in Nineteenth Century Britain* (London: Anthem Press, 2003).
44 Munby Diary, 26 May 1879, quoted in Cathy Carter, *Arthur Munby and Hannah Cullwick: The Collision of Culture, Psychology and Story* (Lafayette: University of Louisiana, 2009), p. 175.
45 Barry Reah, *Watching Hannah: Sexuality, Horror and Bodily Deformation in Victorian England* (London: Reaktion Books, 2002). See also Derek Hudson, *Munby: Man of Two Worlds: The Life and Diaries of Arthur J. Munby 1828–1910* (London: Abacus, 1974).
46 Morris B. Kaplin, *Sodom on the Thames: Sex, Love and Scandal in Wilde Times* (Ithaca: Cornell University Press, 2005); Matt Cooke, *London and the Culture of Homosexuality 1885–1914* (Cambridge: Cambridge University Press, 2003).
47 Walkowitz, *City of Dreadful Delight*, p.11.
48 Margot C. Finn, 'Sex and the City: Metropolitan Modernities in English History', *Victorian Studies*, 44, 1, 2001, pp. 25–32; Elaine S. Abelson, *Ladies Go A-thieving: Middle Class Shoplifters in the Victorian Department Store* (Oxford: Oxford University Press, 1992) focuses largely on the USA but gives some European examples.
49 Judith R. Walkowitz, 'Going public: shopping, street harassment and streetwalking in late Victorian London', *Representations*, 62, 1998, pp. 1–30.
50 *Leeds Mercury*, 2 November 1839
51 *Bristol Mercury*, 14 July 1838. For Booth see Gertrude Himmelfarb *Poverty and Compassion: The Moral Imagination of the Late Victorians* (New York: Vintage Books, 1991), Ch. 15 passim.
52 *The Day's Doings*, 30 January 1872.

53 *The Times*, 15 January 1858.
54 Anon., *Tempted London,* pp. 174–5, 186, 195, 242–3.
55 Gustave Dore and Blanchard Jerrold, *London: A Pilgrimage* (1872; Newton Abbot: David and Charles, 1971), Ch. 10.
56 J. Ewing Richie, *The Night Side of London* (London: William Tweedie, 1858), pp. 218–25.
57 J. Traies, 'Jones and the Working Girl: Class Marginality in Music Hall Song', in J.S. Bratton (ed.), *Music Hall: Performance and Style* (Milton Keynes: Open University Press, 1986), 23; J. Earl, 'Building the Halls' in P. Bailey (ed.), *Music Hall: The Business of Pleasure* (Milton Keynes: Open University Press, 1986), p. 32.
58 Paul Maloney, *Scotland and the Music Hall 1850–1914* (Manchester: Manchester University Press, 2003), pp. 72–4.
59 *Illustrated Midland News*, 16 April 1870.
60 *Town Talk*, 23 November 1878.
61 Rev. Thomas Best, 'The Sinners in Zion are Afraid': A sermon preached at St James' Church, Sheffield (Sheffield: Pawson and Brailsford, 1864); James Greenwood, *The Seven Curses of London* (London: Rivers, 1869), Ch. 3; *Illustrated Sporting and Dramatic News*, 9 August 1879.
62 Barry J. Faulk, *Music Hall and Modernity: The Late-Victorian Discovery of Popular Culture* (Athens, OH: Ohio University Press, 2004), pp. 76–7.
63 *Western Mail*, 9 December 1895.
64 William Acton, *Prostitution, Considered in its Moral, Social and Sanitary Aspects* (London: John Churchill, 1857).
65 *The Times*, 13 December 1876.
66 Warwick Wroth, *Cremorne and the Later London Gardens* (London: Elliot Stock, 1907).
67 *Town Talk*, 13 September 1879.
68 *Birmingham Weekly Post*, 17 July 1880 shows one such prosecution.
69 Joe Wilson, 'Sunday Neets at Jesmond Gardens' in *Tyneside Songs and Drolleries* Part 1 (Newcastle: Wilson, c. 1865), p. 16.
70 *Sunderland Herald*, 18 May 1849.
71 David Kerr Cameron, *The English Fair* (Stroud: Sutton, 1998), p. 194.
72 Gary Moses, 'Reshaping Rural Culture? The Church of England and Hiring Fairs in the East Riding of Yorkshire c. 1850–1880', *Rural History*, 13, 1, 2002, pp. 61–84.
73 Hugh Cunningham, 'The Metropolitan Fairs: A Case Study in the Social Control of Leisure', in A.P. Donadgrodzki (ed.), *Social Control in Nineteenth Century Britain* (London: Croom Helm, 1977), p. 170.
74 Cunningham, 'Metropolitan Fairs', p. 178.
75 S. Boase, The Leicester Pleasure Fairs at Humberstone Gate, 1837–1904 (University of Leicester, MA in English Local History, 1979); Sally Alexander, 'St Giles Fair, 1830–1914', in R.J. Morris and Richard Rodger (eds), *The*

Victorian City: A Reader in British Urban History 1820–1914 (London: Longman, 1993); R.A. Church, *Economic and Social Change in a Midland Town: Victorian Nottingham* (London: Frank Cass, 1966), pp. 213–14.
76 *Waddington's List of Fairs, Feasts, Statutes and Rushbearings* (York: T.A.J. Waddington, 1896).
77 Mike Huggins, *Flat Racing and British Society 1790–1914* (London: Frank Cass, 2000).
78 Lord Henry Curzon, 'The Horse as an Instrument of Gambling', *Contemporary Review*, 20 August 1877, pp. 376–92.
79 'Epsom', *Household Words*, 3, 63, 7 June 1861.
80 Wilkie Collins and Charles Dickens, 'The Lazy Tour of Two Idle Apprentices', *Household Words*, 1857, p. 395.
81 *The Free Lance*, 15 June 1867.
82 Mike Huggins, *Flat Racing and British Society 1790–1914*, p. 206.
83 T. Houston, *The Evils Associated with Horseracing and the Steeplechase and their Demoralising Effects* (Paisley: Houston, 1853).
84 R.M. Bevan, *The Roodee, 450 Years of Racing in Chester* (Northwich: Cheshire County Publishing, 1989), pp. 30–31.
85 Bevan, *The Roodee*.
86 *The Times*, 10 June 1858.
87 Sir Arthur Conan Doyle, 'The Adventure of the Copper Beeches' in *The Complete Sherlock Holmes, volume 1* (New York: Barnes and Noble, 2003), p. 384.
88 Robert Moore, *Pit-men, Preachers and Politics: The Effects of Methodism in a Durham Mining Community* (Cambridge: Cambridge University Press, 1974); Alan Metcalfe, *Leisure and Recreation in a Victorian Mining Community: The Social Economy of Leisure in North-East England 1820–1914* (Abingdon: Routledge, 2006).
89 J.K. Walton, *The English Seaside Resort: A Social History 1750–1914* (Leicester: Leicester University Press, 1983), p. 225.
90 *Cleveland News*, 10 July 1885.
91 J.K. Walton, 'Respectability takes a holiday: disreputable behaviour at the Victorian seaside', in Martin Hewitt (ed.), *Unrespectable Recreations* (Leeds: Leeds Centre for Victorian Studies, 2001), pp. 176–93; J.K. Walton, *Blackpool* (Edinburgh: Edinburgh University Press, 1998), p. 72.
92 Ronald Hyam, *Empire and Sexuality: The British Experience* (Manchester: Manchester University Press, 1992); Ian Littlewood, *Sultry Climates: Travel and Sex Since the Grand Tour* (London: John Murray, 2001); Robert Aldrich *Colonialism and Homosexuality* (London: Routledge, 2003).
93 *The Times*, 23 October 1843. See Martin J. Wiener, 'Homicide and Englishness: Criminal Justice and National Identity in Victorian England', *National Identities*, 6, 3, 2004, pp. 203–15.
94 Mrinalini Sinha, *Colonial Masculinity: The Manly Englishman and the Effeminate Bengali in the Late Nineteenth Century* (Manchester: Manchester University Press, 1995).

Chapter 3: The Vice of Drunkenness

1. *The Era*, 8 September 1872.
2. *Sheffield Independent*, 30 August 1873.
3. *Leeds Mercury*, 28 December 1872; *Sheffield Independent*, 29 August 1873; *Sheffield Daily Telegraph*, 9 June 1874.
4. *The Bradford Observer*, 30 August 1873.
5. John Greenaway, *Drink and British Politics Since 1830: A Study in Policy Making* (Basingstoke: Palgrave Macmillan, 2003), provides a clear overview of the political 'problem' of drink; Lilian Lewis Shiman, *The Crusade Against Drink in Victorian England* (Basingstoke: Macmillan, 1988).
6. See M. Valverde, *Diseases of the Will: Alcohol and the Dilemmas of Freedom* (Cambridge: Cambridge University Press, 1998).
7. Minutes of Evidence of Select Committee on Friendly Societies, 1849 (458) Q. 1444 (T. Barlow).
8. Alexander Thompson, *Social Evils: Their Causes and Their Cure* (London: James Nesbit, 1852), p.12.
9. *The Times*, 15 June 1855.
10. Rev. W. Reid, *Our National Vice* (Glasgow: Scottish Temperance Society, 1858), p. 1.
11. Report by the Committee on Intemperance for the Lower House of Convocation (London: Longman, 1869), p. 3.
12. F. Richardson, *The Crusade* (London: R. Washbourne, 1873), p. 1.
13. J.B. Brown, 'The Pig or the Stye: Drink and Poverty in Late Victorian England', *International Review of Social History*, 18, 1973, pp. 380–95.
14. Charles Booth, *Life and Labour of the London Poor, Vol. I* (London: Griffin Bohn, 1861), pp. 147–8.
15. Harry G. Levine, 'Temperance Cultures: Alcohol as a Problem in Nordic and English-Speaking Cultures', in Griffith Edwards, Malcolm Lader and D. Colin Drummond (eds), *The Nature of Alcohol and Drug-Related Problems* (New York: Oxford University Press, 1992), pp. 16–36; Brian Harrison, *Drink and the Victorians: The Temperance Question in England, 1815–1872* (1971; 2nd edn, Keele: Keele University Press, 1994).
16. *The Times*, 5 January 1845.
17. *The Times*, 15 January 1868.
18. H.G. Levine. 'The discovery of addiction: changing conceptions of habitual drunkenness in America', *Journal of Studies on Alcohol*, 39, 1978, pp. 143–74.
19. Letter to *The Times*, 24 October 1856.
20. R.M. MacLeod, 'The Edge of Hope: Social Policy and Chronic Alcoholism, 1870-1900', *Journal of the History of Medicine*, 22, 3, 1967, pp. 215–45; Terry Parssiner and Karen Kerner, 'Developing the Disease Model of Drug Addiction in Britain 1870–1926', *Medical History*, 24, 3 (1980), pp. 275–96.

21 George R. Sims, *How the Poor Live* (London: Chatto and Windus, 1883), pp. 15–16.
22 House of Lords Select Committee Inquiry into the Prevalence of Habits of Intemperance, 2nd Report 1877 (271), p. 47; 3rd Report 1877 (418) QQ. 9844–57.
23 *The Yorkshireman*, 19 March 1849.
24 *The Times*, 30 January 1868, 23 June 1869.
25 Rob Donovan, 'Drink in Victorian Norwich' (PhD thesis, University of East Anglia, 2003), pp. 41, 193–4, 208.
26 For the following section see Shiman, *Crusade against Drink in Victorian England*; Harrison, *Drink and the Victorians*; W.R. Lambert, *Drink and Sobriety in Victorian Wales* (Cardiff: University of Wales Press, 1983).
27 Aaron Hoffman,' "Distilled death and liquid damnation": the temperance movement in Aberdeen, Scotland, 1830–45' (PhD thesis, Aberdeen University, 2004).
28 J. Read, 'Joseph Livesey of Preston, business, temperance and moral reform', *Northern History* 35, 1999, pp. 269–70.
29 Allan Harty, *A Concentration of Moral Force: The Temperance Movement in Sunderland, 1830 to 1853* (Sunderland: University of Sunderland Press, 2004).
30 Lambert, *Drink and Sobriety*, pp. 67–77.
31 Olwen Claire Niessen, *Aristocracy, Temperance and Social Reform: The Life of Lady Henry Somerset* (London: I.B. Tauris, 2007).
32 *The Times*, 25 May 1857.
33 See A.E. Dingle, *The Campaign for Prohibition in Victorian England. The UK Alliance 1872–1895* (London: Croom Helm, 1980).
34 Harrison, *Drink and the Victorians*, p. 176.
35 See for example, David Gardiner, 'The Nature and Development of Conservatism in Wolverhampton 1886–1910' (MA dissertation, University of Wolverhampton, 1991), p. 34.
36 Heather J. Creaton, *Victorian Diaries: The Daily Lives of Victorian Men and Women* (London: Mitchell Beazley, 2001) contains this and several similar examples.
37 J. Dunlop, *The Philosophy of Artificial and Compulsory Drinking Usage in Great Britain and Ireland* (London: Houlston and Stoneman, 1839).
38 Henry Mayhew, *London Characters: Illustrations of the Humour, Pathos and Peculiarities of London Life* (London: Chatto and Windus, 1881).
39 Anon. *A Memorial to Dean Close, by one who Knew Him* (London: George Rives, 1885), p. 84.
40 Third Report of the Select Committee of the House of Lords for Inquiring into Habits of Intemperance, 1877 (418), QQ.9731–9776 (Levi).
41 Salford Watch Committee Minutes, 29 September 1847.
42 John Burnett, *Liquid Pleasures: A Social History of Drinks in Modern Britain* (New York: Routledge, 1999), p. 124.

43 Charles E. Hardy, *John Bowes and the Bowes Museum* (Newcastle: Frank Graham, 1970), pp. 55–65.
44 *The Times*, 17 May 1865, 25 July 1866.
45 *The Times*, 24 November 1855.
46 Rhodes Boyson, *The Ashworth Cotton Enterprise* (Oxford: Oxford University Press, 1970).
47 Magdalen Goffin, *The Diaries of Absalom Watkin: A Manchester Man, 1787–1861* (London: Sutton Publishing, 1993); *Weekly Record*, 12 September 1857.
48 J. Ewing Ritchie, *About London* (London: William Tinsley, 1860), p. 110.
49 *The Yorkshireman*, 29 September 1838; *The Times*, 19 May 1842.
50 Nataniel Hawthorne, 'At a dinner in London', in *Our Old Home: A Series of English Sketches* (Boston: Houghton, Mifflin and Co., 1883).
51 G.E. Mingay, *Rural Life in Victorian England* (Stroud: Alan Sutton, 1990), p. 77.
52 *The Times*, 23 February 1857.
53 Norman Moorsom, *The Demon Drink in Mid-Victorian Middlesbrough* (Middlesbrough: Middlesbrough Temperance Association, 2000), p. 8.
54 *Star of Gwent*, 15 November 1889. See also Andy Croll, 'Mabon's Day: The Rise and Fall of a LibLab Holiday in the South Wales Coalfield 1888–1898', *Labour History Review*, 72, 1, 2007, pp. 49–68.
55 *Chambers' Edinburgh Journal*, January–June 1850, pp. 165–7.
56 *The Weekly Record*, 12 September 1857.
57 Joseph Rowntree and A. Sherwell, *The Temperance Problem and Social Reform* (London: Hodder and Stoughton, 1899), p. 491.
58 Susan Margaret Kling, 'Spare Time: Pub Culture in Nineteenth Century London: A Social and Cultural History of Working Class Pub Patronage' (PhD dissertation, University of California Los Angeles, 2001); Paul Jennings, *The Public House in Bradford 1770–1970* (Keele: Keele University Press, 1995).
59 Brian Harrison, 'Pubs', in H.J. Dyos and M. Wolff (eds), *The Victorian City. Images and Reality. Vol. 1* (London: Routledge and Kegan Paul, 1973), pp. 161–90; R.C. Riley and Philip Eley, 'Public Houses and Beerhouses in Nineteenth Century Portsmouth', *Portsmouth Papers*, 38 (1983); Rudolph Kenna and Anthony Mooney, *People's Palaces: Victorian and Edwardian Pubs of Scotland* (Edinburgh: Paul Harris, 1983).
60 John Lowerson and John Myerscough, *Time to Spare in Victorian England* (Hassocks: Harvester Press, 1977), p. 64.
61 Henry Solly, *Working Men's Social Clubs and Educational Institutes* (London: Working Men's Club and Institute Union, 1867); R.N. Price, 'The Working Men's Club Movement and Victorian Social Reform Ideology', *Victorian Studies* 19, 15, 1971, pp. 117–47.
62 *The Times*, 25 June 1850.

63 Hugh Cunningham, 'Leisure and Culture' in F.M.L. Thompson (ed.), *The Cambridge Social History of Britain 1750–1950 Vol. II* (Cambridge: Cambridge University Press, 1980), pp. 289–90.

64 Mike Huggins, 'The First Generation of Street Bookmakers in Victorian England', *Northern History*, XXXVI, 2000, pp. 129–45.

65 1889 letter quoted in C.F. Wood, *Kings of Amateur Soccer* (Bishop Auckland: privately printed, 1985), p. 17.

66 *Yorkshire Post*, 22 March 1893, quoted in Tony Collins and Wray Vamplew, *Mud, Sweat and Beers: A Cultural History of Sport and Alcohol* (Oxford: Berg, 2002), p. 1. See also, John Weir, *Drink, Religion and Scottish Football, 1873–1900* (Renfrew: Stuart Davison, 1992).

67 J. Fairfax-Blakeborough, *Northern Turf History, Vol. III, York and Doncaster* (London: J.A. Allen, 1950), p.50.

68 J. Ewing Ritchie, *The Night Side of London* (London: William Tweedie, 1858), p. 143; Geoff Brandwood, Andrew Davison and Mick Slaughter, *Licensed to Sell: The History and Heritage of the Public House* (London: English Heritage, 2004) is good on pub architecture.

69 Rowntree and Sherwell, *The Temperance Question and Social Reform*, pp. 10–11.

70 Brian Spiller, *Victorian Public Houses* (Newton Abbot: David and Charles, 1972); Mark Girouard, *Victorian Pubs* (London: Studio Vista, 1975).

71 David W. Gutzke, *Pubs and Progressives: Reinventing the Public House in England 1896–1960* (DeKalb IL: Northern Illinois University Press, 2006).

72 Richard Tames, *The Victorian Public House* (London: Shire Publications, 2003).

73 Mike Huggins, *The Victorians and Sport* (London: Hambledon, 2004), p.12.

74 *The Times*, 24 February 1838.

75 J.M.V. Paisano, 'Tipplers, Drunkards and Backsliders: The Temperance Movement in England 1830–72' (PhD thesis, Universidade do Minho, Braga, Portugal, 2002), p. 441.

76 *The Times*, 14 April 1854.

77 John Burnett, *Liquid Pleasures: A Social History of Drinks in Modern Britain* (New York: Routledge, 1999), p. 129. See also, R.G. Wilson, 'The Changing Taste for Beer in Victorian Britain', in R.G. Wilson and T.R. Gourvish (eds), *The Dynamics of the International Brewing Industry since 1800* (London and New York: Routledge, 1998), pp. 93–104.

78 Rowntree and Sherwell, *The Temperance Question and Social Reform*, pp. 10–11.

79 A.E. Dingle, 'Drink and Working-class Living Standards in Britain, 1870–1914', *Economic History Review*, 2nd ser., XXV, 1972, pp. 608–22.

80 Dingle, 'Drink and Working-class Living Standards in Britain, 1870–1914', pp. 608–22.

81 Burnett, *Liquid Pleasures*, pp. 68–9.

82 For example, *Barrow Herald*, 25 January, 1 February, 8 February, 15 February, 22 February 1868.

83 Dingle, 'Drink and Working-class Living Standards in Britain, 1870–1914'; T.R. Gourvish and R.G. Wilson, *The British Brewing Industry 1830–1980* (Cambridge: Cambridge University Press, 1994); Burnett, *Liquid Pleasures*, p. 126.

Chapter 4: Vice and Profligacy: Betting and Gaming

1 John Pinfold, 'Dandy Rats at Play: The Liverpudlian Middle Classes in the Nineteenth Century', in Mike Huggins and J.A. Mangan, *Disreputable Pleasures: Less Virtuous Victorians at Play* (London: Frank Cass, 2004), p. 74.

2 Michael Flavin, *Gambling in the Nineteenth-Century English Novel* (Brighton: Sussex University Press, 2003).

3 1844 (297) Select Committee on Statutes Against Gambling, Starkie Q. 9; Baxter Q. 1083.

4 Modern national surveys such as South Oaks Gambling Screen (USA), Victorian Gambling Screen Australia, the Canadian Problem Gambling Index and the Gambling Prevalence Survey (UK) all provide details of the extent of problem gambling. See *International Gambling Studies* 6, 2, 2006 for recent examples.

5 See Michael Flavin, *Gambling in the Nineteenth-Century Novel* (Brighton: Sussex Academic Press, 2003), especially pp. 42–64.

6 *The Sheffield and Rotherham Independent*, 27 March 1869.

7 *Manchester Times*, 9 February 1867.

8 D.C. Itzkowitz, 'Victorian bookmakers and their customers', *Victorian Studies*, 32, 2 (1988), pp. 15–17; Mark Clapson, *A Bit of a Flutter: Popular Gambling and English Society, c. 1823–1961* (Manchester: Manchester University Press, 1992), p. 71; Carl Chinn, *Better Betting with a Decent Feller: Betting and the British Working Class, 1750–1990* (London: Aurum Press, 2004), pp. 197, 281.

9 Carl Chinn, 'Pickersgill, Joseph (1849/50–1920)', *Oxford Dictionary of National Biography* (Oxford: Oxford University Press, 2004 [http://www.oxforddnb.com/view/article/56617, accessed 6 February 2014]).

10 Mike Huggins, 'The First Generation of Street Bookmakers in Victorian England: Demonic Fiends or Decent Fellers?', *Northern History*, XXXVI, 2000, pp. 129–45.

11 *Fraser's Magazine*, May 1838, p. 538.

12 Andrew Steinmetz, *The Gaming Table: Its Votaries and Victims, Vol. 1* (London: Tinsley Bros., 1870), pp. 194–7.

13 *The Satirist*, 16 September 1848.

14 T.H. Bird, *Admiral Rous and the English Turf* (London: Putnam, 1939), pp. 225–50; Roger Munting, *An Economic and Social History of Gambling in Britain and the USA* (Manchester: Manchester University Press, 1996), p. 24; F.M.L. Thompson, *Gentrification and the Enterprise Culture: Britain 1780–1980* (Oxford: Oxford University Press, 2001), p. 33.
15 James Grant, *Sketches of London* (London, 1838), p. 355.
16 *The Times*, 1 December 1836, 11 and 12 February 1837.
17 Sir M. Havers et al., *The Royal Baccarat Scandal* (London: William Kimber, 1977).
18 Mike Huggins, *Flat Racing and British Society 1790–1914* (London: Frank Cass, 2000), pp. 38–67; Chinn, *Better Betting with a Decent Feller*, pp. 7–50.
19 George Plumptre, *The World of Edwardian Racing* (London: Andre Deutsch, 1985), pp. 80–4.
20 *Lloyd's Weekly Newspaper*, 26 April 1874.
21 *Reynolds's News*, 16 December 1877.
22 *Reynolds's News*, 16 December 1877; 26 May 1899.
23 *Reynolds's News*, 16 December 1877; 26 May 1899; see David Camper, 'Popular Sunday newspapers, respectability and working class culture', in Huggins and Mangan, *Disreputable Pleasures*, pp. 83–102.
24 *Hull Daily Mail*, 2 July 1891.
25 Quoted in *Shields Gazette*, 4 September 1894.
26 *Sporting Chronicle*, 9 February 1899.
27 For coins, cards and other forms of non-horse-race betting see Mark Clapson, *A Bit of a Flutter: Popular Gambling and English Society, c. 1823–1961* (Manchester: Manchester University Press, 1992), pp. 79–107.
28 *Alnwick Mercury*, 8 June 1878.
29 *Burnley Gazette*, 28 January 1882
30 Clapson, *A Bit of a Flutter*, p. 81.
31 Alan Metcalfe, *Leisure and Recreation in a Victorian Mining Community* (London: Routledge, 2006), pp. 87–9.
32 Ross McKibbin, 'Working-class gambling in Britain, 1880–1930', *Past and Present*, 82, 1979, pp. 147–76.
33 Clapson, *A Bit of a Flutter*; Chinn, *Better Betting with a Decent Feller*. Other useful works on betting include David Dixon, *The State and Gambling: Developments in the Legal Control of Gambling in England, 1867–1923* (Hull, 1981); Huggins, *Flat Racing*, pp. 88–116; Pamela Horn, *Pleasures and Pastimes in Victorian Britain* (London: Sutton Publishing, 1999), ch. 7; David C. Itzkowitz, 'Fair Enterprise or Extravagant Speculation: Investment, Speculation, and Gambling in Victorian England', *Victorian Studies*, 45, 1, 2002, pp. 121–47.
34 McKibbin, 'Working-class gambling'.
35 *Liverpool Review*, 5 September 1896, p. 7.
36 Clapson, *A Bit of a Flutter*, pp. 44–78.

37 Clapson, *A Bit of a Flutter*, p. 210.
38 Huggins, *Flat Racing*, pp 110–11.
39 Anon., *English Liberty in Danger: A pamphlet exhibiting the Imminent Peril Insidiously Threatening British Freedom by the Proposed Bill for the Suppression of Gaming Houses* (London: J.A. Allen, 1854).
40 *Illustrated Sporting and Dramatic News*, 11 March 1899.
41 See Clapson, *A Bit of a Flutter*, p. 23 for details.
42 *The Times*, 19 July 1853.
43 *The Times*, 3 May 1860; H. Shimmin, *Liverpool Life: Its Pleasures, Practices and Pastimes* (Liverpool: 1856), Chs 15–19.
44 *The Era*, 7 December 1862.
45 A Chester Tradesman, *Chester Races. Do they Pay* (Chester), 1 March 1871.
46 Mathew McIntire, 'Odds, Intelligences, and Prophecies: Racing News in the Penny Press 1855–1914', *Victorian Periodicals Review*, 41, 2008, pp. 352–73, 353.
47 George Stutfield, *The Law Relating to Betting* (London: Waterlow and Sons, 1884) went through three editions. See also Lawrence Duckworth, *The Law Affecting the Turf, Betting and Gaming Houses* (London: Wilson, 1899); J.C. Patterson, *The Citizen's Handbook for Scotland* (Glasgow: Aird and Coghill, 1900).
48 Itzkowitz, 'Victorian bookmakers and their customers', pp. 15–17, 29–30; Chinn, *Better Betting with a Decent Feller*.
49 *Sporting Life*, 21 September 1859.
50 *Hansard*, 11 July 1853, col. 87.
51 S. Petrow, *Policing Morals: The Metropolitan Police and the Home Office 1870–1914* (Oxford: Oxford University Press, 1994), pp. 239–93.
52 *North-Eastern Daily Gazette*, 5 August 1898.
53 *Falkirk Herald*, August 1868.
54 *Nottingham Evening Post*, 5 July 1889
55 James Grant, *Sketches of London* (London: 1838), p. 35.4.
56 David Miers, *Regulating Commercial Gambling* (Oxford: Oxford University Press, 2004), pp. 50–2.
57 *The Satirist*, 10 June 1848.
58 *The Times*, 3 August 1869.
59 J. Ashton, *The History of Gambling in England* (London: Leadenhall Press, 1969, first published 1898), p. 149. For a useful overview of later nineteenth-century gaming see Miers, *Regulating Commercial Gambling*, pp. 61–72.
60 Harding Cox, *Coursing* (London: The Field, 1892), pp. 8–29 gives details.
61 Huggins, *Flat Racing*, pp. 68–87.
62 *The Times*, 4 January 1869.
63 *The Times*, 19 October 1854.

64 J.K. Walton and A. Wilcox, *Low Life and Moral Improvement in Mid-Victorian England* (Leicester: Leicester University Press, 1991), p. 79.

65 Huggins, *Flat Racing*, pp. 68–87.

66 For the racing press see Mike Huggins, *The Victorians and Sport* (London: Hambledon, 2004), pp. 141–56.

67 J. Caminada, *Twenty-Five Years of Detective Life: A Fascinating Account of Crime in Victorian Manchester* (Manchester: Prism, 1985), pp. 7–17; John Pinfold, 'Dandy rats at play: the Liverpudlian middle classes and horse-racing in the nineteenth century', in Huggins and Mangan, *Disreputable Pleasures*, p. 72.

68 *The Sheffield and Rotherham Independent*, 27 March 1869.

69 *The Times*, 26 July 1869.

70 *The Times*, 4 December 1838.

71 *The Times*, 27 June 1854; Wray Vamplew, *The Turf* (London: Allen Lane, 1976), p. 108.

72 Anon., *Illustrated Life and Career of William Palmer of Rugeley* (London: Ward Lock, 1856), p. 27.

73 Peter Ferentzy, Nigel E. Turner and Wayne Skinner, 'The prevention of pathological gambling: An annotated bibliography', *Journal of Gambling Studies*, 17, August 2006, summarizes current research on this subject.

74 Anon., *Illustrated Life and Career*, p. 28. See also Anon., *The Most Extraordinary Trial of William Palmer* (London: W.M. Clark, 1856); Anon., *The Queen Versus Palmer: Verbatim Report of the Trial of William Palmer at the Central Criminal Court, Old Bailey* (London: J.A. Allen, 1856); Alfred S. Taylor, *Poisoning by Strychnia: Comments on the Medical Evidence given at the Trial of William Palmer* (London: Longmans, Brown and Green, 1856).

75 *Lloyd's Weekly Newspaper*, 20 August 1865.

Chapter 5: Sexuality, Pornography and Prostitution

1 Friedrich Engels, quoted in W.H. Chaloner, 'How Immoral were the Victorians: A Bibliographical Consideration', *Bulletin of the John Rylands University Library*, 60, 2, 1978, p. 373.

2 *Manchester Times*, 11 August 1852.

3 *Birmingham Journal*, 21 March 1868.

4 Hera Cook, *The Long Sexual Revolution: English Women, Sex and Contraception 1800–1875* (Oxford: Oxford University Press, 2004); Hera Cook, 'Sexuality and Contraception in Modern England', *Journal of Social History*, 40, 4, 2007, pp. 915–32.

5 John Tosh, *A Man's Place: Masculinity and the Middle Class Home in Victorian England* (New Haven: Yale University Press, 1999).

6   F. Mort, *Dangerous Sexualities: Medico-Moral Politics in England Since 1830* (London: Routledge, 2000), pp. xii–xiv; Lesley Hall, *Hidden Anxieties: Male Sexuality 1900–1950* (Cambridge: Polity Press, 1991), pp. 19–20; Roy Porter and Lesley Hall, *The Facts of Life: The Creation of Sexual Knowledge in Britain 1650–1950* (London: Yale University Press, 1995) see a complex variety of discourse between 1850 and 1885. Michel Foucault, *History of Sexuality: An Introduction, Vol. 1* (New York: Random House, 1978) was amongst the first to challenge the 'repressive' hypothesis; Andrew H. Miller and James E. Adams (eds), *Sexualities in Victorian Britain* (Bloomington: Indiana University Press, 1996); H.G. Cocks and Matt Houlbrook (eds), *The Palgrave Guide to the Modern History of Sexuality* (London: Palgrave, 2005).

7   John Tosh, *A Man's Place: Masculinity and the Middle Class Home in Victorian England* (New Haven: Yale University Press, 1999), Ch. 5.

8   Claire Tomalin's *The Invisible Woman* is full of detail here.

9   William A. Cohen, *Sex Scandal; The Private Parts of Victorian Fiction* (Durham, NC: Duke University Press, 1996), p. 2.

10 *Cheltenham Chronicle*, 31 May 1870.

11 See J.M. Robson, *Marriage or Celibacy: The Daily Telegraph on a Victorian Dilemma* (Toronto: University of Toronto Press, 1995), p. 51.

12 Simon Szreter, *Fertility, Class and Gender in Britain 1860–1940* (Cambridge: Cambridge University Press, 1996).

13 *The Times*, 19 April 1856; *The Times*, 16 December 1864.

14 S. Amos, *Laws in Force for the Prohibition and Regulation of Vice in England and Other Countries* (London: Stevens, 1877), pp. 245–6; John Faulkner Potts, *The Leading Vice of the Age and the Divine Method of Dealing with it* (London: James Spiers, 1881).

15 See for example Josephine Butler, *Gender Trouble: Feminism and the Subversion of Identity* (London: Routledge, 1990).

16 David W. Bartlett, *London by Day and Night* (London, 1852), p. 125.

17 Tom Winnifrith, *Fallen Women in the Nineteenth-Century Novel* (London: St Martin's Press, 1994); Deborah Anna Logan, *Fallenness in Victorian Women's Writing* (Columbia: University of Missouri Press, 1998).

18 *Reynolds's News*, 10 January 1886 and 25 July 1886.

19 Françoise Barret-Ducrocq, *Love in the Time of Victoria: Sexuality, Class and Gender in Nineteenth Century London* (London: Verso, 1991).

20 House of Commons Committee of Inquiry into the Pathology and Treatment of Venereal Disease with a view to Diminish its Injurious Effects on the Army and Navy 1867–8 (4031), pp. xxx–lii.

21 Wendell S. Johnson, *Living in Sin: The Victorian Sexual Revolution* (Chicago: Nelson Hall, 1979), p. 126.

22 George Watt, *The Fallen Woman in the Nineteenth Century English Novel* (London: Croom Helm, 1984); Roxanne Eberle, *Chastity and Transgression in Women's Writing, 1792–1897* (London: Palgrave Macmillan, 2001).

23 Henry Mayhew, *London Labour and the London Poor Additional Volume* (London: Griffin, Bohn & Co., 1851), p. 468; Royal Commission on the Employment of Children, Young Persons and Women in Agriculture 1867–8 (4068), Appendix, Mr Henling's Report.

24 Mary Prior, *Found Hopes: Breach of Promise Cases in Shetland, 1823–1900* (Lerwick: Shetland Times, 2005); Ginger S. Frost, *Promises Broken: Courtship, Class and Gender in Victorian England* (Charlottesville: University Press of Virginia, 1995), pp. 98, 100; Françoise Barret-Ducrocq, *Love in the Time of Victoria: Sexuality, Class and Gender in Nineteenth Century London* (London: Verso, 1991).

25 John R. Gillis, 'Servants, Sexual Relations, and the Risks of Illegitimacy in London, 1801–1900', *Feminist Studies*, 5, 1, 1979, pp. 142–73.

26 *Manchester Courier*, 5 June 1886.

27 St Paul, first Epistle to the Corinthians vi: 9.

28 *The Times*, 22 April 1852.

29 *Cambridge Chronicle*, 31 December 1859.

30 Trevor Fisher, *The Sexual Politics of Late Victorian Britain* (Stroud: Alan Sutton, 1995).

31 F. Finnegan, *Poverty and Prostitution: A Study of Victorian Prostitutes in York* (Cambridge: Cambridge University Press, 1979); J.R. Walkowitz, *Prostitution and Victorian Society: Women, Class and the State* (Cambridge: Cambridge University Press, 1980); Paul McHugh, *Prostitution and Victorian Social Reform* (London: Croom Helm, 1980); Linda Mahood, *The Magdalenes: Prostitution in the Nineteenth Century* (London: Routledge, 1990); Trevor Fisher, *Prostitution and the Victorians* (New York: St Martin's Press, 1997); Paula Bartley, *Prostitution: Prevention and Reform in England, 1860–1914* (London: Routledge, 2000); Maria Luddy, *Prostitution and Irish Society, 1800–1940* (Cambridge: Cambridge University Press, 2007); Julia Laite, *Common Prostitutes and Ordinary Citizens: Commercial Sex in London, 1885–1960* (London: Palgrave Macmillan, 2011).

32 W.E.H. Lecky, *A History of European Morals* (New York: D. Appleton, 1869), pp. 282–3.

33 *The Times*, 19 February 1847.

34 Jean Hawkes (ed.), *The London Journal of Flora Tristan* (London: Virago, 1982), pp. 83–7.

35 *The Times*, 15 January 1858.

36 *Manchester Evening News*, 15 May 1872.

37 See http://www.guywoolnough.com/nineteenth-century-prostitution/mary-reynolds-or-letitia-farrell-prostitute/ (accessed 2 December 2014).

38 *The Times*, 24 and 25 February 1858.

39 William Tate, *Magdalenism: An Inquiry into the Extent, Causes and Consequences of Prostitution in Edinburgh* (Edinburgh: Rickard, 1842).

40 The Newcastle Temperance Society, *The Devil's Mudbath: The Unholy Slave Traffic in Newcastle-upon-Tyne* (Newcastle: Watson, 1883).

41 *Liverpool Mercury*, 23 May 1892.
42 H.G.C. Matthew, *Gladstone* (Oxford: Clarendon Press, 1997), pp. 90–5; Anna Isba, *Gladstone and Women* (London: Continuum, 2007).
43 Paula Bartley, *Prostitution: Prevention and Reform in England, 1860–1914* (London: Routledge, 2000).
44 Alfred Dyer, *The European Slave Trade in English Girls* (London: Dyer Bros, 1880).
45 *The Shield*, 1 May 1880.
46 1881 (448) Select Committee of House of Lords to Inquire into State of Law Relating to Protection of Young Girls from Artifices to induce them to lead Corrupt Life. Report, Proceedings, Minutes of Evidence, QQ. 1–154 (Snagge); 253 (Jeffes).
47 Roger Davidson and Lesley Hall (eds), *Sex, Sin and Suffering: Venereal Disease and European Society Since 1870* (London: Routledge, 2001).
48 *London Daily News*, 28 December 1869.
49 S. Amos, *Laws in Force for the Prohibition and Regulation of Vice in England and Other Countries* (London: Stevens, 1877), pp. 138–9.
50 Paul McHugh, *Prostitution and Victorian Social Reform* (London: Croom Helm, 1980).
51 Matthew, *Gladstone*, pp. 90–5; Isba, *Gladstone and Women*, pp. 90–1.
52 Lisa Sigel, *Pornography and Social Change in England 1851–1914* (New Brunswick, NJ: Rutgers University Press, 2002).
53 Jeffrey Weeks, *Sex, Politics and Society: The Regulation of Sexuality Since 1800* (London: Longman, 1981); Iain McCalman, *Radical Underworld: Prophets, Revolutionaries and Pornographers in London, 1795–1840* (Cambridge: Cambridge University Press, 1988); Ian Gibson, *The Erotomaniac: The Secret Life of Henry Spencer Ashbee* (London: Faber and Faber, 2001); James Nelson, *Publisher to the Decadents: Leonard Smithers in the Careers of Beardsley, Wilde, Dowson* (University Park: Pennsylvania State University Press 2000).
54 *The Standard*, 24 December 1846.
55 *Illustrated London News*, 26 September 1857. For Holywell Street and Dugdale see Lynda Nead, *Victorian Babylon* (New Haven: Yale University Press, 2000), pp. 149–203.
56 Edward Sellon, *The Ups and Downs of Life* (London: William Dugdale, 1867).
57 Sellon, *The Ups and Downs of Life*, p. 60.
58 J.R. Walkowitz, *City of Dreadful Delight* (Chicago: University of Chicago Press, 1992), p. 21.
59 Ian Gibson, *The English Vice: Beating, Sex and Shame in Victorian England and After* (London: Duckworth, 1978).
60 Allison Pease, *Modernism, Mass Culture, and the Aesthetics of Obscenity* (Cambridge: Cambridge University Press, 2000).
61 Iain McCalman, *Radical Underworld: Prophets, Revolutionaries and Pornographers in London, 1795–1840* (Cambridge: Cambridge University Press, 1988), p. 236

62 Lynda Nead, *Victorian Babylon* (New Haven: Yale University Press, 2000), pp. 182–4.

63 Geoff Nicholson, *Sex Collectors: The Secret World of Consumers, Connoisseurs, Curators, Creators, Dealers, Bibliographers, and Accumulators of Erotica* (London: Simon and Schuster 2006), p. 68.

64 *Wiltshire Independent*, 16 December 1841.

65 Diane E. Mason, 'The Secret Vice: Masturbation in Victorian Fiction and Medical Culture' (PhD, Bristol, 2003).

66 H.G. Cocks, *Nameless Offences: Homosexual Desire in the Nineteenth Century* (London: I.B. Tauris, 2003); Graham Robb, *Homosexual Love in the Nineteenth Century* (New York: W.W. Norton and Co., 2004).

67 H.G. Cocks, 'Safeguarding Civility: Sodomy, Class and Moral Reform in Early 19th Century England', *Past and Present* 190, 1, 2006, pp. 12–46.

68 *Reynolds's News*, 14 May 1870; Charles Upchurch, 'Forgetting the Unthinkable: Cross Dressers and British Society in the Case of the Queen versus Boulton and Others', *Gender and History* 12, 1, 2000, pp. 127–57.

69 Chris White (ed.) *Nineteenth-century Writings on Homosexuality: A Sourcebook* (London: Routledge, 1999).

70 Cocks, *Nameless Offences*.

71 Linda Dowling, *Hellenism and Homosexuality in Victorian Oxford* (Ithaca: Cornell University Press, 1994).

72 H.G. Cocks, 'Making the Sodomite Speak. Voices of the Accused in English Sodomy Trials c. 1800–1896', *Gender and History* 18, 1, 2006, pp. 87–107.

73 Morris B. Kaplan,' "Did My Lord Gomorrah Smile?": Homosexuality, Class and Prostitution in the Cleveland Street Affair', in George Robb and Nancy Erber (eds), *Disorder in the Court: Trials and Sexual Conflict at the Turn of the Century* (New York: New York University Press, 1999), pp. 78–99

74 Quoted in *Northern Echo*, 18 October 1895.

75 Sharon Marcus, *Between Women: Friendship, Desire, and Marriage in Victorian England* (Princeton: Princeton University Press, 2007).

Chapter 6: From Vice to Virtue

1 The following section is based in part on Helen Rappaport, *Encyclopedia of Women Social Reformers*, Volume 1 (Santa Barbara, CA: ABC-CLIO, 2001), pp. 102–4.

2 *Lancaster Gazette*, 7 June 1879.

3 A useful list is given by Brian Harrison, 'Drink and Sobriety in England 1815–1872. A Critical Bibliography', *International Review of Social History*, 12, 1967, pp. 204–76.

4 Ian Campbell Bradley, 'Titus Salt: Enlightened Entrepreneur', *History Today*, May 1987, pp. 30–7.

5   For Quaker moral views see James Walvin, *The Quakers: Money and Morals* (London: John Murray, 1997).

6   Anne Vernon, *A Quaker Business Man: The Life of Joseph Rowntree* (London: George Allen and Unwin, 1958).

7   Asa Briggs, *A Study of the Work of Seebohm Rowntree 1871–1954* (London: Longmans, 1961).

8   Seebohm Rowntree, *Poverty, a Study of Town Life* (London: Macmillan and Co., 1901), pp. 144–5; Ian Packer, 'Joseph and Seebohm Rowntree', *Journal of Liberal History*, 45, 3, 2004, pp. 4–11.

9   *The Times*, 8 June 1894.

10 B. Harrison, 'Traditions of Respectability in British Labour History' in Brian Harrison, *Peaceable Kingdom: Stability and Change in Modern Britain* (Oxford: Oxford University Press, 1982); Charles E. Muse, *Poverty and Drunkenness, A Socialist's View* (London: Labour Press Society, 1899).

11 See Robert Colls, *The Pitmen of the Northern Coalfield: Work, Culture and Protest 1790–1850* (Manchester: Manchester University Press, 1987), pp. 118–203.

12 Sue Morgan, ' "Wild Oats or Acorns?" Social Purity, Sexual Politics and the Response of the Late-Victorian Church', *Journal of Religious History*, 31, 2, 2007, pp. 151–68; Paula Bartley, 'A Passion for Purity: Ellice Hopkins and the Politics of Gender in the Late Victorian Church', *Women's History Review*, 9, 3, 2000, pp. 629–50.

13 Helen Meller, *Leisure and the Changing City 1870–1914* (London: Routledge, 1976).

14 *The Times*, 27 June 1858.

15 Harry G. Levine 'Temperance Cultures: Alcohol as a Problem in Nordic and English-Speaking Cultures' in Griffith Edwards, Malcolm Lader and D. Colin Drummond (eds), *The Nature of Alcohol and Drug-Related Problems* (Oxford: Oxford University Press, 1992), pp. 16–36.

16 Herbert Schlossberg, *The Silent Revolution and the Making of Victorian England* (Athens, OH: Ohio University Press, 2000).

17 Simon Gunn, *Political Culture of the Victorian Middle Class: Ritual and Authority in the English Industrial City 1840–1914* (Manchester: Manchester University Press, 2000).

18 For example, John Clifford, 'The Church's War on National Intemperance', Conference of the Baptist and Total Abstinence Association, Newcastle, 8 October 1874 (British Library).

19 M.J.D. Roberts, *Making English Morals: Voluntary Association and Moral Reform in England 1787–1886* (Cambridge: Cambridge University Press, 2004), p. 83.

20 Celia Marshik, *British Modernism and Censorship* (Cambridge: Cambridge University Press, 2007); Records of the National Vigilance Association, Women's Library, London, Reference GB 0106 4/NVA.

21 Allan Harty, *A Concentration of Moral Force: the Temperance Movement in Sunderland, 1830 to 1853* (Sunderland: University of Sunderland Press, 2004).

22 *The Times*, 10 April 1841.
23 Andrew Aird, *Glimpses of Old Glasgow* (Glasgow: Aird, 1894), p. 218.
24 *The Times*, 15 May 1840.
25 *The Times*, 19 May 1842.
26 Gerald Wayne Olsen, 'Anglican Temperance Movements in England 1859–73: An Example of Practical Ecumenicalism', *CCHA Study Sessions*, 40, 1973, p. 42.
27 David Dixon, *From Prohibition to Regulation: Bookmaking, Anti-Gambling and the Law* (Oxford: Clarendon Press, 1991).
28 See M. Milne, *The Newspapers of Northumberland and Durham* (Newcastle: Graham, 1971), pp. 85–7.
29 Charles Kingsley, 'A Letter to the Young Men of Chester' (*Chester Observer*, 1 February 1871) and subsequent letter to the *Chester Observer*, 15 February 1871.
30 *The Times*, 25 May 1837.
31 *Barrow Herald*, 22 February 1868.
32 Robert Carr, *Lost and Found: An Autobiography of Robert Carr, Reformed Drunkard of Castleforth* (Sheffield: J. Drake, 1873).
33 Lilian L. Shiman, *The Crusade Against Drink in Victorian England* (London: Macmillan, 1988), p. 26; J.C. Farn, 'The Temperance Movement: Causes of Failure', *The Reasoner*, 28 October 1857.
34 *The Times*, 14 October 1868.
35 J. Crump, 'The Great Carnival of the Year: Leicester Races in the Nineteenth Century', *Transactions of Leicester History and Archaeological Society*, 58, 1982–3, p. 7.
36 R.W. Proctor, *Our Turf, Our Stage, and Our Ring* (Manchester: Loder, 1862), p. 40.
37 Lillian. L. Shiman, 'The Band of Hope Movement: Respectable Recreation for Working-class Children', *Victorian Studies*, 17, 1973, pp. 49–74.
38 Mark Clapson, 'A Bit of a Flutter', *History Today*, 41, 10, 1991, pp. 38–44.
39 Martin Hewitt, 'The Travails of Domestic Visiting: Manchester 1830–1870', *Historical Research*, 71, 175, 1998, pp. 196–227.
40 HMI Dr Woodford's report in Committee of Council on Education 1852 (1579–80), p. 665.
41 Thomas Archer, *The Terrible Sights of London* (London: S. Rivers, 1870), p. 255.
42 Maude Stanley, *Work About the Five Dials* (London: Macmillan, 1878).
43 *Bradford Observer*, 27 December 1849; *Bradford Observer*, 7 March 1850.
44 *Coffee Public House News and Temperance Hotel Journal*, later the *Temperance Caterer*, first published in 1878, disseminated information.
45 'The Good Templar's Happy Home', in Marshall Cresswell, *Local and Other Songs* (Newcastle: J.W. Chator, 1883).

46 John W. Frick, *Theatre, Culture and Temperance Reform in Nineteenth-Century America* (Cambridge: Cambridge University Press, 2003), compares American to British temperance productions.
47 Written by S.C. Hall and held in the Livesey Collection of the British National Temperance League at University of Central Lancashire.
48 Carol Dyhouse, *Girls Growing up in Late Victorian and Edwardian England* (London: Routledge and Kegan Paul, 1981), p. 113.
49 Archer, *Terrible Sights of London*, p. 466.
50 J. Crump, 'The Great Carnival of the Year: Leicester Races in the Nineteenth Century', p. 67.
51 *Newcastle Daily Journal*, 27 June 1883.
52 Evidence of Manchester Chief Constable R. Peacock, 1902 Select Committee of the House of Lords on Betting (389), v. 445, Qs 152, 300.
53 For a Sheffield example see Tony Mason, *Association Football and English Society 1863–1915* (Brighton: Harvester Press, 1980), p. 197.
54 *The Times*, 5 March and 27 April 1869.
55 Quoted in Brian Harrison, *Drink and the Victorians: Temperance Question in England, 1815–1872* (Keele: Keele University Press, 1994), p. 221.
56 Norman Moorsom, *The Demon Drink in Mid-Victorian Middlesbrough* (Middlesbrough: Middlesbrough Temperance Society, 2000), p. 23.
57 Mike Huggins, 'Victorian Seaside Resorts Around the Mouth of the Tees', *Northern History*, 20, 1984, p. 190.
58 *The Times*, 6 July and 14 December 1877.
59 Wray Vamplew, *The Turf: A Social and Economic History of Horse Racing* (London: Allen Lane, 1976), p. 99.
60 Jack Fairfax-Blakeborough, *Extinct Race Meetings: Northern Turf History Vol. II* (London: J.A. Allen, 1949), pp. 107–8.
61 For example, *The Times*, 21 February 1844; 15 January 1858.

Chapter 7: Vice and Respectability

1 For example, *South Bucks Free Press*, 14 February 1862; *Louth and North Lincolnshire Advertiser*, 15 February 1862.
2 Woodruff Smith, *Consumption and the Making of Respectability, 1600–1800* (Abingdon: Routledge, 2002).
3 F.M.L. Thompson, *The Rise of Respectable Society: A Social History of Victorian Britain 1830–1900* (London: Fontana 1988); Geoffrey Best, *Mid-Victorian Britain 1851–1875* (London: Fontana, 1979).
4 Peter Bailey, 'The Politics and Poetics of Modern British Leisure', *Rethinking History* 3, 2, 1999, pp. 131–75.
5 Peter Stallybrass and Allon White, *The Politics and Poetics of Transgression* (London: Methuen 1986).

NOTES

6 Mary Poovey, *Making a Social Body: British Cultural Formation, 1830–1864* (Chicago: University of Chicago Press, 1995).
7 Richard W. Schoch, 'Theatre and Mid-Victorian Society 1851–1870', in Joseph Donohue, Jane Milling and Peter Thomson (eds), *The Cambridge History of the British Theatre, Vol 2 1660–1885* (Cambridge: Cambridge University Press, 2004), p. 332.
8 Mary Poovey, *Making a Social Body*.
9 Quoted in 'Henry Longhurst Looks Back at 1900', *Golf Illustrated*, 31 May 1935, p. 207.
10 Henry Mayhew, *London Labour and the London Poor* (London: Griffin Bohn, 1851, 1861–2).
11 *Manchester Times*, 18 June 1870.
12 *Daily Telegraph*, 12 January 1892.
13 D. Gutzke, 'The Social Status of Landed Brewers in Britain Since 1840', *Histoire Sociale/Social History*, 17, 1984, pp. 93–113.
14 Geoffrey Crossick (ed.), *The Lower Middle Class in Britain 1870–1914* (London: Croom Helm, 1977).
15 William Knox, *Industrial Nation: Work, Culture and Society in Scotland, 1800–Present* (Edinburgh: Edinburgh University Press, 1999), pp. 40–6, 94–103; C.W. Master, *The Respectability of Late Victorian Workers: A Case Study of York, 1867–1914* (Newcastle: Cambridge Scholars Publishing, 2010), pp. 4–5.
16 Charles Walter Masters, 'The Respectability of Late Victorian Workers: A Case Study of York, 1867–1914' (PhD, York, 2010).
17 Neville Kirk, *Change, Continuity and Class: Labour in British Society, 1850–1920* (Manchester: Manchester University Press, 1998), pp. 111–43.
18 S. Cordery, 'Friendly Societies and the Discourse of Respectability in Britain, 1825–1875', *Journal of British Studies*, 34, 1, 1995, p. 37.
19 Ellen Ross, 'Respectability in Pre-World War I London Neighborhoods', *International Labor and Working-Class History*, 27, 1985, pp. 39–59.
20 Barry Haynes, 'Working-class Respectability in Leicester c. 1845–80', *Transactions of the Leicestershire Archaeological and Historical Society*, 65, 1991, pp. 55–67.
21 Geoffrey Best, *Mid-Victorian Britain, 1851–1875* (London: Fontana, 1971), p. 286.
22 Peter Bailey ' "Will the Real Bill Banks Please Stand Up?" Towards a Role Analysis of Mid-Victorian Working-Class Respectability', *Journal of Social History*, 12, 3, 1979, pp. 336–53.
23 Peter Bailey ' "Will the Real Bill Banks Please Stand Up?", p. 20.
24 Peter Andersson, *Streetlife in Late Victorian London: The Constable and the Crowd* (London: Palgrave, 2013).
25 M.J. Huggins, 'More Sinful Pleasures: Leisure, Respectability and the Male Middle Classes in Victorian England', *Journal of Social History*, 23, 3, 2000, pp. 585–600.

26 Ian Miller, 'Representations of suicide in urban North-West England c. 1870–1910: The formative role of respectability, class, gender and morality', *Mortality*, 15, 3, 2010, pp. 191–204.
27 *London City Press*, 15 August 1857.
28 *Lincolnshire Echo*, 31 October 1895.
29 Jessica A. Sheetz-Nguyen, *Victorian Women, Unwed Mothers and the London Foundling Hospital* (London: Continuum, 2012).
30 *Lloyd's Weekly Newspaper*, 25 January 1857.
31 *Spectator*, 7 May 1870.
32 Susan McPherson, 'Companionship and Collaboration; Marian Evans, George Henry Lewes and *The Life and Works of Goethe*', *The Victorian* 1, 3, 2013, pp. 1–12, http://journals.sfu.ca/vict/index.php/vict/article/viewFile/60/33, accessed 21 October 2014.
33 T. Winnifrith, *Fallen Women in the 19th Century Novel* (London: Macmillan 1994), pp. 49–51.
34 M. Huggins and J.A. Mangan (eds), *Disreputable Pleasures: Less Virtuous Victorians at Play* (London: Frank Cass, 2004).
35 B.G. Orchard, *Liverpool's Legion of Honour* (Birkenhead: Orchard, 1893), pp. 65–6.
36 Anon., *The Nemesis of Drink: Passages in an Autobiography* (London: Harchard, 1863), preface by Dean Close, pp. 15–29.
37 C. Hosgood, 'Knights of the road: Commercial travellers and the culture of the commercial room in Victorian and Edwardian England', *Victorian Studies*, 37, 4, 1994, p. 533.
38 Jonathan Reinartz, 'Promoting the Pint: Ale and Advertising in Late Victorian and Edwardian England', *Social History of Alcohol and Drugs* 22, 1, 2007, pp. 26–44.
39 Dahn Shaulis, 'Pedestriennes: Newsworthy but controversial women in sports entertainment', *Journal of Sport History*, 26, 1, 1999, pp. 29–50; Ellen Ross, 'Respectability in Pre-World War I London Neighborhoods', *International Labor and Working-Class History*, 27, 1985.
40 *Lloyd's Weekly Newspaper*, 20 August 1865.
41 *The Era*, 29 May 1870.
42 *Cheshire Observer*, 5 October 1895.
43 J.K. Walton, 'Respectability takes a holiday: disreputable behaviour at the Victorian seaside', in Martin Hewitt (ed.), *Unrespectable Recreations* (Leeds: Leeds Centre for Victorian Studies, 2001), pp. 176–93.
44 M.J. Huggins. 'Culture, Class and Respectability: Racing and the English Middle Classes in the Nineteenth Century', *International Journal of the History of Sport*, 11, 1, 1994, pp. 19–41.
45 J.A. Mangan, 'Bullies, Beatings, Battles and Bruises: Great Days and Jolly Days at One Mid-Victorian Public School', in M. Huggins and J.A. Mangan (eds), *Disreputable Pleasures*, pp. 3–34.

46 Saki (Hector Munro), 'The Baker's Dozen', in *Reginald in Russia and Other Sketches* (London: Methuen, 1910).
47 J. Springhall, *Youth, Popular Culture and Moral Panics: Penny Gaffs to Gangsta-Rap, 1830–1966* (Basingstoke: Macmillan, 1998), pp. 38–70.
48 Peter Bailey, *Leisure and Class in Victorian England: Rational Recreation and the Contest for Control 1830–1885* (London: Methuen, 1987), p. 71.
49 For the life of one medical student see Shephard Taylor, *The Diary of a Medical Student During the Mid-Victorian Period 1860–1864* (Norwich: Jarrold, 1927).
50 *Town Talk*, 'Mad Medical Students', 20 March 1880.
51 Royal Commission to Inquire into the State, Discipline, Studies and Revenues of the University and Colleges of Oxford 1852 (1482), report and minutes of evidence.
52 J.A. Mangan, 'Bloods, Blues and Barbarians: some aspects of Late Victorian Oxbridge', in M. Huggins and J.A. Mangan (eds), *Disreputable Pleasures*, pp. 35–56.
53 *Liverpool Mercury*, 22 March 1859.
54 *Belfast Newsletter*, 29 August 1856.
55 Bob Clarke, *The Basingstoke Riots; Massaganians v Salvation Army, 1880–1883* (Basingstoke: Basingstoke Archaeological and Historical Society, 2010).
56 L. Davidoff, M. Doolittle, J. Fink and K. Holden, *The Family Story: Blood, Contract and Intimacy 1830–1960* (Harlow: Addison, Wesley Longman, 1999), p. 27.
57 C. Hall, 'The early formation of Victorian domestic ideology', in C. Hall, *White Male and Middle Class: Explorations in Feminism and History* (London: Polity Press, 1992).
58 Susie L. Steinbach, *Understanding the Victorians: Politics, Culture and Society in Nineteenth Century Britain* (Abingdon: Routledge, 2012), p. 120.
59 William Acton (1813–75) quoted in Lynda Nead, *Myths of Sexuality: Representations of Women in Victorian Britain* (Oxford: Basil Blackwell, 1988), p. 19.
60 M. Poovey, *Uneven Developments: the Ideological Work of Gender in Mid-Victorian England* (London: Virago, 1989).
61 Elaine Showalter, *Sexual Anarchy* (London: Virago, 1992).
62 Susie L. Steinbach, *Understanding the Victorians: Politics, Culture and Society in Nineteenth Century Britain* (Abingdon: Routledge, 2012), p. 110.
63 J. Sterngass, 'Cheating, Gender Roles and the Nineteenth Century Croquet Craze', *Journal of Sport History*, 25, 3, 1998, pp. 398–418.
64 'Sylvie and Bruno Concluded', in Lewis Carroll, *Complete Works* (New York: Modern Library, 1936), p. 597.
65 *Hampshire Advertiser*, 20 November 1897.
66 Thompson, *The Rise of Respectable Society*, p. 256.
67 Thompson, *The Rise of Respectable Society*, p.256.

Epilogue

1. W.R. Lambert, *Drink and Sobriety in Victorian Wales* (Cardiff: University of Wales Press, 1983), p. 23.
2. J.C. Whyte, *History of the British Turf, Vol. I* (London: Henry Colborn, 1840), p. 187.
3. *North-Eastern Daily Gazette*, 4 May 1883.
4. *Glasgow Herald*, 31 January 1891.
5. *Glasgow Herald*, 4 December 1897.
6. *Reynolds's Newspaper*, 30 May 1897.
7. *Reynolds's Newspaper*, 21 October 1894.
8. Christie Davies, *The Death of Moral Britain* (London: Transaction Publishers, 2004).
9. Gertrude Himmelfarb, *The De-moralization of Society: From Victorian Virtues to Modern Values* (London: Vintage Books, 1996).

SUGGESTIONS FOR FURTHER READING

Readers wishing to carry out further reading will find below a list of some of the more useful secondary sources on the topics covered here. The list is not intended as comprehensive, but as a valuable and accessible starting point for deeper study.

Chapter 1: The Language of Vice

R.P.T. Davenport-Hines, *The Penguin Book of Vice* (London: Penguin, 1995).
Michael Diamond, *Victorian Sensation or The Spectacular, the Shocking and the Scandalous in Nineteenth Century Britain* (London: Anthem Press, 2003).
Peter Gay, *Schnitzler's Century: The Making of Middle-Class Culture, 1815–1914* (London: W.W. Norton, 2001).
Mike Huggins and J.A. Mangan (eds.), *Disreputable Pleasures: Less Virtuous Victorians at Play* (London: Frank Cass, 2004).
Douglas A. Read, 'Playing and Praying' in *Cambridge Urban History of Britain, Vol. 3* (Cambridge: Cambridge University Press, 2000).
Matthew Sweet, *Inventing the Victorians* (London: Faber, 2001).

Chapter 2: The Spatial Dimension of Vice

Catherine Arnold, *City of Sin: London and its Vices* (London: Simon and Schuster, 2010).
Andy Croll, *Civilizing the Urban: Popular Culture and Public Space, Merthyr c. 1870–1914* (Cardiff: University of Wales Press, 2000).
Seth Koven, *Slumming: Sexual and Social Politics in Victorian London* (Princeton: Princeton University Press, 2004).
Deborah Epstein, *Walking the Victorian Streets: Women, Representation, and the City* (Ithaca: Cornell University Press, 1995).
Margaret Harkness, *In Darkest London* (Cambridge: Black Apollo Press, 2003).
Simon Joyce, *Capital Offences: Geographies of Class and Crime in Victorian London* (Charlottesville: University of Virginia Press, 2003).
Fergus Linnane, *London: The Wicked City: A Thousand Years of Vice in the Capital* (London: Robson Books, 2007).
Lynda Nead, *Victorian Babylon: People, Streets and Images in Nineteenth Century London* (New Haven: Yale University Press, 2000).
Judith R. Walkowitz, *City of Dreadful Delight: Narratives of Sexual Danger in Late-Victorian London* (London: Virago Press, 1992).

John K. Walton and Alastair Wilcox (eds), *Low Life and Moral Improvement in mid-Victorian England: Liverpool Through the Journalism of Hugh Shimmin* (Leicester: Leicester University Press, 1991).

Chapter 3: The Vice of Drunkenness

John Burnett, *Liquid Pleasures: A Social History of Drinks in Modern Britain* (London: Routledge, 1999).
E. Dingle, *The Campaign for Prohibition in Victorian England* (London: Croom Helm, 1980).
Mark Girouard, *Victorian Pubs* (London: Studio Vista, 1975).
John Greenaway, *Drink and British Politics Since 1830: a Study in Policy-Making* (Basingstoke: Palgrave Macmillan, 2003).
Brian Harrison, *Drink and the Victorians: The Temperance Question in England, 1815–1872* (first published 1971; Keele: Keele University Press, 1994).
James Nicholls, *The Politics of Alcohol: a History of the Drink Question in England* (Manchester: Manchester University Press, 2009).
Lilian L. Shiman, *Crusade Against Drink in Victorian England* (Basingstoke: Macmillan, 1988).
Richard Tames, *The Victorian Public House* (Princes Risborough: Shire, 2003).
R.L. Williams, *Drink and Society in Victorian Wales c. 1820–1895* (Cardiff: University of Wales Press, 1989).

Chapter 4: Vice and Profligacy: Betting and Gaming

Mark Clapson, *A Bit of a Flutter: Popular Gambling and English Society c. 1823–1961* (Manchester: Manchester University Press, 1992).
Carl Chinn, *Better Betting with a Decent Feller: Betting and the British Working Class 1750–1990* (Hemel Hempstead: Harvester, 1991).
David Dixon, *From Prohibition to Regulation: Bookmaking, Anti-Gambling and the Law* (Oxford: Clarendon Press, 1991).
Mike Huggins, *Flat Racing and British Society 1790–1914: A Social and Economic History* (London: Frank Cass, 2000).
David Miers, *Regulating Commercial Gambling: Past, Present and Future* (Oxford: Oxford University Press, 2004).
Roger Munting, *An Economic and Social History of Gambling in Britain and the USA* (Manchester: Manchester University Press, 1996).

Chapter 5: Sexuality, Pornography and Prostitution

Paula Bartley, *Prostitution: Prevention and Reform 1860–1914* (London: Routledge, 2000).

Lucy Bland, *Banishing the Beast: English Feminism and Sexual Morality 1885–1914* (London: Penguin, 1995).
Matt Cook, *London and the Culture of Homosexuality 1885–1914* (Cambridge: Cambridge University Press, 2003).
Richard Dellamora (ed.), *Victorian Sexual Dissidence* (Chicago and London: University of Chicago Press, 1999).
Lesley A. Hall, *Sex, Gender and Social Change in Britain Since 1880* (London: Macmillan, 2000).
Maria Luddy, *Prostitution and Irish Society, 1800–1940* (Cambridge: Cambridge University Press, 2007).
Diane Mason, *The Secret Vice: Masturbation in Victorian Fiction and Medical Culture* (Manchester: Manchester University Press, 2008).
Michael Mason, *The Making of Victorian Sexual Attitudes* (Oxford: Oxford University Press, 1994).
Michael Mason, *The Making of Victorian Sexuality* (Oxford: Oxford University Press, 1995).
Steven Marcus, *The Other Victorians: A Study of Sexuality and Pornography in Mid-Nineteenth Century England* (New Brunswick: Transaction Publishers, 2009).
Ronald Pearsall, *The Worm in the Bud: The World of Victorian Sexuality* (London: Sutton, 2003).
Roy Porter and Lesley Hall, *The Facts of Life: The Creation of Sexual Knowledge in Britain, 1650–1950* (New Haven: Yale University Press, 1995).
Judith Walkowitz, *Prostitution and Victorian Society: Women, Class and the State* (Cambridge: Cambridge University Press, 1980).
Tom Winnifrith, *Fallen Women in the Nineteenth Century Novel* (London: Macmillan, 1994).

Chapter 6: From Vice to Virtue

Paula Bartley, *Prostitution: Prevention and Reform in England 1860–1914* (London: Routledge, 1999).
David Dixon, *From Prohibition to Regulation: Bookmaking, Anti-Gambling and the Law* (Oxford: Clarendon Press, 1991).
Brian Harrison, *Drink and the Victorians: the Temperance Question in England 1815–1872* (Keele: Keele University Press, 1994).
Allan Harty, *A Concentration of Moral Force: the Temperance Movement in Sunderland, 1830 to 1853* (Sunderland: University of Sunderland Press, 2004).
Annemarie Mcallister, 'The lives and souls of the children: the Band of Hope in the North West', *Manchester Region History Review*, 21 (2011), pp. 1–18.
M.J.D. Roberts, *Making English Morals: Voluntary Association and Moral Reform in England 1787–1886* (Cambridge: Cambridge University Press, 2004).
James Walvin, *The Quakers: Money and Morals* (London: John Murray, 1997).

Chapter 7: Vice and Respectability

Peter Andersson, *Streetlife in Late Victorian London: The Constable and the Crowd* (London: Palgrave, 2013).

Geoffrey Best, *Mid-Victorian Britain, 1851–1875* (London: Fontana, 1971).
Geoffrey Crossick (ed.) *The Lower Middle Class in Britain 1870–1914* (London: Croom Helm, 1977).
Gowan Dawson, *Darwin, Literature, and Victorian Respectability* (New York: Cambridge University Press, 2007).
Gertrude Himmelfarb, *The De-moralization of Society: From Victorian Virtues to Modern Values* (London: Vintage Books, 1996).
C.W. Master, *The Respectability of Late Victorian Workers: A Case Study of York, 1867–1914* (Newcastle: Cambridge Scholars Publishing, 2010).
Woodruff Smith, *Consumption and the Making of Respectability, 1600–1800* (Abingdon: Routledge, 2002).
Susie L. Steinbach, *Understanding the Victorians: Politics, Culture and Society in Nineteenth Century Britain* (Abingdon: Routledge, 2012).
F.M.L. Thompson, *The Rise of Respectable Society: A Social History of Victorian Britain 1830–1900* (London: Fontana Press, 1988).

INDEX

Abstainers' Union 166
abstention, from alcohol 68, 149. *See also* teetotalism
Act for the Protection of Women 1849 120
activists
   middle-class women 135
   purity 168, 169
   upper-class 149
Acton, William 48–9, 193
Adam Bede 124–5
addiction
   and alcohol 64
   gambling 91
addicts, invisibility of 199
Adelphi Club 110
adolescence 189. *See also* young people
adultery 125, 127–8
Adventures of a Schoolboy, The 139
age of consent 133, 148
Ainsworth, William Harrison 35
alcohol. *See also* drink; temperance movement
   abstention from 68, 149
   and addiction 64
   deaths from 67
   dependency 63
   expenditure on 84
   falling consumption of 195
   and medical profession 75
   as mind-altering drug 65
   moderation in consumption 67–8, 70, 198
alcoholism 64
Alliance News 158
Alliance prohibitionists 70–3. *See also* UK Alliance
allotments, for the poor 165

Ally Soper's Half Holiday 43
Ancient Order of Foresters 79
Anglicanism 4
animal cruelty, and horse racing 87–8
Anne, Queen 3
anti-contagious diseases movement 135
anti-gambling campaign 24, 90, 103, 114, 156–7
anti-gaming laws 100
anti-prostitution campaigns 131
Anti-Smoker and Progressive Temperance Reformer 158
Anti-Tobacco Journal 7
Anti-Tobacco Society 10
anti-vice campaigners, and theatres/music halls 46–7
anti-vice campaigns 23, 25, 27, 152–4, 197–200
anti-vice groups 155, 197
anti-vice leaders 149
anti-vice movements 151, 161, 171
anti-vice organizations 154–7
anti-vice reformers, effectiveness of 169–71. *See also* reformers
anti-vice societies 151, 157–9, 161
appearances, and respectability 179–80
army
   gambling debts 94
   and venereal disease 21–2, 27, 120–1, 134–5
Army Temperance Association 155
Arnold, Matthew 171
Art Nouveau movement 136
art, nudity in 134, 136
Ashbee, Henry Spenser 139
Ashton, J. 110
Aston Lower Grounds 49

attitudes
  to sexual morality 120
  to sexuality 119
  to vice 22, 28

baccarat 94
Balfour, Clara Lucas 151
Bands of Hope 71, 151, 162, 163, 171
Baptists 149
Barker, Thomas Halliday 150
Basingstoke 192
bathing regulations 55–6
Baum, John 49
Baxter, Robert 90
Baxter, Robert Dudley 84
beards, and respectability 178
Beardsley, Aubrey 136
beauty, and virtue 38
Beer Act 1830 68, 84
beer consumption 78, 84
Beer House Licensing System Amendment Association 168
beer houses 67, 68, 70, 71, 78, 81, 167, 168. *See also* drinking; public houses
behaviour, seen as normal/abnormal 17
Bell's Life in London 110, 111
Benefit Societies 179
Besant, Annie 123
betting. *See also* gambling; gaming
  demand for 105
  on horse-racing 53, 88, 95, 101–3, 110–12
  legislation 103
  local authorities responses to 110–11
  and middle classes 24–5, 188
  as a moral sin 90
  and newspapers 103–4, 105–6, 110, 112
  opposition to 90–3
  and public houses 80, 105
  scandals and cheating 98, 113
  street 108, 156, 168
  vice of 7, 90
  and women 103, 111, 194
  working-class 103–5

Betting and Gambling: A National Evil 150
betting clubs 111
betting houses 104
Betting Houses Act 1853 107, 108, 114
betting offices 104
Bible Christian Church 179
biblical teachings, waning power of 171
Bibury Club 194
Birmingham 40, 49, 51, 52
birth control information 134
births, illegitimate 121, 126, 127, 184, 200
Blackburn 151
Blackpool 56
blame, and venereal disease 22
Blight of Respectability, The 200
Blue Ribbon Army 151
Blue Ribbon Temperance campaign 165
bookmakers 88, 92–3, 104–5, 106
books, temperance cause 159
Booth, Catherine 147–8
Booth, Charles 84
Booth, William 37, 45, 147
Bowes, John 75
Boys' Brigade 166
Bradford 78, 80, 164
Bradford Empire 48
Bradlaugh, Charles 123
Brandon, Alfred 49
breach of promise 127
brewing industry 27
'Bridge of Sighs, The' 184
Brighton 40
British and Foreign Bible Society 10, 68
British and Foreign Society for the Suppression of Intemperance 156, 157
British and Foreign Temperance Society 26, 161
British Anti-Tobacco Society 7
British Association for the Promotion of Temperance 158
British Empire, and new forms of vice 27

British League of Juvenile Abstainers
    162
British Medical Association 64
British Medical Journal 123, 141
British Medical Temperance
    Association 155
British society, and democracy 152
British Temperance Advocate, The 158
British Women's Temperance
    Association 149, 155
Brontë, Anne 18
brothels 16–17, 28, 118, 129, 131,
    132, 133, 143
Brown, Baker 120
Brussels 132
Builder, The 40
Bulletin 158
Burdett-Coutts, Angela 26
burial clubs 181
businesses, and respectability 175–6
Butler, Josephine 135, 151
bylaws 167–8, 169, 170

café culture 42
Cambridge University students 190
campaigns, anti-vice 23, 25, 27, 152–4,
    197–200
capitalism 27
Card, Nathaniel 70
Carpenter, Edward 142
Carr, Robert 160–1
Carroll, Lewis 194
catholic lotteries 108
Catholic temperance movement 149
Catholics, and drink 16
*Causes and Prevention of Immorality
    in Schools* 12
change agents 148–9
Chaplin, Harry 96
Chapman, John 186
charity, as a passion 39–40
charity organizations, and prostitutes
    132
charity work, and women 151
Charles II, King 3
Charrington, Frederick 24
Chartism 150
cheating at betting 98
cheating at gambling 96–7, 112–13

cheating at sport 194
Cheltenham Chronicle 9
Cheshire Observer 188
Chester 104
Chester, Dean of 54
Chester, Miss 117–18
Chetwynd, George 98
Child of the Jago, A 37
child sexuality 141
children
    moral corruption of 189
    and pornography 140
    and reform organizations 162–3,
        171
    sexual exploitation of 133
    trained in vice 10
Christian churches, and sex outside of
    marriage 127
Christian duty, as motivator of urban
    reformers 153
Christian ethics, and drinking 61
Christian faiths, and secularism 171
Christian mission stations 147
Christianity
    and fornication 124
    muscular 141
    and respectability 191
    support for 153
    and teetotalism 69, 85
Church attendance 153, 164
Church Discipline Act 127
Church of England 127, 149, 199
Church of England Purity Society 159
*Church of England Temperance
    Magazine* 158
Church of England Temperance Society
    10, 148, 153, 156, 159
Church Penitentiary Association 132,
    163
churches
    and prostitutes 132
    relief programmes 164
    waning power of 171
cities
    and anonymity 187
    as places of moral danger 41
City and North of London Auxiliary
    Society for the Suppression of
    Intemperance 155

city missions 164
civic improvement schemes 40
civic leaders, as reformers 149
civilizing movement 152, 164
class. *See also* middle classes; upper classes; working classes
  dangerous classes 10, 34, 37
  and drink 61
  and drunkenness 65
  and gambling 89, 90, 114
  and gambling law 108
  and homosexuality 141–2, 143
  and pornography 136–7, 139
  pride 181
  and prostitution 130–1, 135
  and reform movements 4–5
  and reformers 151
  and religion 153
  and respectability 179–82
  and sexual vices 117, 124–7
  stereotypes 125
  and vice 8–9, 10, 22–5
  and virtue 17
Clay, John 15
Close, Dean 22
Close, Francis 9–10, 75
clothing, and gentility 178
Coatham 169
codes, upper-class 20
coin-gambling games 101
Coleman, Henry 36
Collins, Wilkie 53, 57
colonies, scandals in 56
commercial aspects of vice 195
commercial leisure 5, 26, 122, 175
Commissioners in Lunacy 140
conception, control of 120
Condition of the Working Class in England, The 35
Congress of the British and Continental Federation for the Abolition of the State Regulation of Vice 1883 135
consent, age of 133, 148
Conservative governments 72–3, 195
construction, of meanings of vice 14
consumer culture, and pornography 136–7
consumer demand, for vice 4
consumer product, vice as 195
Contagious Diseases Acts 22, 120–1, 134–5, 163
contraception 123
control
  drink as agent of 151
  weakening of traditional means of 152
  of working-class behaviour 189
Cook, Thomas 7, 55, 167
Cooperative Education Tours 55
Corrupt Practices Act 1883 75
corruption 23, 107
cottages 54–5
cottaging 143, 188
Cotton, Vincent Hynde 96
Coulson, W.L.B. 7
countryside
  drinking in the 76–7
  as location for vice 54–5, 102
Cremorne Gardens 48–9
crime(s)
  and drunkenness 63
  homosexuality as 143
  statistics 15, 16
  and vice viii, 7
Criminal Law Amendment Act 1885 121, 133, 143
criminality
  of dangerous classes 37
  and gambling 91
  and slum dwellers 34
Crockford's Club 94
Cromwell, Canon 49
croquet 194
cross-dressing, male 142
Crystal Palace 49
cultural capital 178, 196
cultural cleansing 40
cultural codes, of respectability 176
cultural construction, of pleasures 26
cultural function, of drinking places 78–9
cultural hierarchy, of drinking places 81
cultural institutions, reformers in 178–9
cultural power, and respectability 173, 179

cultural role, of drinking 74, 86
cultural significance, of gambling 88–9
cultural understanding, and vice 17
cultural values, social change in 152
culture
    and attitudes to vice 2
    and working-class gambling 101
Cumberland 200
Cumming, William 97
Curzon, Henry 53
Customs Consolidation Act 1876 140
cycling 194

Daily Telegraph 122
danger, of attacking vice 24
dangerous classes 10, 34, 37
dangerous, poor people as 23, 27
dangerous vice, and the proletariat 8–9
Darwin, Charles 192
data on vice, problems of 15–17
David Copperfield 124
Dawson, William 25
de Ros, Lord 97
debates
    about vice 2–5, 22, 25
    drunkenness 59, 60–1
    and economic depression 27–8
debts, gambling 25, 89, 93, 94, 100
decadence, and 'Naughty Nineties' 28
decency 179
Declaration on Gambling, Wesleyan Conference 91
demand
    for betting 105
    for vice 4, 195
democracy, and British society 152
dens of vice and iniquity 7, 31, 41, 46
'dependence on the rates' 7
'Derby Day' 53
desire, control of personal 152
Devereux, Thomas 80
Diary of a Nobody 180
Dickens, Charles 7, 26, 34–5, 53, 57, 122, 124, 126, 193
Dickens, Charles Culliford 42
Dickens's Dictionary of London 42
Dilke, Charles 128
disciplining, of drinking 73

discourses
    temperance 62–3
    on vice 14, 26, 28–9
Disorderly Houses Acts 120
disreputability, statistics on 200
divorce 20, 120, 125, 127–8, 182
Divorce Law 1857 125
dog handicaps 101
Doré, Gustave 46
double standards
    in behaviour 20, 21
    gender 183, 200
    and sexuality 121
Douglas, Alfred 144
'Dover Beach' 171
Doyle, Conan 55
drink. *See also* alcohol
    as agent of control 151
    and Catholics 16
    and class 61
    consumption 175
    popularity of 73–7, 199
    as social evil 71
    statistics 84–5
    trade 199
    types of 82–3
    and women 19–20
drinking. *See also* beer houses; public houses
    1960s 201
    of beer 78, 84
    and Christian ethics 61
    in the countryside 76–7
    cultural role of 74, 86
    decline in 85–6
    disciplining of 73
    of middle classes 24, 75–6
    social support for 199
    of upper classes 70, 75
    of working classes 75, 85
drinking booths, at race meetings 53
drinking houses, as dens of vice 7
drinking places
    cultural hierarchy of 81
    economic function of 78–9
drunkards 63–6
drunkenness
    and class 25
    and crime 63

debates 59, 60–1
European attitudes to 28
and fairs 51
and insanity 62–3
statistics 66–7
vice of 15, 61–7
women 64–5
and working classes 73
Dublin Turf Club 194
Dugdale, William 137
Dunlop, John 74
Durham 66, 130
Durham, Lord 98
Dyer, Alfred 132

Eagle Tavern 46
East London Chronicle 36
Eastern and Western Scottish Temperance Unions 156
Eastlake, Elizabeth 176
economic boom 27
economic depression, and morality debates 27–8
economic function, of drinking places 78–9
economic power, and respectability 179
economy, and gambling 93
Edge, John 149
Edinburgh 131
Edinburgh Journal 77
Edinburgh Review 186
education
  enforced 27
  and respectability 179–80
Education Act 1870 86
Education Act 1872 196
educational schemes 164
Edward, Prince of Wales 4, 94, 95, 97, 99, 131
Egg, Augustus 184
elections, and 'treating' 75
Elementary Education Acts 1886 8
Eliot, George 122, 124, 125, 186
elites. *See also* upper classes
  fast set 97, 175
  female behaviour 20
  and gambling 93, 94
  and societal order 25

Empire Music Hall 47
Engels, Friedrich 35, 117
English Illustrated Magazine 40
Enlightenment movement 5, 153
entrepreneurs, publicans as 80–1, 101
erotic picture trade 140
ethic of respectability 181
Etty, William 136
Evangelical Christians 4, 5, 16, 121, 149
Evans, Ann 122
Evans, Mary 122, 186
Evans, Polly 117–18
evolutionary ideas, of male sexuality 121
excursions, temperance 167
Exeter, Bishop of 120
expenditure on alcohol 84

facial hair, and respectability 178
fairs 50–2, 77
Fairs Act 1871 51
fallen women 21, 27, 125–6, 127, 135
family honour, women embodying 183
family planning 120
fast set 97, 175
fear
  of masturbation 140
  of moral decay 26, 152
  of slums 32–3
  of social unrest 152
Feist, Henry 88
Female Virtue: Its Enemies and Friends 149
feminism, and sexual vices 120
feminist propaganda, and prostitution 131
Fenwick, G.L. 65
Ferguson, Niall 22
Field Club 94
figging 5
financial stability, and respectability 180
flagellation, masochistic 139
flaneurs 43
food, and vice 8
football 81, 106, 110
Forbes-McKenzie Act 1853 83

foreign vice 132
foreigners, morality of 56
fornication 123, 124, 134, 190
foundling hospitals 126, 184
Fowler, J.C. 15
France 28, 36, 132, 134
Frane, John 55
Fraser's Magazine 94
fraud, white-collar and betting 113. *See also* cheating
Free Lance 53
freedoms, of urban life 43
friendly societies 79, 181
Frith, William Powell 53
fund-raising, and women 151

gamblers, pathological 96
gambling. *See also* betting; gaming
    1960s 201
    anti-gambling campaign 24, 90, 103, 114, 156–7
    attractions of 100–1
    and class 89, 90, 114
    compulsive 102
    and criminality 91
    debts 25, 89, 93, 94, 100
    and the economy 93
    excess 91, 97
    and gender 102–3
    governmental responses to 107–9, 113–14
    and industrial production 91
    industry 27, 92–3
    laws 108, 112, 114, 115
    legislation 89, 114
    local authorities responses to 108
    losses 112
    media support for 105–6
    of middle classes 24–5, 90, 109–14
    moral/social arguments against 91
    and policing 99–100, 108–10, 113–14
    prevalence of 100–1, 109–10
    problems and consequences of 106–7, 112–13
    at race meetings 53
    resilience of 114
    scapegoating of those in the industry 92–3
    social/cultural significance of 88–9
    support for 103–5, 109, 170, 199
    of upper classes 89, 93–100, 114
    and vacations 94–5
    visibility of 90, 107
    of working classes 89, 100–9, 114–15
gaming. *See also* betting; gambling
    debts 93
    high-stakes 95
    opposition to 90–3
    prevalence of 93–5, 109–10
    at race meetings 53
    scandals 96–7
Gaming Act 1845 100, 114
gaming houses 109–10
Gaming Houses Act 1854 114
gardens, for the poor 165
Gaskell, Mrs 35
gay subculture 142. *See also* homosexuality; lesbian relationships
gaze, male 44
gender. *See also* girls; men; women
    and betting 103, 111, 194
    changing gender roles 193–4
    double standards 183, 200
    and gambling 102–3
    ideological construction of 193
    politics 200
    and respectability 183–4, 192–4
    and same-sex relationships 144
    and sexual vices 124–7
    and vice 19–22
    and vice debates 22
gentility, and clothing 178
gentlemen's clubs 42, 75, 94, 95, 96, 114, 194
geographical zoning, of moral/immoral pleasures 42
George III, King 3
Georgian immorality 3
Germany 28
gin 85
gin palaces 65, 130
Girdlestone, Charles 23
girls
    idealization of 20
    trafficking of 132, 133

girl's clubs 166
Girls' Friendly Society 166
Gladstone, Robert 104
Gladstone, William 27, 59, 71, 104, 132, 136, 168
Glasgow 40, 47, 166
Glasgow Herald 200
Goldsmid, Howard J. 35
golf 194
Golf Illustrated 179
gonorrhoea 134. *See also* venereal disease
Good Templars 72
Good Templar's Happy Home, The 166
Gospel Temperance 72, 165
governmental responses, to gambling 107–9, 113–14
governments
　motivations for reform 154
　and pressure groups 168, 171
Graham's Club 97
'Greek' or Platonic relationships 142
Greenwood, James 39, 47
greyhound-coursing 110
gross indecency 143, 144
Grossmith, George and Weedon 180
Guest, John 166
Gulland, John 150

habitual drunkards 65
Habitual Drunkards Act 1879 64
Halifax 170
'Hallelujah Lasses' 148
Hampson, William 127
Harcourt, William 72
Hardy, James Keir 151
Hardy, Thomas 125, 126, 182, 184
Harley, John 73
Harris, Henry Vigar 35
Harvey, Augustus John 8
Hastings, Henry 96
'haunts' 31
Hawke, John 91, 150, 170
Hawthorne, Nathaniel 76
Hayler, Henry 140
hedonism, of students 190
heterosexuality, as the norm 141
High Church Oxford Movement 4

hiring fairs 50, 51
History of Gambling in England 110
holiday resorts 56, 188
holidays, and gambling 94–5
Holman, George 87–8
Holyoake, G.J. 9
homes
　middle-class 176
　and roles of women 20, 192–3
Homes for Hope 132
homo-social race clubs 194
homophobia 143–4
homosexuality 28, 44, 56, 121, 141–4, 145, 182, 188
Honest Joe 92
Hope, John 162
Hopkins, Ellice 151
Hopkins, Gerard Manley 182
horse-races, as locations for vice 52–4
horse-racing. *See also* race meetings
　betting on 53, 88, 95, 101–3, 110–12
　cruelty to animals 87–8
　and middle classes 24–5, 88, 188
　support for 170
　and upper classes 95–6
　and women 194
　and working classes 101–3
hotels 81
'Hotspur' 87
House of Commons Commission on the Sanitary Condition of the Labouring Population of Great Britain 1842 40
House of Lords Committee into the Supply and Consumption of Beer 1850 70
House of Lords Select Committee on Betting 1901 91
Household Words 53
housing conditions 40, 54–5, 165. *See also* slums
Houston, T. 54
Hoyle's Hymns and Songs for Temperance Societies and Bands of Hope 166
Hull 52
human bodies, and vice 38

human rights, and Contagious Diseases Act 1864 135. *See also* rights
hymns, temperance 166
hypocrisy 8

idealization, of girls and married women 20
identities
  multiple of Victorians 196
  self-identity of women 193
illegitimate births 121, 126, 127, 184, 200
Illustrated Midland News 47
Illustrated Police News 13, 122
Illustrated Sporting News 103
images, of the anti-vice movement 161
immigrant workers, and cities 41
immigrants, and moral corruption 38
immoral pleasures, geographical zoning of 42
immorality, Georgian 3
Importance of Being Earnest, The 181–2
improvidence 6
impurity, term 11–12
In Darkest England and The Way Out 37
incomes, rising and leisure 26, 44, 114. *See also* wages
indecency in public 143
Indecent Advertisements Act 1889 134
Independent Labour Party 151
Independent Order of Good Templars 156
Independent Order of Oddfellows 79
Independent Order of Rechabites 69
India 57
individual responsibility, and legislation 27
individuals, vices of 9
industrial production, and gambling 91
industrial schools for girls 163
industrialists, as reformers 149–50, 154
industrialization 4–5, 27, 33
industry
  brewing 27
  pornography 136–7
infanticide 126

information, on sexual issues 123, 134
innocent, portrayals of women as 20
inns 81
insanity
  and drunkenness 62–3
  and respectability of women 183–4, 186
intelligentsia, and homosexuality 142
intemperance 62–3
Intemperance in Food: A National Vice 8
International Association for the Suppression of the Gaming Tables of Monte Carlo 95
Ireland 83, 163
Irish immigrants 38
Is the Pleasure worth the Penalty: A Common-Sense View of the Leading Vice of the Age 124
Islam 153
Italy 28

Jack the Ripper 23, 37
Jackson, John 185
James, Henry 39
Jerome, Jerome K. 47
Jerrold, Blanchard 46
Jewish immigrants 38
Jockey Club 97, 194
journalism, and moral crusading 27. *See also* newspapers
Judaism 153

Kaggs family 173
Kennard, Mrs Edward 185
kept women 125. *See also* fallen women; mistresses
Kerr, Norman 64
Kingsley, Charles 157
Kirwan, Daniel 36

Labouchère, Henry 143
Ladies' Association for the Care of Friendless Girls 132, 163
Lancet, The 7, 123, 131, 134
language, of vice 5–14, 29, 37, 123, 144
lasciviousness 18

law(s). *See also* legislation; names of individual laws and acts
  anti-gaming 100
  gambling 108, 112, 114, 115
  and homosexuality 121
  and upper classes 100
Laws of Betting or Betting Legalised: A Clear Summary of the Acts and Guide to Investors, The 106
Lawson, Wilfred 71, 150
Lazy Tour of Two Idle Apprentices, The 53
League of the Cross 155
Lecky, W.A.L. 128
Leeds Mercury 99, 157
Lees, Frederick 150
legislation. *See also* law(s)
  anti-drink 27
  against betting 103
  against gambling 89, 114
  imposing respectability 194–6
  licensing 85
  and pressure groups 168
  and sexual vices 119–20
Leicester 52, 167, 181
leisure
  commercial forms of 5, 26, 122, 175
  corrupting effects of 22
  increasing time for 28, 195
  offering better alternatives 164–7
  and religion 171
  and rising incomes 26, 44, 114
  urban leisure landscape 41–6
  and women 44, 193
lesbian relationships 144
Levi, Leon 75
Lewes, George Henry 186
Lewis, Elizabeth Ann 151
Liberal governments 71, 195
Liberal Party 72, 199
Liberals, and enforced temperance/education 27
libertinism 124
Licensing Act 1872 59–60, 67
licensing legislation 85
licensing system 73
Life of Jane Johnson, The 161
list houses 104, 107

List of Fairs, Feasts, Statutes and Rushbearings 52
literacy rates
  and newspaper readership 103
  and pornography 137
literature. *See also* pornography
  preventing publication of inappropriate 168
  vicious 14
Liverpool
  beer houses 67
  and betting 104, 109, 111
  brothels 131
  and drunkenness 64, 65
  nightlife 190
  race meetings 87–8
  slums 35
  and vice 32, 36
Liverpool Mercury 11
Liverpool Review 102
Livesey, Joseph 68–9, 71, 151
living conditions, of poor people 37–8, 55
living standards, rising 44
Lloyd, Marie 47
Lloyd's Weekly Newspaper 13, 99, 103, 113, 188
lobbying, of temperance movement 168
local authorities
  provision of leisure facilities 164
  and race meetings 170
  regulation of music halls and theatres by 47
  responses to betting 110–11
  and working-class gambling 108
locations
  linked to vice 45, 46–54
  and respectability 187–9
Lock Hospitals 134, 135
lodging houses 35
London
  anonymity of 187
  and betting 107
  brothels 16–17, 129, 133
  as centre for vice 4
  and depravity 144
  drinking places 78
  erotic picture trade 140

gaming houses 109–10
'immoral localities' 42
night houses 16–17
opium dens 7
pleasure map of 42
port areas 36
prostitution 16–17, 45, 129–30, 131
race meetings 169–70
slums 36, 37–8, 40, 64–5
and vice 33–5
London Baptist Association 99
London Christian Instruction Society 51
London County Council 47
London Foundling Hospital 184
London in 1865: A Handbook for Strangers 42
London Society for the Protection of Young Females 149
London Society for the Protection of Young Females and Prevention of Juvenile Prostitution 132
London Statistical Society 84
London Temperance Hospital 165
London Working Men's Association 151
Lords Committee into the Supply and Consumption of Beer 1849–50 79
Lord's Day Observance Society 26
lotteries 108
Lotteries Act 1823 112
Louise, Princess 186
Lovett, William 151
low list houses 104. *See also* list houses
'lumpenproletariat' 22
Lunacy Act 183
Lunn, Henry 55
Lunn Poly 55
Lyttelton, E. 12, 149

Macarthy, Miss 164
Magdalene Asylums 163
magistrates
  laissez-faire approach of 170
  and middle classes 195–6
  and pressure groups 167
  reluctance to act 195

Maidstone, Lord 96
Maine Law 70
Manchester
  and betting 107, 111
  brothels 118
  bylaws 168
  drunkenness 77–8
  horse-racing 53–4
  music halls 47
  Peterloo Massacre 25
  pleasure gardens 49
  slums 35
  and vice 36
Manchester Evening News 105
Manchester Guardian 107, 157
Mann, Tom 151
market demand, for vice 4, 195
market economy, capitalist democratic 27
marriage
  deferring of 120, 122
  high value given to 120
  and respectability 126
  sex outside of 12, 123, 127–8
Martin, Violet 144
Mary Barton 35
masculine privilege 123
masochistic flagellation 139
mass temperance rallies 165–6
Massaganians 192
masturbation 12, 140–1
Matrimonial Causes Act 1857 120
Mayhew, Henry 32, 35, 37, 74, 179
Mayne, Richard 100
McGonagall, William 165
media
  and anti-vice campaigns 25, 27
  coverage of vice 11–14
  print and sex 121–4
  support for gambling 105–6
  use of by anti-vice societies 157–9
medical discourse, and masturbation 140–1
medical profession, and alcohol 75
medical students 190
meeting places, alcohol free 79
Melbourne, Lord 5
Members of Parliament, and pressure groups 168

Memoirs of Madame Chester of Manchester 118
men
    attitudes to women 183–4
    as causes of vice 135
    having a reputation 185
    as heads of households 192
    male gaze 44
    male prostitutes 44, 143, 144
    male sexuality 121, 144
    middle aged/older 190, 191
    notions of superiority 20
    power of 20
    unmarried 190
mental maps 31, 32
Merthyr 36–7, 66, 199
Methodism 86
Methodist Times 144
Methodists 135, 149
Metropolitan Police 28, 140
Metropolitan Police Act 1839 119
Meyer, F.B. 162
middle classes
    activism of women 135
    attacks on vice 23–4
    bachelors 120, 143
    and betting 24–5, 188
    and church attendance 153
    cultural capital of 196
    deferring marriage 122
    drinking of 24, 75–6, 81
    and drunkenness 65
    families 21
    fear of slums 32–3
    gambling of 24–5, 90, 109–14
    hedonistic notions of fun 200
    and the home 176
    and homosexuality 143
    and horse-racing 24–5, 88, 188
    and magistrates 195–6
    middle aged/older men 190, 191
    moral superiority of 23, 153, 176
    morality of 23, 24
    and the police 65, 109–10, 113–14, 195–6
    prejudices of the poor 37
    professionals as reformers 150
    reformers 4
    reformist leisure culture 22–3
    respectability of 175, 179, 180, 185, 186
    sexual life of 118–19
    urban middle-class men 43
    vice of 19, 23–5
    as virtuous 17
    youth and vice 189
Middlesbrough 37, 66, 77, 109, 169
military, and venereal disease 21–2, 27, 120–1, 134–5
Milky White 47
Mill, John Stuart 199
mining areas 55, 66, 86, 101, 151
ministers of religion, and reform movement 149
Minor St James Club House 97
minorities, Non-Christian 153
Minors' Protection Society 154
missionary and domestic visiting 164
mistresses 127. *See also* fallen women; kept women
moderation, in alcohol consumption 67–8, 70, 198
modernity, and attitudes to vice 28
Molesworth, W.N. 60
moral arguments, against gambling 91
moral campaigns, and new journalism 27
moral concerns 3
moral contagion
    and homosexuality 143
    and prostitution 128
moral corruption
    of children 189
    and immigrants 38
    as threat to social position 19
moral crusading, and journalism 27
moral danger, cities as sites of 41
moral decay, fear of 26, 152
moral degeneracy, of upper classes 23
moral evil, tobacco smoking as 10
moral panics 8, 16, 23, 26, 55, 129
moral pleasures, geographical zoning of 42
moral reform
    opposition to 191–2
    voluntary societies 25–6
Moral Reform Union 158

moral reformers, women 19
moral responsibility, individual 27
moral ruin 184
moral superiority
  of middle classes 153, 176
  of reformers 198
moralism 120
morality
  of foreigners 56
  and the middle classes 23, 24
  new 3
  rhetoric of 190
  sexual 120
morality debates, and economic depression 27–8
Morals of the Midlands: A Sporting Tale 185
Morning Chronicle 35, 199
Morning Post 110
Morrison, Arthur 37
Mortimer, Geoffrey 200
Moss, Horace E. 48
motivations, of anti-vice groups 197
moustaches, and respectability 178
Mumford, Samuel 112
Munby, Arthur 44
Municipal Corporations Act 1882 168
Munro, Hector Hugh 189
Murphy, Francis 165
music halls 46–8, 80, 166, 187–8
music, use of by reformers 166
Musical Entertainer: Songs and Ballads for Penny Readings and Temperance Entertainments 166
My Secret Life 139
Mystery of Edwin Drood, The 7

naïve, women as 20
National Anti-Gambling Association 157
National Anti-Gambling League 92, 150, 156–7, 158, 169, 170
National Association for the Promotion of Social Science 64
National British Women's Temperance Association 158
national identity, and otherness 56
National Society for the Prevention of Cruelty to Animals 87, 88
National Temperance League 7, 71, 75, 156, 165
National Temperance Society 65, 69
National Vigilance Association (NVA) 133, 140, 141, 154–5
'Naughty Nineties' 28
navy, and venereal disease 21–2, 27, 134–5
Netherlands 132
networking skills, of reformers 154
Nevison, Henry Woodd 39
New British and Foreign Temperance Society 156
New Women 136
New York World 36
Newcastle 49, 104, 131, 167
Newcastle, 6th Duke of 96
Newcomes: Memoirs of a Most Respectable Family, The 200
News of the World 198
newspapers
  and betting 103–4, 105–6, 110, 112
  coverage of vice 11–12, 13–14
  and homosexual acts 143
  and prostitution 126
  and sex reporting 122–3
  temperance movement 158
Nicholson, Renton 5
night-clubs 41
night houses 16–17
'Nocturne in Black and Gold: the Falling Rocket' 48
Non-Christian minorities 153
Nonconformist churches 179
Nonconformist conscience 23
Nonconformists, National Temperance League 156
Nonconformity 153
Normand, Ernest 136
North-Eastern Daily Gazette 200
North Woolwich Pleasure Gardens 49
Northern Echo 23, 157
Northern England 66
Northumberland 66
Norwich 78, 167
nudity, in art 134, 136

obesity, as a vice 8
Obscene Publications Act 1857 137, 140
'obscene publications' Squad, Metropolitan Police 140
obscenity 135–40
occupation, and respectability 179–82, 187
Offences Against the Person Act 133
Offences against the Person Amendment Act 1875 189–90
Oh, Mr Porter 47
Oliver Twist 34, 193
On Liberty 199
Onanism 140
opium dens 7
opposition
    to gaming/betting 90–3
    to reformers 191–2
    to Salvation Army 191–2
    to upper-class gambling 98–9
organizations, working-class 150–1
Orientalism 7
otherness, in terms of foreign morality 56
Outcast, The 184
outreach, forms of 159–62
overcrowding, and sexual promiscuity 37
Owen, J.S. 169
Owenism 150
Oxford 52, 190
Oxford, Earl of 120

Paget, Lady 96
Pall Mall Gazette 13, 23, 39, 133
Palmer, William 113
parks, urban 169, 188
Parliament, lobbying of 168
Parliamentary Select Committee of the House of Commons Report on Metropolitan Improvements of 1837–8 40
Parnell, Charles Stewart 128, 185
Parrington, C.H. 25
Past and Present 184
Patmore, Coventry 20
patriarchy 121, 192
pauperism 7

Pearl, The 139
Pearson, Charles 51
penny dreadfuls 190
People, The 103
perception, and vice 6
Permissive Bill 1869 71, 168
personal virtue, of women 12–13
Peterloo Massacre, Manchester 25
philanthropic provision of leisure facilities 164
Phillpotts, Eden 47
photography, and pornography 140
Pickersgill, Joseph 92
Pictorial Handbook of London 35
Pioneer, The 158
pitch and toss 101, 107
places
    and respectability 187–9
    and vice 31–2
Platonic relationships 142
Please Sell No More Drink to My Father 166
pleasure fairs, as locations for vice 50–2. *See also* fairs
pleasure grounds, as locations for vice 48–50
pleasure resorts 66
pleasures, as vicious or virtuous 26
Pole, Edward 187
police
    concern with propriety 15–16
    drinking of policemen 75
    and drunkenness 66
    and gambling 99–100, 108–10, 113–14
    and homosexual acts 143
    and middle classes 65, 109–10, 113–14, 195–6
    powers and venereal disease 135
    and pressure groups 167
    and prostitution 129, 170
    reluctance to act 195
    and slum visits 39
    and upper classes 99–100
    and vice-related behaviour 15–16
    and working classes 108–9
political concern, public drinking as 72
political force, temperance as 70–1
political power, of working class 28

political support, for gambling/
    drinking 199
politicians, and anti-vice movements
    150
politicization, of vice 26, 27, 149
politics
    gender 200
    and pressure groups 167–9
pollution, and slums 37
Poor Drunkard's Child, The 166
Poor Man's Friend Society 165
poor people. *See also* poverty;
    working-class
    as dangerous 23, 27
    female 21
    governance of 4–5
    as idle 23
    living conditions of 37–8, 55
    respectable 180
    undeserving 27
    vices of 29
Pope, Samuel 64
pornography 134, 135–40
ports 36, 66, 135
Portsmouth 36, 78
postal bookmaker offices 108
Potter, John 117
poverty 63, 150. *See also* poor people
Poverty, a Study of Town Life 150
power
    cultural and respectability 173, 179
    male 20
    of upper classes 199
    and vice 19
power relationships
    and definition/use of vice 19
    and same-sex relationships 145
pre-marital sex 12, 123, 127–8
preaching from the pulpit 160, 162,
    199–200
pregnancy, single women 126. *See also*
    illegitimate births
pressure groups 157, 167–9, 171
Preston Guardian 69
Preston Temperance Advocate 69
prevalence of gambling 100–1, 109–10
prevalence of gaming 93–5, 109–10
Prevention of Gaming (Scotland) Act
    1869 108

Primitive Methodist preachers, mining
    areas 151
private life, and public life 21
Proclamation against Vice
    King George III 3
    Queen Victoria 2–3, 5, 6
Proclamation against Vice and
    Debauchery, Queen Anne 3
Proclamation Society 3
profligacy, temptation to 18–19
prohibitionist movement 70–3
proletariat 8–9, 22
propriety, new female 44
prostitutes
    compulsory testing of 134–5
    defences of 131–2
    demonization/victimization of 126
    forced emigration of 26
    foreign 131
    Germany 28
    at holiday resorts 56
    locations for 45
    male 44, 143, 144
    outcast identity of 129
    police powers to arrest 135
    relief organizations for 132
    scapegoating of 129
    upward mobility of 126, 129
    and venereal disease 22, 134–5
    as victims 131
prostitution
    anti-prostitution campaigns 131
    and class 130–1, 135
    as a female vice 128
    as great social evil 128–34
    London 16–17, 45, 129–30, 131
    numbers involved in 130
    and the police 129, 170
    prevention of 26
    as a profession 126
    visibility of 128–9
Prostitution in London 131
Protestant British, and vice 28
Protestant Christianity, and anti-vice
    campaigns 153
Prude's Progress, The 47–8
public behaviour
    new female 44
    and prostitution 128

public drinking, as political concern 72
Public Health Acts Amendment Act 1890 80
public health concerns, and alcohol 64
public houses
   and Beer Act 1830 68
   and betting 80, 105
   licensing system 73
   prosecutions of landlords 167
   respectable 188
   and vice 62, 77–84
   and viciousness 7
   women drinkers in 64
public indecency 143
public libraries 168
public life
   corruption in 23
   and private life 21
public meetings 160–1
public morality, and the press 123
public order, and prostitution 128
public parks 169, 188
public schools 141, 189
public spaces 32
public toilets, and homosexual acts 143, 188
publicans, as sporting entrepreneurs 80–1, 101
pubs. *See* public houses
Puritans 152
purity campaigners 132, 133, 168, 169
purity movements 28, 148, 154, 165–6, 201
Pygmalion and Galatea 136

Quakers 24, 132, 149, 191

race meetings 9, 52–4, 77, 169–70, 194. *See also* horse-racing
Racing Calendar 95
Racing Times 105
Ragged Schools 6, 164
rallies, temperance 165–6
Ranyard Bible nurses 40
rape 126, 185
Recent Legislation on Contagious Diseases 22
recreational function, of drinking places 78–9
recreations, respectable 176
Reddie, James 139
Redgrave, Richard 184
reform, motivations for 152–4
reform movements
   and class 4–5
   denominational divisions 26
   effectiveness of 197–200
reform of manners movements 3
reform organizations, targeting children 162–3, 171
reformatory schools for girls 163
reformers 148–51
   anti-vice 23
   and class 151
   effectiveness of 169–71, 196
   female 12, 147
   industrialists as 149–50, 154
   and Liberal Party 199
   marginalization of 27
   middle-class 4
   moral superiority of 198
   need for unrespectability 177
   networking skills of 154
   number of 197
   opposition to 191–2
   and respectability 178–9
   satirization/ridiculing of 199–200
   self-interest/hypocrisy of 198
   targeting of slums 33
regulation
   of drinking 73
   of music halls and theatres 47
   self-regulation 102, 152
   weakening of traditional means of 152
Reid, W. 24, 62
relief organizations, for prostitutes 132
relief programmes, Churches 164
religion
   and class 153
   decline in 201
   and leisure 171
   as motivator of urban reformers 153
   and respectability 191–2
religious groups, and differing views of vice 16–17

reputation(s)
  having a 185
  of women 193
rescue activities 163–4, 171
respectability
  in 1960s 201
  and age/generation 189–90
  appearance of 177–9, 185, 188, 196
  'being found out' 185
  and class and occupation 179–82
  consequences of loss of 182–7
  and cultural capital 178
  and cultural power 173, 179
  as currency 25
  decline in popularity of 200–1
  and economic power 179
  and education 179–80
  ethic of 181
  external 185–6
  and financial gain 173–4, 178
  and gender 183–4, 192–4
  importance of 175–7
  legislation 194–6
  and marriage 126
  middle-class 175, 179, 180, 185, 186
  multiple dimensions of 176, 182
  as normal 183
  and occupation 179–82, 187
  offences against 187
  and place and time 187–9
  and reformers 178–9
  and religion 191–2
  revolt against 200–1
  as a role to be played 181–2
  and social mobility 179
  and social networks 178–9, 193
  term 174, 176
  visual features of 177–8
  and women 181, 186, 193
  working-class 175, 176, 180–1, 200
respectable
  prefix of 180
  and unrespectable 18
respectable classes/society 179, 196
respectable poor 180
Revelations of London 35
Reynolds, G.M.W. 122
Reynolds, Thomas 7

Reynolds's News 13, 99, 125
Reynolds's Newspaper 198, 200
rhetoric, of morality 190
'Rich and Poor' 23
Richards, James 25
Richardson, Fr. 62
rights
  and Contagious Diseases Act 1864 135
  of women 120, 127, 147, 151
Riot Act 192
Robinson, Henry Crabb 176
Rochdale 59–60, 130
Roman Catholic Church 128, 155, 191
Romance of Chastisement, The 139
Rosebery, Lord 170
Rowley, Henry 17
Rowntree, Joseph 84, 150
Rowntree, Seebohm 150
Royal Caledonian Hunt Club 194
Royal Commission on the Houses of the Working Class 1885 40
Royal Commission on the Licensing Laws 72–3
'Ruined Maid, The' 184
ruined women 183, 184
rules, of respectability 186
rural areas, and vice 54–5, 76, 77, 102
Ryan, Michael 131

Sabbath breaking 3
sailors, and venereal disease 21–2, 27, 110, 112, 134–5
Salford 130
Salt, Titus 149–50, 169
Saltaire 149, 169
salvation 163
Salvation Army 40, 148, 191–2
same-sex relationships 141–4. *See also* homosexuality; lesbian relationships
sanitation, poor 55
Sapphic 144
Satirist, The 97
Saturday Review 42
scandals
  betting 98, 113
  in the colonies 56
  gaming 96–7

scapegoating
  of bookmakers/those in the gambling industry 92–3
  of prostitutes 129
  of upper classes 23
  of women 135
scientific study of sex 120, 121
Scotland 83, 156, 158
Scottish Temperance League 69
Scottish Temperance League Journal 158
Scottish Temperance Union 156
scrutiny, of women 193
seaports, and drunkenness 66. *See also* port areas
seaside casinos 95
seaside holidays 55–6
seaside resorts 169, 188
Secret Ballot Act 1872 75
secular counter-attractions 165
secularism 153, 171
Select Committee on Statutes Against Gaming 1844 90
Select Committee on the Gaming Laws 100
Select Committee on the Married Women's Property Bill 1867/8 63
Select Committee on the Regulation of Public Houses 15
Select Committee on the Sale of Liquors 8
Self-Help 8
self-identity, of women 193
self-improvement 150
self-regulation 102, 152
Sellon, Edward 137–8
sex
  modern conceptualizations of 122
  pre-marital 12, 123, 127–8
  and print media 121–4
  as problematic 122, 123
sex industry, Georgian times 3–4
sex tourism 56, 57
sexual agency, of women 138
sexual attitudes, 1960s 201
sexual desire, female 119–20
sexual exploitation, of children/women 133, 134
sexual indecency 185

sexual misbehaviour, and holiday resorts 56
sexual misconduct, by women 193
sexual promiscuity, and overcrowding 37
sexual temptation, and deferring of marriage 122
sexual vices 117, 119–20, 124–7
sexuality
  child 141
  control of women's by men 120
  human 120
  male 121, 144
  male/female 120, 121
  as problematic 118–19
  transgressive 142
  Victorian 119
  of women 120, 122
sexually transmitted diseases. *See* venereal disease
Shadows of Slum Life 38
shame 182, 183, 191
Shawcross, W.T. 60
She'd Never Had Her Ticket Punched Before 47
Sheffield 59, 60, 112
Sherlock Holmes 55
Sherwell, Arthur 84
Shields Daily News 35
Shimmin, Hugh 42
shopping, of women 44–5
Sidebottom, John 112–13
Silas Marner 124
Silent Friend 123
Sims, George 64–5
slumming 39, 143
slums
  fear of 32–3
  Liverpool 35
  London 36, 37–8
  misrepresentation of 36
  slum dwellers 37, 38, 39, 64–5
  vice in 7, 32–8, 57
  visits and clearances 38–40
Smiles, Samuel 8
Smith, C.E. 156
Smith, Sydney 18
smoking 7, 10
Snowdrop Bands 166

social activism, of middle-class women 135
social arguments, against gambling 91
social campaigners, working-class 150–1
social change, in cultural values 152
social class. *See* class
social constraints 183
social contagion, and prostitution 128
social control
   and moral reform 153
   and Sunday schools 163
social cost, of gambling 89
Social Democratic Federation 151
social differentiation, in public houses 82
social disorder, and drunkenness 63
social division, and attitudes to vice 22. *See also* class
social drinking 75
social force, temperance as 70–1
social function, of drinking places 78–9
social geography, of dangerous classes 37
social mobility
   of prostitutes 126, 129
   and respectability 179
social networks, and respectability 178–9, 193
social norms 122
social order
   and drunkenness 61
   threat of vice to 5
social purity 149
Social Purity Alliance 12
Social Purity Association 158
Social Purity campaign 121
social reformers. *See* reformers
social significance, of gambling 88–9
social spaces, socialization in new 122
social status, inability to recognise 44
social support, for gambling/drinking 199
social unrest, fear of 152
socialist leaders, working-class 151
societal order, and elites 25
Society for the Study and Cure of Inebriety 64

Society for the Suppression of Vice 16–17, 45, 137, 139, 154
Society for the Suppression of Vice and the Encouragement of Religion 3
Society for the Suppression of Vicious Practices, Liverpool 36
Society for the Suppression of Vicious Resorts, Liverpool 32
Society of Vice, The 137
sodomy 141, 143, 144
soldiers, and venereal disease 21–2, 134–5. *See also* army
Solly, Henry 79
Somerset, Lady Henry 149
Somerville, Edith 144
song and supper clubs 46
spaces
   socialization in new 122
   urban and homosexuality 44
   and vice 31–2
Spectator, The 185
spirits, consumption of 85. *See also* alcohol
spiritual revival 153
sport
   and public houses 80–1
   women taking part in 194
Sporting Chronicle 105
sporting entrepreneurs, publicans as 80–1, 101
Sporting Life 105
Sportsman, The 105
sportsmen, and corruption 107
St Helena Gardens Music Hall and Pleasure Grounds 49
standards of living, rising 26, 28
Stanhope, John Roddam 184
Stanhope, Lord 156
Stanley, John 96
Stanley, Maude 164
Star, The 13
Starkie, Thomas 90
statistics, on disreputability 200
Stead, W.T. 23, 133, 154, 155
stereotypes
   class-based 125
   upper-class debaucher 124
   of women 21
Stevens, Samuel 60

Stevenson, Robert Louis 18
Stock Exchange 99, 111, 112
Stock, George 139
Strange Case of Dr Jekyll and Mr Hyde, The 18
street betting 108, 156, 168
street bookmakers 105
suicide 182–3
Sunday
   opening of pubs 83
   and respectability 188–9
   Sabbath breaking 3
Sunday Observance movement 6
Sunday schools 162–3, 164, 167, 171
Sunderland 50
superiority
   male notions of 20
   moral of middle classes 23, 153, 176
   moral of reformers 198
support
   for gambling/drinking 199
   for horse-racing 170
Suppression of Betting Houses Act 1874 108
surveillance, formal/informal 183
sweepstakes 112
swells 43
Swinburne, Algernon Charles 18
Sykes, Tatton and Jessica 20
symbols, of the anti-vice movement 161
syphilis 134. *See also* venereal disease

table games 94
tableaux vivants 48
Taine, Hippolyte 36
Tattersall's Rooms 95
Taylor, John 65
Taylor, William 118
tea, and respectability/morality 69
teetotalism 68–70, 71, 85, 150, 151, 179
Telegraph, The 88
temperance
   and control of personal desire 152
   discourse 62–3
   enforced 27
   and excursions 167

   organizations 151, 155
   rallies 165–6
   reformers 149–50
   and respectability 178
   temperance movement 26, 67–73, 82, 85, 86, 168
   and upper classes 199
Temperance Bells 158
Temperance Building Society 165
Temperance Chronicle 158
Temperance Provident Institution 165
Temperance Question and Social Reform, The 150
Temperance Society, Church of England 10, 148, 153, 156, 159
temporal dimension, of urban vice 41
temptation
   and vice 7
   to vice and profligacy 18–19
Tempted London: Young Men 11, 46
Tenant of Wildfell Hall, The 18
tennis 194
Ternan, Ellen 122
Tess of the d'Urbervilles 125, 182
Thackeray, William 200
theatres 46–8, 187–8
theatrical literature/performance, temperance movement 166
Thompson, Rev. Dr 127
Thornton, Richard 48
Thoughts of the Past 184
Tillett, Ben 151
time, and respectability 187–9
Times, The 19, 42, 54, 56, 62, 75, 77, 110, 111, 112, 123, 129, 185
tobacco smoking 7, 10
Tories, support of vice-related industries 27. *See also* Conservative governments
tourism
   sex 56, 57
   vice 42
Town Talk 13–14, 47, 49, 190
Town, The 5
towns, civilization of 23. *See also* urbanization
trade societies and unions 79, 151
trafficking, of girls 132, 133

transgressive sexualities 142
travel agents 55
'treating' and elections 75
Trevelyan, Walter 149
Trewint Industrial Home 166
Trial of Sir Jasper: A Temperance Tale in Verse, The 166
Tristan, Flora 129–30
truancy 8
Truck Act 1887 76–7
Turf Club 95
Tyneside 35

ugliness, and vice 38
UK Alliance 64, 70–3, 150, 156, 159, 160, 161–2, 168, 169
Ulrichs, Karl Heinrich 142
undeserving poor 27
Unitarians 5, 191
United Kingdom Alliance. *See* UK Alliance
university students 190
upper classes. *See also* elites
 activism of 149
 attacks on vices of 23
 codes of 20
 debaucher stereotype 124
 divorce cases 20
 drinking of 70, 75
 fast set 97, 175
 gambling of 89, 93–100, 114
 and homosexuality 142, 143
 and horse-racing 95–6
 and the law 100
 and police 99–100
 power of 199
 prevalence of gaming 93–5
 scapegoating of 23
 and sexual vices 125
 and teetotalism 70
 and temperance 199
upward mobility, of prostitutes 126, 129
Urania Cottage 26
Uranians 142
urban areas
 and anonymity 187
 as places of pleasurable opportunity 41

urban life 33, 43
urban populations, civilization of 164
urban pub culture 80
urban space, and homosexuality 44
urban vice 41
urbanization 4–5, 27, 28, 38, 126

vacations, and gambling 94–5
Vagrancy Act 1837 136
values, concept of 201
variety theatres 46–8. *See also* theatres
Vaughan, Rev. Dr 110
venereal disease 21–2, 27, 120–1, 134–5
vice
 meanings of over time vii–viii
 term 5–6
 for the Victorians 1
vicious
 preaching to the 162
 and the virtuous 18
vicious habits 7
vicious literature 14
victims, prostitutes as 131
Victor Albert, Prince 143
Victoria Club 95
Victoria, Queen, Proclamation against Vice 2–3, 5, 6
Victorian, term 1–2
Vigilance Association 17, 154
Villiers, Frank 96
Vincent, Henry 152
virtue(s)
 and beauty 38
 and vice 17–19
virtuous, and the vicious 18
virtuous classes 10
virtuous women 12–13
visual materials, of the anti-vice movement 161
voluntary societies, moral reform 25–6

wages, rising and leisure 28, 102, 195. *See also* incomes
Wakefield 50
Wales 83, 158
Walters, Catherine 131
War Cry, The 148
Watkin, Absalom 75–6

wayward girls 125, 132
wealth, and respectability 179–80
Webb, Beatrice 37
Weekly Journal of the New British and Foreign Bible Society 158
Weekly Record 158
Wesleyan Conference, Declaration on Gambling 91
Wesleyans 149
Westminster Gazette 99
Westminster Review 186
Westmorland 200
Whistler, James McNeill 48
White Ribbon 158
white slavery 133
Whittaker, Thomas Palmer 150
Wilde, Oscar 28, 121, 136, 144, 181
Wilkinson, Mary 127
Williams, George 151
Wilson, Arthur 97
Wilson, Joe 50, 166
Wilson Patten Act 1854 83
Wilson, William 54
Wolverhampton 168
Woman's Christian Temperance Union 72
women
   anti-drink activities 85
   and anti-vice movement 151
   and betting 103, 111, 194
   and blame for sexual vices 125
   as carriers of social/religious virtue 192–3
   changing role of 20, 135
   and drink 19–20
   drunkenness 64–5
   fallen women 21, 27, 125–6, 127, 135
   and the home 20, 192–3
   and horse-racing 194
   the ideal 193
   idealization of married 20
   and insanity 183–4, 186
   and leisure 44, 193
   and loss of respectability 183–4
   male attitudes to 183–4
   men controlling sexuality of 120
   moral reformers 19
   moving to private sphere 192
   and new public behaviour/propriety 44
   New Women 136
   public role of 85, 151
   reformers 12, 147
   reputations of 193
   and respectability 181, 186, 193
   rights of 120, 127, 147, 151
   ruined 183, 184
   scapegoating of 135
   scrutiny of 193
   as second class citizens 21
   self-identity of 193
   sexual agency of 138
   sexual exploitation of 133, 134
   sexual misconduct by 193
   sexuality of 120, 122
   shopping of 44–5
   stereotypes of 21
   taking part in sport 194
   targeting of working-class 19, 20
   upper-class gambling 94
   and urbanization 126
   victimization of 131
   in Victorian times 21
   virtuous 12–13
   working 21, 44, 187
   working-class 21, 185, 191
   young at risk 166
Worcester Journal 109
workforce, and commercial forms of leisure 5
working classes. *See also* poor people
   betting 103–5
   control of 189
   as dangerous class 10
   drinking of 75, 85
   drunken women 64–5
   and drunkenness 73
   excursions 55
   gambling of 89, 100–9, 114–15
   and homosexuality 141–2
   and horse-racing 101–3
   leisure 164
   male prostitutes 143, 144
   organizations of 150–1
   and police 108–9
   political power of 28

and pornography 136–7
prostitutes 130, 135, 143, 144
and public houses 82
rape of women 185
respectability of 175, 176, 180–1, 200
as respectable/rough 180, 181
social campaigners 150–1
and street betting 156
targeting of female behaviour 19, 20
women 21, 185, 191
Working Men's Club and Institute Union 79
working women 21, 44, 187

workplaces, and respectability 175–6
Wright, Thomas 8

York 150
York Herald 110
Yorkshire Gazette 110
Young Crusader's Hymn and Song Book 153
Young Men's Christian Association (YMCA) 151
Young Men's Improvement Societies 166
young people
  at risk 166, 189
  and vice 41

www.ingramcontent.com/pod-product-compliance
Lightning Source LLC
Chambersburg PA
CBHW050136240426
43673CB00043B/1693